ENTERPRISE NETWORKING

FOREWORD

Author - David Palmer-Stevens

I started my career as an Engineer, often repairing equipment constructed of up to 45 thousand valves. Life became simpler with the introduction of transistors, followed in quick succession by Integrated Circuits, LSI and the VLSI. These technology advancements made an engineer's task more interesting, allowing us to involve ourselves with the application of the technology.

In 1981, while working for Wordplex as its Engineering Training Manager, I volunteered, along with the training staff, to install PLANET. PLANET was a new dual copper ring network from Racal Milgo that contained many of the operating features of FDDI. We worked over the weekend and by Monday, the network was up and running. Before then we were considered the oddballs from training, but on Monday morning we were venerated by colleagues and elevated into a new class of employee: the networking experts.

In my career I have worked for Racal Milgo, Northern Telecom, Ungermann-Bass, Cabletron Systems, Xylan, Madge Networks, GigaLabs and currently, Enterasys Networks. I have lived through all of the technology changes and I even believed some of the exaggerated claims of life-enhancing or world-changing technology

ENTERPRISE NETWORKING

FOREWORD

advancements. I have also enjoyed the lighter side of our industry such as in November 2000 when a hacker stole the new, security-enhanced operating system from a major software manufacturer.

My reason for writing this book was to enable new colleagues to gain a fresh perspective on the industry, to obtain an understanding of the technology that is installed out there and why it was considered so vital in its time and, of course, share a little who did what to whom.

The author would like to acknowledge technical contributions from:

Manek Dubash

Manek Dubash is an independent consultant. He started his career in 1984 as an IT journalist focusing on networking, working for well-known industry titles such as PCW and Practical Computing. He joined PC Magazine in 1991 and became Editor-in-Chief in 2000. He moved to become E-Commerce Technology Strategist at analyst firm Datamonitor, before launching his consultancy service in 2001.

Samuel Liddeatt

Samuel is a Technical Consultant at Enterasys Networks. As a technical trainer specialising in security products, he has worked internationally with a wide range of customers whose networks are built with existing and emerging products from Enterasys Networks.

Tim Wansbourgh

Tim is a Networking Specialist at Enterasys Networks. He has gained his experience through working on a varied selection of national and international projects. Tim is currently training the Enterasys Security Solutions throughout EMEA.

Introduction

ENTERPRISE NETWORKING

EVERYTHING YOU NEED TO KNOW
AND A FEW THINGS YOU DIDN'T WANT TO KNOW

INTRODUCTION

I first wrote this book in 1990 as an easy guide to get everyone used to the jargon used in this fast-moving industry. Recent developments include a huge wave of mergers between Local Area Network (LAN) equipment manufacturers and the dominant companies in Wide Area Networks (WANs). This was a response to both industries migrating towards a single unified solution for integrating voice, video and data over a common transport medium.

One other major technology shift is a move away from shared media networking to a switched infrastructure with the key features of virtual, policy-based and application-aware networking.

With these challenges in mind, the problem we all face is finding skilled staff and, once hired, ensuring they understand the wide range of technologies used by your organisation. So the objective of this network guide is to provide an overview for your new staff that's both easy to read and to understand. My intention is to save the time and effort of network managers who need to bring staff up to date on networking technology.

The sections are independent so no one has to read the whole book. Readers can select the topic they need to bone up on and only read that section. If you're a network manager who spends more time managing people than technology, should find this guide useful in keeping you abreast of the latest developments and networking trends.

Finally, before I sat down to update this guide, I visited some of our blue-chip customers and was surprised to see technology that was over 20 years old still in productive service. So I've decided to keep the historical aspect to the book, as people new to our industry might find it interesting to know how we got to today's dominant technologies.

The exponential rate of change of technology is making it extremely difficult to keep up to date with new communications products. You never know what you will find in a new consignment of bananas. This Communications Guide should reduce the surprises.

ENTERPRISE NETWORKING

WIND OF CHANGE

PROLOGUE

It has become somewhat of a tradition in the networking industry for technologists to present to their would-be clients a network solution that is the answer to all their prayers. The client collects several of these presentations and, on quiet evenings, mulls over the perceived benefits of networking and the relative merits of policy-based networking, service level agreements, security, and whether wireless can really deliver acceptable performance.

But it never works like that. The hard fact is very little planning and strategy goes into many of the decisions taken. A user in an organisation discovers the perfect application that is going to automate their particular task, improving productivity and quality of work. It is then up to the MIS staff to make it work. This in order of importance is achieved by first selecting a platform to run the application, providing correct memory sizes and adequate disk capacity. The power of the platform is always pushed to the economic limit on the understanding that today's whizzy processor is tomorrow's antique. Having settled on the platform, the problem of providing access to corporate resources has to be solved. It is during this phase that networking is considered.

Many of my colleagues in the networking industry have not got their brains around the fact that no one buys a network, businesses buy applications and networking is just an enabling technology. But the wind of change is blowing through European businesses. At the moment, it's a light breeze but the prospect is definitely changeable with possible storm fronts approaching.

Technology and therefore end user expectations are changing at an accelerating rate. The business wants technology not only to deliver business process efficiency but to deliver the competive edge. Yesterday the network had to work today it has to perform. Network Managers have to meet these challenges head to or be swept aside by outsourcing.

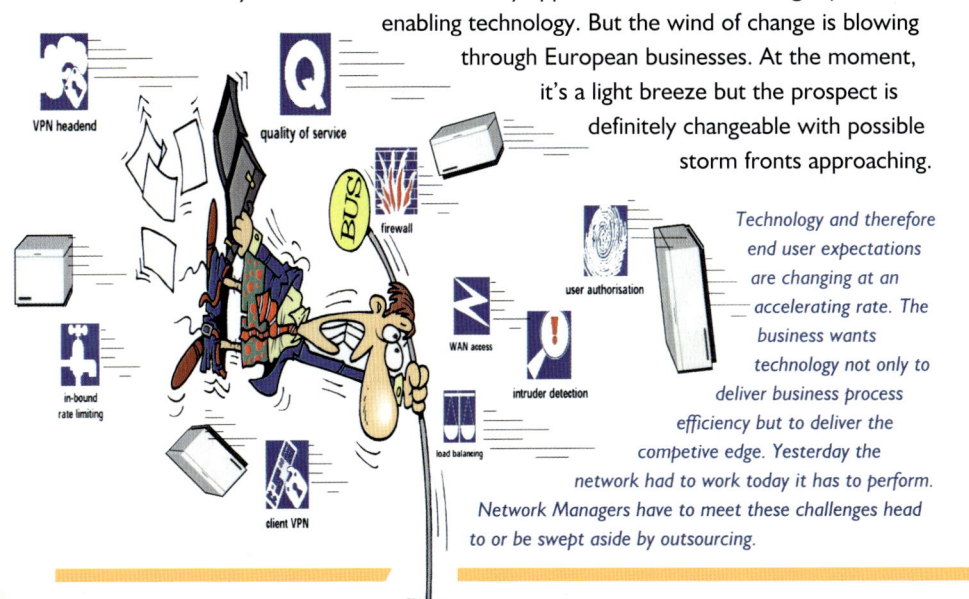

ENTERPRISE NETWORKING

WIND OF CHANGE

What's happening is that organisations are starting to believe that 'content is king'. If you know more and you are informed first, then your decisions can be taken quickly and the change resulting from your decision means your competition, who are not so equipped, making later decisions on incorrect assumptions. The net result is that you cannot fail to succeed.

This change has focused the CEO's attention on networking. The ramifications of this are in two areas: strategic planning and quality of service (QoS). Networking has become involved in both areas and, with it, jobs have moved into the 'at risk' category. From a strategic planning standpoint, the network manager is faced with a dilemma.

All networks run across cabling infrastructures but networking products are classed as hardware. Most corporate organisations view cabling as part of the building facility. As with electricity supply, air conditioning and so on, this is written-off over 10 to 15 years but the hardware is transient and written-off over three to five years. So the network manager is trying to build a long-term strategy around short-term product life cycles. Different manufacturers have different product strategies, even though they all profess to support the Institute of Electrical and Electronic Engineers (IEEE) 802.x networking standards. What this means is that feature sets and therefore the ability of a product to support business applications varies from manufacturer to manufacturer. The chances of making the wrong decision are highly likely, putting network managers' jobs at risk. The position taken by network managers has been to accelerate the changes and to accept the inevitable. *"I will make the wrong decision. Therefore, I want the option when I purchase a product to swap out this equipment for the equipment I should have bought in the first place."* Hence today's successful manufacturers all support some form of product 'Buy Back' programme.

This guaranteed buy back and replacement trend is forcing

When the CIO selects SAP R3 as the application, he assumes that the communications infrastructure can deliver the required service level for each business department. Next week, when he decides to run voice over IP across the same network, he also assumes this will not cause any technical problems.

ENTERPRISE NETWORKING

WIND OF CHANGE

manufacturers to establish not only upgrades and backward compatibility strategies but also migration strategies through the whole gambit of available technologies. This is a considerable financial burden for any new manufacturer to the networking industry.

The second breeze, which is definitely a cold front that's picking up speed as it sweeps from the US into Europe is Quality of Service (QoS). Here the CEO's demand that as the water supply and toilets must always be available, so must network services be available to all users 24 hours a day, 7 days a week, 52 weeks a year. The CEO knows about servicing so you are permitted 1% down-time for preventative maintenance. If the network manager fails to achieve this level of service, to the CEO this is no problem, he can outsource to a facilities management company. By imposing financial penalties on this company if it fails to achieve the stated level, he is in a win-win situation.

Here the wind of change has, once again, struck hardware manufacturers as they see network managers - their allies in an organisation, especially in the USA - dropping like flies. The problem is to define QoS, measure it and provide tools for the network manager to improve it end-to-end. This shift has caused even big systems vendors to develop partnerships with other manufacturers. Such partnerships require standards to reduce the costs of co-operating.

The task is to integrate under one platform the management and control of the network, cabling, fixed assets, applications and configuration. A further challenge is to provide this platform with real-time monitoring, decision making and automation of recovery and repair procedures. The network manager then needs to present information that is available from the system to non-technical CEOs ensuring they can understand the improvements being made.

To understand the enormity of this task, consider asking a network manager how the network is. If it is a five-node PC network, the chances are the manager will have a picture in his mind of the whole network, how it's connected, what files are in use and who is logged on. Extend this to a medium-sized network of 3,000 devices spread over several continents encompassing maybe five to six different technologies the question *"how is the network?"* is very hard to answer - and it's even harder to provide an answer the CEO will understand.

The wind of change has just started as a breeze, however, it's at force 7 in the USA and rising. A recent Industrial Survey showed that the highest category of redundancies in the IT industry were network managers, displaced for failing the QoS hurdle and having their job outsourced. With such a world-wide shortage of good engineers it's a sad state of affairs.

Contents

ENTERPRISE NETWORKING

CONTENTS

SECTION 1:
NETWORK QUESTIONS AND ANSWERS

This section will answer the questions of the inquisitive user focused on Local Area Networking but touching on some relevant Wide Area Networking topics and an over view of Storage Area Networking. Ideal reading if you need a general overview rather than an in-depth, technical explanation.

SECTION 2:
LANS ARE BUILT ON A CABLE FOUNDATION

The importance and current implementations of cabling systems for data networks are reviewed in this section. The relevant cable standards are reviewed and the final section is a quick reference for current cabling specifications for Ethernet installations.

SECTION 3:
NETWORKING TECHNOLOGY REVIEW

This section reviews Ethernet, Token Ring and FDDI. Token Ring was not so rigorously specified so some of the issues are illustrated to ensure the reader is aware of the nuances. This section will bring a new entrant to networking bang up to date and give an understanding of why we are where we are.

SECTION 4:
INTRODUCTION TO FDDI AND TP-PMD

Gives a good overview of Fibre Distributed Data Interface (FDDI) and reviews the copper standard for this technology TP-PMD. This is included because users of this technology are reluctant to replace it as it has given great reliable networking service.

SECTION 5:
ATM TECHNOLOGY REVIEWED

Asynchronous Transfer Mode (ATM) is reviewed and some of the issues considered. This is a serious technology in carrier voice delivery services. It had found a niche solution in many corporate backbone networks so the support of Ethernet and Token Ring legacy networks is reviewed. However, it failed to capture any significant market share in the true LAN implementations.

ENTERPRISE NETWORKING

CONTENTS

SECTION 6:
HOW PCs GREW INTO THE NETWORK WORKSTATION

Explains PCs in a networking environment and the position of PCs with respect to the standards available for communication. This is an historical journey to positioning the PC at the centre of corporate computing and with the pervasiveness of the Internet the centre of all our lives.

SECTION 7:
BRIDGES, ROUTERS AND SWITCHES

Bridging and routing have become increasingly important as networks increase in size and new technologies mean that every port accessing the network will be a switched router port by the middle of this decade. This section illustrates the major differences and some applications. The two technologies are merging and being implemented directly into silicon these fast bridges are now called switches and the router as a hardware device is now considered a software service.

SECTION 8:
SWITCHES AND VIRTUAL NETWORKS

Networks today are moving over to switched infrastructures. And to map the system onto business functions and processes, a feature known as virtual networking has become dominant. The options are reviewed with the resulting benefits.

SECTION 9:
CHANGES IN WIDE AREA COMMUNICATIONS

There is a whole range of network technologies competing to be the best foundation for Wide Area Networks (WANs). Although LANs traditionally are seen as quick and reliable compared to WANs, this is changing fast. This section reviews Fast Packet technology options and brings the reader up to date with all the jargon used around VPN technology.

ENTERPRISE NETWORKING

CONTENTS

SECTION 10:
WIRELESS LANS

Cable-free networking is now possible. Recent improvements have boosted bandwidth and so broadened the scope of applications for which wireless LANs are appropriate solutions. And as the standards bodies focus on even greater speeds, applications will become more widespread. Compare the latest wireless network standard IEEE802.11a with its speed of 54Mbit/sec with the days when the industry said that twisted-pair copper wire had reached its limit at 112Kbit/sec!

SECTION 11:
NETWORK MANAGEMENT

A complete study of the problems facing network administrators and some technology recommendations as potential solutions. Developments in networking hardware have also made some management features more usable, such as one of the latest tools, policy-based management. Moves to build network management standards are also discussed.

SECTION 12:
SNMP, RMON AND SMON

Underlying the modern graphical user interface is a series of protocols that the technically oriented network manager will need to understand. So for those who want to know the details, here is a more detailed overview of Simple Network Management Protocol (SNMP), the Remote MONitor standard (RMON) and Switch MONitor (SMON) are highlighted.

SECTION 13:
NETWORK MANAGEMENT WITH ARTIFICIAL INTELLIGENCE

Following on from network management there is a major move to introduce artificial intelligence (AI) into managing a network. This section discussed the options of rules-based AI against inductive modelling-based AI.

ENTERPRISE NETWORKING

CONTENTS

SECTION 14:
RISK MANAGEMENT

Networks today are built on technology that works for many thousands of hours between failures. The more tasks that are performed in hardware the longer the gaps between failures. But hardware fails eventually so manufacturers have devised features to work around them. Recently the standards committees have defined a minimum set of standards to provide a degree of failsafe so you can now build networks with 100% service delivery guaranteed.

SECTION 15:
SECURITY - INFORMATION ACCESS IS AN ISSUE FOR TODAY

The Internet has changed the dynamics of networking. We now have the freedom to surf the Internet, intranets to service our own employees, and extranets to service business partners. This opening up of company resources puts a business at risk from hackers from both within and without. Here is a summary of today's defences.

SECTION 16:
SNA NETWORKING IN AN OPEN MULTI-PROTOCOL NETWORK

SNA is IBM's proprietary networking specification. Being old, it is widespread but users have been moving their SNA networks to open, IP-based multi-vendor solutions for the last 10 years. This section gives an overview of the environment and the issues to be considered when migrating to standards-based LAN solutions.

SECTION 17:
MULTI-SERVICE TECHNOLOGY

Rationalising technology spending is all the rage and, in the area of networking, this means moving to a multi-service communications infrastructure that can carry voice, video and data. Yet networks have grown organically over the past decade, with some having morphed into complex technology nightmares. We look at how today's networks can meet tomorrow's demanding challenges.

ENTERPRISE NETWORKING

CONTENTS

SECTION 18:
INTRODUCTION TO STANDARDS

This explains the OSI Seven Layer communications model, which is mandatory in any communications publication. There is no denying that OSI never made it but TCP/IP did. We keep it short and sweet.

SECTION 19:
THE HISTORY OF THIS INDUSTRY

If you are reading this and have got this far then you must be working in or with communications products. I have lived through all the changes in our industry and I can remember many of the significant milestones. However, if you remember them differently, let me know.

SECTION 20:
GLOSSARY OF LAN TERMS

section one

General Network Questions and Answers

Section 1: Network questions and answers

The section will answer the questions of the inquisitive user focused on Local Area Networking but touching on some relevant Wide Area Networking topics and an overview of Storage Area Networking. Ideal reading for those who do not require any real depth of explanation but just want a general overview.

ENTERPRISE NETWORKING

GENERAL NETWORK QUESTIONS AND ANSWERS

Q   What is a LAN?

A   An efficient cabling system that enables all computer resources to connect to each other. Installing a private cabling system (to which computer equipment can be connected) and using agreed procedures (protocols) enables communication. Prior to this cabling system, communications were point-to-point links dedicated from one terminal to one host connection port. This new cabling system and interconnection ability has become known as a Local Area Network, or 'LAN' for short. The IEEE802 official definition of a LAN:

"A Local Area Network is distinguished from other types of data networks in that the communications are usually confined to a moderately sized geographical area, such as a single office building, warehouse, or a campus area, and can depend on a physical communications channel of moderate to high data rate which has consistently low error rate."

Q   What is a WAN?

A   A WAN is a wide area network. This is used to describe the connections that computer systems use to get to a remote site, usually involving the rental of a line or service from the local telephone company. Some users get a wide area connection by using their telephone connection. Once a line is rented (normally known as leased line) then different communications methods are used to get the best price/performance for moving data between the remotely connected sites. These include modems, x25, ISDN, and Frame Relay; more techniques are discussed in Section Nine.

Cabling on the floors is not too congested but when you get the cables converging on to the host it is quite easy to see that the number of cables required is going to cause a problem. This is compounded by the fact that unused cables are never removed.

ENTERPRISE NETWORKING

GENERAL NETWORK QUESTIONS AND ANSWERS

Q Why do you require a cabling system?

A If you buy a host computer that has 20 terminals, then you have to lay 20 point-to-point cables from host to terminal. This means that next to the host there are cable ducts with 20 cables in them. When you add two more terminals, an installer will just lay two more cables since removal of existing cables costs just as much as installing new ones. You then have 22 cables to the host.

This has a number of disadvantages. While the re-cabling is carried out, it wastes cables, cost in re-laying the cable, productivity and causes discomfort. Furthermore, your cable ducts will eventually fill up and, the more cables you have, the harder it is to monitor, manage, diagnose and fix faults - and cable faults are common.

Q What is the cabling scheme?

A The cabling scheme is the plan you construct to lay appropriate cables and connectors and is determined by the type of cable used and the topology of the network solution. The cabling type decides the performance, all other things being equal and the topology decides the installation costs, future expansion costs and, in some cases, the actual resilience of the network.

Q What types of cable are available?

A There are four basic types of cable available: Unshielded Twisted Pair, Shielded Twisted Pair, Coaxial Cable and Fibre Optic Cable. Today there are also two main types of fibre optic cable: multi-mode and single mode.

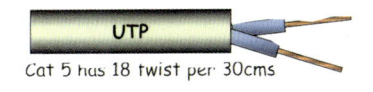

Cat 5 has 18 twist per 30cms

UNSHIELDED TWISTED PAIR (UTP)
This is the lowest cost cable and is often said to be the cheapest to install mainly due to low termination costs. A possible disadvantage of twisted pair cabling has been the low transmission speeds. However, with modern technology this is no longer true. Many networks use UTP today and super-grade cable is certified for 100Mbit/sec over 100 metres using 2-pair cable and 1000Mbit/sec over 100 meters using 4-pair cable.

ENTERPRISE NETWORKING

GENERAL NETWORK QUESTIONS AND ANSWERS

SHIELDED TWISTED PAIR (STP)
This cabling system was primarily promoted by IBM, it is more expensive than UTP but has the advantage of exceeding 100Mbit/sec and being less susceptible to electro-magnetic interference.

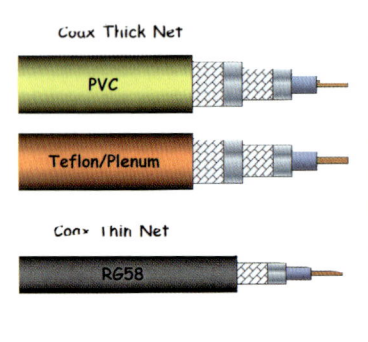

CO-AXIAL CABLE (CO-AX)
Supplied in varying diameters, the larger the diameter the greater the data throughput but also the cost. The connectors are more expensive and terminating the cable with these connectors results in the installation costs being higher. Co-ax has the advantage of being very resilient to interference and consequently can support large distances between devices, compared to twisted pair.

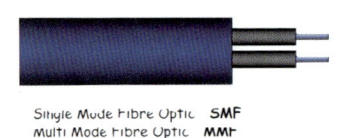

FIBRE CABLE
This is an exciting development and has shown a rapid acceptance in all areas of communications. Connection to the cable requires an active device to turn electrical signals into light signals and vice-versa. The world of fibre optics is rapidly developing to facilitate easier installations and termination techniques. There are two main types of fibre multi-mode, which is good for communications up to 2km, and mono - or single mode fibre, which is works over distances up to 40km. Fibre has the greatest data throughput capability of all the types of cable, making it attractive for future developments. Following heavy investment by telephone companies in fibre, manufacturing volumes have increased and prices have fallen considerably.

Q Are there any other methods?

A Yes, Wireless LANs, also known as Wi-Fi. These LANs can use infrared technology similar to the familiar, domestic remote control unit, or radio frequency (RF) similar to those employed delivering radio signals to telephone handsets on a military battlefield. The main disadvantage of infrared is the need to have a line of sight between stations. RF has overcome all of its early disadvantages - such as speed and security - and is fully covered in Section 10.

ENTERPRISE NETWORKING

GENERAL NETWORK QUESTIONS AND ANSWERS

Wireless communications are now being implemented as an overlay network to the wired solution. This provides freedom of movement and encourages collaborative working.

Q What choice of topology is there?

A There are three basic LAN topologies: STAR, RING and BUS LAN. Manufacturers offer combinations of these topologies to provide the benefits of each type within a single solution. The current trend is to design a fully meshed network giving improved redundancy in the backbone.

STAR - A central hub, providing the switching of data, is interconnected with devices on a 'point-to-point' basis producing a star configuration. A major advantage is there is minimal effect if a spur fails, although it is very reliant on the central hub which could be a single point of failure. Re-cabling can also be a problem, as it utilises point-to-point connections. This is offset by the low installation costs of the twisted pair cabling it uses and by pre-cabling an office using structured wiring solutions to create a grid system, thus enabling the quick and cheap relocation of terminals. This is the modern trend and is the main thrust of Section Two.

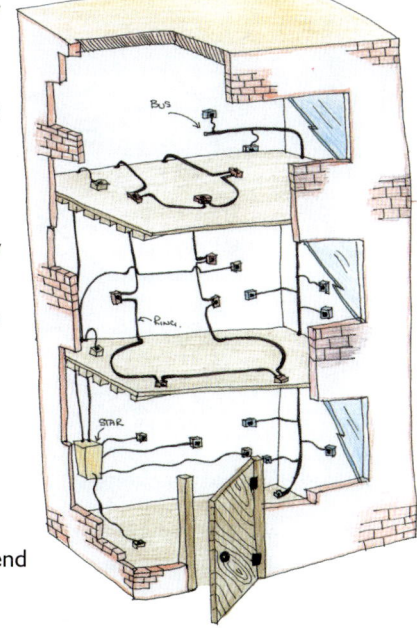

ENTERPRISE NETWORKING

GENERAL NETWORK QUESTIONS AND ANSWERS

RING - A ring of cable is placed round an installation and devices attached to it. One degree of cable fault tolerance is now available because if you break the ring once everything is still connected. However, rings are losing out to structured wiring today, mainly because additions and changes to the ring are harder to implement compared to the structured wiring approach.

BUS - A single cable run with devices tapping in. This involves installing a cable throughout the building which, once done, allows equipment to be freely moved, eliminating re-cabling costs. Cable failure would result in part of the network being lost and extending the network requires skilled staff. Bus techniques use co-axial cable but cable costs and the bulk of the cable makes installation difficult, so managers now favour systems using structured wiring.

FULLY MESHED TOPOLOGY - Here, redundant paths are used to cross-connect the core backbone switches and create back up paths, allow load sharing and routing on failure using recognised IEEE standards. From the backbone departments will be a STAR connected via the network switches. The redundancy features are covered in Section 14, Risk Management.

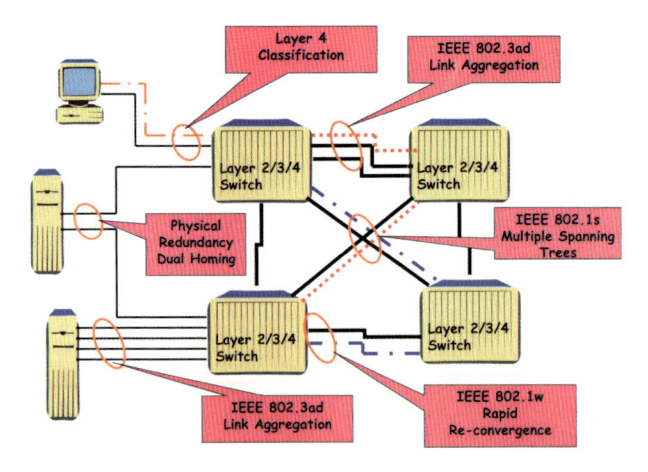

Q   Having installed a cabling system, how do I use it?

A   This usually involves purchasing an interface box which enables connection to the cabling. Different manufacturers have different names for the interface, such as Network Interface Unit or Terminal Access Point. The major difference is the

ENTERPRISE NETWORKING

GENERAL NETWORK QUESTIONS AND ANSWERS

method used to put the signals onto the cable. There are two aspects to consider: modulation and the access protocol.

Modulation - Here there is a choice of baseband, a digital signal carried on the cable or broadband, a radio frequency signal carried on the cable.

Baseband - Interfaces are relatively inexpensive as they require no special devices for generating the digital signal. Only one channel is available over the cable for communications.

Broadband - These interfaces generate signals at different frequencies and are effectively multiplexers, making them more expensive. One cabling system can carry many communications channels each using a different frequency. The frequency separation is laid down in the broadband standard. The easy way to think of it is to consider having several televisions on in a family room. You can all watch BBC1 or you could tune to different frequencies and some watch BBC2 and others watch ITV. You change neither the room nor the medium the radio waves are travelling in. That's how one or many networks can utilise a single cabling system. Broadband cabling is normally high-grade co-axial, which is bulky and relatively costly. Both planning for and installation of broadband LANs are typically more complex than baseband LANs.

Access Protocol - The function of the access protocol is to control the use of the cabling system so devices can share the cable and communicate with the desired recipient. (If you are in a room full of people and everyone spoke at once the information exchange would be very low, but if you all take turns to speak then the information exchange could be 100%). There is a choice of access methods specified by a standards committee, the Institute of Electrical and Electronic Engineers (IEEE). This is so all manufacturers make equipment that can inter-communicate. The IEEE standards for network equipment include: 802.3 Ethernet using CSMA/CD, 802.4 Token Bus using Token Passing, 802.5 Token Ring using Token Passing, 802.11 Wireless LANs. Common ANSI standards are Fibre Distributed Data Interfacing (FDDI) using multiple Token Passing and TP-PMD - A copper version of the FDDI specification.

CSMA/CD - (Carrier Sense Multiple Access/Collision Detection) Each 'node' listens before transmitting on the network and will only talk if the network is quiet. If a collision between simultaneous transmissions occurs, the transmitting nodes

ENTERPRISE NETWORKING

GENERAL NETWORK QUESTIONS AND ANSWERS

detect it and re-transmit the data after a random time interval. On this shared media network only one device may use the network at any one time.

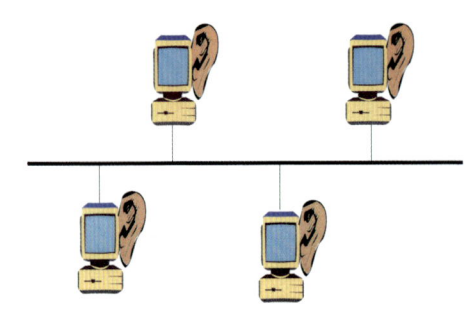

All workstations listen to the network. If it is silent, then a station can send information on the network. It then listens again to make sure what it sent is what is on the network. If the data is corrupted, another station must have done the same. Both stations wait for a random interval and try again.

The token-passing access method is controlled by a special frame or token that is passed from node to node throughout the network.

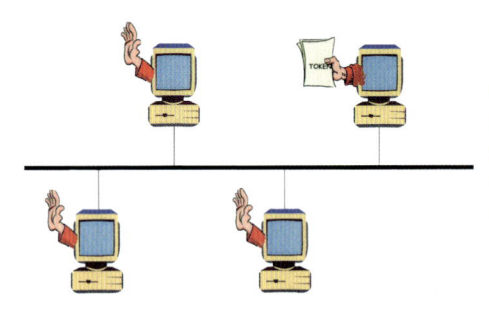

Each station accepts the one token in turn. If it does not want to communicate, it passes on the token. If it wants to communicate, it keeps the token until it's finished. On completion of sending out a packet, it hands on the token.

A node may only transmit data when in possession of the token, which is normally passed in order of network priority. This is also a shared media technology in that, with only one token, only one device can communicate on the cable at any one time.

Slotted Ring - this is a little-used IEEE standard today, and forms the basis of the FDDI Token Ring technique. Each node is allocated a time slot in which it may transmit on the network. Nodes monitor the token in turn which establishes an order of priority. When a device wishes to communicate it sets a free token and enters information into the packet.

ENTERPRISE NETWORKING

GENERAL NETWORK QUESTIONS AND ANSWERS

Here the networking infrastructure maintains a continuous stream of empty packets. The empty packets are denoted by a special token. If a station wishes to communicate, it sets the token and places its packet onto the network. When the packet returns with an acknowledgement, the workstation resets the token to 'free'.

Q These are baseband explanation (one communications channel) How would these technologies be achieved on broadband?

A You can have different access methods supported by broadband. In fact, you can support all three on one broadband system. Transmissions on broadband require the signal to be sent down the cable, then turned round and sent back up the cable. This is achieved by using a device known as the head end. Thus one channel is used for transmitting, and the other for receiving. You can think of this as being like having a number of sets of radios. You can set several to Radio One and another group to Radio Four, with each set representing a separate network. As with listening to the radio, Radio One doesn't interface with Radio Four so co-existence is fine.

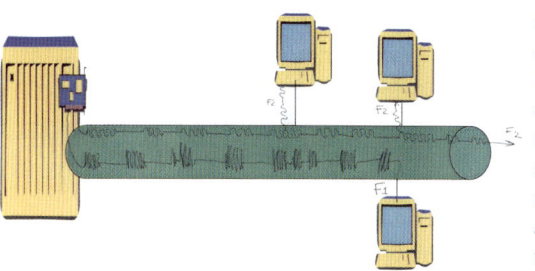

Here we have a 'master slave' configuration. The master is known as the 'Head End'. When a workstation wants to communicate, it sends a radio signal to the Head End. This will contain the packet of information. The Head End converts from the 'received' radio frequency to the 'send' radio frequency. All workstations working on that frequency will see the packet.

Q What will LANs do for me?

A To answer this question you should read Section Three. However, a basic LAN will enable interconnection of your computer equipment allowing you to move information between users/decision makers and share commonly used hardware

ENTERPRISE NETWORKING

GENERAL NETWORK QUESTIONS AND ANSWERS

such as modems, printers, plotters and host ports, all of which can be used by all without individual cabling. Office reorganisations are cheaper and easier when cabling already exists to provide the new connection.

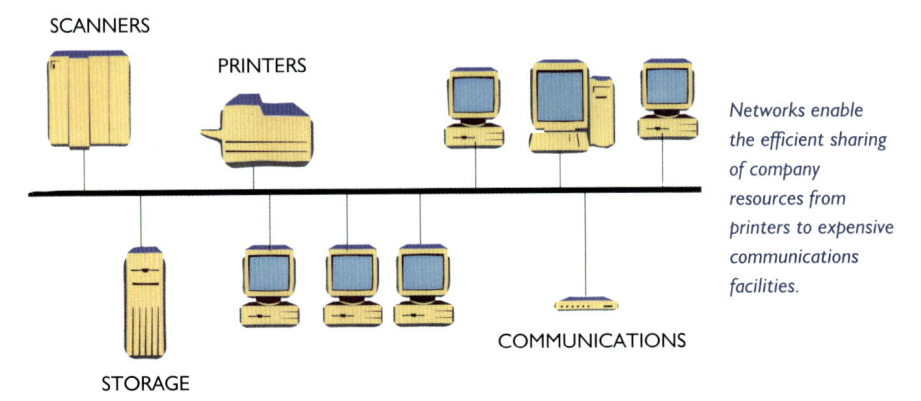

SCANNERS
PRINTERS

Networks enable the efficient sharing of company resources from printers to expensive communications facilities.

STORAGE
COMMUNICATIONS

Q   What is management of a LAN?

A   LANs are broadcast communications networks therefore they can be managed similarly to other communications networks. Some suppliers provide network management devices, others provide software for an intelligent terminal to perform the task. The basic job of the management unit is to monitor the communications, enable network diagnostics, provide security, control contention for ports, control queuing of calls to a shared resource and provide usage statistics. The statistics form the basis of service billing, future purchasing of hardware and future expansion of the system.

The latest focus for network management is to provide bandwidth management and billing services. MIS departments want to control the usage of resources so that an employee browsing the Web does not take resources away for the sales order processing running on an SAP application. Once the bandwidth is allocated, the MIS department wants to monitor and record traffic flow to enable the correct allocation of communications costs against the departments using the resources.

Q   What type of equipment can I connect to a LAN?

A   There are basically two types of LAN vendor, providing either closed or open systems. This describes the equipment that can connect to a given LAN

ENTERPRISE NETWORKING

GENERAL NETWORK QUESTIONS AND ANSWERS

technology. A closed system is manufactured by a company that wants its customers to have the benefits provided by a LAN but use only its products. Other vendor's equipment may ir will not inter-operate. Open systems are one those whose vendor whose main objective is to allow the communications between all equipment, irrespective of vendor and protocol.

If the LAN is closed, then the host supplier will provide a list of model numbers that will connect. If the LAN is open, then equipment is specified by international standards such as IEEE802.3 (Ethernet) and IEEE802.5 (Token Ring). Interface cards complying to these standards can be provided to fit most computer hardware.

Q   This sounds very simple. Is it as simple as Open and Closed LANs?

A   There is another complication. When we use a LAN, the idea is to pass data between two devices securely. We have already mentioned that we use the cable and need a standard access method for sharing the cable such as IEEE802.3, IEEE802.4 or IEEE802.5. Methods both of addressing the information so it gets to the correct destination and error checking are required which requires communications software to be available on the LAN. There are five possible choices of software:

1. Proprietary owned and used only by the host supplier.
2. XNS Xerox Networking Systems published by Xerox used by many of the early (1980's) LAN suppliers and which was the first documented protocol generally available.
3. TCP/IP Transmission Control Protocol Internet Protocol specified by the U.S. Department of Defence for use on its Area net installation. IP is the dominant networking protocol today providing vendor-independent networking.
4. IPX Internetworking protocol used by Novell in its PC networking solutions.
5. Open Systems Interconnect (OSI) which is a suite of protocols defined by the International Standards Organisation. All LAN vendors conform to the OSI architecture for communications products known as the OSI 7-layer model. However the imminent development of a complete OSI protocol stack is not on anyone's agenda. The main problem slowing down the implementation of OSI is the amount of memory and processing power needed by the networking devices to understand these protocols.

ENTERPRISE NETWORKING

GENERAL NETWORK QUESTIONS AND ANSWERS

Q   What is a Terminal Server?

A   During the early 80s, before the PC became pervasive, the way to use Host and Mini computer resources was to use a terminal. These devices, which were predominantly asynchronous in nature, had limited intelligence to allow low speed communications with the host at 9.6Kbit/sec to 19.2Kbit/sec and supported local screen displays and keyboards. The most popular terminal was the VT100 replaced later with the colour-capable VT220. IBM supported synchronous terminals generically known as 3270 terminals. To connect these low speed devices to a high-speed network required a device that could buffer data and had enough intelligence to run the required protocol stack. These devices were known as terminal servers. Many of the early LAN manufacturers produced asynchronous terminal servers but Ungermann-Bass and Bridge Communications were the only companies who produced the early synchronous terminal servers that supported 3270 devices. These used the LAN as a transport mechanism not as a resource-sharing medium. The idea of an intelligent buffer to connect low speed communications devices to the high speed resources of a LAN still survives today in the form of the Remote Access Server (RAS). The RAS connects users of remote PCs who are connecting to the LAN via a dial-up modem. Modems support speeds of 9.6Kbit/sec to 64Kbit/sec, the secondary rate ISDN speed. The RAS acts as the speed converter from WAN speeds to LAN speeds. Processor-driven devices, they are able to run other applications alongside their RAS ability. They can run security applications to authenticate the individual trying to dial in.

Q   How do I connect to other LANs?

A   There are several options available for interconnecting LANs by using local or wide area communications techniques. The products used are known as bridges, routers, switches and gateways. The major manufacturers of router products now include bridging capabilities. These products are known as brouters, although the growing dominance of switching has resulted in switch/router being the currently accepted nomenclature.

A bridge - the networks are interconnected locally or remotely but to the connected device they appear as the same network. The bridge will establish the connection but the devices will have to be compatible to exchange meaningful data across the connection. Bridges are also known as a datalink bridges.

ENTERPRISE NETWORKING

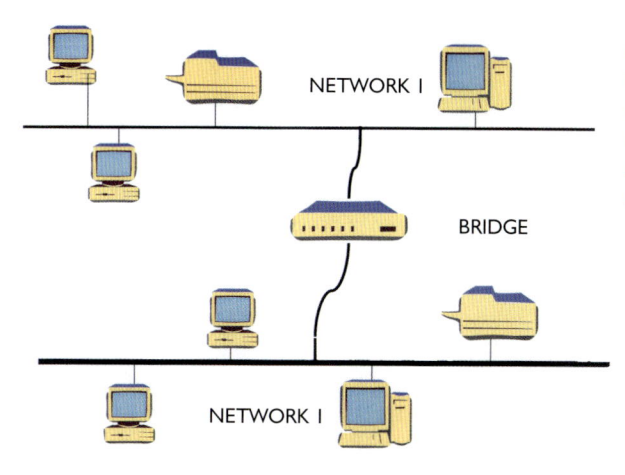

GENERAL NETWORK QUESTIONS AND ANSWERS

Bridges link multiple segments but they are all part of the same network. the bridge will only send information that needs to be on the distant segment to save bandwidth.

A router - this links two different networks that use the same network protocol. They have the advantage of being able to find a way through large networks. Also if one router is down it can find an alternative route to the destination. A router is capable of linking different media types such as linking Ethernet to Token Ring. These devices tend to have very complex software so they are more expensive than bridges and need very skilled engineers to support them.

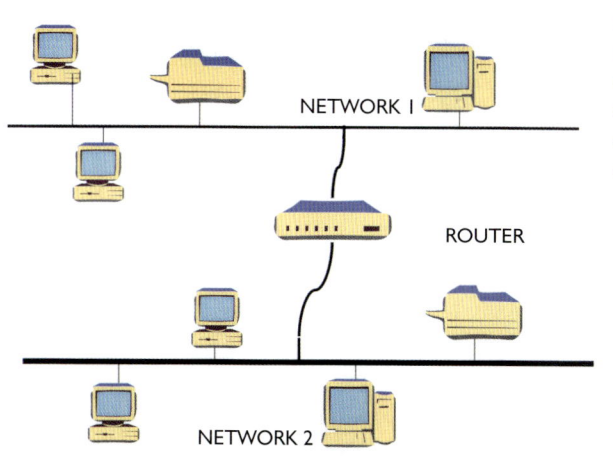

Routers were designed to connect to different networks and can use different technologies to do this. Routers give extensive control over traffic and form the backbone of the Internet.

ENTERPRISE NETWORKING

GENERAL NETWORK QUESTIONS AND ANSWERS

A switch - this initially was a bridge implemented in silicon providing pure wire speed communications and very large port densities in the networking devices.

More recently manufacturers have been able to put routing functions into specialist Application-Specific Integrated Circuits (ASICs) enabling wire speed switches to segment between different broadcast domains. Switches can now offer wire-speed performance - that is, they don't hold up any data while processing packets - while switching at Layer 2, Layer 3 and Layer 4.

A brouter - a multi-protocol router with in-built bridging technology. If the LAN has to support say TCP/IP and XNS, the brouter will be configured to route these protocols. If it fails to recognise the protocol it then bridges the data behaving as a datalink bridge.

A gateway - this device is used to convert from one type of system into a completely different system. Therefore it not only physically links the system, but converts one protocol into another. Gateways are commonly used to link LANs to WANs. They rely heavily on software because they accept information from one network, remove the protocol that was used and reassemble the information into the new protocol of the next network in the communications path.

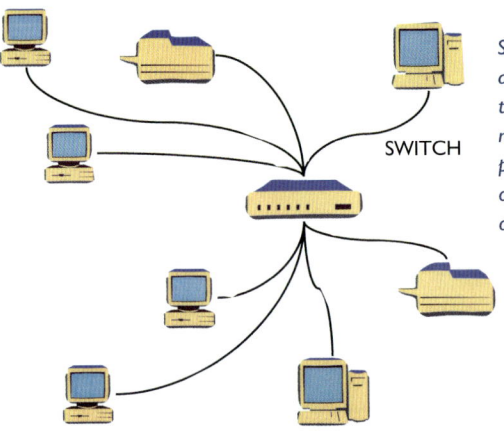

SWITCH

Switching treats every connection as a separate network, even though they could be the same network. Switches bring performance and greater control over networking traffic than any other technology.

ENTERPRISE NETWORKING

GENERAL NETWORK QUESTIONS AND ANSWERS

Q   I can connect dissimilar equipment on an Open LAN, but how can I get this equipment to communicate sensibly?

A   There are three options open to you, emulator software, protocol converter gateways, or OSI standards.

Emulator - the device runs proprietary software to pretend to be the same machine that it is to be connected to. Thus dissimilar machines can communicate by emulating each other or by emulating a well-known standard; for instance for file transfer, IBM's Bisync protocol was very common. The disadvantage is that each manufacturer can produce its own version of that unpublished application specification which can lead to incompatibility.

Gateway - as previously mentioned, a device that provides a network connection to a host, enables several network users to access the host and provides protocol conversion in both directions. A disadvantage is that it is usually restricted to one type of device, so a PC gateway works only for PCs. Gateways can be provided for hosts and communications services such as X25 or Frame Relay.

Protocol Converters - here a device translates the protocol in both directions much like a gateway, but protocol converters are designed and built for a specific task whereas gateways also provide the network connections along with software to perform the protocol conversion. The protocol converter can be configured for a terminal type such as VT220, and all devices emulate the VT220 and access the host the protocol converter is connected to. The disadvantage is that

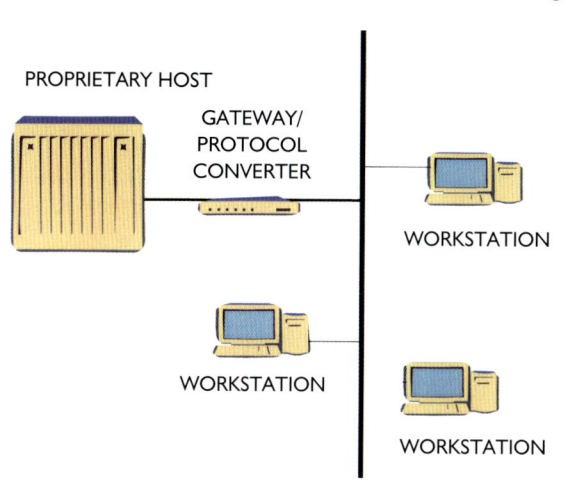

Here the standards based workstations access the proprietary host via the gateway

ENTERPRISE NETWORKING

GENERAL NETWORK QUESTIONS AND ANSWERS

you rely on a third-party supplier to keep up to date with the protocol, and host manufacturers are slow to inform other vendors of changes.

OSI Standards - by conforming to an international detailed standard, each supplier can provide, support and concentrate their resources on providing better applications. It then becomes the responsibility of all suppliers to take on the OSI standards. The purchaser of the LAN need not worry about the range of protocols to be supported, as only the one OSI protocol was required. Due to commercial pressure from widespread implementation TCP/IP has replaced the original OSI protocols.

Q I've heard of ATM. What is it?

A ATM is Asynchronous Transfer Mode a specification for transmitting information over a cell relay based infrastructure. You should read section seven for an understanding of this technology. It was first released as a new LAN standard but only gained acceptance in the backbone. Today, it is mainly used in WAN infrastructure communications.

Q What is the difference between LANs and WANs?

A LANs are local based around a privately owned cabling scheme. WANs connect geographically displaced locations and come in two commercial types. Either a WAN is private in which case the company leases a set of lines between the different sites or it is public, using a shared service for connections such as X25, ISDN, Frame Relay or a high speed service like SONet (USA) or SDH (Europe). LANs also tend to have much higher data rates than WANs. ATM was a technology used by both industries but lack of business applications has seen its popularity in the LAN area fade and it now forms the basic infrastructure of SONet (Synchronous Optical Networks) or SDH (Synchronous Digital Hierarchy).

Q Do WANS have the same OSI communications model?

A Yes, but the technology differs across the Wide Area. Communications have to interface into the existing telecommunications networks that were originally built for analogue voice communications. The old telephone systems relied on making a physical connection between the two end points. This type of connection has been termed connection-oriented networking. Technology has advanced however, and

ENTERPRISE NETWORKING

GENERAL NETWORK QUESTIONS AND ANSWERS

now we take advantage of the ability to create small blocks of information and send this information out of order and via different routes to a destination, reassembling it into its original order and form at the destination point. Such networks are known as connectionless. These small blocks of digital information are known as packets so the networks are also known as packet networks. This upgrade to convert into digital systems is not yet complete for all voice networks so devices such as modems retain their usefulness today. Section Nine covers the different access methods and protocols for the WAN looking at connectionless and the fast packet technologies.

The initial idea of creating easy access to remote resources and data for the American Department of Defense has grown to become a global phenomenon. The Internet is a global network of routers. Access to these routers is via a PoP (Point of Presence). This is a strategic location where an Internet Service Provider (ISP) has installed banks of modems connected to a router which in turn is directly connected to the Internet. All you have to do is make a local telephone call to the PoP, phone the number and as long as your membership is paid up, you get connected to the world for the price of a local call. PC, Televisions with set-top boxes and WAP phones can communicate with humanity.

Q   **What is the Internet?**

A   The US Department of Defense wanted a method of interconnecting its locations

ENTERPRISE NETWORKING

GENERAL NETWORK QUESTIONS AND ANSWERS

which did not rely on fixed connections. The result of the work was the ARPANet, work that was lead by Robert Morris senior who has since been referred to as the father of the Internet. This work also led to the invention of the TCP/IP protocol. ARPANet achieved its objectives of providing a packet-based network with equal access and the ability for anyone to connect to anyone else on the network.

The basic building blocks were the forerunners of today's router technology using the Internet Protocol (IP), and resulted in the birth of the Internet. This communications system outgrew its military birthright to include university research and information-sharing. To make using the Internet easier and more in line with the way professional people – as opposed to engineers - would access a system, a physicist at CERN devised a page-based way of adding links - which became known as hyperlinks - from the current page of information to pages of related topics. The protocol invented was HyperText Transfer Protocol (HTTP). HTTP enables the basic look and feel of what you see in your Web browser, particularly page layout and mouse clicks for jumping around and linking from document to document without knowing the location of the information. This ease of use and the later introduction of graphics support fuelled the proliferation of so many servers offering information and resources became known as the World Wide Web and the communications network linking them grew into the Internet as we know it today. Each country funded its own Internet and many companies formed new businesses to give people Internet access: the Internet Service Providers (ISPs).

"Here you are Grandma, I told you Johnny would be in his room. He's connected to the World Wide Web, and that's not his spider collection. For the cost of a local telephone call, Johnny can communicate with his friends in Japan, look around the art in the Louvre in Paris and send mail to all his school friends with one click of the mouse. And that's nothing to do with rodents."

ENTERPRISE NETWORKING

GENERAL NETWORK QUESTIONS AND ANSWERS

The Internet is a meshed connection of routers. The ISP enables anyone with access to a phone line to use a modem and dial into the ISP, who for a small fee will connect caller into an Internet-connected router. These connection points are known as points of presence (POPs). An ISP can provide local access for a whole country by establishing a Point of Presence in each telephony region. Therefore, every user pays only a local telephone call to get into the Internet and the Internet enables global communications.

Q What is an intranet?

A Businesses wanting to link all its employees from multiple sites to common information services use the Internet as a private resource. Using security tools to protect its servers, businesses can connect its server resources to the Internet and enable employees to be authorised to access company information. Remote users dialling up from home via a modem usually connect to a RAS (Remote Access Server) that checks their security details and enables access to company resources. A whole security industry has grown up to protect this connection to the Internet, delivering such technologies as firewalls, host intruder detection, network intruder detection and the widespread use of data encryption. See Section 15 for a complete overview.

Q What is Internet2?

A Internet2 is a research and development project advancing Internet communications to meet the needs of research and education. Over 170 US universities, working together with industry and government, are leading the Internet2 project. Internet2 is enabling applications like telemedicine, digital libraries and virtual laboratories to run. This would not be possible without the technology underlying today's Internet. The Internet2 backbone must provide limitless bandwidth with traffic classification for the appropriate Quality of Service to be applied over a global infrastructure. This requires a GigaPoP (Gigabit Point of Presence) that connects the Internet2 backbone to commercial businesses and university campuses.

Q What is VPN?

A Virtual Private Network is a networking technique for creating secure links across any communication infrastructure. Normally used to describe using a public,

ENTERPRISE NETWORKING

GENERAL NETWORK QUESTIONS AND ANSWERS

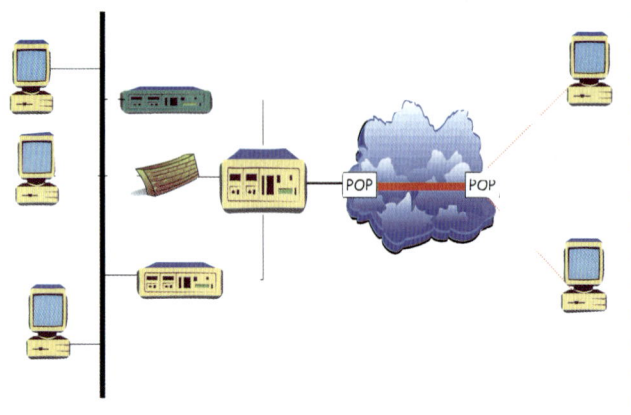

Virtual Private Networks (VPN's) are used by businesses to enable remote workers to log on to the corporate network securely. This is done at a very low cost via the Internet. All access to the Internet via a point of presence owned by an ISP (Internet Service Provider). All calls are local calls, so a remote worker can travel around the world and access his corporate network like a directly connected worker at local telephony rates.

Q What is SAN?

A   SAN stands for Storage Area Network and is for disk drive systems whereas LANs was for any computer and its peripherals. Since its inception in 1986, Small Computer System Interface (SCSI) has provided a standard for storage devices, SCSI accounts for more than 90% of the installed base. But SCSI has some limitations for today's data centres including short cabling distances and support for a limited number of devices on the SCSI bus. Several new technologies have emerged such as Serial Storage Architecture (SSA), Fibre Channel-Arbitrated Loop (FC-AL), Fibre Channel switching and FireWire.

An aside SCSI limitations

SCSI is limited to six metres for the single-ended bus and 25 metres for the differential bus. SCSI is share bandwidth maximum through put of 40 megabytes per second (40MB/sec) in a daisy-chain topology. Each device on the SCSI bus has a permanent ID number and an assigned permanent priority status based on that ID. Unfortunately, when several servers are connected, low priority servers have difficulty gaining access to storage during busy times. Also SCSI supports a limited number of devices, seven or 15 devices on the bus, depending on the SCSI version.

Fast Ethernet is the leading network connection for the server, this is capable of transmitting data at 8MB/sec - even ATM155 technology would limit the transfer to 12MB/sec in a practical application. Therefore Gigabit Ethernet and Fibre channel at 80MB/sec is a major improvement for storage communications.

ENTERPRISE NETWORKING

GENERAL NETWORK QUESTIONS AND ANSWERS

Packet-based network - connectionless technology - to behave like a private connection-orientated network. More recently, VPN technology has been developed to enable business users to use the Internet as a secure communications medium. The advantage of this is that Internet access is universal and cheap compared to private leased lines which are anything but. See Section 9 for a full description.

section two

The Cable Foundation

Section 2: Local Area Networks are built on a Cable Foundation

The importance and current implementations of cabling systems for data networks are reviewed in this section. The relevant cable standards are reviewed and the final section is a quick reference for current cabling specifications for Ethernet installations.

ENTERPRISE NETWORKING

THE CABLE IS THE LAN FOUNDATION

In the 1990s, local area networking changed from enabling the sharing of expensive resources into a strategic company resource, which for many enterprises is their competitive advantage. The emphasis is on information flow. This information is transported by the active LAN components and the associated communications software in a secure, error-corrected, resilient environment across the cable. As the vehicle enabling the information flow, the cable supports a company's business. Irrespective of networking technology - whether Ethernet, Token Ring, LocalTalk or FDDI - its cabling infrastructure is the most significant investment an organisation makes.

A project to install a network into a medium-sized business can give managers a shock, especially if it is the company's first foray into local area networking. It is surprising to discover that the LAN technology rarely accounts for more than 30% of the costs. The design, procurement, project management and installation of the cabling infrastructure will account for the lion's share of the projects budget. Once this major investment is undertaken, the corporate purchaser has historically considered the cable infrastructure as a 10 to 15 year investment. Technologies can change, indigenous host suppliers can be usurped by new competitive start-ups, but all modifications to the IT solution must live with the cable infrastructure.

Companies are in business to make money and to grow to make more money. Any IT solution is therefore destined to grow in parallel. It is vital for any organisation investing in information technology that it should have a network strategy. This strategy is more about the cable infrastructure than the technology that makes use of it.

Cabling is viewed the same as any utility such as the water supply or the electricity supply. this is at odds with the technology that connects to the cabling infrastructure which has a life cycle of two to three years.

ENTERPRISE NETWORKING

THE CABLE IS THE LAN FOUNDATION

A significant technological achievement reached by the LAN companies is the ability to provide Ethernet 802.3 10Mbit/sec, 100Mbit/sec and 1000Mbit/sec, Token Ring 802.5 4Mbit/sec, 16Mbit/sec and 100Mbit/sec on unshielded telephony twisted pair cabling. Electro-magnetic interference (EMI) and other sources of outside interference have traditionally been a concern with UTP wiring but transmission technologies combined with modern UTP's physical characteristics have eliminated this concern. When wires are twisted together, each receives the same amount of noise through the cable's jacket. Since the signal is sent as a difference of two lines, the noise is common to both lines and the difference is not affected. This cancellation effect is known as common-node rejection. Today several of the major LAN vendors have developed products for unshielded twisted pair supporting speeds of 1000Mbit/sec with 100 metres between nodes. This technology, on the face of it, appears to offer major cost savings in cable plant installations. However, the cable may be cheaper on termination cost and components are significantly less expensive, but the manpower to lay the cable in a building still costs the same. So where do the cost savings come from by using unshielded twisted pairs?

Cost of Ownership

The first insight into the costs resulting from the ownership of IT products was provided by the Gartner Group, an American-based, business information service organisation. In 1987, the Gartner Group published the results of its survey of major organisations across the USA. It discovered that it costs, on average, $1,500 to move a computer user, while a telephony user was only costing an organisation $300 for the same move, amounts that are significantly higher today. Why the difference in cost? The answer was found in the saturation wiring provided by telephone wiring schemes. Wherever the employee moved, a phone jack could always be found within a few metres. With data cabling, a special team often working out of hours, had to be called in with inevitable expense. The team would design and install the specialist type connections required to extend a traditional LAN installation. The conclusions were that an organisation using an unshielded saturation wiring system could afford to provide a connection to every location, whereas a traditional solution was neither economical nor practical in providing a saturated installation.

The immediate question that arises is, *"Is it important for saturation wire as I don't have the need at present for a connection at every location?"* The Gartner Group report also found that in an average organisation, 22.5% of all employees will move within a year - the churn rate. This is the rate of additions, moves and changes that will effect the computer

ENTERPRISE NETWORKING

THE CABLE IS THE LAN FOUNDATION

installation over a year. If you are in any doubt about the benefits, add up your computer users, find 22.5% of them and multiply by $2,500 (using today's prices) and you're losing this operational cost year on year by not having saturation wiring. In the financial sector, churn rates of up to 80% are common. To provide a managed solution to saturation wiring, several companies have devised modular wiring schemes that have all the cable/components for a total solution but which can be installed in a modular fashion. These are known as structured wiring schemes. AT&T's is most probably the best known, the Premises Distribution System. IBM had a structured wiring scheme but initially heavily promoted shielded twisted pair, although UTP was part of the scheme. British Telecom offered its Open System Cabling Architecture (OSCA) and most leading IT suppliers had similar offerings under a variety of names.

These structured wiring schemes had a similar approach to enable modular introductions if a big bang approach was out of the question. The wiring schemes supported all types of connectivity including LANs, voice, and port to port terminal host capabilities. So at any time, you could start to implement a solution with your existing technology.

There are lots of arguments about which is the cheapest cabling system but the cost of cable installation is a function of manpower time so installation costs are similar across technologies. The component and cable costs make the difference: it boils down to whether your organisation is willing to invest in the future or go for a quick fix today.

The Structured Solution

A structured wiring solution is broken down into a set of sub-systems. Each sub-system has a range of cables and products designed to provide an economical saturated wiring solution for a given area.

Work Location Sub-System

Starting at the user, there is a work location sub-system. This sub-system can be both unshielded and shielded or fibre with a range of baluns to physically interface a user

ENTERPRISE NETWORKING

THE CABLE IS THE LAN FOUNDATION

device or computer resource into a wall socket. Baluns (BALanced/UNbalanced) match the impedance characteristics of co-ax, twin-ax, or dual co-ax to that of twisted pair, enabling conversion from twisted pair to the appropriate type of connector. As a result, IBM's 3270 terminals, System/3X, and AS/400, as well as computer systems from Wang Laboratories Inc., and other vendors that require exotic cabling schemes, will function in a twisted pair environment.

Horizontal Sub-System

The second module is the horizontal wiring sub-system. This sub-system can be provided on co-ax, fibre, shielded or unshielded twisted pairs, however, few people use co-axial cable here because it is relatively expensive, less flexible and occupies more space in ducts or cable trays. This provides connectivity from the wall sockets to a wiring punch down block or patch panel. This is usually housed in the wiring closet, which is part of the administration sub-system.

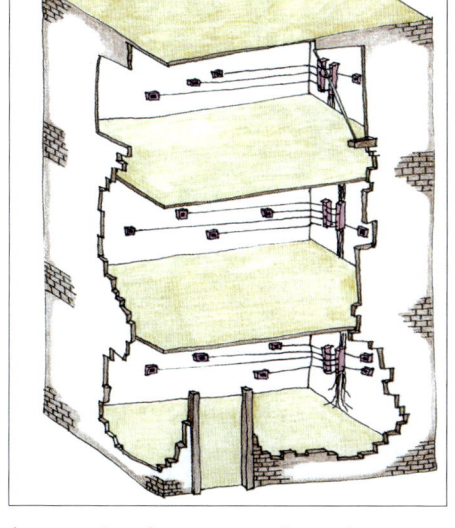

Administration Sub-System

This consists of the cross-connects or physical connections between patch panels or punch-down blocks, consisting of multiple connections, interconnects, a single connection between patch panels or punch-down blocks, and interfaces that provide a method of linking other sub-systems. A building may already have one or more of the sub-systems in place to support voice services. These sub-systems can be adapted or augmented to support other types of communications such as data or video. The existing twisted pair wiring in most buildings provides flexible, low cost data cabling solution that eliminates proprietary media schemes such as co-axial, twin axial or dual co-axial cable, while still allowing for high transmission rates. But you would need to find a LAN supplier who is prepared and capable of testing the existing cable and certifying it for these high-speed transmissions. Most companies insist that a building is rewired with the new cabling scheme.

ENTERPRISE NETWORKING

THE CABLE IS THE LAN FOUNDATION

Back Bone Sub-System

The backbone sub-system provides the interconnection of the administration sub-systems. Once again, fibre, co-ax and unshielded twisted pairs are supported. However, there is a definite trend in new installations to use fibre for the data traffic. Although more fibre interfaces have recently become available, they are often thought of as expensive. New multimedia, video, data and voice, applications will increase demand and this increase in production will enable the price to fall. Splicing and terminating fibre optic cable used to require a high level of expertise, but with the latest fibre splicing kits available, the operation can be performed by most technicians. Fibre optic is clearly the medium of choice for this type of sub-system. Characteristics such as immunity to electromagnetic interference, security, high bandwidth, and small diameter make it an ideal medium for the interconnection of horizontal sub-systems.

Fibre optic cable provides an order of magnitude increase in bandwidth over copper. A strand of fibre, only one sixth of a human hair can carry as much data as 800 pairs of copper wire. With the increase of clutter in conduits and cable trays, size has become an important consideration when choosing cabling.

Campus Sub-System

Finally the Campus Sub-system, which interconnects the various buildings in a linked geographical area. Co-ax or fibre can be utilised but fibre is easily the preferred solution, thus connecting various building backbone sub-systems into a cohesive enterprise wide network.

LAN Industry Support

Networking on these structured wiring schemes has been the major focus for many LAN companies. The solutions are generically termed intelligent hubs. A hub provides a high number of LAN connections for all types of cabling, fibre, co-ax, and twisted pair. Each hub also supports a mix of networking concentrators to provide a range of services. Many of these products are advanced technologies that enable data to co-exist with voice and video in the same twisted pair sheath. While this may seem desirable, it is more common to run individual four pair sheaths for each termination point. You can install two, four-pair sheaths for a small incremental cost instead of installing either a single eight-pair or 12-pair sheath.

In addition, this four-pair wiring configuration conforms to the integrated services digital

ENTERPRISE NETWORKING

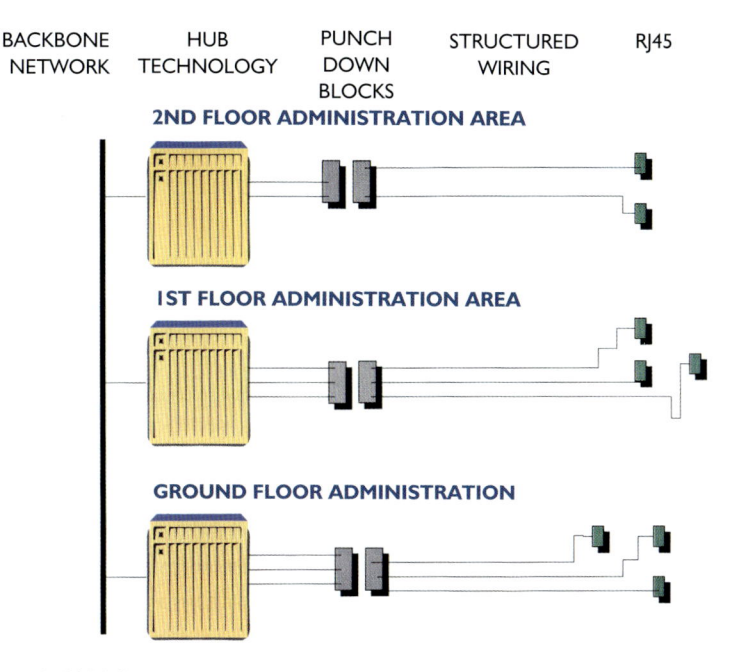

THE CABLE IS THE LAN FOUNDATION

BACKBONE NETWORK | HUB TECHNOLOGY | PUNCH DOWN BLOCKS | STRUCTURED WIRING | RJ45

2ND FLOOR ADMINISTRATION AREA

1ST FLOOR ADMINISTRATION AREA

GROUND FLOOR ADMINISTRATION

network (ISDN) standard and ensures you will not have problems with technologies such as video-conferencing systems. These products all support a modified star topology where point to point connections can form a star of UTP (Unshielded Twisted Pair) along the horizontal, and fibre/co-ax on the vertical risers. This modular structure in the horizontal wiring subsystem allows for the rapid connection and movement of devices. Since the topology is a physical star, it eliminates many of the traditional problems of bus and ring architectures, such as a single point of failure. It also provides for fault tolerance, hubs that support Ethernet and Token Ring and can provide management of individual ports. This gives multi-vendor solutions a degree of management by monitoring and managing individual cable runs.

If a given threshold of traffic or number of errors is reached then automatic segmentation occurs, isolating the offending equipment and preserving the remainder of the network. Not only LAN companies believe that this implementation of structured wiring on the horizontal and fibre backbone sub-system on the vertical, is the correct solution. The internetworking manufacturers, who provide complementary product to the LAN manufacturers, supply router technology products for interconnecting large, geographically displaced networks believe that box product solutions are not the way of

ENTERPRISE NETWORKING

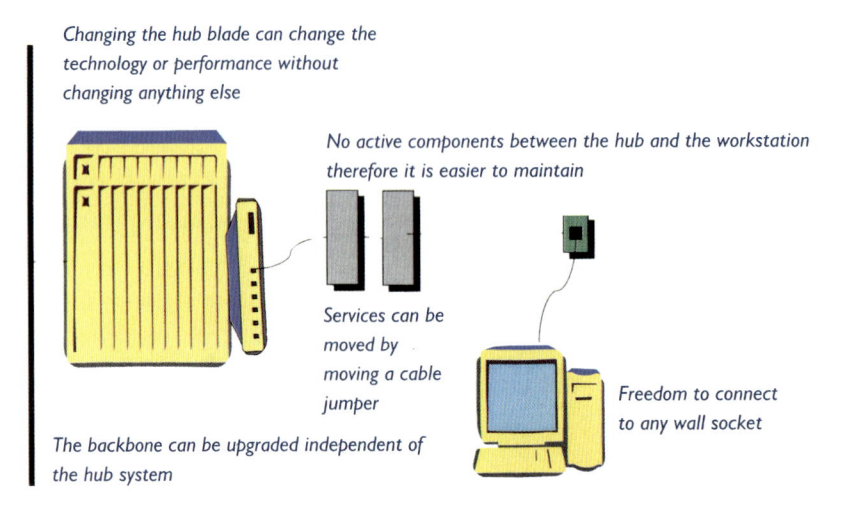

THE CABLE IS THE LAN FOUNDATION

Changing the hub blade can change the technology or performance without changing anything else

No active components between the hub and the workstation therefore it is easier to maintain

Services can be moved by moving a cable jumper

Freedom to connect to any wall socket

The backbone can be upgraded independent of the hub system

the future. Router products have to go into the wiring closet and utilise the structured wiring infrastructure. LAN/WAN joint developments have become the norm over the last few years resulting in integrated solutions supporting common hub platforms. These developments have resulted in hardware-based switching. The hubs have migrated into modular switches supporting existing cabling systems.

Tomorrow's Infrastructure

Networking has moved into key business areas as the strategic weapon in providing the competitive edge. This is changing the way organisations make their purchasing decisions. A realisation of the importance of the cable plant and the savings delivered by moving to structured wiring makes this the solution of choice. Organisations who are used to the technology are now reviewing the cost of ownership. Once you own a network it grows and your churn rate causes additions, moves and changes. Clearly the cost of ownership is lower with a structured wiring solution. The communications industry is supporting it and your choice of technology is available today with Ethernet 10/100Mbit/sec including the newer 1000Mbit/sec, Token Ring 4/16Mbit/sec and 100Mbit/sec, FDDI as TP-PMD 100mbit/sec supported on unshielded twisted pairs. The technology invented to provide integrated services networking was Asynchronous Transfer Mode (ATM) technology. This was designed to carry data, video and voice over a common infrastructure. However, the commercial interest and investment into Ethernet has pushed this technology into new areas by enabling features like Quality of Service, traffic priority and huge increases in

ENTERPRISE NETWORKING

THE CABLE IS THE LAN FOUNDATION

bandwidth (up to 10Gbit/sec). Ethernet dominates and there is no sign of any technology challenging its position. ATM resides in the WAN network as a transport mechanism.

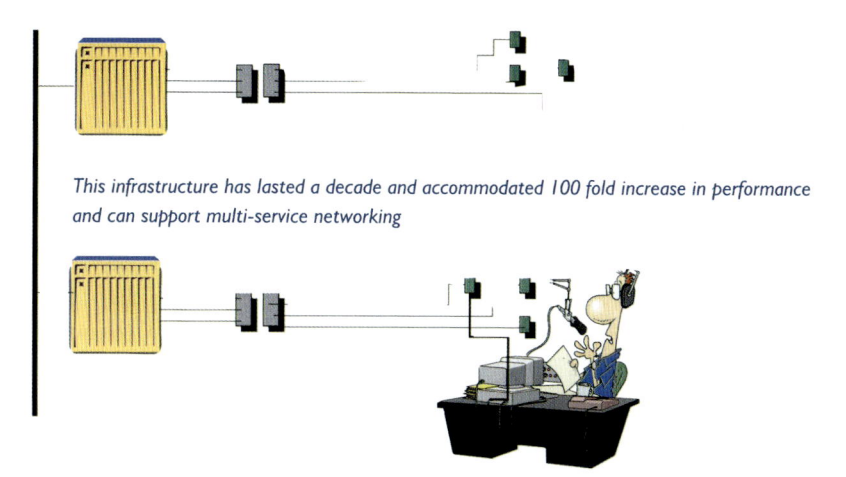

This infrastructure has lasted a decade and accommodated 100 fold increase in performance and can support multi-service networking

ATM is a cell- (rather than packet-) based technology that provides switched dedicated connections unlike the traditional shared-bandwidth solutions of Ethernet, Token Ring and FDDI which have had to go through several iterations till we reached the switched solutions available today. The good news is that these switched solutions require a star-wired cabling infrastructure. So your next technology change will be supported on these existing structured wiring schemes providing that the category 5 (see below) cabling was used. The issue you have to wrestle with is the progress made by wireless networking currently at 10Mbit/sec, moving shortly to 54Mbit/sec and many research dollars trying to ratify a 100Mbit/sec solution. To cable or not to cable? That is the question.

Cable Specifications

In November 1991, the Electronic Industries Association published a document entitled 'Technical Systems Bulletin Additional Cable Specifications for Unshielded Twisted Pair Cables', Document. (TSB-36 can be obtained from Global Engineering Documents, 2805 McGaw Avenue, Irvine CA 92714). This document describes the specifications for categories of UTP cables. It also describes the techniques for measuring these specifications. It includes definitions for category 3 which is specified up to 16MHz, category 4 specified up to 20MHz, and category 5 specified up to 100MHz. When purchasing cables you should ask your vendor to meet or exceed the specifications

ENTERPRISE NETWORKING

THE CABLE IS THE LAN FOUNDATION

defined in TSB-36. The specified parameters are mutual capacitance, attenuation, near end cross talk (NEXT), and impedance. The impedance of the data grade categories of cable including cat3, cat4 and cat5 must be 100Ohm (Ω) +/- 15% at all frequencies. By following these guidelines, your cable plant should be compatible with all LAN systems up to each specified frequency.

Twisted pair cables for LANs are marked up and certified according to an accepted standard developed by Underwriters Laboratories Inc. This programme, announced in November 1991, takes of the guesswork out of ordering the correct grade of twisted pair for 10BaseT, 16Mbit/sec Token Ring and TP-PMD applications. This programme is for the marking on the cable jacket to verify that the cable does meet EIA/TIA 568. This programme certifies 100Ω TP, but is not limited to UTP. UL has left the door open for shielded versions of 100Ω UTP. Note that IBM Type 1 STP commonly used in Token Ring is a 150Ω cable, and 10BaseT, 16Mb Token Ring on UTP uses 100Ω cable.

The objective of these universal cable markings was to make life easier for end users. You can call your favourite cable manufacturer and order their TP wire by a UL certification level. You can tell by looking at the jacket on the cable if it is the right stuff. This makes life much easier for the technical staff, who has to try and figure out if the connections are working. You would be surprised at the number of installations where so-called wet string has been used instead of quality cable. The UL certification levels break down in five levels, one being the lowest, and five being the best. For 10BaseT the customer will need to order UL level-3 (or category 3), for 16Mbit/sec Token Ring the customer needs UL level-4, and for TP-PMD the customer will need UL level-5. The best advice that you can offer the customer is to buy the highest level they can afford! 10BaseT will work on level-5, but TP-PMD will not work on level-3. So if they want to plan for the future, install level-5 in the first place. The customer should also use the same level grade for all jumpers/patch cables. Also be aware that there are currently no 25-pair cables that are graded higher than level-3. Token Ring and TP-PMD will not work in multi-bundle cables!

The cables that have been UL certified will carry a marking on the jacket that must appear in one of the following manners: 'Verified level #' or 'Classified level #' (LVL or LEV may be substituted for level), and the # must be displayed as a roman numeral. You can call UL and request a document called 'UL's LAN Cable Certification Programme' at 1 800 676 WIRE on the East Coast or 1 800 786 WIRE on the West Coast. This programme is good for our industry and we should help promote it. Technology Distance Specifications

ENTERPRISE NETWORKING

THE CABLE IS THE LAN FOUNDATION

CABLE GUIDE

Technology Distance Specifications
Copper:

Standard IEEE	Data Rate	Medium	Maximum Cable Segment Length in meters	
			Half Duplex	Full Duplex
10Base-5 802.3	10Mbit/sec	Single 50-Ω RG58 co-axial cable (thick Ethernet) 10mm thick	500 meters	N/A
10Base-2 802.3a	10Mbit/sec	Single 50-Ω RG58 co-axial cable (thin Ethernet) 5mm thick	185 meters	N/A
10Base-T 802.3i	10Mbit/sec	Two pairs of 100-Ω Category 3 or better UTP cable	100 meters	100 meters
100Base-TX 802.3u	100Mbit/sec	Two pairs of 100-Ω Category 5 UTP cable	100 meters	100 meters
1000Base-T 802.3ab	1Gb/s	Four pairs of 100-Ω Category 5 or better cable	100 meters	100 meters

ENTERPRISE NETWORKING

THE CABLE IS THE LAN FOUNDATION

Standard IEEE	Data Rate	Medium	Maximum Cable Segment Length in meters			
			MMF		SMF	
			Half Duplex	Full Duplex	Half Duplex	Full Duplex
10Base-FL 802.3j	10Mbit/sec	Two optical fibres	2km	2km	5km	10km
100Base-FX 802.3u	100Mbit/sec	Two optical fibres	412	2km	5km	20km
		short wavelength laser (850nm) over:	**Maximum Cable Segment Length in meters**			
			Half Duplex		Full Duplex	
1000Base-SX 802.3z	1Gb/s	62.5um multi-mode fibre	275		275	
		50um multi-mode fibre	316		55	
		long wavelength laser (1300nm) over:				
1000Base-LX 802.3z	1Gb/s	62.5um multi-mode fibre	316		550	
		50um multi-mode fibre	316		550	
		10um single-mode fibre	316		5km	

Quick cable notes

COPPER:

10Base-5

Transmission Rate: 10Mbit/sec (full-duplex not supported)
Maximum Number of Transceivers per Segment: 100
Signal Encoding: Manchester encoding
Typical connectors used: N-type co-axial connectors, barrel connectors, and terminators

10Base-2

Transmission Rate: 10Mbit/sec (full-duplex not supported)
Maximum Number of Transceivers per Segment: 30
Signal Encoding: Manchester encoding
Typical connectors used: BNC T-piece co-axial connectors, barrel connectors and terminators

ENTERPRISE NETWORKING

THE CABLE IS THE LAN FOUNDATION

10Base-T

Transmission Rate: 10Mbit/sec (20Mbit/sec in optional full-duplex mode)
Signal Encoding: Manchester encoding
Typical connectors used: RJ45/RJ21

100Base-TX

Transmission Rate: 100Mbit/sec (200Mbit/sec in optional full-duplex mode)
Signal Encoding: 4B/5B
Typical connectors used: RJ45/RJ21

1000Base-T

Transmission Rate: 1000Mbit/sec (2000Mbit/sec in optional full-duplex mode)
Signal Encoding: PAM5
Typical connectors used: RJ45

FIBRE:

10Base-FL

Transmission Rate: 10Mbit/sec (20Mbit/sec in optional full-duplex mode)
Signal Encoding Manchester encoding
Typical connectors used: ST

100Base-FX

Transmission Rate: 100Mbit/sec (200Mbit/sec in optional full-duplex mode)
Signal Encoding: 4B/5B
Typical connectors used: MTRJ/SC

1000Base-SX

Transmission Rate: 1000Mbit/sec (2000Mbit/sec in optional full-duplex mode)
The 'S' in 1000Base-SX stands for 'short wavelength lasers' to transmit data over fibre optic cable. Short wavelength lasers have the advantage of being less expensive than long wavelength lasers.
Only multi-mode optical fibre is supported.
Signal Encoding: 8B/10B
Typical connectors used: SC

1000Base-LX

Transmission Rate: 1000Mbit/sec (2000Mbit/sec in optional full-duplex mode)
The 'L' in 1000Base-LX stands for 'long wavelength lasers' to transmit data over fibre

ENTERPRISE NETWORKING

THE CABLE IS THE LAN FOUNDATION

optic cable. Long wavelength lasers are more expensive than short wavelength, but have the advantage of being able to drive long distances.

Both single mode and multi-mode optical fibres are supported, in conjunction with the Mode Conditioning Patch Cord.

Signal Encoding: 8B/10B

Typical connectors used: SC

Mode Conditioning Patch Cord:

The Mode Conditioning Cables are solely for running MMF over LX technology. LX equipment (Mode Conditioning Patch Cord and LX card) must be deployed on both sides of the connection.

Cable Definitions

568A is an EIA/TIA standard for the termination of an 8-wire RJ-45 cable. 568A, 568B and AT&T 268A are functionally identical, but uses different colour wire identification. They both differ from the older USOC termination pattern that was widely used by AT&T.

AUI (Attachment Unit Interface) is an IEEE 802.3 standard name for the cable connecting an Ethernet transceiver to a networked device. An AUI cable is equipped with a 15-pin connector that mates with a 15-pin connector on the networked device. Also called 'Thick Ethernet' or 'Thick Net'.

Attenuation is the decrease in magnitude of a signal as it travels through any transmission medium such as copper cable or optical fibre. Measured in dB per unit of length.

BNC (Bayonet Neill Concelman) is a co-axial connector that uses a bayonet-style turn and lock mating method. Used with RG-58 or smaller co-axial cable. Used with 10Base2 Ethernet thin co-axial cable 'Thin Net'.

Category 1 - Cat 1 Unshielded Twisted Pair used for transmission of audio frequencies. Used as speaker wire, doorbell wire, etc. Not suitable for networking applications.

Category 2 - Cat 2 Unshielded Twisted Pair used for transmission at frequencies up to 1.5MHz. Used in analogue telephone applications. Not suitable for networking applications.

ENTERPRISE NETWORKING

THE CABLE IS THE LAN FOUNDATION

Category 3 - Cat 3 Unshielded Twisted Pair with 100Ω impedance and electrical characteristics supporting transmission at frequencies up to 16MHz. Defined by the TIA/EIA 568-A specification.

Category 4 - Cat 4 Unshielded Twisted Pair with 100Ω impedance and electrical characteristics supporting transmission at frequencies up to 20MHz. Defined by the TIA/EIA 568-A specification.

Category 5 - Cat 5 Unshielded twisted pair with 100Ω impedance and electrical characteristics supporting transmission at frequencies up to 100MHz. Defined by the TIA/EIA 568-A specification.

Category 5e - Cat 5e, Enhanced Cat 5, Cat 5+

Category 5e is a new standard that will specify transmission performance that exceeds Cat 5. Cat 5e has improved specifications for NEXT, PSELFEXT, and Attenuation. Like Cat 5, it consists of Unshielded Twisted Pair with 100Ω impedance and electrical characteristics supporting transmission at frequencies up to 100MHz. To be defined in the TIA 568-A-5 update.

Category 6 - Cat 6 is a proposed standard that aims to support transmission at frequencies up to 250MHz over 100Ω twisted pair.

Category 7 - Cat 7 is a proposed standard that aims to support transmission at frequencies up to 600MHz over 100Ω twisted pair.

Cladding - the material surrounding the core of a fibre optic cable. The cladding must have a lower index of refraction than the core in order to contain the light in the core.

Conduit - a rigid or flexible metallic or non-metallic casing for supporting cabling for protection and to prevent burning cable from spreading flames or smoke in the event of a fire.

Core is the central region of an optical fibre cable through which light is transmitted.

Crossover Cable - a twisted pair patch cable wired in such a way as to route the transmit signals from one piece of equipment to the receive signals of another piece of equipment, and vice versa. Contrast with straight-through cable.

Dark fibre is unused optical fibre. Usually pre-installed for later use a practice of carriers and large businesses. The user is responsible for adding the transmission system at both ends when the service is required.

ENTERPRISE NETWORKING

THE CABLE IS THE LAN FOUNDATION

DB Connectors come in 9, 15, 25, 37 and 50-pin sizes and are widely used connect computer and communications devices.

Hybrid Cable is an assembly of two or more cables (of the same or different types or categories) covered by one overall sheath.

Hydra describes a cable that is spliced into eight or more breakout cables. There is one connector on one end and multiple connectors on the other (Typically RJ71/RJ21 to RJ45 connectors).

MMF - Multi-Mode Fibre is optical fibre with a core diameter of from 50 to 100 microns. It is the most commonly used optical fibre for short distances such as LANs. Light can enter the core at different angles, making it easier to connect the light source. However, light rays bounce around within the core causing some distortion and providing less bandwidth than Single-Mode fibre.

MTRJ - also known as mini-MTRJ, brings the size, cost and simplicity benefits of RJ-45 copper connections to fibre optics. This was designed for ease of use for networking applications such as FDDI, ATM, Fibre Channel, Gigabit Ethernet, and general premises cabling. The MTRJ housing, while maintaining polarity of the cable, provides smooth insertion and removal of the connector pairs, and yet it's one of the smallest connectors available. It's actually a little smaller than a standard phone jack, and just as easy to connect and disconnect. It's half the size of the SC connector it was designed to replace.

N - connector a co-axial connector used for Ethernet 10Base5 thick co-ax segments.

NTI is the equipment required to convert from the two-wire U interface to the four wire S/T interface. This equipment is NOT REQUIRED outside of North America.

Octopus cable is a cable that is spliced into eight breakout cables (octopus has eight tentacles). There is one connector on one end and multiple connectors on the other, typically RJ71/RJ21 to RJ45 connectors. Some companies make even bigger octopuses.

Optical Fibre is a thin glass or plastic filament used for the transmission of information via light signals. Fibre optic technology offers high bandwidth and gives protection from electromagnetic interference, eavesdropping and radioactivity.

Pin-outs are the descriptions and purpose of each pin in a multi-line connector.

Plenum - a cable that is plenum-rated is suitable for running through air ducts and spaces between the floor and ceilings without being enclosed in conduit. It uses a fire retardant coating that must comply with local building codes.

ENTERPRISE NETWORKING

THE CABLE IS THE LAN FOUNDATION

FEP - Plenum-rated. Designates copper cabling with cladding made of Fluorinated Ethylene Polyethylene thermoplastic.

PVC is not plenum-rated (must be run through conduit). Designates copper cabling with cladding made of PolyVinyl Chloride.

RJ-21 - (Registered Jack-21) An Ethernet (CAT 5) cable that uses a 50-pin Telco connector.

RJ-45 - (Registered Jack-45) Eight-wire RJ-45 connectors are used with Ethernet.

RJ-71 - (Registered Jack-71) An Ethernet (CAT 3) cable that uses a 50-pin Telco connector.

RS-232 - (Recommended Standard-232) An TIA/EIA connection standard for serial transmission between computers and peripheral devices. It uses a 25-pin DB-25 or 9-pin DB-9 connector.

RS-449 - (Recommended Standard-449) Defines a 37-pin connector for RS-422 and RS-423 circuits.

RS-530 - (Recommended Standard-530) Defines a 25-pin connector for RS-422 and RS-423 circuits. It allows for higher speed transmission up to 2Mbit/sec over the same DB-25 connector used in RS-232, but is not compatible with it.

SC Connector - a fibre optic connector having a 2.5mm ferrule, push-pull latching mechanism, and the ability to be snapped together to form duplex and multi-fibre connectors. SC connectors are the preferred fibre optic cable for premises cabling, and are recommended by the TIA/EIA-568-A Standard for structured cabling. Used with Ethernet 100Base-FX and 1000Base-LX/SX fibre optic media systems.

SMF - (Single-Mode Fibre) is an optical fibre with a core diameter of 10 microns or less. Used for high-speed transmission over long distances, it provides greater bandwidth than multimode.

ST Connector is the designation for the 'straight tip' connector developed by AT&T. This fibre optic connector features a physically contacting, non-rotating 2.5mm ferrule design and bayonet connector-to-adapter mating. Used with Ethernet 10Base-FL and FIORL links.

STP - (Shielded Twisted Pair) twisted pair cable in which the pairs are enclosed in an outer braided shield, although individual pairs may also be shielded. STP most often refers

ENTERPRISE NETWORKING

THE CABLE IS THE LAN FOUNDATION

to the 150Ω IBM Type 1, 2, 6, 8, & 9 cables used with Token Ring networks.

Straight-through Cable - a twisted pair patch cable that the wires do not cross. Contrast with Crossover Cable.

TIA - (Telecommunications Industry Association) Body which authored the TIA/EIA 568-A 'Commercial Building Telecommunications Wiring Standard' in conjunction with EIA.

UTP - (Unshielded Twisted Pair) cabling that includes no shielding. UTP most often refers to the 100Ω Category 3, 4, & 5 cables specified in the TIA/EIA 568-A standard.

section three

Networking Technology Review

Section 3: Networking Technology Review

This section reviews Ethernet, Token Ring and FDDI. Token Ring was not so rigorously specified so some of the issues are illustrated to inform the reader of the nuances. This section will bring a new entrant to networking bang up to date and give an understanding of why we are where we are.

ENTERPRISE NETWORKING

NETWORKING TECHNOLOGY REVIEW

SETTING THE SCENE

Networking Standards and even more networking products have been developed and deployed in enterprise networks only to be replaced by yet another round of innovations. All these innovations are destined to revolutionise the way we do business and provide the organisation with the latest technical edge. Today, the Ethernet standard dominates the LAN connectivity industry in all its forms. This is not because it was the best technology but because of the sheer number of manufacturers who support it. The research and development dollars invested into Ethernet totals the total spent on all other LAN developments. However businesses have strict financial rules and no organisation can just change its IT investment overnight. Therefore in the real world there are many networking technologies that you will come across for many years to come. Therefore we will take the next few sections to review the legacy you are most probably dealing with on a day to day basis.

The IEEE802.3 Ethernet and 802.5 Token Ring standards together account for all but a small portion of corporate LAN installations worldwide. FDDI was the first major backbone and server connectivity solution but was short-lived and superseded by ATM as standard in the backbone of many enterprise class networks. This, in turn, was surpassed by Ethernet.

The IEEE802.3 Ethernet standard started life at 1Mbit/sec but quickly moved to the 10Mbit/sec variant supported by various media including co-ax, fibre, and twisted pair cables IEEE802.3i. Its popularity has resulted in a flurry of standards activity to push its capabilities even further. We now have 100Mbit/sec Fast Ethernet IEEE802.3u, 1000Mbit/sec Gigabit Ethernet IEEE802.3z and soon we will have 10,000Mbit/sec Ethernet 10GbE ratified as IEEE802.3ae. The IEEE802.3 standard was adopted by the International Standards Organisation (ISO) in 1983 and is now in widespread use around the world. The IEEE802.5 Token Ring standard, introduced in 1985, was originally developed by IBM and had limited vendor support. Token Ring operated at 4Mbit/sec but was quickly upgraded to run at 16Mbit/sec. Then, during 1998, the first 100Mbit/sec IEEE802.5t products were introduced and by late 1999 we received 1000Mbit/sec Token Ring IEEE802.5v. The question is which standard is best? Before answering that question, let us review the history and current status of Ethernet and Token Ring standards.

ENTERPRISE NETWORKING

NETWORKING TECHNOLOGY REVIEW

IEEE802.3 ETHERNET STANDARDS

Ethernet was invented at Xerox in Palo Alto in the USA, 1976. The patent for CSMA/CD was awarded to the Xerox Corporation in 1977. Commercialisation of Ethernet was achieved by an industry consortium of DEC, Xerox and Intel in 1981 as Ethernet Version 1.0 using CSMA/CD at 10Mbit/sec. The Ethernet technology that dominates today started with a specified by the IEEE in 1983 as the 802.3 10Base5 LAN standard. This specified thick co-ax cable up to 500 metres in length and up to 1024 devices connected to a single cable. Most people still refer to this standard as Ethernet, even though there are some minor differences between original Ethernet and the IEEE802.3 specifications. Users and vendors quickly learned that what works well in the lab is not always practical in the real world. Thick Net co-axial cables were unsuited to the office environment. The cable was not only expensive and bulky but difficult to install and maintain. Early Ethernet users began installing lower cost, easier to work with, RG58 Thin Net co-axial cable in place of Thick Net co-ax. This rapidly gained acceptance and was adopted by the IEEE802.3 committee as the 10Base2 Thin Net standard in 1985. This limits the length of a Thin Net segment to 185m with a maximum of 30 connections. Because of these limitations, 10Base2 Thin Nets are usually connected into Thick Net backbones using multi-port repeaters.

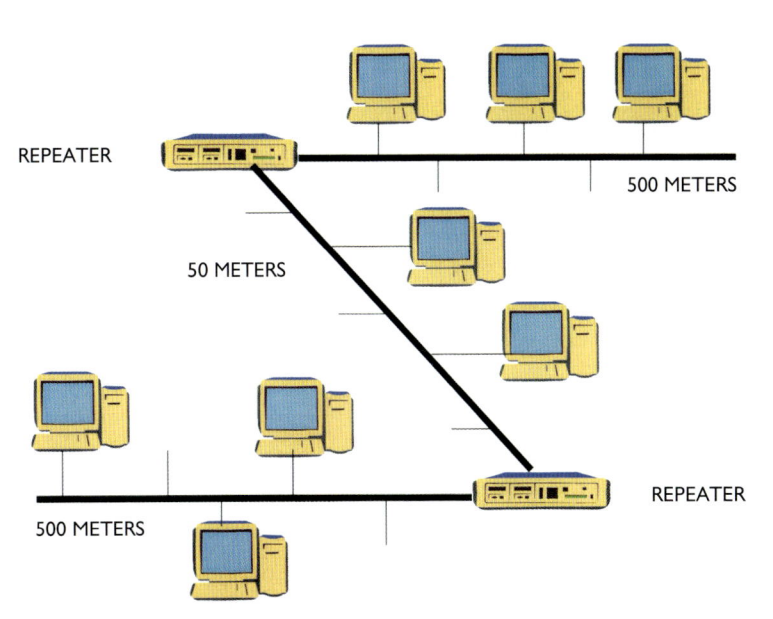

ENTERPRISE NETWORKING

NETWORKING TECHNOLOGY REVIEW

The IEEE802.3 repeater standard was approved in 1985. The repeater provides for the regeneration of Ethernet packets as they move from one cable segment to another. The repeater also provides a level of fault protection. The basic repeater rules enable a damaged cable segments to be effectively disconnected from the rest of the network until the fault is corrected. In an Ethernet network, the standard states that only two repeaters can be in any signal path. This would allow three segments to be linked together giving a distance of 1500 metres. To gain further distances the idea of having half-repeaters evolved. This is where the input and output of a single repeater are separated by a cable connection, usually a fibre cable. This cable cannot have device connections to the cable itself, it is only to support the link connection. This technique is used to gain several kilometres of network coverage. Depending on the network's configuration, packets can pass through up to four half-repeaters when travelling from source to destination.

Another important standard developed with the repeater standard is the Fibre Optic Repeater Link (FOIRL) standard. The FOIRL standard defines the requirements for a fibre optic transceiver (MAU-media access unit) that can be used to link repeaters together over distances of up to 1Km. Although the FOIRL standard was developed to connect repeaters together, it is also widely used for connecting end-user devices into the Ethernet when optical fibre is the media of choice.

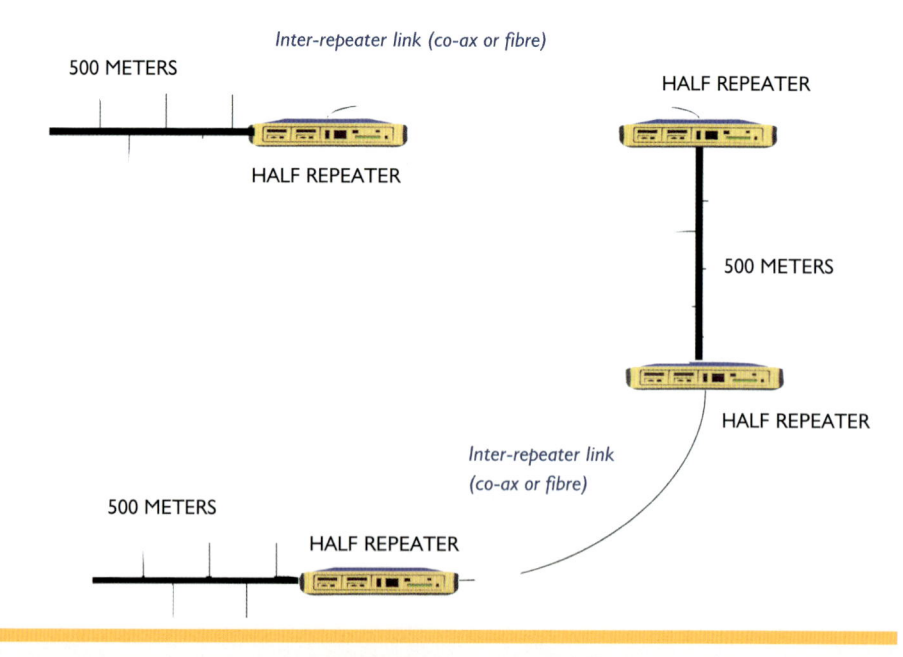

ENTERPRISE NETWORKING

NETWORKING TECHNOLOGY REVIEW

In 1992, the IEEE802.3 10BaseF task force developed additional fibre optic Ethernet standards. There were three elements to this standard, IEEE 10Base-FA for active star, defines a new fibre optic MAU and hub. This scheme is similar to the FOIRL standard except that data is synchronised at the transceiver, not at the hub. This method allows the data packets to travel through more hubs than the 'four repeater' limit set by FOIRL. Unfortunately, these differences require the definition of a new hub in place of the current repeater standard. With the widespread use of bridges, the 'four repeater' limit was rarely an issue. So FOIRL remained the dominant standard implementation.

The second FOIRL standard, IEEE 10BaseFP, was known as the passive star implementation. This scheme makes use of an optical splitter for the hub. Its chief benefit is that it requires no power at the hub. It does have some serious problems, the most significant being that in most installations the network will require tuning or balancing of the optical power received at each node whenever the network's configuration is changed. This problem was solvable by increasing the dynamic range of each receiver but that increases the manufacturing cost. Finally the IEEE adopted FOIRL as an IEEE standard IEEE 10Base-FL. One wonders why they bothered.

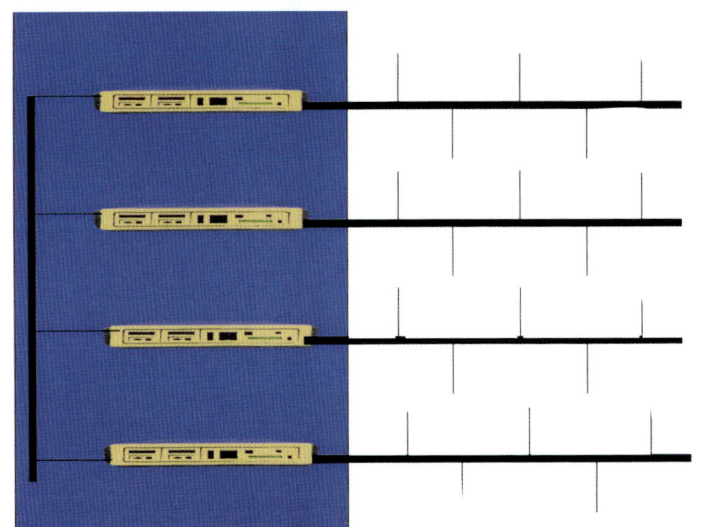

Put all the repeaters into a single unit and you have a multi-port repeater

Subnets support 30 users per net on Thin Net

ENTERPRISE NETWORKING

NETWORKING TECHNOLOGY REVIEW

10BASET TWISTED PAIR ETHERNET

The use of Thick and Thin Net co-axial cable was overshadowed by the use of Unshielded Twisted Pair (UTP). Various vendor-specific products had been available since 1987 to permit Ethernet operation over UTP. The IEEE802.3 10BaseT committee first met in August of 1987 at a meeting sponsored by Hewlett Packard. This became an official standard for networking in August 1990 the IEEE802.3i standard. However, diehards still call it 10BaseT after the committee. The IEEE802.3 committees did not give up and by 1994 we had a standard for 100Mbit/sec Ethernet on category 5 UTP cabling the 100BaseT specification. By 1997 the IEEE responded to the fact that installations

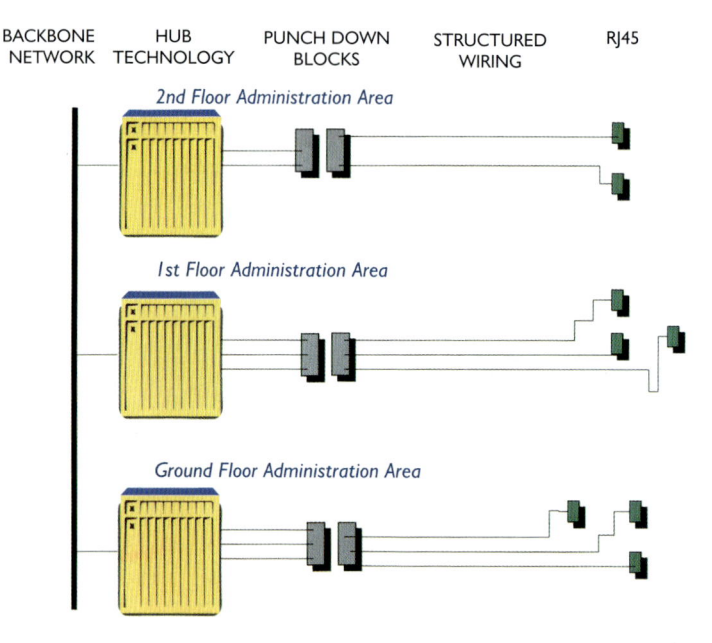

BACKBONE NETWORK	HUB TECHNOLOGY	PUNCH DOWN BLOCKS	STRUCTURED WIRING	RJ45

2nd Floor Administration Area

1st Floor Administration Area

Ground Floor Administration Area

were now all star-wired, with Ethernet workstations being on their own individual connection. This paved the way for IEEE802.3x the full duplex derivative of Ethernet, which permeated through all of the subsequent Ethernet derivatives. Gigabit Ethernet IEEE802.3z was specified in 1998, operating at 1000Mbit/sec over fibre and gained widespread adoption during 1999 and 2000. The UTP version of Gigabit Ethernet was ratified in 1999 as IEEE802.3ab specifying category 5 four-pair UTP cabling. In 2001 we will start to see the introduction or 10,000Mbit/sec products using the specifications

ENTERPRISE NETWORKING

NETWORKING TECHNOLOGY REVIEW

developed by the GEA (Gigabit Ethernet Alliance). This will only be available in a fibre version and is initially aimed at the Metropolitan Area networking requirements and will use Dense Wave Division Multiplexing (DWDM) at the Data Link layer.

There is a cautionary note that the reader should be aware of in the march for world dominance of Ethernet. When networks are built today they are usually constructed on structured wiring schemes, which are described in section two. One of the main aims was to save money on the additions, moves and changes the churn rate of a network. Ethernet, Token Ring, TP-PMD copper FDDI and ATM standards based products can move freely across these cabling schemes. But as we have striven for pure, available bandwidth this flexibility has started to diminish. Even the 100Mbit/sec Fast Ethernet standard created differing distances for whether a product is an active device or a passive device and what function the device is performing. This means caution has to be taken when connecting a 100Mbit/sec Ethernet device.

IEEE802.5 TOKEN RING STANDARDS

The IEEE802.5 Token Ring LAN standard was first approved in December of 1984. This was for networking 260 devices on a logical ring of shielded twisted pair cabling. The current 802.5 standard, which deals primarily with medium access control (MAC) sub-layer requirements, defines only basic physical layer functions including symbol encoding and decoding, symbol timing and latency buffering for 1Mbit/sec and 4Mbit/sec ring speeds.

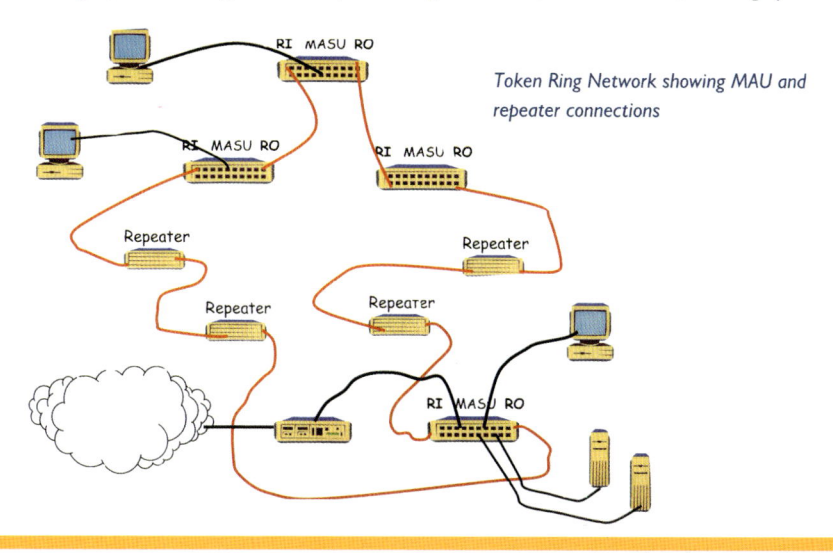

Token Ring Network showing MAU and repeater connections

ENTERPRISE NETWORKING

NETWORKING TECHNOLOGY REVIEW

Section seven of this standard provides specifications that define the shielded twisted pair cable Media Interface Connectors (MIC), and Trunk Coupling Unit (TCU) that should be used when building a Token Ring LAN. For most of its early years Token Ring had no IEEE802.5 media attachment standards for either unshielded twisted pair or fibre optic cabling. Lacking these standards, many proprietary Token Ring networks have developed which was one of the contributory factors in the lack of widespread Token Ring support from LAN manufacturers. Unfortunately, not all of the systems will inter-operate. The best known proprietary Token Ring was IBM, whose standards differ slightly from the IEEE802.5 standard but are generally compatible. In truth, most vendors actually manufactured their products to the IBM standards.

IEEE802.5 standard was first published in 1984 and included networking on 1Mbit/sec and 4Mbit/sec networks however the 1Mbit/sec was dropped in 1989. At the same time 16Mbit/sec was proposed but no media specifications existed. Over the next couple of years feverish work had being carried out on IEEE802.5m, the Source Routing Committee; IEEE802.5l the early Token Release committee; IEEE802.5f the 16Mbit/sec standards committee; IEEE802.5j Token Ring Fibre Optic Station Attachment; IEEE802.5k Token Ring Media Specifications. Today, the IEEE802.5 committee has completed the missing media specifications covering active and passive hubs, and the use of UTP and fibre optic cabling for station to hub connections and stretched the specifications to include 100Mbit/sec and 1000Mbit/sec Token Ring.

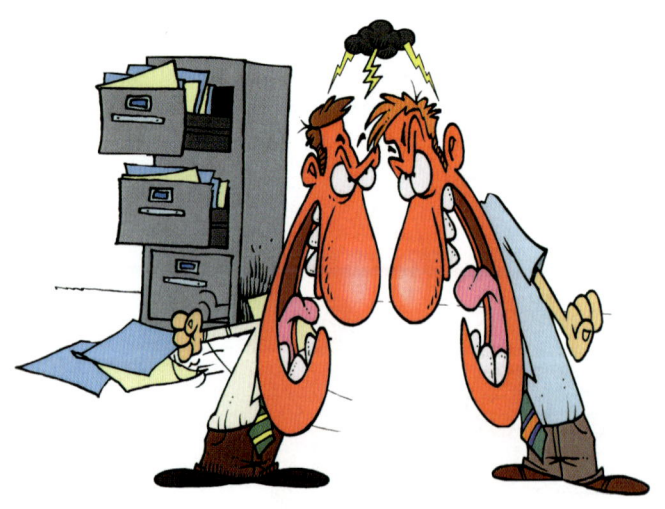

Today, Token Ring or Ethernet is not the question, as many organisations have made their investment in the last century. The issue today is, how does the Token Ring network migrate into an Ethernet Network for the simple reason that there is choice and investment in Ethernet but very few manufacturers of Token Ring products in a diminishing market place.

ENTERPRISE NETWORKING

NETWORKING TECHNOLOGY REVIEW

WHICH IS THE BEST TECHNOLOGY ETHERNET OR TOKEN RING?

Since 1985 there has been a long-running debate over which LAN standard is best, Ethernet or Token Ring. While each has some clear advantages over the other, experience has proven that from a data flow point of view, either method is acceptable. The main issue was not transfer speed, since both are more than fast enough for most applications, but ease of implementation and reliability. The real winner here is unshielded twisted pair. Both Ethernet and Token Ring LANs were implemented using UTP. Ethernet does have a clear advantage over Token Ring due to the fact that the IEEE802.3 committee had approved the 10BaseT standard early giving a clear cost advantage to enable Ethernet to dominate in the marketplace. Now in 2001, the latest market figures has Token Ring's installed base at 20-30 million nodes depending which LAN report you read, while Ethernet is more like 250-350 million nodes.

Token Ring today is still lagging behind Ethernet in terms of chip vendor support. National Semiconductor, AMD, Intel, NCR and other chip vendors manufacture Ethernet chip sets. Only one major chip manufacturer Texas Instruments manufactured an IEEE802.5 Token Ring Chip set. Initially TI's Token Ring chip set operated at the slower 4Mbit/sec data rate, TI's 16Mbit/sec chip set did not reach LAN vendors until spring 1990. This delay had further slowed the implementation of Token Ring based LAN's outside of the 'IBM only' world.

IBM recommended that users install Type 1 Shielded Twisted Pair (STP) cable for their networks. This made a significant difference in the cable installations costs of Token Ring, further disadvantaging it in favour of the simpler, cheaper Ethernet solutions. On initial introduction the 16Mbit/sec products were available to operate over UTP. Also when operating a 4Mbit/sec IBM Token Ring over UTP, the maximum number of stations is reduced from 260 to 72. This limit was often a problem for corporate LANs where the number of users can be many hundreds, if not thousands of nodes. However, over time, standardisation of active Token Ring networking products had gone some way to bring param,eters such as the number of stations and specific UTP, STP multimode fibre and monomode fibre cabling into line. But in terms of dominating the market place it's a case of too little too late.

FAULT TOLERANCE

It is often said by Token Ring enthusiasts that Token Ring is more reliable than Ethernet. This claim is based on a Token Ring being made up of cables in a point-to-point star

ENTERPRISE NETWORKING

NETWORKING TECHNOLOGY REVIEW

topology, simple unpowered MAUs and a cable wrap feature on the main ring. On the other hand, an Ethernet requires an active, powered transceiver attached to a single co-axial cable in a bus topology. It is true that cutting the co-axial cable of a basic 10Base5 or 10Base2 Ethernet would cause a failure of that cable segment. Ethernet designs that make use of multi-port repeaters and UTP cabling have made this problem non-existent since Ethernet has changed from a bus to a star-based logical network and physical star wiring. Today all networks are based on hardware switching and the topology of a LAN can be identical, regardless of its access method Ethernet or Token Ring.

Now that we have all the background information we can concentrate on all the considerations required in designing a network that is adaptable to changing technologies, flexible to company additions, moves and changes and upgradeable to newer standards as the evolve. The basic concept of Token Ring was to support a ring of Multi-Station Access Units that were passive. The connection of the station to the MSAU was via a lobe cable.

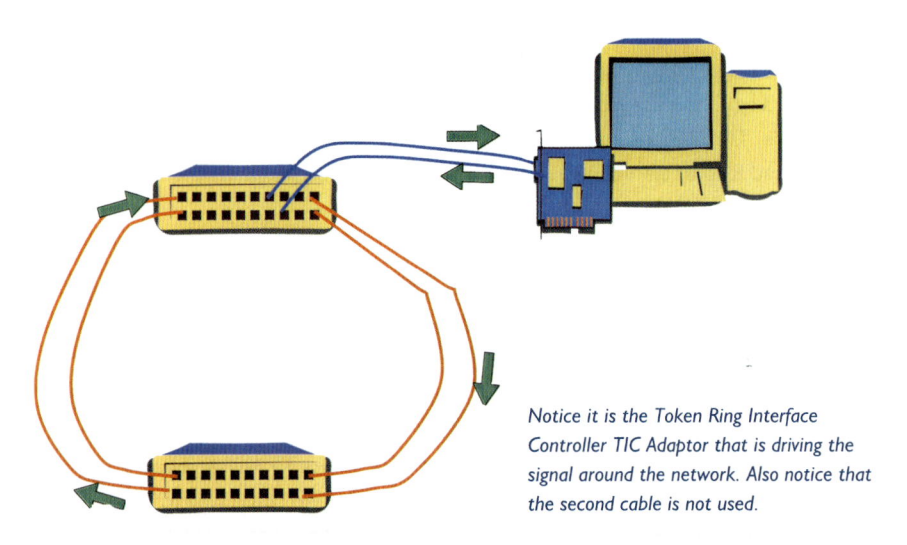

Notice it is the Token Ring Interface Controller TIC Adaptor that is driving the signal around the network. Also notice that the second cable is not used.

Therefore, a Token Ring network could be set up in the wiring closet connecting the MSAU's to the structured wiring and these star-wired lobes are provided to each location. There are however, several flaws with this passive approach. Firstly, being passive there is no re-generation of the signal at the MSAU. Therefore it is the actual workstation/host connection which is generating the signal and driving it round the network. So if you had a network of one device with a large MSAU concentration, the

ENTERPRISE NETWORKING

NETWORKING TECHNOLOGY REVIEW

device has to send its signal all the way around the network to its own receiver side to know it is the only device.

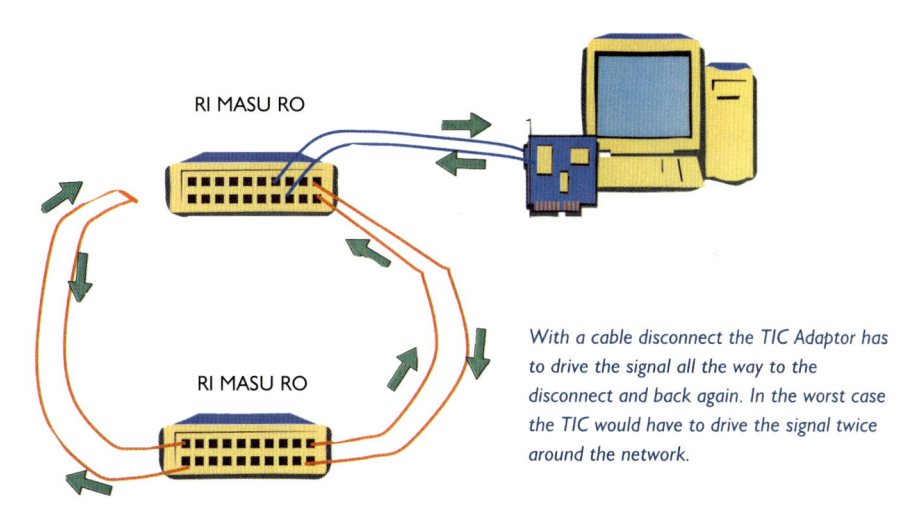

With a cable disconnect the TIC Adaptor has to drive the signal all the way to the disconnect and back again. In the worst case the TIC would have to drive the signal twice around the network.

Secondly, if an intermediate MSAU connection (Ring in/Ring out) is open, the device would send the signal out all the way to the disconnection after which it is mechanically looped back and returned to the sending station's receive side. In order to know there is a problem, a device has to be able to drive a signal twice the distance actually covered by the physical installation.

To ensure a system keeps working, the installation has to stay within these 'signal driving' capabilities that is calculated by the Adjustable Ring Length calculation. The effect of having to do this is to complicate an installation and make it difficult to increase the size of a ring (all networks get bigger after installation) and removes some of the flexibility in being able to move equipment around an installation, which is one of the major benefits of a structured wiring solution. This fixing of cable lengths is detrimental to changing the installation to say, Ethernet, where the consistent cable requirements make interchanging technology easier. To overcome this many suppliers had developed Active Networking MSAU's that actually drives the signal to the devices and drives the signal between the MSAU's. Thus a standard structured wiring system can be supported with the flexibility to move users freely and change technology at will.

The initial problem with active MAUs was that these products were late to be addressed by the IEEE802.5j standard. Therefore there were many non-standard products actually

ENTERPRISE NETWORKING

NETWORKING TECHNOLOGY REVIEW

installed, so network engineers had to be especially conscious when working on existing networks and introducing newer, standards-based products. To preserve the signal at 16Mbit/sec on UTP wiring schemes, filters were required at the workstation end of the connection. These filter devices were not covered by the standard bodies. Having an active hub driving a Token Ring signal to a device with a filter can cause inoperability of the Token Ring device unless the filtering mechanism matches the signal driving mechanics. The message was to be extremely careful out there.

Addressing the need for solutions in a structured wiring environment, manufacturers produced modular hubs. During the 90's there were more than 60 different hub manufacturers. Hubs are units which support structured wiring schemes and can house multi-port adapters providing resilient power and air cooling systems. Most are intelligent, giving port control over all connections. These differ from modular hubs because of the in-built management features; manageable hubs are now known as intelligent hubs.

The success of the Ethernet standards committees means that it is quite safe to purchase any vendors' hubs and link them together. However, Token Ring was late in having a complete set of specifications for media support and even longer to achieve agreement on active products. This means you must be careful when adding products to an existing network.

There was a problem in the fault tolerance built into the Token Ring cabling scheme between MSAU's. This cable is known as 'Trunk' or 'Main Ring' cable to distinguish it from lobe cable that runs from the station to the MSAU. When an inter MSAU/hub ring in/ring out connection is removed from the MSAU/hub, it will mechanically loop back on the cable end and on the MSAU/hub socket. This had the effect of maintaining the ring for data traffic. If these trunk cables were broken in the middle, the ring fails because it is relying on the physical disconnection of the cable for the loop-back facility. Since the network was down, how could you use management to find the broken cable to repair it? You've guessed correctly - you couldn't.

As the trunk connections were usually the ones that interconnect floors in a building and interconnect buildings on site, they were vulnerable to unauthorised manhandling. The response by the hub manufacturers to this serious deficiency was to put auto-loop-back circuitry into the ring in/ring out ports.

So as the standards committee had not provided a solution, manufacturers used their own mechanisms to save the network from collapse on a ring in/ring out failure. This meant that mixing different vendors' hubs was a major problem in testing for

ENTERPRISE NETWORKING

NETWORKING TECHNOLOGY REVIEW

Ethernet had a complete set of standard ratified by the IEEE802.3 standards committee. Token Ring however, initially relied on manufacturers trying to mirror IBM solutions with all the incompatibilities.

Therefore single vendor solutions worked but multi-vendor systems were prone to problems. Therefore, the end user had to exercise extreme caution in selecting Token Ring products.

compatibility of different schemes. The IEEE802.5J specification solved this problem but not for the existing pre-standard installations. I think you are getting a picture of Token Ring being a problem if multiple suppliers are used to provide a solution. This is always true when you have un-ratified standards.

Before we started, the general impression was that to design a Token Ring network an engineer had to consider what Token Ring speed was to be used, the number of stations to be connected, the overall ring length for the adjustable ring, lengths calculation and finally, the type of cable to be used. You now know all the supplementary issues that had to be covered before any manufacturer was selected to ensure that you were receiving a solution, which was flexible and extendible.

CONSTRUCTING NETWORKS

Once the decision was made on the cabling scheme, physical layout, Ethernet or Token Ring, the task of assessing the network usage must be performed to work out where the bulk of the network traffic is likely to be. This can then be filtered out onto a sub-network, making more bandwidth available for the main network. This filtering out of traffic could be applied to the whole installation by putting each department on its own network then linking these sub-networks onto a corporate-wide backbone network. The products that achieve this design feature are known as datalink bridges or routers. Detailed information is in Section 7 but to complete the story so far . . .

ENTERPRISE NETWORKING

NETWORKING TECHNOLOGY REVIEW

Datalink bridges are devices which link networks together at layer two of the OSI model and use low level addressing to send information to devices. They are quite intelligent and can filter out traffic not destined for global use. Hence, they will keep departmental traffic local and only pass relevant information on to the backbone network. Most bridges were configurable to either prevent unauthorised access across to the backbone network or prevent specific protocols crossing it.

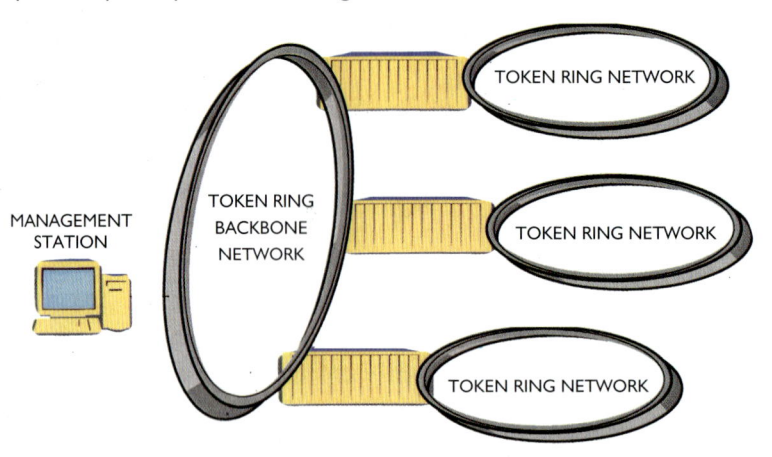

The hub technology supports sub-networks of Token Ring bridged onto a backbone network. The backbone uses Ring-in and Ring-out connections on the bridges.

Routers can perform the same function as the datalink bridges but because they have considerably more intelligence they can control the use of the internetworking links more efficiently. For example, they can send information over the shortest or more cost effective path to the destination. Routers are normally associated with addressing at layer three of the OSI communications model.

The architecture that was being increasingly adopted was that of the backbone feeder network where departmental LANs are bridged onto a backbone LAN which was generally of higher performance than the departmental solutions. The implementation of the network is on structured wiring with intelligent hubs providing the networking technology and housing the bridge/router functionality to separate the department from the main backbone network. The final consideration in the design was *"how is the network to be managed and what are the functions of Network Management?"* If we are focusing on Ethernet the network management problem was well solved and understood. We would use SNMP (Simple Network Management Protocol) as the standard and this would

ENTERPRISE NETWORKING

NETWORKING TECHNOLOGY REVIEW

provide multi vendor management of all infrastructure products.

However, in the case of Token Ring, network management was implemented in the chipsets. The network devices, all by themselves, with no human intervention, readily communicate network status, problems and recovery information via the media access control (MAC) frames. This is low-level, layer two function where the state of the infrastructure is continually monitored. IBM's LAN Network Manager programme was a window onto this source of vital information. Token Ring provided comprehensive and inherent benefits in monitoring a network. Consider an installation where an Intelligent Hub is connected to a dumb passive MSAU, which in turn supports an intelligent workstation adapter. You can control the hub and the workstation but not the MSAU. By integrating the hub on one side of the MSAU and the workstation adapter on the other, a full and accurate picture of how the MSAU is performing is achievable using the MAC frames. This was also true of using third party products, which had proprietary management schemes. All standards-based Token Ring adapters 4 and 16Mbit/sec support these management MAC frames. Therefore, it was irrelevant where you purchased your adapter, you could be sure the MAC monitoring and diagnostics had been implemented. So it looked like Token Ring had all the answers, but the market trends never supported single vendor solutions. The bulk of the networking products in the market were Ethernet, so mixed technology and mixed vendors were more likely on Token Ring sites. To address this, a standard management protocol was needed, and, by consumer demand, SNMP from the TCP/IP arena grow into acceptance. Management is covered in Section 11.

FDDI MOMENTARILY MOVES INTO THE PICTURE

FDDI stands for Fibre Distributed Data Interface. The FDDI standard had been developed by the American National Standards Institute (ANSI) X3T9.5 committee. The 100Mbit/sec line speed of FDDI was 10 times that of Ethernet in the early 90's, however Ethernet has outpaced them all. Products based on FDDI standards were widely available and were seen as preferred high-speed solutions, especially since the newer ATM specifications were not fully ratified and ATM's costs were higher than FDDI for the first two years of its introduction.

Due to the high cost per connection compared to Ethernet, the greatest use for FDDI has been in the high-speed backbones for Ethernet and Token Ring LANs and as a large server connection. As ATM costs came down, FDDI was certainly displaced in the

ENTERPRISE NETWORKING

NETWORKING TECHNOLOGY REVIEW

backbone and for high-speed server connections. However, over time the faster Ethernet solutions were easier to implement and took over from FDDI as the preferred connection. In an early attempt to get FDDI used for high-powered workstation or server access, the ANSI committee had specified a copper version - the TP-PMD standard for 100Mbit/sec on both UTP and STP cabling schemes. But it was too little, too late and Ethernet has overtaken DDI speeds and at a very much lower cost point. FDDI however was around long enough to establish itself and will exist for some of this decade because it works; there's no incentive to fix things that are not broken. FDDI is reviewed in the following section, Section 4.

IMPLEMENTING NETWORK TOPOLOGIES

The physical limitations in building design, in that they are levels separated by concrete floors, restrict the installation of the cable to a backbone feeder network topology. This is where a high-speed LAN such as FDDI is implemented as the backbone installed into the building's risers or just in the computer room. Then the departmental solutions are connected to the backbone via a network concentrator or intelligent hub - today's choice would be a switch - distributed onto each floor.

This backbone feeder network cable implementation is generally a fibre backbone and UTP saturation wiring to the desk. The intelligent hubs house the Ethernet and Token Ring concentrators along with the repeaters, bridges or routers. Often the hub may perform more than one operation. An Ethernet could contain a repeater and a bridge. The repeater provides a port to each desktop while the bridge would be used to link the hub into the backbone. The backbone could be an Ethernet, Token Ring or an FDDI LAN. The newer backbone solutions were initially based on ATM technology till the Ethernet standard rolled on to yet greater speeds.

By structuring the network cabling using this backbone feeder approach, the network planner can provide a topology that is essentially technology independent, thus making it easily upgradeable as new networking standards emerge. To conclude this section here is a review of the current LAN committees supported by the IEEE.

The IEEE802.1 Working Group is chartered to develop standards and recommended practices in 802 LAN/MAN Architecture, Internetworking, Network Management and Protocol layers above the MAC & LLC layers.

The IEEE802.2 Working Group develops standards for Logical Link Control.

ENTERPRISE NETWORKING

NETWORKING TECHNOLOGY REVIEW

The IEEE802.3 Working Group develops standards for CSMA/CD (Ethernet) based LAN's. Active projects include IEEE802.3ae, 10Gb/s Ethernet and IEEE802.3af DTE Power via MDI.

The IEEE802.4 Working Group develops standards for Token Bus.

The IEEE802.5 Working Group develops standards for Token Ring.

The IEEE802.6 Working Group develops standards for Metropolitan Networks.

The IEEE802.7 Broadband Technical Advisory Group (TAG) develops recommended practice for Broadband Local Area Networks. This group is inactive today, but is supported by 802.14.

The IEEE802.8 Technical Advisory Group (TAG) develops recommended practices for fibre optics.

The IEEE802.9 Working Group develops standards for Isochronous LAN's, this was seen as a LAN solution for integrated Voice and Data communications over a common infrastructure.

The IEEE802.10 Standards for Interoperable LAN/MAN Security (SILS)

The IEEE802.11 Working Group develops standards for wireless communications. The two significant standards are IEEE802.11b 11Mbit/sec and IEEE802.11a the 54Mbit/sec standard.

The IEEE802.12 Working Group develops standards for Demand Priority.

The IEEE802.15 Working Group develops Personal Area Network consensus standards for short distance wireless networks, the most visible of which is Bluetooth.

The IEEE802.16 Wireless MAN™ Standard for Broadband Wireless Metropolitan Area Networks.

IEEE802.17 Resilient Packet Ring Working Group

The IEEE has a work group reviewing standards for 10 Gigabit Ethernet (10GbE) using Dense Wave Division Multiplexing at the data link layer and there will only be a fibre standard for 10GbE. The IEEE802.3ae standard is expected early 2002 and has an objective of supporting existing multi-mode fibre at distances up to 100 metres, new multi-mode fibre installations using higher specification connectors 300 metres and Single mode fibre installations up to 40km. These distances are without any signal regeneration.

section four

FDDI - An early Backbone Solution

Panel of Experts

Section 4: Introduction to FDDI and TP-PMD

This section gives a good overview to Fibre Distributed Data Interface (FDDI) and reviews the copper standard for this technology TP-PMD. This is included because users of this technology are reluctant to replace it as it has given great reliable networking service.

SECTION FOUR

ENTERPRISE NETWORKING

FDDI - AN EARLY BACKBONE SOLUTION

FDDI had been around in draft form for nearly a decade as a solution without a problem. But true to history it did not take us long to create a real need for high bandwidth. The major vendors in the communications market place all got together at Interop '90 in California. The purpose of the gathering was for 40 vendors of FDDI product to show their commitment to supporting the ANSI specification and the latest revision of station management 6.2 at the time.

Interop 1990 reminded the world that the cable infrastructure is the network. The best technology and the best applications are reliant on a solid foundation. The least expected must be planned for.

The 40 vendors far outstripped the number of FDDI customer installations, but it was a memorable event. Some say it showed the ability of a maturing industry to work together in the customers' best interests. I think it is memorable because a forklift truck drove through the fibre cable looms destroying the fibre cabling and wrecking the demonstrations. However, 40 vendors were prepared to work together to provide customers with an open fibre solution. Tradition has it that new product sales are required to gain a return on the millions of dollars invested in providing the solution. The practicality was that many companies could not justify the cost of a move to FDDI which at this time was ten times the price of an Ethernet connection. It took till 1994 to create a viable FDDI market to justify the millions invested to develop the products. Today FDDI is installed in many fibre backbones and the copper version TP-PMD has been used for server connections. It did not take too long for Ethernet to catch up on FDDI's speed advantage and it first displaced the high-speed server connection.

ENTERPRISE NETWORKING

FDDI - AN EARLY BACKBONE SOLUTION

Then, just as FDDI was getting established, the ATM Forum ratified the first ATM specifications, which gave FDDI a direct competitor in the backbone. Long term, ATM was set to dominate because of a feature called Quality of Service (see Section 5). The adoption by many manufacturers of QoS features into mainstream products meant many organisations did not have to implement ATM. This competition for high-speed connections has not eroded the dominance of 10/100Mbit/sec Ethernet for the majority of desktop connections.

In the early days of structured wiring solutions, far-sighted companies looking at saving costs in the long-term laid fibre in the backbone. This would have been either using 10Mbit/sec Ethernet or 16Mbit/sec Token Ring on fibre and bridging to departmental sub-nets using copper on the horizontal, or they laid dark fibre, in other words unterminated fibre but laid to each desk ready for a potential increase in demand for networking bandwidth.

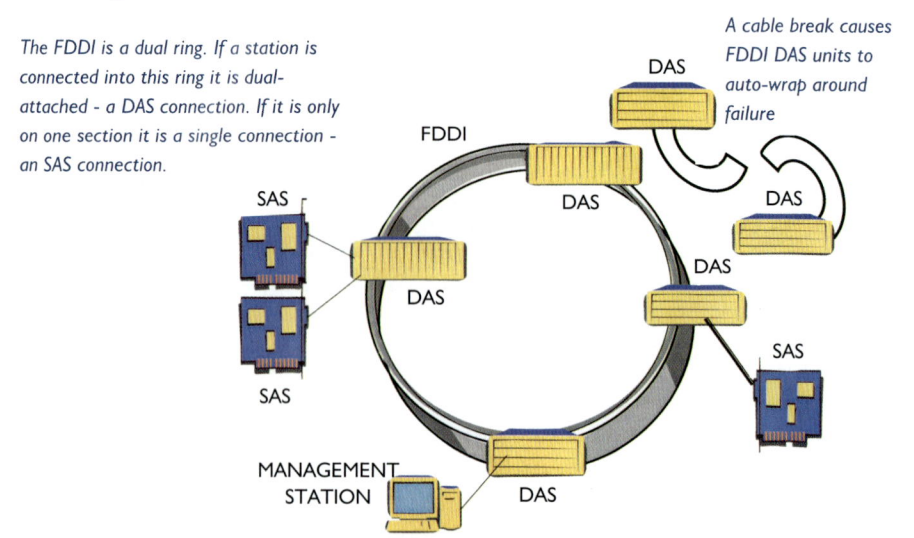

The FDDI is a dual ring. If a station is connected into this ring it is dual-attached - a DAS connection. If it is only on one section it is a single connection - an SAS connection.

A cable break causes FDDI DAS units to auto-wrap around failure

THE SPECIFICATION

The FDDI standard defines a physical layer and data link layer (OSI levels 1 and 2 - see Section 18) using fibre optics at a data rate of 100Mbit/sec. The standard sets a maximum limitation of 500 stations, 2Km between stations, and a maximum total distance of 100Km.

ENTERPRISE NETWORKING

FDDI - AN EARLY BACKBONE SOLUTION

FDDI is characterised by its dual ring topology. The dual attachment stations contain two sets of physical layer and physical media connections for fault tolerance. When connected, the physical links of the dual attachment stations form two counter-rotating rings. FDDI uses a token-passing algorithm to pass packets, which may be no larger than 4500 bytes, from one active station to the next.

The dual ring topology requires at least four fibres (62.5/125 micron) be installed between stations (two transmit/receive pairs). Placing additional fibres in the initial cable installation is recommended to allow for the replacement of faulty fibres and providing flexibility for future bandwidth needs. Even though the FDDI is a ring the physical installation is a star. This enables the FDDI to be replaced by newer technologies such as ATM when the FDDI capacity has been reached.

The benefit of the counter-rotating ring is that if a fault occurs, the FDDI device can re-route data to the fault-free connection and retain ring integrity. During a station failure, the connection management mechanisms of FDDI will cause the primary and secondary rings to be wrapped into a single ring. For the duration of the break in the physical media, the topology will be collapsed into a single logical ring. Optionally, an optical bypass switch may be used to bypass a station that has lost power on the ring or, in the case of intelligent hubs, enables hot-plug card insertion.

CABLE REQUIREMENTS

The fibre available is 50/125 microns and 62.5/125 microns. Both fibres are supported under the FDDI specification. However the technology driving signals down this cable is the Light Emitting Diode (LED). Therefore, the 62.5/125 micron fibre was favoured as more light gets down the larger aperture of 62.5 microns. However, European telephony companies have historically favoured the 50/125 micron fibre from the range of fibre multiplexers that were early implementations of fibre technology. The way such backbones have been implemented is to install an active star, usually using an intelligent hub in the computer room, and star wire quad-fibre to each floor's wiring closet using Ethernet FOIRL between the active stars to the concentration on the floor. The spare fibre is left as dark fibre or used for fault tolerance backup. This installation topology is capable of upgrading to FDDI by replacing the FOIRL adapters with FDDI adapters MIC to ST fibre cable adapters to save replacing the cable.

Telephony companies during the 1990s, in France and Germany especially, favoured the use of 8-12 micron cable which has caused customers to request single mode signalling. A

ENTERPRISE NETWORKING

FDDI - AN EARLY BACKBONE SOLUTION

laser has to be used to light the fibre but distances over 40Km are achievable while for LED technology, 1-2Km between stations is normal. However, using laser-based technology results in pricier single-mode fibre products; at the time the average price delta was three-fold over multi-mode.

This tentative approach to fibre caused the networking industry to try again at a solution. It was certain the requirement was for high networking bandwidths and it was only the fibre aspect which was slowing down the uptake. So, obviously what was needed was 100Mbit/sec on copper.

The background to the copper standard TP-PMD Twisted Pair - Physical Media Dependency, manufacturers developed the technology to transmit FDDI for distances up to 100 metres on 'Data Grade' Unshielded Twisted Pair (UTP) cable, and for distances up to 150 metres on Shielded Twisted Pair (STP) cable while maintaining a class A FCC compliancy, and not requiring a change to the existing FDDI encoded scheme (the FDDI encoded scheme is defined by the physical layer protocol [PHY] standard). The research including the draft proposal was presented to the FDDI ANSI TP-PMD (Twisted Pair - Physical Medium Dependent) committee back in June of 1991. This task was completed by National Semiconductor.

These developments have been based on AT&T's 1061 and 2061 'Data Grade' cable. This is a four-pair level 5 cable that has the consistent characteristics required to transmit extremely high rates of data. Note that regardless of the type of cable - whether it's data or voice grade - because of crosstalk, each workstation connection will require a dedicated four-pair cable, that is, no 25-pair bundles).

In addition to efforts by National Semiconductor, there were two other groups developing twisted pair products for FDDI. One group developed an STP-only solution. This was targeted at companies locked into IBM solutions and STP customers. However, due to the cost and installation issues of STP, the industry did not see this as a desirable solution. The standards committee therefore rejected this proposal in February of '92 saying that the committee would work for a combined UTP/STP solution. The other group, dubbed the Unshielded Development Forum (UDF), was looking for an FDDI interface for voice grade or DIW cable (level 2-3). Though a technically noble endeavour, this technology is still limited on low-grade cable, the problem being to keep radio frequency emissions within FCC specified levels. Below is a quote from the International Data Corporation (IDC) document entitled *'The Prospects for Twisted Pair FDDI Technology'*, dated September 1991.

ENTERPRISE NETWORKING

FDDI - AN EARLY BACKBONE SOLUTION

ANALYST: LEE DOYLE

"IDC believes sales of twisted pair FDDI products will be extremely limited until several vendors deliver proven products which enable FDDI to run over UTP. Sales of STP products will be small due to a limited number of organisations with installed STP that will implement FDDI to the desktop. Given a solution to the technical challenges presented by UTP FDDI, IDC believe the standards committee will approve a 'compromise' UTP FDDI standard by late 1993. The standard will encourage a large number of vendors to introduce products and legitimise the market, and result in a ramp up of TP-PMD sales during late 1994 and 1995."

IDC also forecast that the demand for FDDI bandwidth would increase substantially by 1995. The result was exactly as predicted, 30% of installed networks using FDDI products with TP-PMD having a 15% penetration of the installed FDDI nodes. What was not seen at the time was the move to provide 100Mbit/sec Ethernet, which eventually displaced TP-PMD as a server connection.

The TP-PMD committee ratified the standard for 100Mbit/sec per twisted pair including both Unshielded and Shielded Twisted Pair (UTP/STP) cable, and clearly defined minimum performance requirements.

TP-PMD REQUIREMENTS

- The transmit distance is 100m for UTP and STP
- The same Bit Error Rate (BER) as FDDI over fibre (2×10^{-10})
- FCC class A commercial certification
- European EN55022 class A commercial certification
- There is one standard comprising UTP and STP
- UTP - Category 5 cable (as specified in EIA/TIA TSB-36)
- STP - Type 1, individually and over shielded, 150Ω cable

In 1991 the standard document ANSI EIA/TIA 568 was completed and laid the foundation for cabling installations capable of supporting data rates up to 100Mbit/sec. This document specifies multi-mode fibre to be installed for vertical riser applications and horizontal wiring distances greater than 100m. Horizontal desktop cabling is specified for desktop wiring up to 100m, and data rates up to 100Mbit/sec. In addition, two Technical System Bulletins (TSB) were issued by EIA/TIA after the ANSI EIA/TIA 568 was published. TSB-36 classifies UTP cables into categories 3,4 and 5 and provides characteristics and

ENTERPRISE NETWORKING

FDDI - AN EARLY BACKBONE SOLUTION

performance values at particular data rates. TSB-40 classifies connector hardware (punch-down blocks, patch panels, wall jack, etc.) into categories 3, 4 and 5 and also provides characteristics and performance values at particular data rates. Together these three documents provide all the information required to construct a cable plant that has known and measurable performance at a desired data rate. Anyone considering installing a new cable plant for any data communications application should consult all three documents.

LINK LAYER CONSIDERATIONS

When utilising FDDI as a high speed backbone connecting lower speed networks such as 802.3, the FDDI protocol can be utilised in one of two formats: Encapsulation or Translation.

Encapsulation (transparent bridging) places an Ethernet packet within the information field of an FDDI packet. Translation (source routing) actually converts, or translates, the Ethernet packet into an FDDI packet.

It is important to note that encapsulation is used in bridging applications, thus it is a lower OSI-layer device that filters/ forwards between the same protocol, and translation is used in routing applications (i.e. converting from one protocol to another).

In standard transparent/mapping bridging, each side of the bridge must know the Node IDs accessible on that side of the bridge, not just on that segment but through all other bridges.

This may be done via separate tables or one consolidated table. In either case the total number of entries for both sides of the bridge must equal the total number of Node IDs in the network.

When a packet is received, the table is searched for the destination address. If it is found or if its origin is on the other side of the bridge, the packet is forwarded. If it is found and its origin is on this side of the bridge, the packet is discarded. In either case, the table is then updated with the source address as the address of the device that originate on this side of the bridge.

With Encapsulation, an additional step takes place on the Ethernet side, and one less step on the FDDI side. On the Ethernet side, when a packet is to be forwarded, the Bridge Node ID address of the other bridge is retrieved from the table as filed under the destination Node ID address. A new MAC header is prefixed to the original packet and the frame transmitted to the other bridge. Since the frames are specifically addressed to the Bridge Node ID, filtering is not necessary on the FDDI side.

ENTERPRISE NETWORKING

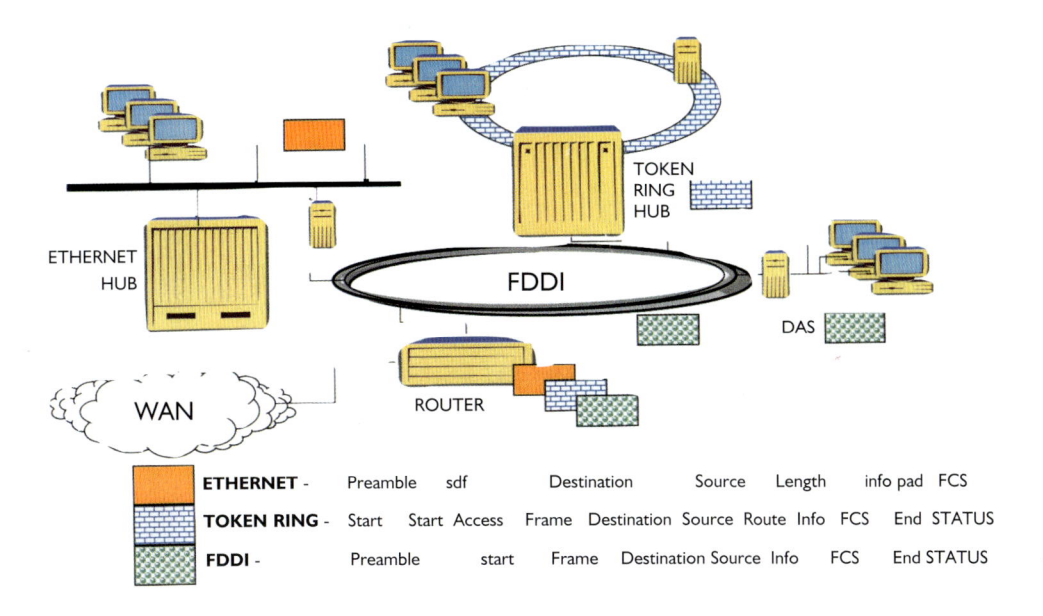

FDDI - AN EARLY BACKBONE SOLUTION

ETHERNET -	Preamble	sdf		Destination	Source	Length	info pad	FCS
TOKEN RING -	Start	Start Access	Frame	Destination	Source Route Info	FCS	End	STATUS
FDDI -	Preamble		start	Frame	Destination Source Info	FCS	End	STATUS

Multi technology sites that have the requirement to 'interconnect' all devices for meaningful communications will have to worry about Encapsulation or Translation. Network to network, just using the backbone as a transport mechanism, Encapsulation works fine. If the corporate resources are connected directly to the backbone, then Translation is required.

When a frame is received on the FDDI side, the packet is forwarded without the additional MAC header. The filter table is then updated placing the Bridge Node ID of the source bridge in the record for the original source address. This is how the bridge learns which Bridge Node ID to use when a response is processed or any other device communicates with that particular Node ID. SMT (Station Management) compliance will not guarantee interconnection with other FDDI vendors. SMT does not address compatibility above the MAC level. ANSI X3T9.5 is only specified to ensure that FDDI stations will not interfere with each other and assuring that the network maintains the highest integrity of operations. In order to guarantee full interconnection at the MAC layer, one must also adapt to the mapping bridging algorithm on the FDDI upgrade.

ENTERPRISE NETWORKING

FDDI - AN EARLY BACKBONE SOLUTION

A FINAL OPTION

If a company today is either moving to a new building or is in the process of re-cabling and it already needs 100Mbit/sec to the desktop, experience shows that its bandwidth requirements will grow along with the number of nodes. So the correct future-proof solution is to install fibre in the backbone as a minimum.

It is the only medium capable of supporting the multi-gigabit bandwidths of the future. To advise a company that copper is the future is to limit the expansion capabilities and cause it to undergo the upheaval and expense of recabling for fibre at some point in the future. This is true as long as you believe that the organisation will embrace multi-media applications - applications providing users with data, graphics, images, voice and full motion video to every desktop.

section five

ATM - An Efficient Networking Technology

Section 5: ATM Networking Reviewed

Asynchronous Transfer Mode (ATM) is reviewed and some of the issues considered. This is a serious technology in carrier voice delivery services. It had found a niche solution in many corporate backbone networks so the support of Ethernet and Token Ring legacy networks is reviewed. However, it failed to capture any significant market share in the true LAN implementations.

SECTION FIVE

ENTERPRISE NETWORKING

ASYNCHRONOUS TRANSFER MODE (ATM)

EVOLUTION NOT REVOLUTION

Time Division Multiplexing (TDM) was developed to allow a single physical connection to carry a number lower-performance sources by enabling the signals to be combined in a single communications channel without interfering with each other. This technique has been used for digitised voice communications to enable many phone users to be mixed onto a single carrier while maintaining uninterrupted bandwidth. This was achieved by allocating a specific time slot to a given call, guaranteeing the performance of individual calls but proving wasteful because it cannot reallocate unused bandwidth to other users during a lull in the original call. The ability to dedicate a connection to a communicating device is known as circuit switching.

To make better use of the bandwidth, labels or tags were attached to identify the separate connections so that any time-slot could be used as long as it were free. The basic Packet Switching techniques formed the basis of X25. X25 offered connections speeds up to 64Kbit/sec. While this work was developing, telephony companies under the

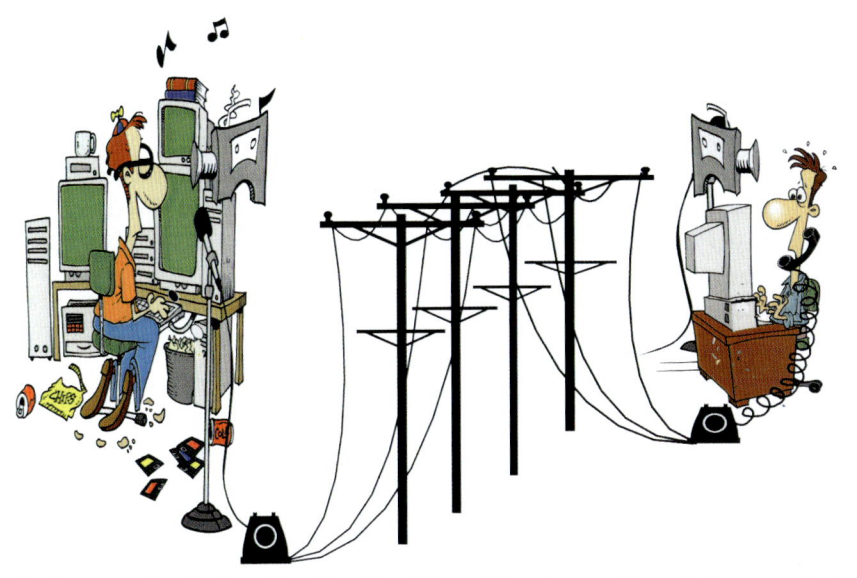

The future is predicted to be multi-media - Voice, Video and Data integrated into a single communications channel. ISDN is already providing this service but at too low a speed for full motion video. ATM was seen as the solution for end to end communications but commercially missed its window of opportunity. XDSL is the new kid on the block to capture the local loop connection. ATM is still the delivery mechanism across the carrier connections.

ENTERPRISE NETWORKING

ASYNCHRONOUS TRANSFER MODE (ATM)

European standards body, the Comité Consultatif International Téléphonique et Télégraphique (CCITT - now called the ITU) developed a digital communications mechanism known as Integrated Services Digital Network (ISDN).

ISDN was first specified in the 1970s and used a 16Kbit/sec signal channel to control the call and two 64Kbit/sec data channels. These were multiplexed together, up to 32 channels at a time, to form the Megastream (1.028Mbit/sec) services. The high speed provides a primary rate service, the 64Kbit/sec low speed provides the secondary rate. ISDN originally used circuit switching techniques similar to TDM's and suffered the same bandwidth inefficiencies. This was not addressed until the mid-1980s when broadband ISDN began to solidify as a standard for high-speed digital communications.

This was in response to the widely held view that the future would see voice communications replaced with full-motion video communication, with phones replaced by interactive television sets. You will have noticed similar marketing hype happening today with respect to mobile phones. Full-motion video must be continuous - users will not tolerate broken speech and jerky motion yet data communications used by business computing needs to support random and bursty traffic profiles.

If you are using a PC and you request a file from the server, the server sends you the file in blocks of data. You as a user do not see that some blocks were lost and re-transmissions had taken place. This is because you are working in batch mode: request the file, pause, then work on the file. You would not try and type amendments while the file rolls up your screen, you wait till it stops. This is acceptable as it reflects how we work so sending data in bursts is fine. So circuit switching provides continuous uninterrupted data flows but is inefficient while packet switching is more efficient but cannot offer the guarantee of service needed by voice and video. This caused the engineers to revisit some old technology of cell switching and a means of asynchronously accessing the network.

This technology is Asynchronous Transfer Mode (ATM) and is used as the infrastructure by carriers today. ATM could not displace Ethernet, so Ethernet had to develop features that gave the same services as circuit switching. See Section 17 for the ATM story.

ENTERPRISE NETWORKING

ASYNCHRONOUS TRANSFER MODE (ATM)

THE ROOTS OF ATM

ATM was born in an AT&T laboratory in Naperville, Illinois, USA in, 1980. Developed as a switching technique that would satisfy voice as well as data in a packet format. At a 1988 meeting in Seoul, South Korea, the CCITT recommended the use of ATM for Broadband ISDN (BISDN) which is now a standard public telecommunications infrastructure supporting broadband services for both home and business.

ATM's packet-switching technique is achieved by using short fixed length packets called cells. As the cells are of a fixed length, ATM switch design is simpler, both the processing of and the variability of delays are reduced, both of which are essential for time-sensitive services such as video and voice. The cell length is 53 bytes, comprising five header bytes and 48 bytes of data. The 48 bytes are an IEEE specification that represents a compromise between the 64 bytes recommended by a North American proposal and the 32 bytes recommended by the Europeans.

The reason for the Europeans wishing for a smaller cell is due to the fact that it would have had a lower latency when used on the slower circuits that existed in Europe at the time. Fixed length cells means fixed length buffers to handle congestion, and simpler buffering techniques generally. Another advantage is predictable network delays, especially queuing latencies at each switch. This is achieved through the implementation of switching within silicon itself. Hardware-based switches are the only way to build high

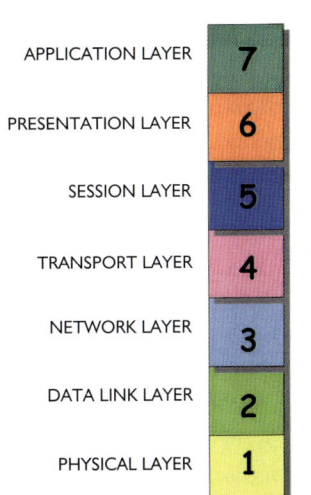

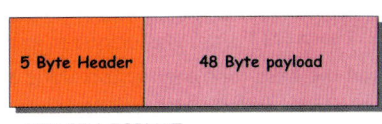

APPLICATION LAYER	7
PRESENTATION LAYER	6
SESSION LAYER	5
TRANSPORT LAYER	4
NETWORK LAYER	3
DATA LINK LAYER	2
PHYSICAL LAYER	1

5 Byte Header	48 Byte payload

ATM CELL FORMAT

ATM Adaptation Layer is responsible both for understanding the requirements of application such as voice which requires constant bit rate service, and ensuring the connection is established with the correct QoS parameters.

ATM Layer is responsible for Virtual Circuits and Virtual Paths. It is also responsible for transporting and multiplexing cells. UNI flow control is in this layer.

Physical Layer Media Access and UNI specification support at this layer.

ENTERPRISE NETWORKING

ASYNCHRONOUS TRANSFER MODE (ATM)

performance products today because the current state of processor technology cannot run software at the speeds required by high-speed ATM devices. ATM can be seen as the true implementation of ISDN's goals in that it provides seamless voice, video and data services using the SONET/SDH transport mechanism.

ATM can provide both LAN and WAN services with adaptable capacity. With one technology providing desk to desk seamless communications the concept of LAN/WAN will cease - so the story went. However the large installed base of Ethernet precluded widespread adoption of ATM in the LAN. The merge of the LAN/WAN industry has changed the focus and the merger of all these services is now not a function of the hardware but the communications protocols used, at the IP layer, but that's another story . . . back to ATM.

ATM FORUM

In 1991, the ATM Forum was founded with an initial membership of four companies. The objective was to accelerate the standardisation of this new technology for LAN implementation. The Forum quickly grew to over 600 members from all branches of computing and communications. It is remarkable that, despite its large size and the fact it was not a standards body but relied on vendor co-operation, it managed to complete, publish and implement enough standards to enable multi-vendor ATM solutions to be integrated into existing networks.

Standards are critical in making the basic ATM services deliverable with any hope of vendor interoperability. The ATM Forum was unique in its approach. It looked for viable solutions and then picked the best, lobbying support using a 'lead, follow or get out of the way' technique. Key to the speed of progress was its two-thirds majority voting rules, radically different to other standards bodies such as ANSI or IEEE which can be stopped in their tracks by an individual serious objection.

KEY ATM FORUM STANDARDS

ATM did not become the mainstream desk to desk connectivity technology envisioned by the early pioneers. The problem was that ATM was an all or nothing solution. To use it meant scrapping your existing networking products which was commercial suicide. If an organisation had 1,000 Ethernet connected PCs, to change them to ATM in those days would have cost $1 million before the company bought the ATM switches. Another

ENTERPRISE NETWORKING

ASYNCHRONOUS TRANSFER MODE (ATM)

ETHERNET

ETHERNET

RFC1483 enables ATM to emulate Ethernet and can act as a data link bridge

ATM BACKBONE

LANE enables ATM to emulate a packet network

NATIVE ATM

ETHERNET

TOKEN RING NETWORK

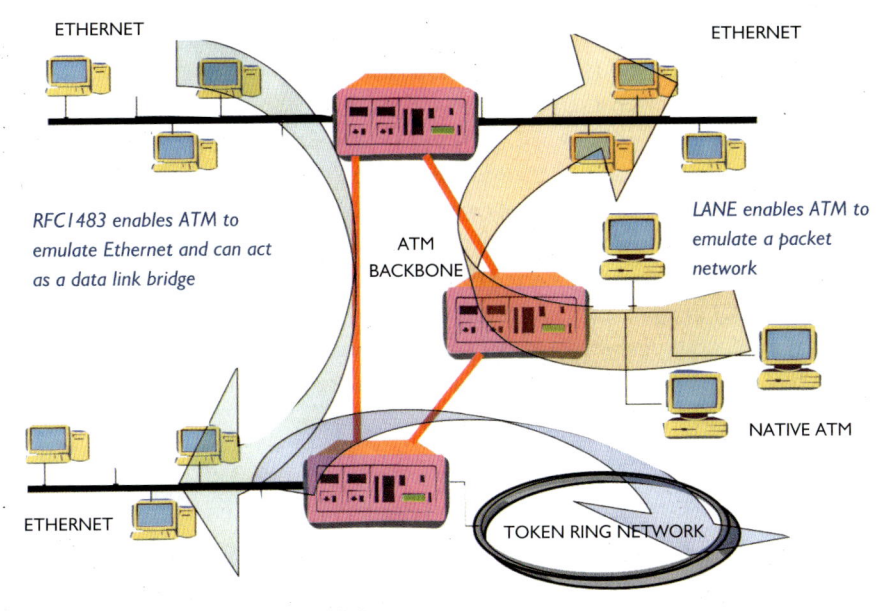

RFC 1577 enables ATM to perform as an IP Router

major issue was business applications, which were designed to run on existing LAN technologies. The only way for ATM to succeed was to simulate a legacy system so the applications would run unchanged. This caused ATM installation to be very complex as reflected in the standards needed to implement a solution - as discussed below.

Primarily for end user nodes such as PCs and workstations, UNI (User to Network Interface) describes the signalling and cable media and specifies how a workstation physically connects to an ATM switch.

LAN Emulation (LANE) enables ATM to integrate into existing networks. RFC 1483 makes ATM emulate Ethernet or Token Ring and supports single technology bridging. The base requirement is that legacy LAN users will not have to change their network drivers or applications in order to work across an emulated LAN. This means that the access points into the ATM network must do the work that is normally done by the original LAN's broadcasting mechanism. LANE clients can be ATM bridges, routers, switches or workstations directly attached to ATM. LAN Emulation Servers (LESs) can either be implemented as part of an ATM switch or run as a process on a workstation to provide the services to allow traditional connection-less LAN traffic to be transported

ENTERPRISE NETWORKING

ASYNCHRONOUS TRANSFER MODE (ATM)

over a connection-oriented ATM backbone.

The way to look at this is to consider what happens on traditional networks today. When a workstation requires a file from a server the network card in the workstation broadcasts a request onto the network asking the server to respond. When the server receives the request it sends its address back to the workstation. This enables the workstation to exchange information explicitly with the server. In an ATM switched network, the broadcast mechanism does not work so LANE provides a mechanism to answer the broadcasts. The device connected to the shared media network uses the LAN Emulation Client (LEC) to capture the broadcasts requesting address information and explicitly calls the LES - this can be viewed as a directory service. The LES returns the ATM address that will achieve a connection to the requested service. There can be many LECs accessing a LES and large networks can have several LESs.

Traffic management, a feature of ATM, is the ability to provide the correct communications service for the type of information being transported. This means that a voice device can request of the ATM communications an uninterrupted connection, while at the same time using the same connection a data device can ask for best efforts to

AAL Type	Service	Application	Control
1	Constant Bit Rate Support		Connection Orientated
2	Variable Bit Rate Support	Video	Connection Orientated
3	Variable Bit Rate Support	Frame Relay	Connection Orientation
4	Variable Bit Rate Support	SMDS	Connectionless Orientated
5	Variable Bit Rate Support	Simple and Efficient Adaptation Layer (SEAL)	Connection Connectionless

ENTERPRISE NETWORKING

ASYNCHRONOUS TRANSFER MODE (ATM)

transfer a file. There are five types of services available which are accessed by the corresponding adaption layer, that have been specified:

P-NNI (Private Network to Network Interface) specifies how multi-vendor hubs, switches or routers interconnect with ATM. There were several steps to achieving a solution. In 1994 the Forum agreed on IISP (Interim Inter-switch Signalling Protocol) and in 1996 approved P-NNI, which was similar in functionality to OSPF in the router world but had the embedded ATM service features of Quality of Service and bandwidth reservation. You'll find it described in Section 7.

ATM MECHANISM

Traditional networking relies on broadcasting to locate the destination of any resource on the network. As they are connectionless systems then the mechanism works fine. However ATM is a connection-based solution so, like the phone system, you need to know the destination number first before you make the call. ATM cells contain addressing information. Rather than addressing to specific destination, ATM cells are addressed to Virtual Channels (VCs) and/or Virtual Paths (VPs). VCs and VPs are similar to voice channels in public networks. The ATM channels and paths are bi-directional depending on the connection mode. These channels are set up between devices on the ATM network prior to transferring cells. To determine which channel or path the cells should follow, Virtual Channel Identifier (VCI) and Virtual Path Identifier (VPI) are included in the cell. Each User-Network Interface (UNI) within an ATM network possesses a number of Virtual Channel Connections (VCC) and Virtual Path Connection (VPC). These VCCs consist of a single point-to-point VC, or combination of adjacent VCs. Virtual Path Connections (VPC) can consist of a single VC, or several bundled VCs. During set-up, the Quality of Service (QoS) and Traffic Management for each VCC and VPC is specified.

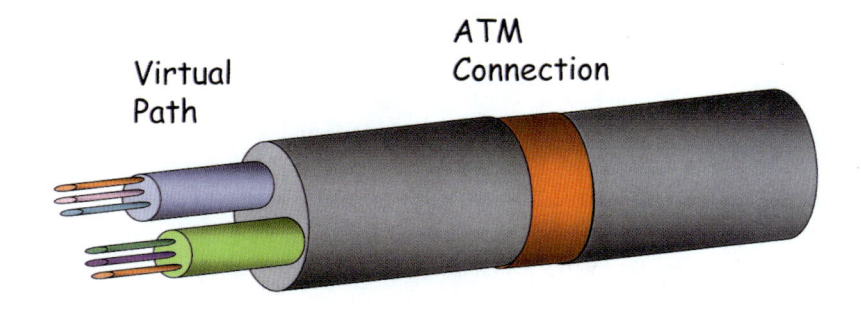

ENTERPRISE NETWORKING

ASYNCHRONOUS TRANSFER MODE (ATM)

There are two types of Virtual Channel in an ATM network: Permanent Virtual Channels (PVC) or Switched Virtual Channels (SVC). The difference between PVC and SVC is the way the channel is set-up. Permanent Virtual Channels (PVCs) are pre-configuring by an administration function, and are similar to static routes in packet-based networks. PVC will be typically established through a local interface or via a remote SNMP management station. SVC however are dynamically set up using a signalling procedure. This essentially requires a routing protocol between the associated AALs. SVCs can be established as needed for a particular service. SVCs allow ATM networks to operate and be managed much like broadcast LANs.

ROUTING IN ATM

The IETF Internet Engineering Task Force provided a specification to enable the routing of IP over ATM. RFC-1577, Classical IP over ATM defined a method of running IP on an ATM backbone. Classical IP is based around the concept of Logical IP Subnets (LIS), which allow users to be in the same IP subnet no matter where they are physically connected into the ATM network. When a workstation needs to resolve an IP address to an ATM address, it contacts an ARP server that is responsible for all users within the LIS. When a user wants to open a connection on a different subnet, the connection must be placed through a virtual router. RFC-1577 also specifies the way IP data is encapsulated directly onto ATM with no MAC layer information.

Encapsulation RFC 1577 users and LANE users cannot communicate directly. LANE is essentially bridging, supports all protocols, and uses MAC layer addressing. RFC-1577 is only for IP and does not use MAC addresses. The ATM forum replaced these RFCs with MPOA (Multiple Protocols Over ATM) specifications.

QUALITY OF SERVICE

One of the main attractions of ATM is its efficient emulation of circuit switching. Although a connectionless technology, it can implement the features of a connection based service. Quality of Service (QoS) is the ability to provide an appropriate communications channel for the traffic passing over the channel. Voice needs low bandwidth but must have a continuous service while data needs very high bandwidth in relatively short bursts. QoS needs to be defined and then mechanisms need to be available to regulate the service to the defined parameters. Some of the parameters that control QoS are the cell loss ratio and cell delay variation. Having set them for the traffic type the mechanisms to control

ENTERPRISE NETWORKING

ASYNCHRONOUS TRANSFER MODE (ATM)

and deliver are defined by the service's supported variable bit rate, available bit rate, constant bit rate and explicit bit rate. Mechanisms such as flow control and congestion management are all required to deliver QoS.

The practicalities in implementing a QoS scheme place a burden on the switches used to construct the network. On a request for a service, a switch needs to know the network topology and whether bandwidth is available to support the call before the switch can accept the QoS request. Network information can be configured on installation but this does not fit well with the user churn rate that affects IT installations. This network knowledge needs to be automated and is an embedded feature of the PNNI. These include Automatic Information Exchange and Dynamic Routing subroutines and then, during call setup, Connection Administration Control to allocate available bandwidth. During the call the Available Bit Rate/Explicit Rate is the most effective means of flow control for the source traffic. In this scheme the 'Explicit Rate Field' inside the 'Resource Management' cell is adjusted to the traffic rate that each element in the proposed path of the network can sustain. The flow control keeps the source at this rate.

ATM WHERE NOW?

As a multi-service delivery technology ATM is a great technology delivering the best of the circuit switched and the packet switched worlds. It was timed correctly for the integration into network service providers' moves to digital services but was commercially defeated by Ethernet in the LAN.

Will it rise like a phoenix out of the ashes? I think not. In the LAN wireless technology has the best chance of a long-term, desk to desk solution as it moves into multi-media support.

section six

Convergence of Standards in the PC

Section 6: How PCs grew into the Network Workstation

Explains PCs in a networking environment and the position of PCs with respect to the standards available for communication. This is an historical journey to positioning the PC at the centre of corporate computing and with the pervasiveness of the Internet the centre of all our lives.

ENTERPRISE NETWORKING

CONVERGENCE OF STANDARDS IN THE PC

The objective of the International Standards Organisation in its development of the Open System Interconnection (OSI) protocols, was to provide two main benefits to the purchaser of computer equipment. Firstly, the freedom to purchase the most cost effective solution to a given problem with the knowledge that the chosen solution would integrate with previous computer solutions. This being the case, the second benefit would be that no costly bespoke software development would be required to provide compatibility and portability of the resulting data. The problem is that we have been working on OSI specifications since its conception in 1978 and the standard bodies have been defining and refining specifications for over two decades. Meanwhile, the computer industry has suffered a revolution and there has been great resistance to some of the consequences of that revolution. The revolution was started by PCs and concluded by PC networking. To enable us all to understand what is feasible today we have to look at the past decade and plot the changing computer environments that have resulted in the changing of the objectives.

The PC has moved from just being a general purpose tool for business to the window, to the world in our homes. This is thanks to the Internet. The path the PC has had to take in achieving global communications is a long and painful one for those of us who had to live with all the changes.

IN THE BEGINNING

In the beginning there were special rooms with special staff who guarded and administered a corporation's computing resources. To get the computer to do any work required a set of specialists to input the data for the required task and yet another set to distribute the results of the computations. Mere mortals could not directly communicate with the computer; this had to be done by the white-coated computer staff who operated punch card readers, paper tape readers and the computer printout delivery trolleys. This was the early 1960s to mid 1970s when large central machines

ENTERPRISE NETWORKING

CONVERGENCE OF STANDARDS IN THE PC

dominated computing.

Then a series of proprietary network architectures and computer terminals arrived, enabling more direct access and avoiding both delays and the layers of administration represented by the white coats. Large computer resources were called mainframes - later shortened to host computers - and access methods were designed to provide reliable, stable connections between a manufacturer's terminals and host computers. All applications ran on the mainframe, and most of the data that passed across the network was textual. Most networks were based on the concept of shared bandwidth through groups of terminals attached to controllers. The most essential elements in the network were front-end processors and cluster controllers. Given the types of data these networks handled, they provided an excellent combination of throughput, fairness of access and cost. The dominant vendor in this period was IBM. The networks from this period ran so well that some of them were still running relatively unchanged over two decades later. Some however migrated into Token Ring linked with bridges and/or routers while others were simply completely replaced.

Token Ring was complex but provided many of the same performance characteristics of the older SDLC-based controller/terminal network coupled with the flexibility and bandwidth of a LAN access method. These host-based systems however were proprietary; single manufacturer solutions were the only choice. It was readily accepted that no one host supplier had all the answers and if they did they were not necessarily the most cost effective. Businesses trying to keep control of IT expenditure and trying to match computer systems to business processes ensured that multi-vendor solutions became the norm. This created an array of incompatibility problems from differing screen and keyboard layouts, to the inability to exchange the simplest of files.

Early solutions adopted a given supplier's protocol with IBM, as the dominant player, usually the vendor chosen. A range of emulation programmes and file transfer packages evolved which relied heavily on IBM's protocols remaining static. However, the real world dictates new software releases so the adoption of another vendor's protocol was not practical in the long term. The host vendor has no commitment to inform the emulator vendor of either new features or withdrawal of features. As a result, compatibility could only be maintained until the next release and then everyone started again.

It was in this environment that the International Standards Organisation evolved the seven-layer OSI model with the idea of to interconnecting systems. A single standard independent of any individual manufacturer was required to provide system compatibility.

ENTERPRISE NETWORKING

CONVERGENCE OF STANDARDS IN THE PC

The OSI seven layer model defines the architecture of all communications products. Devices that function at layer two are known as 'Data Link Bridges' and devices that function at layer three, the network layer, are known as 'Routers'. Devices that can operate at both layers are known as Brouters.

Being independent, every manufacturer had access to the specification at the same time so no commercial advantage could be gained by leading the way. In the meantime, minicomputers became technically feasible and proved cost-effective, and many organisations shifted technical and business applications to them. Terminal access started in a very basic way, using asynchronous terminals, each connected directly to a port on the minicomputer. Statistical multiplexers evolved to provide wide area line sharing and error protection. Data PBXs became central to many networks, enabling terminal users to select which minicomputer to log on to. The nature of business usage of computers meant that these data PBXs could multiplex more users than computer ports, leaving users to contend for expensive computer ports.

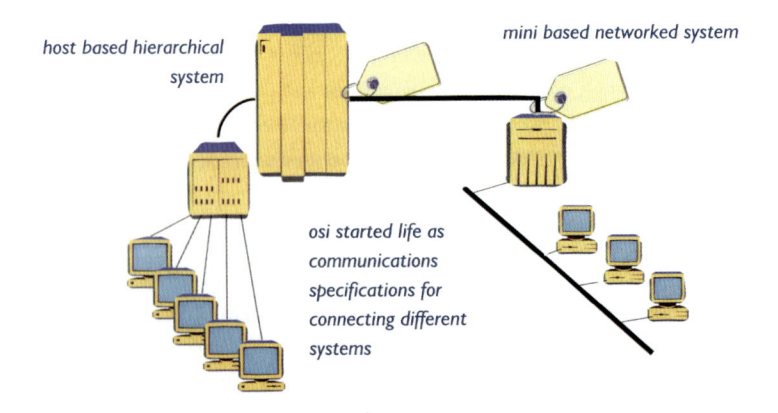

host based hierarchical system

mini based networked system

osi started life as communications specifications for connecting different systems

ENTERPRISE NETWORKING

CONVERGENCE OF STANDARDS IN THE PC

A key change in networking had taken place. It was now typical for multiple vendors to provide the various components of a network. This rapidly accelerated the rate of change in networking technology as an increasing number of small manufacturers entered the market. The largest of the mini-computer manufacturers, Digital Equipment Corporation (DEC), was an early leader in asynchronous minicomputer networks. The same terminals as before were connected to terminal servers which were connected to the minis across a 10Mbit/sec Ethernet cable. Local bridges, and the inherently shared nature of the technology, replaced data PBXs. Remote bridges replaced statistical multiplexers. The age of the LAN had started.

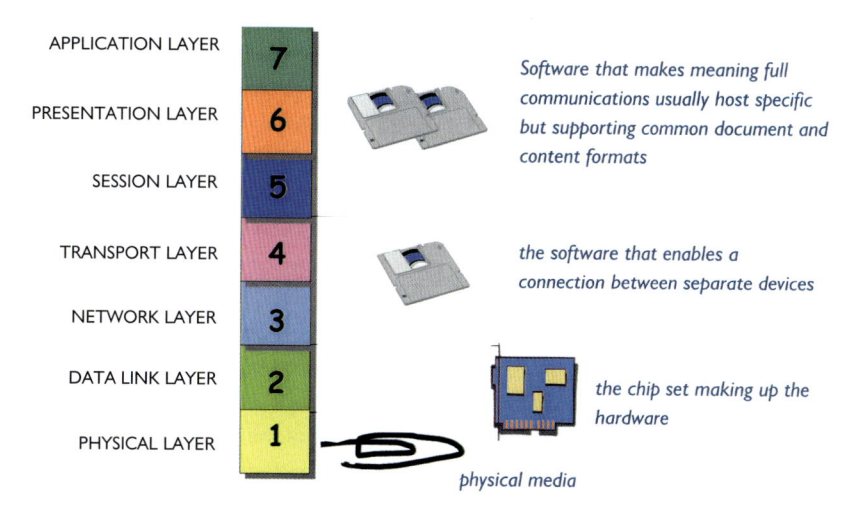

APPLICATION LAYER	7	*Software that makes meaning full communications usually host specific but supporting common document and content formats*
PRESENTATION LAYER	6	
SESSION LAYER	5	
TRANSPORT LAYER	4	*the software that enables a connection between separate devices*
NETWORK LAYER	3	
DATA LINK LAYER	2	*the chip set making up the hardware*
PHYSICAL LAYER	1	*physical media*

The acceptance of LAN technology as a solution to point to point wiring problems within a limited geographical area occurred in 1981. Then Ethernet, an informal networking standard produced by Xerox, Intel and Digital Equipment Corporation was quickly mapped onto the seven-layer model. The LAN industry promoted standard solutions as the only viable way to build communications networks. 'Don't buy proprietary' was the sales pitch, even though each supplier supplied proprietary versions of the standard because a complete profile did not exist. A profile is a specification selection for all seven layers. This early standard solution had XNS, Xerox Networking Systems, as the defined communications protocol. This was the *'de facto'* standard adopted by Xerox, DEC, Ungermann-Bass and 3Com, to name a few. In each of the early solutions, layers 5, 6 and 7 of the OSI model either did not exist or, where code did exist, it was proprietary to each supplier. This prevented file transfers and terminal access across multi-vendor

ENTERPRISE NETWORKING

CONVERGENCE OF STANDARDS IN THE PC

systems. It was not all bad news: a major step forward had been achieved in that multi-vendor solutions could exist on and share the same cable even though they could not exchange data. The popularity of the TCP/IP protocols today is attributed to the fact that a complete profile did exist - but we are getting out of chronological order.

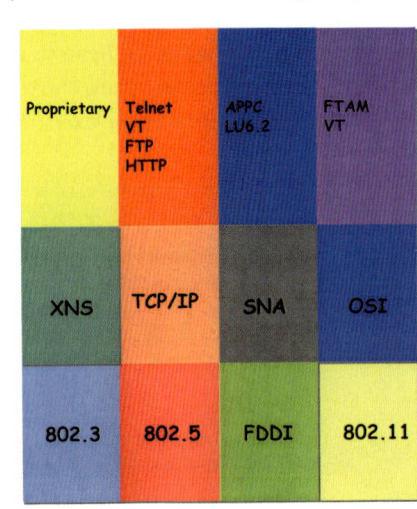

Layer				
7	Proprietary	Telnet VT FTP HTTP	APPC LU6.2	FTAM VT
6				
5				
4	XNS	TCP/IP	SNA	OSI
3				
2	802.3	802.5	FDDI	802.11
1				

A significant corporate contribution to the OSI momentum came from the General Motors Corporation. More victimised by multi-vendor incompatibilities than most because of pure size, it decided enough was enough and became the driving force behind the Manufacturing Automation Protocol (MAP) standard. MAP was a complete specified profile for an OSI-based networking standard for industrial environments. In a parallel effort, Boeing drove the development of the Technical and Office Protocols or TOP standard. TOP is an OSI-based standard for administrative, scientific, engineering and office environments. What this work did to the early development of the open system interconnect was firstly the adoption of all the IEEE802 committee specifications for layers 1 and 2. Therefore, LANs were firmly in placed on the OSI model. This in turn focused the standards committee on providing connectivity down to the device level which became Open Device Interconnect. This subtle change in the ground rules from SYSTEMS to DEVICE caused a significant change in what manufacturers were to develop. Enter the PC.

1981 saw the release of the new concept in desktop computing, even though 1983 saw the PC's rise to prominence. Prior to 1983 there was a vast array of different modules with differing processors and variations on the CP/M Operating System. IBM firmly established the PC bus in 1983 and Microsoft's Disc Operating System (MS-DOS) became the operating system of choice. All developers now produced products for this MS-DOS environment. The corporate purchaser resisted the PC invasion because there was no standard way to control them or link them to the host. PCs as a result became islands of information.

ENTERPRISE NETWORKING

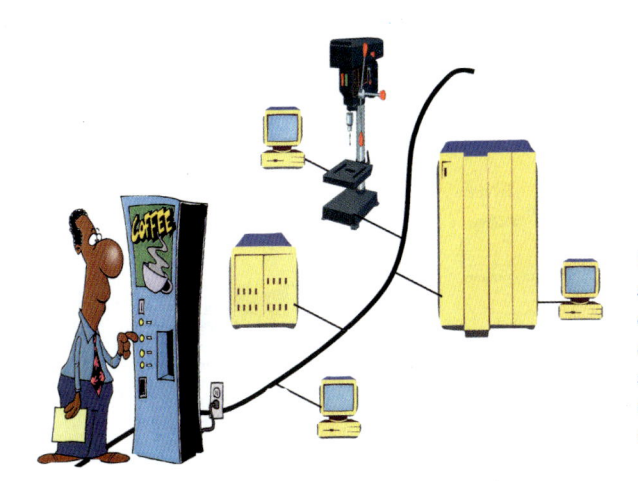

CONVERGENCE OF STANDARDS IN THE PC

With the introduction of MAP specifications OSI was seen as defining the communications for devices. Therefore instead of separate systems being linked, all devices were expected to support the MAP profile

Meanwhile, the LAN industry was forging ahead and the new PC networking market, which started life as selling disk sharing systems, quickly migrated to file and print sharing. To make PC networking acceptable to the corporate DP department, a standard was required to guarantee interoperability, so IBM gave the world NetBIOS (Network Basic Input Output System). NetBIOS provides access to the network specific functions that are not available from the standalone MS-DOS. The idea is to enable software developers to access network functions and produce network specific applications, in much the same way that the ROM BIOS enables developers to access the PC hardware. Virtually all network vendors provided NetBIOS-compatible network interfaces. It was considered safe to network PCs and inter-operability was guaranteed by the NetBIOS interface at the session layer. NetBIOS has become firmly established and has been

The early attempts at integrating the PC into the Mainframe environment were difficult with limited functionality. In many cases, the PC emulated a dumb terminal, which is hardly using the PC at its best. The term 'Islands of Information' is how the market viewed the use of PCs. The introduction of PC networking was the driver that pushed PCs into world domination as the new window onto corporate resources.

ENTERPRISE NETWORKING

CONVERGENCE OF STANDARDS IN THE PC

extended by Microsoft to move PC networking from the age of file sharing to the age of client-server networking.

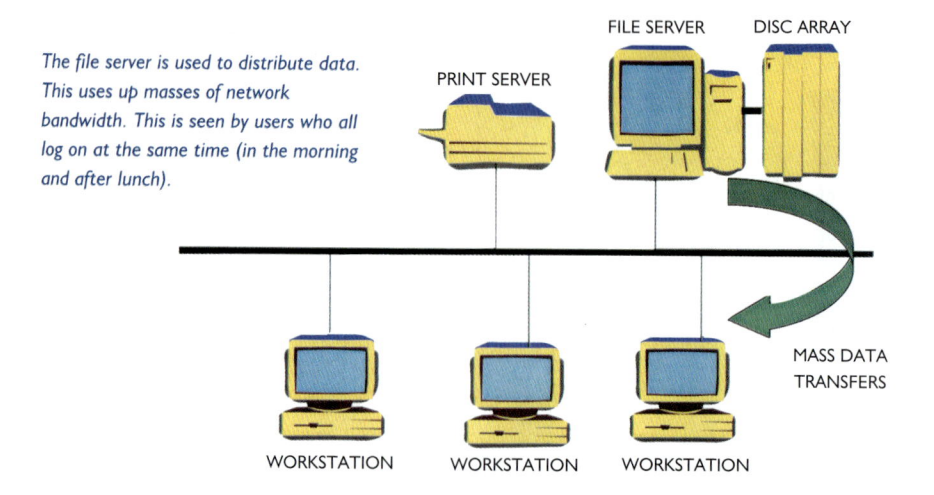

The file server is used to distribute data. This uses up masses of network bandwidth. This is seen by users who all log on at the same time (in the morning and after lunch).

FILE SERVER DISC ARRAY
PRINT SERVER
MASS DATA TRANSFERS
WORKSTATION WORKSTATION WORKSTATION

I would like to acknowledge the contribution to PC networking from Novell which, in my opinion, pioneered and drove PC networking into the mainstream of computer resources for the enterprise. Possessing worldwide market leadership for much of the late 1980s and early 1990s, Novell focused on pure PC networking and provided PC access to PC file servers. The development of its NetWare product centred on user-friendly interfaces and PC network supervisor facilities to control the working environment. Later developments included print sharing and then, very much later, communications servers and access to host computer resources. Therefore apart from becoming a de facto standard, Novell was more about PCs sharing PC resources than addressing the grander scheme of things. And this story is following the underlying standards and not the user facilities.

Returning to the mainstream of our story, networking moved ahead with extensions to NetBIOS. These extensions were provided by an application known as named pipes. This was an integral part of LAN Manager, the new generation of networking software from Microsoft. This new networked computing model was based firmly on economic reality. The servers are shared facilities therefore purchasers buy relatively expensive, high performance machines while the user population in comparison is vast. OS/2 provided the multi-tasking environment required by the central resource while LAN Manager

ENTERPRISE NETWORKING

CONVERGENCE OF STANDARDS IN THE PC

formed the communications mechanism enabling the user device - the intelligent workstation - to deliver a user-friendly environment and window onto the corporate resources.

To achieve open systems and the resulting freedom of choice, any standard must be supported and implemented by all vendors. There was an acceptance by all equipment manufacturers that the personal computer was winning the race, with over 300 million installed by the beginning of the 90s. Communications solutions had to include facilities that were required by these users. Therefore, the environments that had traditionally supported PCs, begrudgingly, now provide PC services as mainstream options. LAN Manager for UNIX, developed by Hewlett Packard, brought UNIX-based host services. DEC, the other great terminal supporter, had purchased a LAN Manager licence and fell in line to support the new model. This enabled freedom of choice to purchase the server of choice, with no restrictions and the knowledge it would integrate into a client server system.

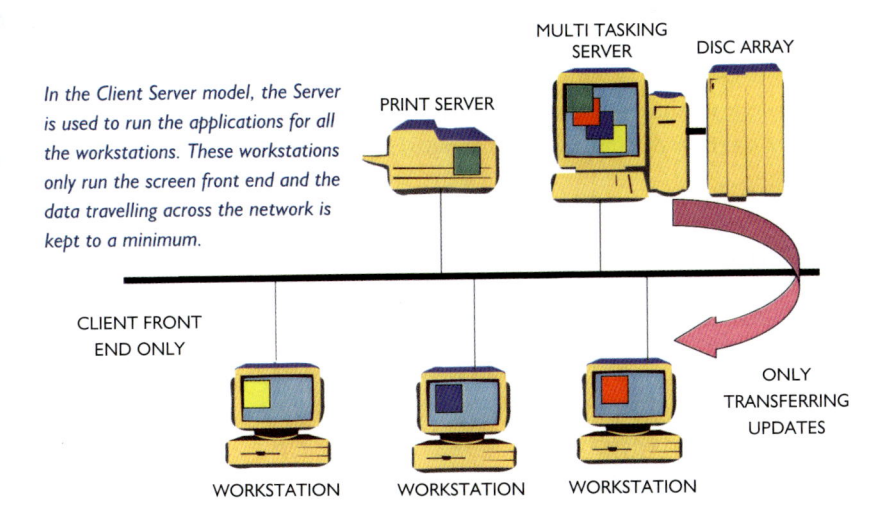

In the Client Server model, the Server is used to run the applications for all the workstations. These workstations only run the screen front end and the data travelling across the network is kept to a minimum.

PRINT SERVER

MULTI TASKING SERVER

DISC ARRAY

CLIENT FRONT END ONLY

ONLY TRANSFERRING UPDATES

WORKSTATION   WORKSTATION   WORKSTATION

Next we have to address the interconnection problems faced by PC machines in a multi-vendor environment. The hosts would all use a LAN manager communications interface but could still possibly be running a range of protocol stacks XNS, TCP/IP, ISO(4), and SNA. Instead of trying to replace the multiple stacks while waiting for all suppliers to adopt OSI standards and the same conformance-tested profiles, the solution was to run

ENTERPRISE NETWORKING

CONVERGENCE OF STANDARDS IN THE PC

multiple stacks in the workstation. To do this, the protocol stacks had to be removed from any hardware dependency.

Microsoft provided a de facto specification NDIS (Network Driver Interface Specification), which was a software interface for these protocol stacks that removed hardware dependencies and enabled the automatic selection of multiple stacks. We now had complete freedom of choice at the workstation end.

Novell addressed the same problem and produced Open Datalink Interface (ODI) to provide a common software interface for all protocol stacks. There was also one major commercial benefit resulting in support of NDIS and ODI. The additional requirement came about as corporate purchasers began to realise what standards were about. A corporate purchaser telephones his PC dealer and said *"Send me 50 Token Ring cards"*. The dealer enquired, *"Which supplier's cards do you want?"* the response was *"Who cares, they are all standard aren't they"*. What was required was a software interface to enable the communications software to be independent of the networking hardware. We now had the solution NDIS and ODI which enabled any PC adapter card to be freely interchanged so you could buy any host or workstation and not worry about protocol stacks. Couple this with LAN market reports which showed terminal servers sales declining and PC network sales increasing. A clear trend of client-server was establishing itself. This freedom of choice and communications compatibility was achieved with no OSI protocols in sight.

There are less drastic ways to enable computers to communicate. The international Standards Organisation laid the foundations but the manufacturers only adopted the architecture of the OSI seven layer model. Commercial pressure forced manufacturers to conform and adopt 'de facto' standards for PC communications.

ENTERPRISE NETWORKING

CONVERGENCE OF STANDARDS IN THE PC

But standards never stand still and a new round of developments is being introduced to extend the reach of the PC into multimedia. This implies supporting data, voice and video on a single platform to add to the vast range of tasks PCs already perform. Telephony and video-conferencing functions are also on the agenda. The changes that have been implemented in the PC hardware has put video compression and decompression and voice codecs onto the motherboard.

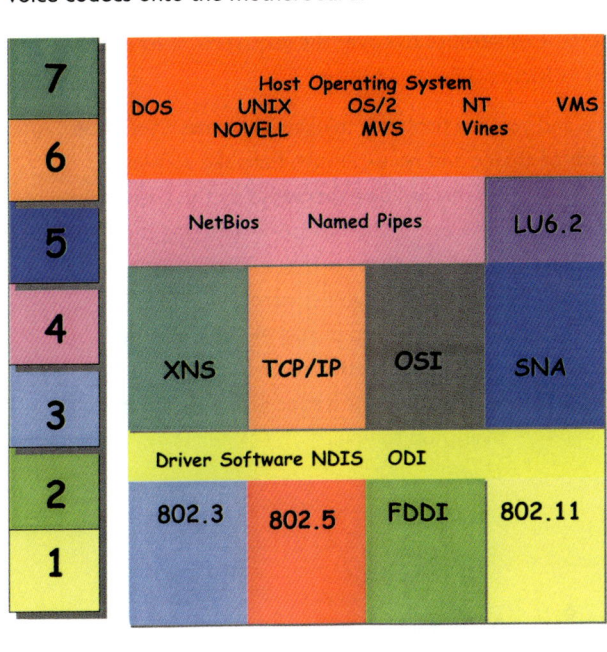

7	Host Operating System				
	DOS	UNIX	OS/2	NT	VMS
6		NOVELL	MVS	Vines	
5	NetBios	Named Pipes		LU6.2	
4					
3	XNS	TCP/IP	OSI	SNA	
2	Driver Software NDIS		ODI		
1	802.3	802.5	FDDI	802.11	

A new PC peripheral connection appeared the Universal Serial Bus (USB), which was designed to interconnect the extra hardware that turned the basic PC into a multimedia workstation. This not only covered printers and scanners but video and telephony devices.

And wireless chip manufacturers are making newer solutions that aim to eliminate cables, a solution is known as Bluetooth with a range of up to ten metres, although there is a secondary standard designed to offer a 100 metre range. The aim is to allow all peripherals - printers, mouse, keyboard, PDAs and so on - to authenticate and connect automatically.

There are also two new wireless network standards, IEEE802.11b at 11Mbit/sec and IEEE802.11a at 54Mbit/sec which are described in Section 10. These wireless products have ranges of 300m to 11Km.

Both Novell with Telephony Server API (TSAPI) and Microsoft with Telephony API (TAPI) are enabling a new generation of applications developers to put voice applications onto PC platforms. To transport the information across the network new protocol stacks are required for voice and video. This does not cause any concern as NDIS and ODI are

ENTERPRISE NETWORKING

CONVERGENCE OF STANDARDS IN THE PC

capable of running multiple protocol stacks.

These newer protocol stacks have to deal with differing transport requirements of the new PC applications of voice, video and data. Voice requires a guaranteed service level even though the absolute bandwidth requirement is relatively low. Video requires a contiguous service at higher bandwidth levels and data has not changed from its original bursty nature. What has been happening is that the TCP/IP protocol stack has been slowly improved and added too with new capabilities to cover the requirement for multi service networking. You will find this in Section 17.

This paints an incredibly rosy picture and you are probably thinking the news cannot be all good you would be right. Freedom of choice and no expensive bespoke software development was what we set out to achieve. This has been achieved by the popularity of the PC as the preferred work platform. However, multi-vendor networking is only a viable solution if it can be managed. The reality of this today is that it is still extremely difficult to put a true service level management solution together across multiple vendors. Most network management solutions are made up of specific task-oriented modules. Today there are a couple of widely supported platforms on which to build systems management but the task of achieving a solution for a specific enterprise is mainly up to you.

Standards give you the freedom to buy any product and guarantee interoperability with your existing equipment. Microsoft has provided a solid standard for the PC platform and the IEEE802. Standards have given flexibility and safety in communications both Locally and in the Wide Area.

ENTERPRISE NETWORKING

CONVERGENCE OF STANDARDS IN THE PC

SERVER FARMS AND NETWORKING

Networks suffer from their own success by growing to the limit of the available bandwidth. Users feel this bandwidth pinch when accessing the server because they tend to start and stop work at the same time. This means they boot up and log off together, creating several specific periods of high demand. The first step taken to alleviate the problem was to concentrate servers into groups, or server farms. This allowed the system administrator to link servers to higher speed connections, isolating them from general user communications.

Server farms too have grown larger and larger and a new phenomenon occurred. The client server brings applications back to the centre of the system so that users have to download client applications with the processing being done on the servers. This places a huge load onto the servers, so servers of popular applications get swamped while other servers sit by with minimal load. When one of these servers buckles under a high load, an entire company can be brought to its knees. So features built into the network infrastructure are required to increase the performance, reliability and security of the servers. The technique is to spread the load over the servers, instead of dedicating one server per function while checking the servers' status such as the amount of processing power available and which applications are current. These features are known collectively as Load Sharing Network Address Translation (LSNAT).

HOW LSNAT WORKS

Load Sharing Network Address Translation (LSNAT) as defined in RFC 2391 allows an IP address and port number to become a Virtual IP (VIP) address and port number that maps to many devices such as a server farm. So the networking device supporting LSNAT sits in the communications path between users and servers, with users seeing a big device with lots of spare capacity. The device translates addresses and balances traffic across the available resources that have spare capacity.

When the VIP is seen as a destination address and destination port number by the LSNAT device, the networking device traps the packet. The device then translates VIP to a real IP address and port combinations, using a selected algorithm such as Round Robin, Weighted Round Robin, Least Load or Fastest Response that allows it to select from a group of server addresses. The network device makes the appropriate changes to packet and header checksums before passing the packet along.

ENTERPRISE NETWORKING

CONVERGENCE OF STANDARDS IN THE PC

On the return path, the networking device will see the source and destination pair with the real IP address and port number, and know that it needs to replace this source address and source port number with the VIP and appropriate checksum recalculations before sending the packet along.

The simplicity of the description above belies the complexity of the feature. The network can see a tremendous increase in performance by optimising traffic among different groups of servers. Reliability is increased by allowing for scheduled maintenance, and also by automatically taking defective servers out of a group when they are detected. Security is improved since only the VIP is publicly accessible, not the specific server addresses, so only the traffic you desire goes to the servers.

The ability to support multiple resources in parallel means that a server farm can be constructed that will deliver 100% service availability, even during routine maintenance of the resources.

section seven

Bridging, Routing and Switching

Section 7: Bridges, Routers and Switches

Bridging and Routing have become increasingly important as networks increase in size and new technology advancements means that every port accessing the network will be a switched router port by the middle of this decade. This section illustrates the major differences and some applications. The two technologies are merging and being implemented directly into silicon. These fast bridges are now called switches and the router as a hardware device is changing with the routing function and now considered a software service which with the latest technology, is embedded in to dedicated hardware chips knows as ASCI's (Application Specific Integrated Circuits).

ENTERPRISE NETWORKING

BRIDGING ROUTING AND SWITCHING

The PCs ability to display complex graphics and images has raised the expectation of the users. They in turn, put greater demand on the communications infrastructure to deliver these complex high content documents.

If anything is certain, it is that networks get bigger and, with more users sharing a wiring scheme, available bandwidth gets consumed and the network slows down. A good LAN is a victim of its own success. By enabling information transfer, improvements in productivity and ease of access to information, it encourages more business functions to be transferred to PC applications there.

And it's the PC's ease of use and adaptability that is at the root of the network's bandwidth problem. Modern PCs have driven the need for applications look and feel the same, largely because it reduces training requirements, enabling new applications to be adopted very quickly with the minimum of assistance. The enabler here is the graphical user interface (GUI).

I first saw the interface in 1980 at Xerox where they had a lab set up running the first network I had seen called the Ether. The workstations connected had real pictures of offices with real filing cabinets and I saw my first electronic mouse at the same time. But I give credit to another company for successfully promoting the user interface: Apple. Microsoft introduced the interface onto MS-DOS-based PCs with the introduction of Windows 3.0 and it's been there ever since.

What this did was to raise users' expectations. Where once they were happy with simple text, now a graphical front-end is standard. Complex data and graphics cause bandwidth

ENTERPRISE NETWORKING

BRIDGING ROUTING AND SWITCHING

utilisation problems as large, complex files move around the network from storage to printer to workstation. You can no longer put a piece of cable round a building and plug in all your computer users into it. You have to think architecture and you have to think bandwidth conservation. The architecture that is winning is a backbone feeder network. This is system involving a LAN backbone with departmental solutions configured as sub-networks which are isolated but connected - bridged - onto the backbone.

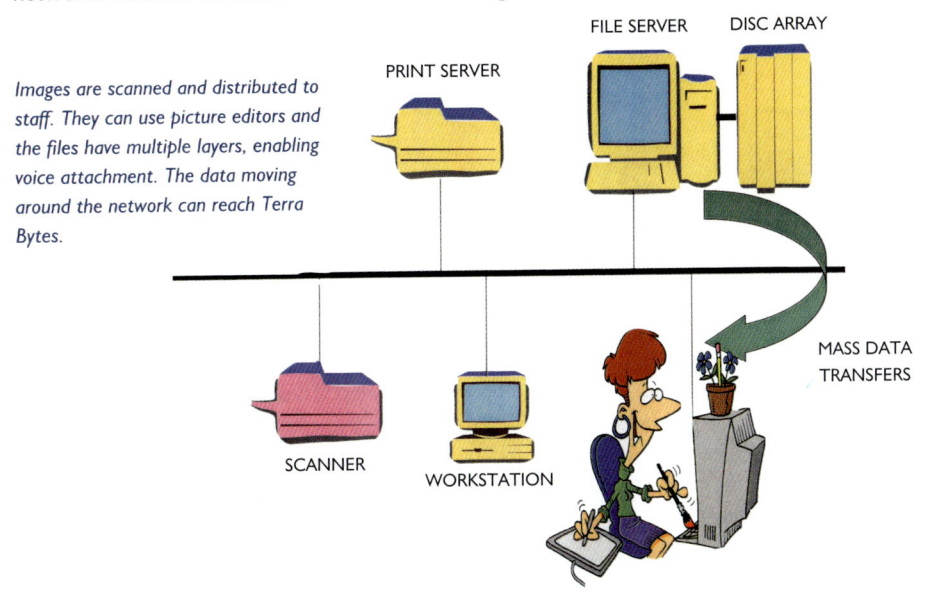

Images are scanned and distributed to staff. They can use picture editors and the files have multiple layers, enabling voice attachment. The data moving around the network can reach Terra Bytes.

Bridging enables filtering of traffic, removing unnecessary packets and only transferring data in and out of the subnet that explicitly needs to traverse the wider network. This mechanism conserves bandwidth by controlling who and what can transfer information onto the backbone. However, bridging is not the only choice - routing performs a similar task.

Bridges and routers are defined by where they sit with regard to the OSI reference model. Layer 1 defines the wiring infrastructure which can be extended within the standards by using repeaters. A repeater cleans up and amplifies the signal and sends it on its way. It has very limited functionality but can extend the physical coverage of the network. Layer 2 describes the access method of sharing the cabling infrastructure and products here are called data link bridges. They behave as a node on the network and can link two networks together. Data link bridges receive information for the second

ENTERPRISE NETWORKING

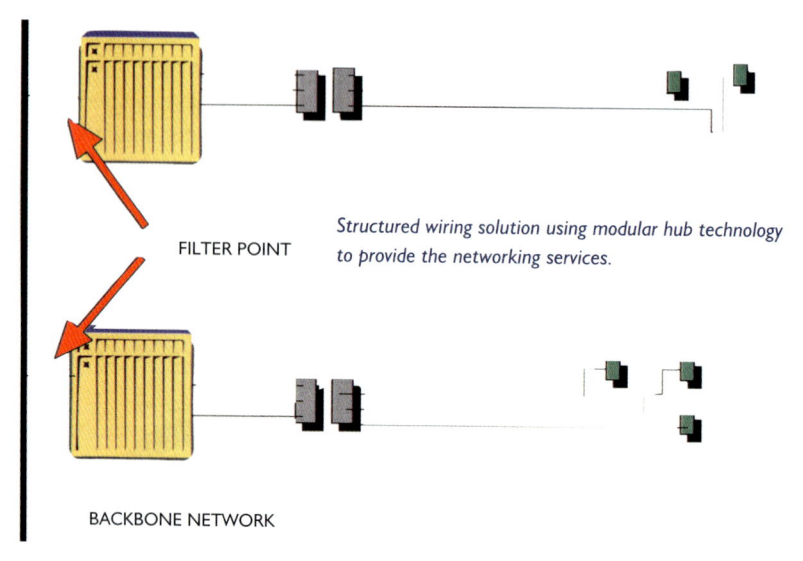

BRIDGING ROUTING AND SWITCHING

FILTER POINT

Structured wiring solution using modular hub technology to provide the networking services.

BACKBONE NETWORK

network and effectively re-send it error-free as new information while suppressing broadcasts and ensuring only relevant information is forwarded. These products enable large networks to be constructed.

But because they do not understand logical network addresses, data link bridges construct one homogeneous network. This can cause problems if you think about how devices locate each other by broadcasting. Large networks can suffer from bandwidth problems caused by excessive broadcast traffic, commonly called broadcast storms. On the upside, bridges work at layer 2 and are independent of the higher level protocols so different communications software can run across them. This enables multi-vendor systems to be constructed, all sharing the same infrastructure. Bridged Ethernet to Ethernet is straightforward, similarly Token Ring to Token Ring. Because bridges are performing a simple task - either forward packet or do not forward packet - they can be installed in a network without being configured and they will automatically learn what devices surround them and make their own forwarding decisions. This has resulted in bridging being termed transparent bridging. In fact bridging any similar technology is a straightforward task, but bridging dissimilar technology creates several problems.

Ethernet has a maximum packet size of 1,500 bytes where Token Ring has a maximum packet size of 4,000 bytes. Moving packets from Ethernet to Token Ring is straightforward but putting Token Ring packets on an Ethernet network causes problems.

ENTERPRISE NETWORKING

BRIDGING ROUTING AND SWITCHING

Bridges need to fragment the bigger packets and sequentially send them at the smaller packet size. Then there is the question of addressing because the differing technologies use different bit patterns to specify the destination. Bridges for linking dissimilar technologies by dealing with the differing addressing schemes while fragmenting and re-assembling packets are known as translation bridges.

Layer 3 products are network-aware - that is, they can read and use the Network Addresses. Therefore routers are specific to the communications being used. On a TCP/IP network a TCP/IP router is required while on a Novell NetWare network you need an IPX router. Routers can build big complex networks and filter out unwanted traffic preserving bandwidth. The router process is to use routing protocols to find out where a specific device is located. Once discovered, this information is entered into a routing table. Routers keep these tables up-to-date and exchange information between themselves using specific routing protocols so, even with no data flowing, routers are continually using the communications paths to keep themselves configured correctly. When information is broadcast onto the network, the router reads the packet to identify the communications protocol and the address the packet is destined for. From its routing tables the router can determine the paths along which a packet may be sent to the desired destination. The router then applies the rules that you have configured into it to

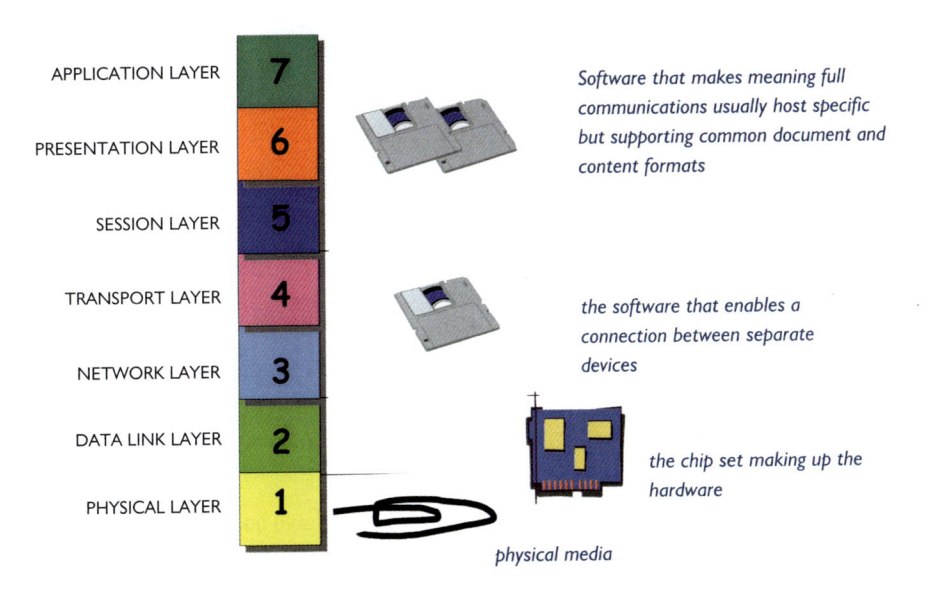

7	APPLICATION LAYER	Software that makes meaning full communications usually host specific but supporting common document and content formats
6	PRESENTATION LAYER	
5	SESSION LAYER	
4	TRANSPORT LAYER	the software that enables a connection between separate devices
3	NETWORK LAYER	
2	DATA LINK LAYER	the chip set making up the hardware
1	PHYSICAL LAYER	physical media

ENTERPRISE NETWORKING

BRIDGING ROUTING AND SWITCHING

ensure that the route taken is the most cost-effective for the desired destination. This intelligent use of communication paths is one of the main advantages routers have over bridges.

We can construct a network from data link bridges or routers with exactly the same topology. If we use data link bridges then it would be a single, vendor-independent network. To prevent data circulating round the bridged network, we employ the IEEE802.1d Spanning Tree algorithm this enables links to the same destination, possibly by a different path, to go into standby. This prevents circulatory packets and, should a failure occur on a live link, the standby will insert itself automatically. Therefore both bridges and routers can build the network, they can both filter traffic so data only goes where you need it. Data link bridges do not process the protocols so they are cheaper, quicker and can support multi-vendor equipment. A disadvantage is that one of your communications paths will not be fully utilised as it is on standby.

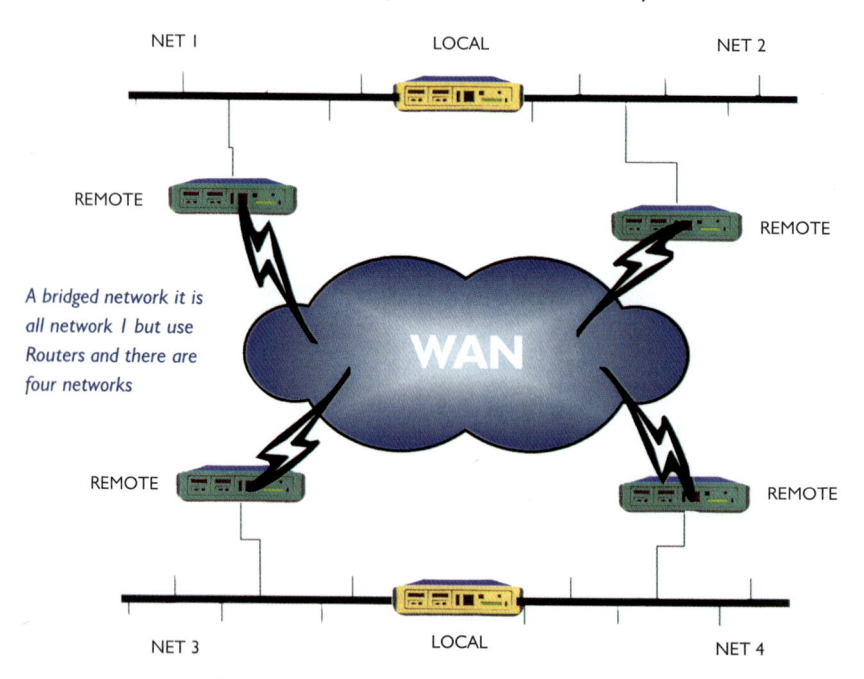

A bridged network it is all network 1 but use Routers and there are four networks

Building the same network using routers would be both more expensive and specific to a given protocol but all your communications paths will be fully utilised. The drawback of routers is that each router has to process the information and determine the path

ENTERPRISE NETWORKING

BRIDGING ROUTING AND SWITCHING

through the network, increasing latency and hence the delay in getting information across the network. So your decision has to be based on price versus performance versus functionality against your actual communications costs.

Token Ring networks approach the problem in a similar way but the implementation of bridging requires the use of a technique known as source routing. Here a device, which is broadcasting to find the location of a particular service sends out a network-wide packet asking the service where it is. On its voyage across the network, each bridge crossed inserts information that it has been part of the path. When the desired service is reached it answers the request and the answers percolate back across the network. Obviously the answer arriving first has found the shortest route across the network so this is the path used for the communication. Standards committees have now integrated the two techniques, Source Routing and Spanning Tree, which is known as the SRT, (Source Routing Transparency) specification.

Bridges are commonly used to increase the size of networks. They can also be used to isolate departments for bandwidth reasons or to keep sensitive information in a given domain. Bridges and routers can be configured for example to block a particular user or protocol from leaving a domain, making them useful security devices. Bridges are also used to link dissimilar networks as in an Ethernet to Token Ring.

Routers are commonly used in this dissimilar network mode because they do not limit any applications. Routers are also used when networks are very big and where complex routes exist as backup paths in the event of line failures. Routers are also commonly used where external communications are a premium. As for brouting - bridging and routing - in one unit, the box primarily routes information but if it does not understand the communications protocol, it reverts to bridging which can move any protocol anywhere.

Bridges and routers have not been immune from technological advance, the latest of which is the development of ASIC technology. ASIC have enabled developers to put a data link bridge into a single IC, resulting in very high performance throughput with very low latency.

These bridges on a single chip are commonly called LAN switches or layer 2 switches, With the progress of technology, we have switches that work at layer 3 and others that can identify the application, a layer 4 function. Thus, we can have layer 2, 3 or 4 or combination switches.

ENTERPRISE NETWORKING

BRIDGING ROUTING AND SWITCHING

Since the mid 1990s, Token Ring and Ethernet switches have been able to work more like simple repeaters than like bridges or routers, examining the header of a frame and forwarding it immediately before waiting for the rest of the frame to arrive. Known as cut-through switches, they do not check the entire frame for errors which made them cheaper than equipment which processed the entire packet, checking its integrity and then making a forwarding decision. These store-and-forward switches formed the second wave of switches and, as ASIC speeds have increased and their price fallen, they now dominate switching.

Note that cut-through switches do not examine an entire frame and so are unable to translate a frame from one LAN format to another; for example, Ethernet workstations can only talk to other Ethernet devices, limiting the ability to connect workstations to high-speed servers. However, store-and-forward switches can reformat the information for a different packet structure, enabling different technologies to be interconnected.

Another key function is workstation support capabilities, that is, how many workstations per port they can support. Some switches function only in workgroup applications, in that they only support a single MAC address per switch port. This means one device per port. System-based switches allow multiple MAC addresses per port, which then allows you to connect downstream hubs and switches. The total number of MAC addresses per unit should be sufficient for the LAN segments that you intend to connect.

Routers have not been immune from these technology advances either. Routers processing routing decisions in software under processor control have always had performance limits that frustrated network managers. The switching of packets in hardware has resulted in massive performance advantages therefore there are now router ASICs. These devices are known as layer 3 switches. Here the router's functions have been separated into two distinct tasks. The routing function, selecting the correct path, is kept in the software and once the path is established the transferring of the information is the second task, which is handled by the ASIC and is called stream switching.

ATM SWITCHING

Asynchronous Transfer Mode (ATM) has become widely accepted as the standard switching mechanism for digital telecommunication networks. It has been deployed within local and wide area networking products, but predominantly by wide area public

ENTERPRISE NETWORKING

BRIDGING ROUTING AND SWITCHING

networks. ATM's small cells keep latency low while being able to combine variable bit rate information, such as LAN packets, and constant bit rate information, such as voice. Because ATM switching is implemented in hardware and switches can be meshed, it can scale to support applications that are orders of magnitude larger than today's largest networks. The issue with ATM is a commercial one. Given that the installed base of Ethernet technology is huge and that businesses employ engineering staff deeply versed in the ways of Ethernet, it would be a major risk to consider switching away from it. Look at the installed networks around today, you can see that the idea of ATM becoming the dominant LAN standard has not happened and looks unlikely to do so.

LAN SWITCHING

Most applications will see an enormous increase in throughput by dedicating Ethernet or Token Ring connections to individual devices, and switching them to higher speed Ethernet, FDDI or ATM servers. This means that two kinds of switches will be needed. Wiring closet switches, working at layer 2 of the ISO model, will connect to workstations and servers with Ethernet, Token Ring and FDDI interfaces. Each device will have its own dedicated connection. Connections between two devices attached to the same wiring closet switch (for example, a workstation and a local file server) will be handled locally at wire speeds. These switches, in turn, will connect to backbone switches. These will act as a multi-gigabit backbone fabrics working at layer 3 and layer 4 of the OSI model, providing true business application services that map to a businesses functions and business processes.

SWITCHES AND ROUTERS TOGETHER

Routing services, not necessarily routers, have a place in their ability to interconnect with security differing network types. In the new infrastructure the routing service will be the primary means to interconnect virtual networks as opposed to today's physically dissimilar networks. This is the subject of the next section. There are solutions competing against routing in a switched network but they have the common theme of separating the routing decision, which is taken in software, from the routed protocol that's processed in silicon.

AN ASIDE: ROUTER CONSIDERATIONS

When using routers there are a few key considerations. Firstly there are routing

ENTERPRISE NETWORKING

BRIDGING ROUTING AND SWITCHING

protocols and routed protocols. Routing protocols are the standard communications used by the routers to find out what the network topology looks like and to keep up to date with the communications links are available for use as communications path to send the data across. Routing protocols include RIP (Router Information Protocol), OSPF (Open Shortest Path First), IS-IS (Intermediate System to Intermediate System) protocol, NHRP (Next Hop Routing Protocol) and RSVP (Resource Reservation Protocol). Routed protocols both carry the data from one end of the communications path to the other, while checking and error correcting the data in the destination device. Examples of routed protocols are TCP/IP, IPX and LAT. At the low end of communication speeds the router employs serial protocols as the routed protocol such as SLIP (Serial Line Interface) Protocol, PPP the Point to Point Protocol.

TCP/IP networks require that all devices have a IP address, currently a four-byte code that the IP protocol uses to identify devices. Users of a IP network have to decide whether to use the standard addressing scheme or a private addressing scheme. A standard scheme is where the addresses conform to the addresses issued by the USA-based Internet Address Numbering Authority which manages the IP standards for connecting into the Internet.

This means that there will be no address conflicts when interconnecting different sites. Using a private scheme means that a gateway would be needed to link to standard or other private schemes. Network Address Translation (NAT) is now a feature available on many layer 3 switches to take account of the private addressing schemes. The reasons for these alternate schemes is that with the exponential world growth in networking, we are running out of addresses.

In the standard addressing scheme, the four bytes can be used in different ways. If you use the first byte for network addresses and then the remaining three bytes for hosts then the world can have only 254 networks and 16 million hosts. You can take it from me that we need more than 254 networks. This is a type 'A' address. You can use two bytes for the network address, then you can have 64K networks and 64K hosts. This is a type 'B' address.

The most common addressing scheme is type 'C', which uses three bytes for the network addresses and one byte for hosts. This provides enough network addresses but still not enough for the hosts on most networks today. This problem is overcome by subnetting and subnet masking helps isolate one part of the network from the other. Here the network manager can decide to use some of the network address space to

ENTERPRISE NETWORKING

BRIDGING ROUTING AND SWITCHING

identify hosts. If we have two bits of the second byte this gives us four permutations so by using these two bits a network manager can have four different hosts with the address 254.

The IP addressing problems are workarounds that will be resolved in the future as the standards bodies work on IP version 6, the next generation of IP. However were ATM to take off and native ATM applications were used, none of this would be necessary. Today the problem IP addresses cause in a router-based network is that to communicate between subnets requires a separate router port for each subnet. So if a user moves to a new location, the IP address would have to be change to match the new location, requiring the efforts of a highly skilled engineer. Companies spend a sizable chunk of their network support budget on managing their IP addressing schemes.

IP BASICS

Internet Protocol is the Internet's *lingua franca* and is similarly dominant in enterprise networks. Note though that some departmental networks still use Novell's IPX although many plan to move to IP. Therefore IP is the de facto communications protocol. As IP is an OSI layer 3 protocol specification it will run over a wide range of underlying communications media.

IP is a common packet format and addressing scheme that provides for connectionless communication of packets across networks that may consist of different types of transport mechanisms. This includes all versions of Ethernet, Token Ring, FDDI, Leased Lines, Dial up Lines, and Frame Relay. The IP packet format contains a header, which holds the Internet address to which the packet is to be sent, a unique end station, the address of the sending station and the actual data to be transferred. Routers are able to interpret the destination address on each packet and, using their own internal tables, determine the connection to be used to send the packet to its next stop on route to the destination. IP packets can range in size from a few bytes in length to a thousand bytes or more.

IP is called a connectionless protocol because the end stations don't have to do anything in advance to set up any kind of link to where they want to talk before they send IP packets. Sending an IP packet is like sending a letter. The letter has an address, which is sufficient in its entirety for the postal system to be able to route it to its final destination. Once the IP packet is passed on by a node, it is forgotten. The packet then becomes the

ENTERPRISE NETWORKING

BRIDGING ROUTING AND SWITCHING

responsibility of the receiving node.

IP is a delivery mechanism; it has no means of checking what it is transporting. As an example, IP itself does not contain any mechanisms to detect if a packet is lost in the network, so if you want to be sure that data has been received at the far end, you need some additional protocol running over IP to keep track of this, hence Transmission Control Protocol (TCP). TCP takes data from the application that wants to send it and puts this data into IP packets to be sent over the network. TCP also adds a sequence number and a process for acknowledging receipt of data and requesting a re-transmit in the event that a packet is corrupted or lost. This way we can guarantee that data transfers are completed successfully which is why data applications use high layer protocols.

REAL-TIME OVER IP

When we want to send real-time communications like voice and video over IP, we are not actually that interested in whether we receive every last bit of the data at the far end. We are much more interested in getting the data through quickly in a known time frame. This is because voice and video are designed for human consumption and we can tolerate missing pixels in pictures and a miss pronunciation but we cannot have picture frames arriving out of sequence and we need the beginning of a sentence before the end of a sentence. TCP is therefore inappropriate. If we lose an IP packet containing a segment of speech from a phonecall, it makes more sense to ignore this, the user just hears a click, than to have TCP request a re-transmit.

What is required, when using IP for real time applications, is some timing information. This is to enable the re-construct it time sequence the real-time voice or video information as a steady stream at the far end. This is specified under the Real-Time Protocol (RTP) proposal as an alternative to TCP over IP for communicating real-time voice or video.

Todays networks already exist and therefore we will be mixing voice packets, video packets and data packets. The voice and video packets will come in steady, measured streams that require limited bandwidth, but require minimum of delay in getting to the desired destination. The data packets however will occur in bursts. This could be bursts of a few data packets when using a transactional application to a file transfer across the network which streams a flood of data packets. With file transfers there is no concerned about delay. If a file transfer takes three seconds instead of two seconds to complete users will not notice but if voice packets take a few fractions of a second longer to arrive

ENTERPRISE NETWORKING

BRIDGING ROUTING AND SWITCHING

we have a unacceptable interruptions in speech. In real networks, bursty data traffic almost always causes transient congestion at concentration points in the network, especially when the information as to cross the WAN. Congestion creates more congestion as packets queued up at router ports waiting to get onto the congested link. If voice and video packets are forced to wait in the queue behind data packets, you will generate unacceptable delays. With IP all packets get treated equally. There is no way that voice and video packets can jump the queue to avoid delay. This is why Bandwidth Reservation Protocol has been adopted. The IEEE has specified Resource Reservation Protocol (RSVP).

RSVP allows real-time traffic to be separated out into separate queues at router ports and given higher priority than data. RSVP also involves negotiation between end stations and routers to reserve bandwidth for real-time communications. RTP and RSVP are new additions to the IP family of protocols and are still in the process of completing standardisation.

IP Multicast Real-time transport of voice and video from point to point is one aspect of a multi-service network. Multicasting is another important aspect. Should a network provide a video source to users then it would be inefficient to have ten point-to-point connections for ten users, a better system would be to have one connection from the source to the nearest switch and then have the switch replicate the information to the other nine users. This is the concept of multicasting. Just as the IP family of protocols is being enhanced to handle real-time point-to-point communications, so it is also being enhanced to handle multicasts. The way this works is that a workstation wishing to receive a particular multicasts stream requests this from its nearest router port on the network, and the routers co-operate in the network to ensure that the stream of IP packets containing the multicast is copied to the router port nearest to the requesting user and thence carried to him over the LAN.

Broadcast and Unicast, to complete the picture, are methods of packet delivery. Unicast packets are directed at one specific destination this is the normal traffic flow on a network. Broadcasts on the other hand are all station announcements. These are packets meant for every destination on the network. They are not intended to cross the network boundary hence bridges forward broadcasts while routers terminate them. A common broadcast is the ARP request, which is sent by a source device that knows the destination device is on an IP sub net but does not know its unique MAC address.

section eight

Networks using Switches and Virtual Networks

Section 8: Switches and Virtual Networks

Networks today are moving over to Switched Infrastructures. To map onto the business functions and processes, a feature known as Virtual Networking has become dominant. The options are reviewed with the resulting benefits.

ENTERPRISE NETWORKING

NETWORKING USING SWITCHES AND VIRTUAL NETWORKING SWITCHING

INTRODUCTION

In the mid-1990s, market research and analysis organisation The Yankee Group surveyed network managers to discover their requirements and priority of achieving these requirements. The summary, which they displayed in order of importance, was displayed as the hierarchy of needs. The working principle was that a network manager must service each slice of the pyramid before he moves up a rung and tackles the next problem.

Network Managers who are trying to provide a reliable and predictable service need all the help they can get. Switching technology helps by providing predictable dedicated services and simplifies the overall communications infrastructure. The added services that can then be deployed across a switched network give network managers control of users and resources never experienced in the shared media world.

A network manager who starts to charge for using services is not going to get a polite response if the same user finds that the services are only 50% available so he must first ensure that a user has 100% access to all appropriate services. The next step would be to tune network performance to match the user's application. With a working network, the network manager now has time to adjust the network configuration to better match the task-orientated workgroups of his organisation. Naturally, security comes into play when isolating the various operations. A combination of configuration control and a security overlay should enable a network manager to match the organisation's functional split onto the communications infrastructure.

Once users are happy with their service levels and managers are confident about each department's confidentiality, it is reasonably safe for a network manager to account for these services. The next step is to negotiate an acceptable service level agreement with the user departments so as to recoup some or all of the costs of maintaining the

ENTERPRISE NETWORKING

NETWORKING USING SWITCHES AND VIRTUAL NETWORKING SWITCHING

infrastructure. With a regular income guaranteed as long as he is can maintain the service levels, automating the process can be considered in an attempt to reduce the network department's overheads and so reduce the cross-charging for any given service. Many network managers who review this hierarchy of needs are frustrated by the fact that they already own the networking products and have no idea on how to get off the first rung of the pyramid. If this is the current state of networking then we need to change things, and I don't mean a forklift change but a redeployment change. The enabling technology for this change is switching and the service provider is virtual networking, which allows switches to address the hierarchy of needs.

Telephony systems have one major benefit over networking systems today. Financial controllers understand the phone system and are very comfortable in making business decisions about its usage, such as, "no international calls after 6pm". These same controllers are very uncomfortable with IP networks as they do not understand IP addressing or subnet masks. The use of policy-based networking and the inclusion of IP accounting will address this discomfort and bring networks under control of the business financial objectives.

Most organisations are familiar with the telephone systems; so much so that we take for granted the service that it provides. If you ask some computer users *"how is your phone"* they would reply, *"it's fine"*. They would be shocked if the phone didn't work because the phone always works. Not only does the phone work but, because the financial people in the organisation understand it, they can make decisions such as *"these phones cannot make international calls, these other phones will be disconnected at 6.00pm"* and so on.

ENTERPRISE NETWORKING

NETWORKING USING SWITCHES AND VIRTUAL NETWORKING SWITCHING

There is no technical barrier to a telephone system as there is today with complicated LAN technology. Also when the boss makes a personal call he's unlikely to worry that another phone user has the knowledge, skill or equipment to tap into his call. Phone systems are inherently secure. The problem facing organisations is that even though businesses run on voice today, the phone is not a major resource for your employees.

All you have to do is say to a PC user *"I will take your phone away for 15 minutes"* or *"I will take your PC away for 15 minutes"*. Which do you think they will give up? The phone, of course. *"I can call some one later but I have to get this task done now!"*

The phone system provides this high level of availability, manageability and security because it is built on a switched infrastructure. The phone system uses circuit switching which provides a dedicated connection between source and destination. In today's IP networking, we use packet switching which does not require a dedicated connection from source to destination. Therefore, the trick is to get circuit-switched features into a packet switched network.

Once the switched infrastructure is in place, how do you get the same service levels that you experience with the phone system? The answer is virtual networking. This is the ability to interconnect everything onto a common, open network infrastructure and impose your organisation's structure onto this secure communications facility.

FRAGMENT BASED SWITCHING

Early Ethernet switches worked more like simple repeaters than bridges or routers. They examined the header of a frame and begin to forward it immediately without waiting for the rest of the frame to arrive or checking the entire frame for errors. This allows these fragment-based or cut-through switches to be less expensive than equipment that processes the packet's payload. By not processing the data, errors propagated across an entire network. There is also no opportunity to translate the information that would enable connection to a dissimilar networking technology. Cut-through switches were only useful for single technology networks in a reliable and error-free environment. One advantage fragment-based switches provided was a reduction in latency, compared to devices that storing an entire frame, check the entire frame, then make a forwarding decision. Low latency is an advantage if the protocol in use is inherently half-duplex. Novell's NetWare Core Protocol (NCP) had this limitation in the past; current options allow a number of packets to be outstanding without an acknowledgement. This is also

ENTERPRISE NETWORKING

NETWORKING USING SWITCHES AND VIRTUAL NETWORKING SWITCHING

TIME 0: SWITCHING PACKET THROUGH SWITCH

TIME 1: SWITCHING PACKET THROUGH SWITCH

TIME 2: SWITCHING PACKET THROUGH SWITCH

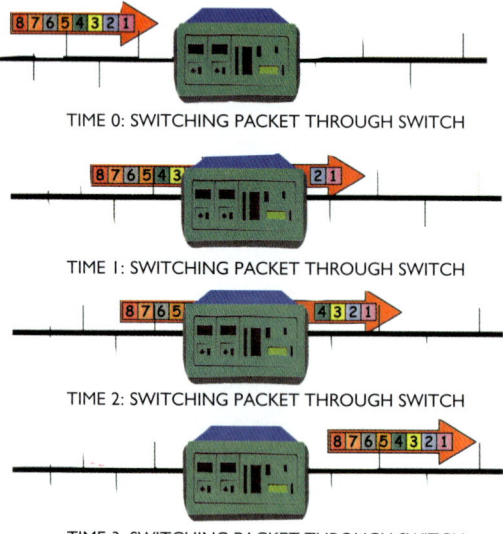

TIME 3: SWITCHING PACKET THROUGH SWITCH

Fragment based switches forward immediately the destination is known.

the case with TCP and NFS, which have very robust open-window transmission. Latency is relatively unimportant if the average packet size is small, since it doesn't take long for a switch to receive the packet in order to check it. For applications that need to use large packet sizes, latency is best dealt with by upgrading the protocols that are inherently slow. This is essential if the applications are to be effectively extended beyond a single site, since wide area links are very high in latency. If you just need to connect Ethernets together and you don't want to be able to add high-speed servers, a high-speed backbone, ATM or routing firewalls, then cut-through switches are fine. Ethernet workstations can only talk to other Ethernet devices, limiting the ability to connect workstations to high-speed servers. There is not much point in giving each workstation its own dedicated bandwidth if they are all contending for the same 10Mbit/sec or 100Mbit/sec server. It makes more sense to use the highest speed technology available for server and share resource connections. However, store-and-forward switches now dominate the networking marketplace.

A number of early switches were single-purpose devices. They connect a number of Ethernet ports together, and usually support one or more high-speed ports, such as full-duplex Ethernet, high-speed Ethernet, FDDI and some supported ATM; the high-speed connection would normally be used as an uplink port. If your requirements meet their

ENTERPRISE NETWORKING

NETWORKING USING SWITCHES AND VIRTUAL NETWORKING SWITCHING

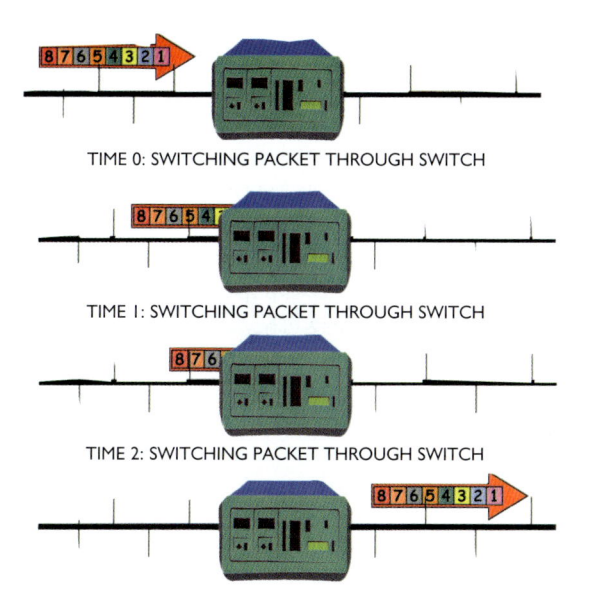

TIME 0: SWITCHING PACKET THROUGH SWITCH

TIME 1: SWITCHING PACKET THROUGH SWITCH

TIME 2: SWITCHING PACKET THROUGH SWITCH

Store and Forward based switches forward after complete packet certification

abilities and you have no networking plans for the future then they are an adequate solution.

However, change is a basic characteristic of networks and the only thing you can be sure of is that it never happens at the pace you plan for. ISDN is still just slowly phasing in, after 20 years while SNMP was accepted almost overnight. FDDI clearly provided high-speed power but was out-marketed by Fast Ethernet. ATM was the central component of the next generation of networks but has since been overshadowed by Gigabit Ethernet. For these reasons there are always going to be choices and you can never be certain what your organisation will need. This means a modular switch will be the safest solution. Just as hubs won the shared media wars, modular switches will win this new campaign. Store-and-forward switches are in fact data link bridges implemented in hardware. This means they can process information extremely fast and new ASICs can reduce the size of the electronics. So where the old software-based bridge products might support four or eight ports and strain to keep two concurrent connections running at wire speeds, today's ASIC-based switches can provide 32 to 64 ports in the same packaging, with all ports running concurrently at full duplex, wire speeds.

ENTERPRISE NETWORKING

NETWORKING USING SWITCHES AND VIRTUAL NETWORKING SWITCHING

Asynchronous Transfer Mode (ATM) has become widely accepted as the standard switching mechanism for wide area public networks. ATM's small cells keep latency low and can combine variable bit rate information, such as LAN packets, and constant bit rate information, such as voice. However, ATM switching having failed to dominate the LAN market we have to consider all switches. Today switching at layer 2, layer 3 and even at layer 4 can be implemented in hardware while retaining full duplex, wire speed performance. Some manufacturers are able to implement all monitoring and metering functions at a flow level without impairing the wire speed performance. These switches can be meshed to provide resilient installations. They can scale to support enterprise wide implementations, which are in orders of magnitude larger than today's largest networks.

VIRTUAL NETWORKING

Network managers have had enough experience to know what works, what doesn't work and, most importantly, what business needs to function efficiently. It is unanimously agreed that network managers do not want yet more new technology but they do need solutions.

The areas that require some engineering focus are in reducing the operational costs of maintaining a network that works but is flexible enough to match the organisational changes that happen in business. These have been addressed earlier as the adds, moves and changes or churn rate of a business which averages out at 22.5% of employees who move or change their physical connectivity to the network but their job function remains

With a flat infrastructure supported by switching, adapting to business needs and new technologies is easier. The advances made in virtual networking means that as new corporate resources are integrated onto the interface, access control and security issues are simplified.

ENTERPRISE NETWORKING

NETWORKING USING SWITCHES AND VIRTUAL NETWORKING SWITCHING

consistent. Then there is the swat team or workgroup orientation of performing business tasks, which are dynamic and fluid in response to any given market condition that the business faces.

The first step in enabling a network to be flexible and respond dynamically to these changing requirements is to move to a flat topology. Removing the hierarchy out of the network removes configuration complications and makes all end nodes equal. The hierarchy can be implemented in the core of the network. The rule of thumb had always been 'bridge where you can and route where you must'. Today, we switch wherever possible, re-connecting layer 2 at the edge and layer 3/4 the core.

Adapting this flat structure to changing business needs will be easier. The technology enabling high performance, flat topologies is switching. Businesses are slow to make unnecessary changes and work on the principle of not fixing something that's not broken. The result is that most networks today have a mix of technology acquired over the last decade. I would bet that at your company there is still some shared media about, at least two different media access methods in use and I would even suspect that more than one protocol is running applications. Switching solutions must support existing multi-technology sites so they must be based on store and forward switches. This switched topology provides a data network system equivalent to the telephone system which is also flat and is switch based. This in turn enables implementation of some of the telephone-style features such as closed user groups, hunt groups and so on but this time at the higher performance and more capable level of LAN-based systems.

Virtual networking is the ability to create logical workgroups of users, isolated in their own private and secure network from the rest of the network users. Quite a clever task as we have just installed switches to create one flat homogeneous network. These logical groups can be created irrespective of the technology that provides the network connection for the individual workstations and spans the whole network. It is possible today to build out a virtual LAN (VLAN) not only to individual connected devices but extend the feature into the older, shared media equipment. Existing shared media networking segments can connect to the switched infrastructure and the individual users can be allocated to different VLANs. This gives extended capabilities to the older legacy systems increasing their usefulness to organisations and can delay the decision to replace them, saving organisations money. Another VLAN feature is to take special resources - a server, communications resource or even a super-user - and configure individual devices to span many virtual networks while not corrupting the separate VLANs.

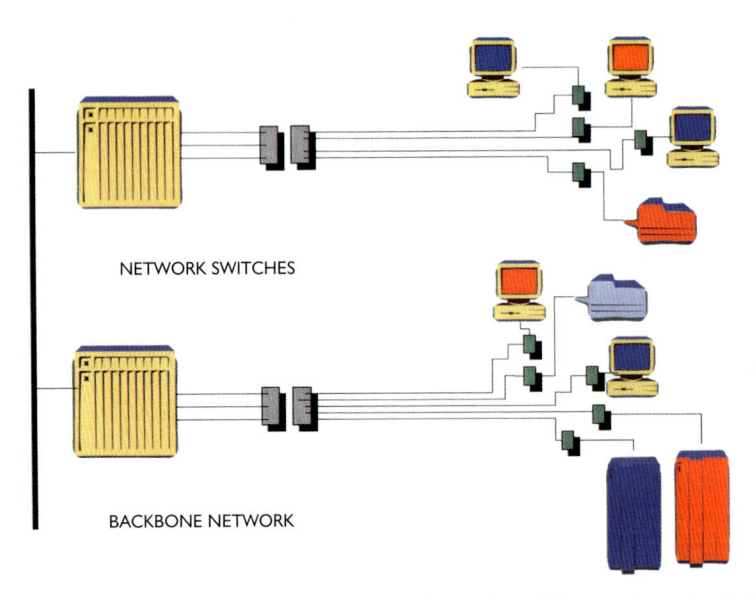

ENTERPRISE NETWORKING

NETWORKING USING SWITCHES AND VIRTUAL NETWORKING SWITCHING

NETWORK SWITCHES

BACKBONE NETWORK

Workstations can be configured into VLANs depending on their job function. the options for identifying the VLANs are MAC address, port ID, protocol, IP subnet or, with layer 4 switches, application

There are three aspects to virtual networking that the technology has to solve. The first is how individuals connected to a switch are divided into the different VLANs. Then, how do we interconnect switches onto a backbone technology that maintains the VLAN separation and, finally, how do we extend the VLANs to go across the wide area and connect remote offices? Organisations are distributed geographically but, operationally, there may be one finance department with 20 employees who work in four different countries.

Today, most companies already own their Ethernet, Token Ring and FDDI networks and they work. So the solution is to use LAN switches and deploy a mechanism that can enable the three areas to be addressed. From the earlier discussion on bridging, routing and switching there are some problems that a switch must solve in a flat topology when we break it into separate, logical workgroups or VLANs. Building networks on store-and-forward devices causes a problem known as broadcast storms. This is where unknown devices or services are broadcast to find out their physical location. On a flat topology, these floods of requests for information would reduce the bandwidth available for data flow and hence provide poor performance. Such broadcasts are a legacy from the

ENTERPRISE NETWORKING

NETWORKING USING SWITCHES AND VIRTUAL NETWORKING SWITCHING

connectionless nature of the protocols used for communications. Ideally switches are connection-orientated and, like the phone system, you need to know the destination number before you call. But we have to integrate switches with the systems already installed so switches have to control and reduce the number of requests from flooding the network. Routers solve the problem by placing a hierarchy on the network and placing physical barriers to prevent flooding. However, routers keep up to date by using router protocols which themselves swallow a great deal of bandwidth with their requests for information.

So how do switches separate the intended broadcast and unicasts into the separate virtual networks in a flat topology? There are techniques for this VLAN separation in the three areas of implementation on the switch across both the backbone and across the wide area. If we consider individual switches then VLANs can be set up by building tables on each port stating which ports are in which VLANs. This however would mean that if 20 devices were on a shared media system and connected to port 4 then they, by default, would be all on the same VLAN. When we come to interconnect switches, port IDs present a problem. If you have four switches, then you have four number one ports, so MAC addresses are a better currency. These port-based VLANs are not very flexible. A better solution would be to create a table of MAC addresses and give the ability to the port to assign multiple VLANs to a port. The MAC address of network devices is a physical address and unique to each network device just as a phone number is unique to a telephone location. Considering the backbone, how can we extend the VLANs across from one switch to another?

There are five options open to us. The first is to make the connection high speed and use time division multiplexing techniques to provide each VLAN with a time slot. The disadvantage here is that the VLANs are limited by the number of time slots and the bandwidth on this type of solution is shared, which detracts from the high performance capabilities of the switches. A second method might be to use a message system where one switch tells connected switches the VLAN configuration of its neighbours. This has two drawbacks, firstly the messaging is proprietary and secondly, on large networks, the synchronisation of information is very difficult to guarantee especially when coping with normal adds, moves and changes. The third option is to use individual dedicated connections for each VLAN. The problem here is the waste of ports in having multiple connections, which wastes cabling, and the inflexibility of having physical restraints on the virtual networks means they are no longer virtual. The fourth method would be to use frame tagging. Here, the technique is to put a preamble onto a communications frame

ENTERPRISE NETWORKING

NETWORKING USING SWITCHES AND VIRTUAL NETWORKING SWITCHING

identifying which VLAN the device belongs to. This is very similar to the IEEE802.10 secure data exchange standard, a standard for security tagging, where frames are tagged to identify the sensitivity and availability of the information. Frame tagging has the advantage of working on shared media as well as switched dedicated media, but could cause frames to exceed the frame size limit, so products that use frame tagging must also monitor frame size and do automatic fragmentation if the limit is exceeded. Frame tagging has the potential for the highest flexibility because many different parameters of a frame could be used to produce a tag. So, virtual networks could be created for MAC addresses, Protocols, IP address, IP subnets or if the switches are layer 4 switches by Application.

The final option is to use the IP address and IP subnet addressing as used by routers as an ID for virtual network identification. This has uses for backbones and for wide area extensions of the VLAN capabilities. IP subnet addresses are layer 3 of the OSI protocol stack, the network layer, hence the layer three switch concept. Layer 3 switching has the advantage of providing VLANs on the switches by using the subnet IDs and when going across the wide area the router uses the IP addresses as normal, so seamless integration is achieved. The disadvantage is the configuration work that the maintenance of the IP and IP subnet addressing causes because of organisational churn rate. While frame tagging based on MAC addresses will completely eliminate the need for IP and IP subnet addressing, it will need a standard protocol to enable interoperability over the wide area. It should be noted that non-routable protocols like NetBIOS cannot be supported by layer 3 switching.

Another requirement for wide area connectivity is to be able to connect to ISDN or frame relay services, the pay as you use variety, without going to the expense of purchasing a router. A means for transferring the frame preamble across with the frame is needed and this will extend the VLAN capabilities across the lower cost WAN service. There were two competing groups working to provide a standard for frame tagging as a means to create virtual networks. IEEE802.10 is the subcommittee that provided the 48-byte frame tagging scheme for network security. There were manufacturers trying to modify this standard to identify VLANs. The second committee is the IEEE802.1Q sub committee. These are the link layer management people. They were working on cross-technology VLAN frame tagging. The IEEE802.1Q won the race and many manufacturers have this facility imbedded in their switches.

If networking staff were free from the mundane tasks of maintaining configurations during adds, moves and changes, then they would have more time to focus on service, planning

ENTERPRISE NETWORKING

NETWORKING USING SWITCHES AND VIRTUAL NETWORKING SWITCHING

and maintenance of service level agreements. In the new infrastructure, the routing service will be the primary means of interconnecting virtual networks as opposed to today's physically dissimilar networks. The implementation of routing services will migrate out of the traditionally expensive, dedicated routing box to be a software service option on a network switch. This makes management easier, fewer products (and icons) to manage, less product to deploy - a major cost saving - and it makes the solution scaleable to match the infrastructure by using one or all the switches as routing service providers. The vast investment already seen in traditional routers can be redeployed from being a collapsed backbone where their performance is not adequate into mixed technology gateways offering a routing service at the periphery of the network.

USEFUL STANDARDS IN SWITCHED NETWORKS

The flow of packet-based information across an enterprise network can be controlled effectively by products supporting two standards: IEEE802.1Q VLANs and traffic prioritisation IEEE802.1p. Products supporting these standards enable data traffic to be analysed, marked with an identifier and then controlled via the identifier. These two standards allow a user to configure VLANs and set priority rules throughout the entire network. As ingress switches classify frames into VLANs and add the identifier, the traffic can be steered to different output queues that define the priority to be given to the particular frame. The specific information (VLAN/priority) is shared among switches in the network via the attached identifier known as a frame tag. When frames reach the final switch in the link, the frame tag is removed and the original frame is delivered to the user. The best place to assign or classify frames to a VLAN and assign priority is at the point a user's frame enters the network fabric, at the network edge. When a frame tag is inserted in the original frame, other switches further upstream will make forwarding decisions based upon the VLAN and the priority placed within the frame tag. Tags can be assigned by port, MAC address, protocol classification, layer 3 addressing classification and layer 4 socket/port classifications all within the input switch. Additional specifications can assist in a switched network, for example, IGMP (Internet Group Management Protocol) snooping (the IGMP is a multi-cast protocol and the snooping enables the removal of non-active members), layer 3 protocol classification and layer 4 socket/port classification, which facilitate VLANs on business functions.

ENTERPRISE NETWORKING

NETWORKING USING SWITCHES AND VIRTUAL NETWORKING SWITCHING

IGMP SNOOPING

The increasing deployment of multimedia and other real-time applications across companies' intranets requires a method of efficient distribution. IP multicast and the IGMP protocol have rapidly emerged as the industry standard technologies for enabling the delivery of one-to-many or many-to-many services such as Web-casting, video-casting, and market data-feeds within an IP-based network. By eliminating the need to replicate and then transmit multiple packet flows to each client participating in a multicast communication, IP multicast technology conserves network bandwidth. In traditional layer 2 switched (bridged) environments however, IP multicast communications are treated in the same way as broadcast transmissions and flood all ports in the broadcast domain (VLAN), which results in bandwidth inefficiency.

The IGMP standard IETF RFC1112 defines the format for establishing IP multicast routes in a network. According to IGMP operation, end-stations access IP multicast applications by transmitting join and leave messages that advertise the client's preferred status in relation to the specific application. IGMP snooping recognises these requests and builds an appropriate multicast distribution tree. Dynamically distributing layer 3 IP, multicast flows only to those end-stations configured and registered to receive the service. The benefit of this feature is not only limited to ensuring the availability of bandwidth within the network but also in eliminating this type of traffic to any or all users who are not permitted to receive it thereby enhancing the security of the communications infrastructure. The network administrator has the control to allow or disallow these types of services by individual user.

PORT BASED

This simplistic method is the default classification method for IEEE802.1Q switches. All frames received on a port are classified as belonging to the same VLAN and receive the same priority assigned to the port.

PROTOCOL CLASSIFICATION

This advanced feature enables the recognition of network traffic by protocols such as IP, IPX, SNA, AppleTalk, NetBIOS, Banyan and DECnet, enabling QoS policies to be applied to these specific protocols. This method works well for containment of protocols within the network for unknown broadcast containment and to filter certain protocols from entering a network.

ENTERPRISE NETWORKING

NETWORKING USING SWITCHES AND VIRTUAL NETWORKING SWITCHING

LAYER 3 ADDRESS

This method of classification allows a user to classify frames based upon their layer 3 network address, service type or protocol type. Using this classification method, a user is capable of assigning VLANs based upon the IP addressing subnet schemes or Novell NetWare address scheme. Assigning priority to frames based upon network address provides a useful priority service for servers. The specific IP address of a server can be specified as high priority and all frames to or from this server will be given preferential treatment throughout the network. This method also works well for security purposes in that a user can specify that a specific IP address, such as the router, is the only access address available to the network.

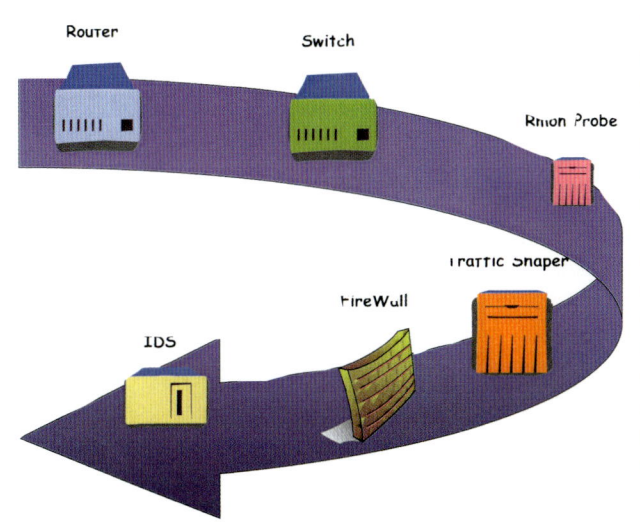

The current installed base of products is heavily reliant on software and processor cycles. This means that all the processing to be performed on a communications packet is done serially.

The more features enabled, the more processor cycles required. This increases latency and where a central resource is used such as a router, the chance of introducing variable delay because of differing packet sizes also increased.

LAYER 4 SOCKET/PORT

This classification allows a user to classify frames based upon layer 4 or application type information. In turn, this makes possible the idea of containment, in that all NetWare server SAP advertisements could be contained within a VLAN boundary where only NetWare servers reside. Such a classification method could be used to identify different priority levels assigned to different applications. The network could reflect the priorities that the business puts on its business processes.

ENTERPRISE NETWORKING

NETWORKING USING SWITCHES AND VIRTUAL NETWORKING SWITCHING

The flexibility to define and create 802.1Q VLANs based on protocol, layer 3 or layer 4 classifications can have many important applications in a switched network such as traffic containment around broadcast-intensive protocols such as IPX and AppleTalk. These protocols can be confined only to the intended users, servers and segments by creating VLANs specifically for that purpose. Traffic filtering against any unwanted protocol types or applications, possibly originating from a shared segment, can be filtered out of the switched network altogether by disallowing that protocol at the ingress switch port. You could implement traffic security by monitoring specific protocols and confining them to specific authorised switched ports or users and QoS and prioritisation for specific, time-sensitive applications such as Voice over IP traffic. This can be prioritised or expedited over less business-critical applications using 802.1D(p) and priority queuing. Giving priority to specific network traffic can assure delivery of mission critical protocols during periods of high bandwidth demand. These standards enable the delivery of key traffic control capabilities without any drastic changes or hardware upgrades. Advanced layer 3/4 services dramatically improve the level of bandwidth management possible in switched networks.

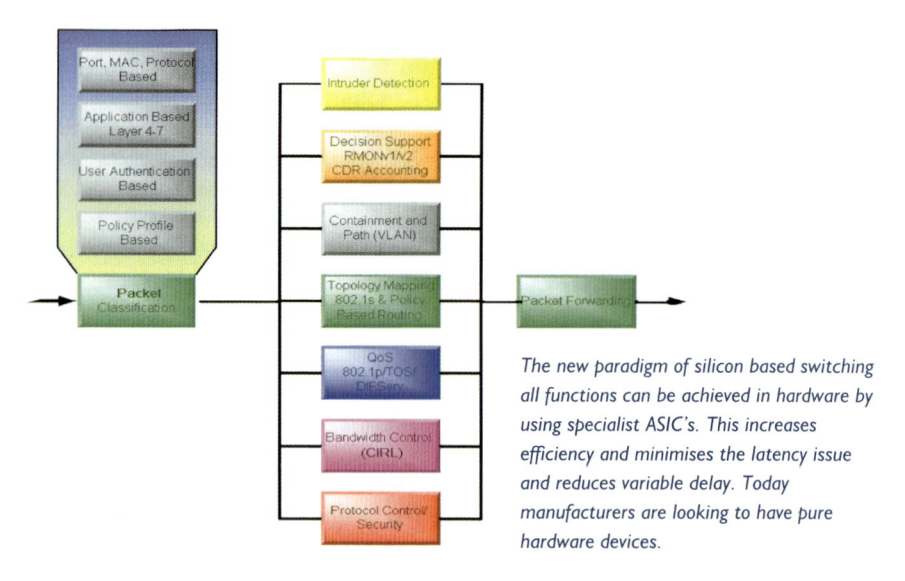

The new paradigm of silicon based switching all functions can be achieved in hardware by using specialist ASIC's. This increases efficiency and minimises the latency issue and reduces variable delay. Today manufacturers are looking to have pure hardware devices.

section nine

Changes in Wide Area Networking

Section 8: Changes in Wide Area Communications

There is a whole range of solutions existing as the best solution for networks to communicate across large geographical distances. The issue has been that LANs are high speed and reliable where as WANs are considered low speed and subject to failures in connections. This section reviews the Fast Packet technology options and brings the reader up to date with all the jargon used around VPN technology.

SECTION NINE

ENTERPRISE NETWORKING

CHANGES IN WIDE AREA COMMUNICATIONS

INTRODUCTION

Purchasers of LAN products used to have to decide on the technology, Ethernet, Token Ring, FDDI or ATM. Now the question is: *"what speed of Ethernet?"*. It's a lot easier. Picking a cabling scheme is a little more complicated: structured wiring using UTP or STP, Multi-mode Fibre or Single-mode Fibre. Unforeseen, except by the experienced hand, is the fact that networks get bigger and pervade all areas of a business which is still not too much of a problem. The choice is whether to bridge or route to the different locations which means a 50% chance of picking the right solution or go for switching with layer 2/3 and 4 support and you can configure to suit your requirements. The final decision is what type of service, either a leased line between locations or pay on demand with a switched service such as ISDN or Frame Relay and do not forget to consider the long-standing question, *"when will xDSL reach my location?"*.

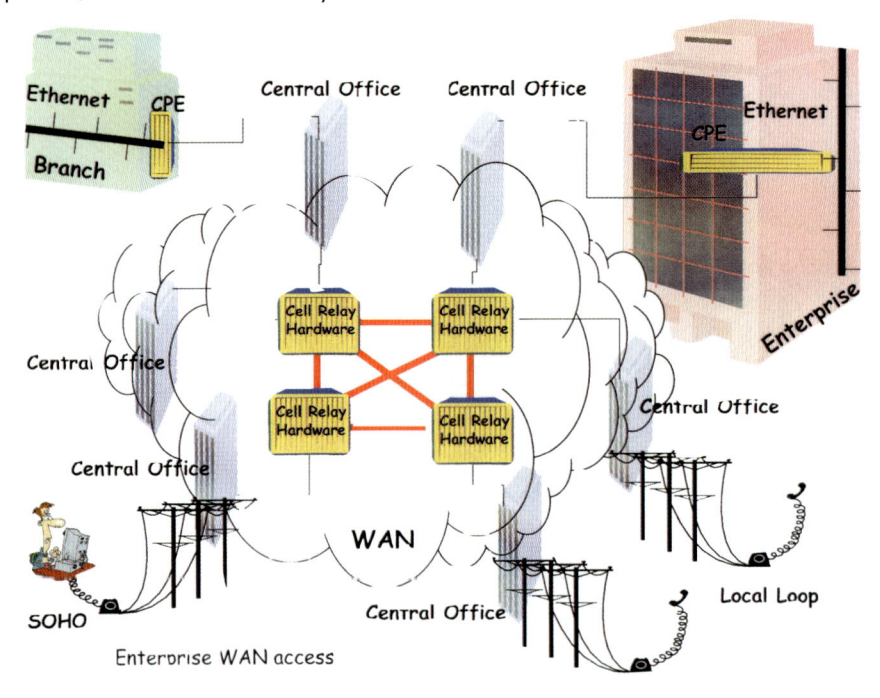

Enterprise WAN access

Over the last decade this simple scenario has exploded into a vast array of choices all under the generic rubric of fast packet technology. A proliferation of standards has evolved from the different market sectors all to address the same problem. How do we

ENTERPRISE NETWORKING

CHANGES IN WIDE AREA COMMUNICATIONS

get maximum data throughput on a wide area connection now that all the communications links are digital, error free and 100% reliable? And do not forget that these services must be paid for on a monthly basis. This makes the best price/performance fit to a given situation critical. This task is not easy to solve. An international call from country A to country B costs $5 per minute for a high performance service. Leasing a connection from country A to the USA with an equivalent service level is $2 per minute. An international call from the USA to country B is 20 cents per minute. Therefore the cost effective solution is to go via the USA. But this would depend on whether I have enough traffic to justify the leased line. The problem is to transport voice, data and video along the most cost-effective route with the minimum of error checking and routing information. The group of standards competing are collected under the term fast packet technology, examples of which are Frame Relay, Cell Relay, SMDs, MANs with DQDB, ATM/B-ISDN, which is disguised as SoNET in the USA and SDH in Europe.

The great confusion about these specifications is that they appear to address the same problem with no clear picture of how the pieces fit together in defining a solution. In the LAN world, it is layered with the cabling, technology such as Ethernet or Token Ring, and services: NetWare, LAN manager, NFS with Unix. If we copy this layering approach and apply it to these fast packet technologies we get the following layers: the service provided which includes the quality of service, the available bandwidth and the security aspects. Next is the access method to connect the services: Frame Relay, ATM, B-ISDN and finally the technology that is providing the services, Frame Relay switches, cell relay switches, DQDB gateways and so on.

The major issue that WAN networks have to content with (that does not apply to LAN installations) is the ongoing charges. LAN communications are considered free once the installation is over. WANs generate a monthly charge depending on the services contracted. The choices available are considerable and they are in constant change as the Internet becomes more stable and VPN technology become accessible and secure.

ENTERPRISE NETWORKING

CHANGES IN WIDE AREA COMMUNICATIONS

I do not want to discuss modem technology - that has always been available for the analogue telephony services supporting speeds from 9.6Kbit/sec to 56Kbit/sec and on the new digital services starting at 64Kbit/sec up to 1.54Mbit/sec. I want to focus on the serious stuff that up until the mid 1980s had been the choice of only two viable WAN methods for transporting data reliably from host to host or for the inter-connection of LANs. That choice was either expensive leased lines for speeds of up to 2.048Mbit/sec - the E1 service - or X.25 packet switching, a public or private network, at speeds from 9.6Kbit/sec up to 64Kbit/sec. Today we have a whole range of competing technologies to choose from. The situation is further complicated as wide area networking splits into the long-haul Wide Area Network (WAN) and the Metropolitan Area network (MAN). These changes are out of our control because it is the carriers who are selecting the solutions and they are offering the services to the enterprise. The question is what price-performance model carriers use to calculate charges for their services. Tariffing, as ever in the wide area, is key.

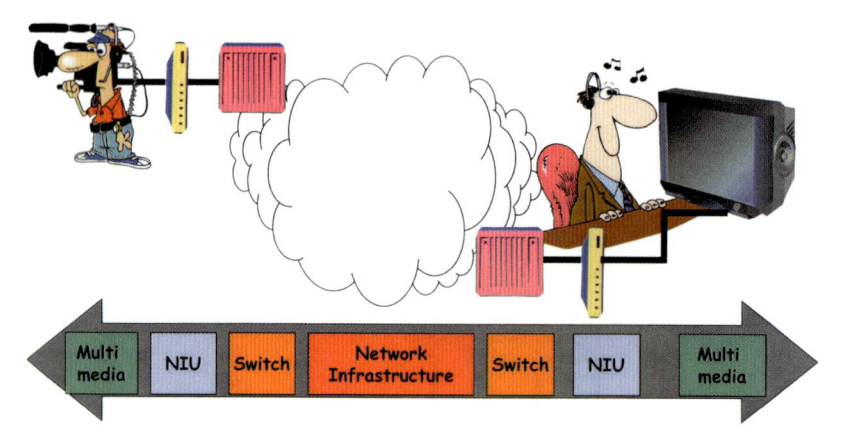

Multimedia Applications need high speed, low latency infrastructure with minimal variable delay. All aspects are continually under review from the standards body.

X.25 is a reliable method to communicate over noisy (compared to today's digital offerings), analogue PTT lines. X.25's ability to identify errors and to request re-transmission guaranteed a respectable service but at a cost. The throughput in terms of packets per second for some infrastructures is already unacceptable and outweighs the benefits gained in reliability. This is because X.25 is considered a heavy protocol in that the data content of the communication is low compared to the error checking protocol

ENTERPRISE NETWORKING

CHANGES IN WIDE AREA COMMUNICATIONS

content. As more and more digital PTT lines came into service the need to be so fastidious in terms of service delivery lessened. Hence, the creation of Frame Relay which is X.25 without the protocol overhead, has caught the imagination and has rapidly gained acceptance.

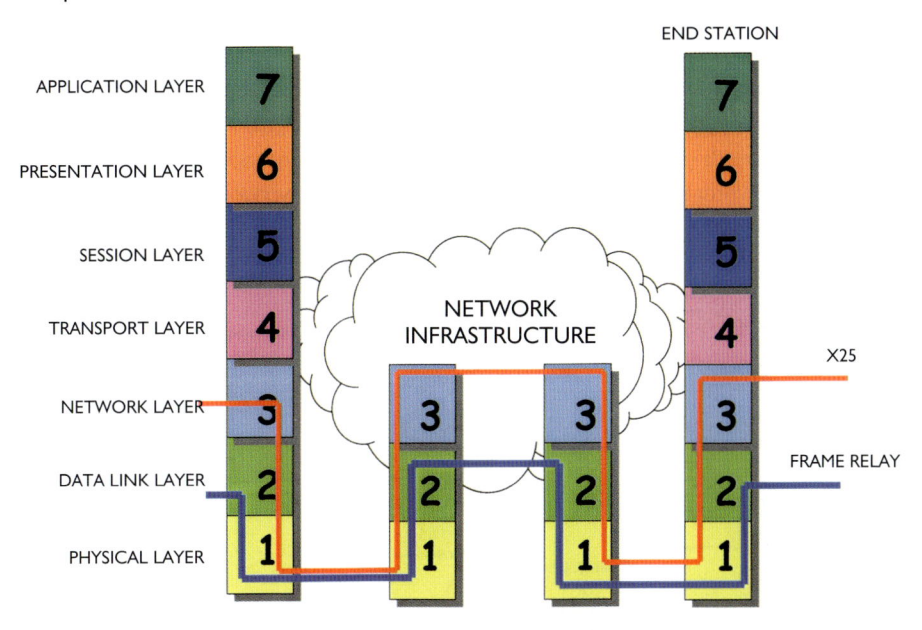

APPLICATION LAYER	7	7
PRESENTATION LAYER	6	6
SESSION LAYER	5	5
TRANSPORT LAYER	4	4
NETWORK LAYER	3	3
DATA LINK LAYER	2	2
PHYSICAL LAYER	1	1

END STATION — NETWORK INFRASTRUCTURE — X25 / FRAME RELAY

Frame Relay is the next generation technology to succeed X.25. Frame Relay is a simple bit-oriented protocol that assumes the lines are relatively error free. Being devoid of the error-checking and recovery mechanisms that slow X.25 down, a typical processing time across the node is about two milliseconds for Frame Relay compared to 5-20 milliseconds for X.25. There is, of course, a greater emphasis placed upon the use of intelligent end points such as a LAN routers to run error correction procedures and be responsible for error recovery. As Frame Relay accomplishes switching with the first two layers (physical and data link layer) any protocol can be run over it without extra overhead. Therefore it is critical that end stations run error checking and flow control to maintain reliable connections.

Another contribution to the rapid uptake is that traditional router products can be software-upgraded to Frame Relay, making it a relatively inexpensive migration. Initially operating like X.25, a Permanent Virtual Circuit (PVC) is established prior to data

ENTERPRISE NETWORKING

CHANGES IN WIDE AREA COMMUNICATIONS

transfer. These specifications allow users to dynamically select their intended destination; in other words, they become Switched Virtual Circuits (SVC). Frame Relay can be run on upgraded TDM (Time Division Multiplexed) switches, upgraded X.25 switches, PTT carrier circuits such as BT GNS LAN Interconnect and AT&Ts Inter Span and MCI Hyper Stream, frame switches or cell relay switches. The most efficient method is cell relay or fast packet in that these switches emulate the same principle as broadband ISDN and utilise short fixed length cells. This obviates the need to use store-and-forward techniques that are implemented by X.25 and frame switches which results in higher and more variable delay. The speeds that are accommodated by Frame Relay technology are from 56/64Kbit/sec up to 1.5Mbit/sec (T1) and 2.048Mbit/sec (E1). Some vendors already support up to 45Mbit/sec today.

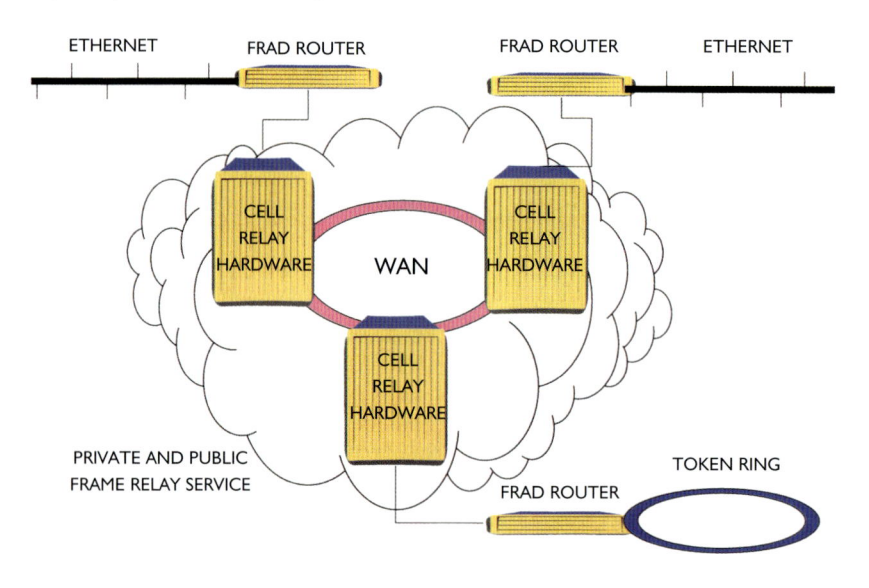

The Frame Relay Forum, formed in July 1991, with about 52 company members whose aim was to provide a set of specifications that would ensure rapid deployment of the technology. They key specifications focused around the User Network Interface (UNI) and the Network to Network Interface (NNI). UNI defined how a user connected to a Frame Relay switch and the NNI defined how two Frame Relay switches interconnected. Frame Relay uses either the LAPD packet format (spec 1.122) or the ITU-T International Telecommunications Union specification Q.931 for ISDN implementations. The latter is

ENTERPRISE NETWORKING

CHANGES IN WIDE AREA COMMUNICATIONS

the preferred transport mechanism throughout Europe due to the implementation of ISDN primary rate services by the various PTTs. Standardisation is continuing at a pace within the auspices of the ITU and the American National Standards Institute (ANSI) providing specifications for service architecture, data transfer, signalling and congestion control.

The deployment of Frame Relay services has been more advanced in America due to the greater coverage of digital services. Europe on the other hand has had to go through extensive upgrades from analogue to digital services with the individual PTTs working to their own specific programme.

INTEGRATED SERVICES DIGITAL NETWORK (ISDN)

ISDN has been a standard in various forms for over a two decades and is only included for the sake of completeness. It became an issue for the PTTs when it became clear they would have to upgrade from analogue to digital. The first phase of that upgrade applied only to the backbone network, and the second extended the service to subscribers.

In 1984 the CCITT (now ITU) specified ISDN as a suitable digital subscriber service. A second version was specified in 1988 by the European Telecommunications Standards Institute (ETSI). ISDN is a digital system providing subscriber services at standard and primary rates across multiple channels using the carrier's circuits. The service is now widely available across the globe and there is a European standard. ISDN Basic Rate service provides two 64Kbit/sec channels that can be used for any digital signal these are commonly called the B channels. Along with the two data channels is a 16Kbit/sec D channel used for signalling and, on telephony connections, to add to the telephone call features that were not possible in the analogue system. These included displaying the caller's phone number while ringing.

Primary Rate ISDN is 30 channels of 64Kbit/sec and 2 channels giving 128Kbit/sec for the common signalling. ISDN can set up a call in under a second, making it ideal as a backup connection for router based networks. If the primary connection fails then an ISDN backup can be dialled immediately. Remote workstations can use an ISDN connection to connect to the main network. Being a switched service, the remote station can dial up the host network establish a connection and start working. While work is being carried out locally the software drops the ISDN connection but when the host network is required, the remote client can establish the old connection undetected by the operator of the workstation. This greatly reduces connection time and hence costs. ISDN has also

ENTERPRISE NETWORKING

CHANGES IN WIDE AREA COMMUNICATIONS

found great favour with video-conferencing suppliers. Using the two B channels for a single 128Kbit/sec connection adequate video is provided. The standard for this is H.261. Regular users of remote video though find that the minimum acceptable performance is achieved with speeds greater than 378Kbit/sec.

DIGITAL SUBSCRIBER LINES

Digital Subscriber Line (DSL) does not really fit in a Local Area Networking guide but as enterprises need to support home workers, many see it as yet another way of making corporate resources directly available to their remote or mobile workers. Most remote workers connect to the corporate resources using dial-up telephony. They use a modem with speeds up to 56Kbit/sec and gain a mediocre service. The lucky employees get a funded ISDN line but this is to expensive for mass deployment. In stepped DSL technology, offering a digital service at low cost but at ten times the performance of current offerings.

To provide the service, the telephony service company has to install a concentrator (or DSLAM) in the central office to connect to all of the subscriber copper connections. Each

ENTERPRISE NETWORKING

CHANGES IN WIDE AREA COMMUNICATIONS

client needs a DSL modem in the home. Most DSL implementations to homes are asynchronous (Asynchronous DSL): they provide an unbalanced service of up to 1.5Mbit/sec out of the home and up to 8Mbit/sec downstream. The idea is that the user may send emails and some low level interactive traffic but the service provider can pump full-motion videos to you and save you going to the rental shop.

Other flavours of DSL include HDSL (High Bit Rate DSL) a straight replacement for ISDN, RADSL (Rate Adaptive DSL) is technology for service providers to vary the service against the application you are renting pay more you get more, and SDSL (Symmetrical DSL). SDSL (Synchronous DSL) is designed to offer VPN services across where the data going out is about the same coming in. this is more appropriate to small to medium-sized companies whose traffic is more two-way. Finally for the moment there is VDSL (Very High Bit Rate DSL) a special high speed services for companies situated very close to the service provider.

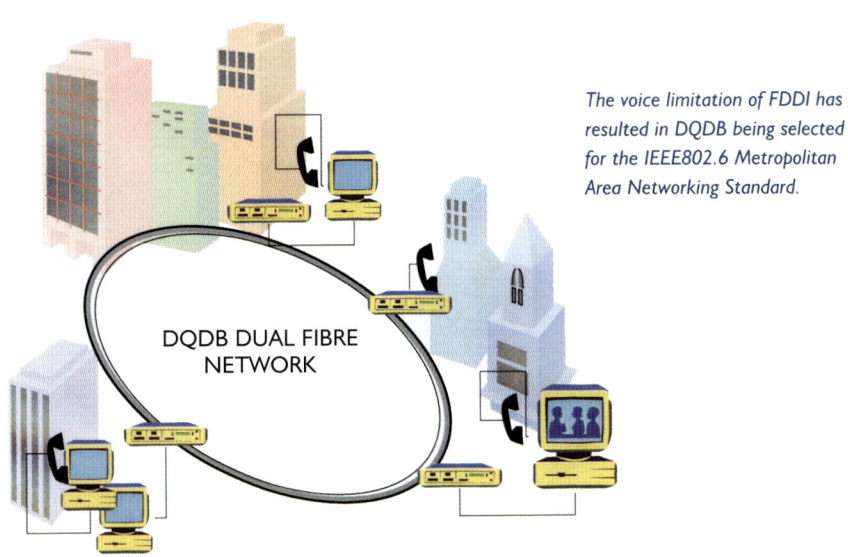

The voice limitation of FDDI has resulted in DQDB being selected for the IEEE802.6 Metropolitan Area Networking Standard.

DQDB DUAL FIBRE NETWORK

METROPOLITAN AREA NETWORKS (MANs)

The Institute of Electronic and Electrical Engineers (IEEE) finalised the 802.6 specifications for MAN technology in 1994. The specification provides for a Distributed Queue Dual Bus mechanism (DQDB) that was based on a technology originally developed at the University of Western Australia by a few post-graduate students. They formed called

ENTERPRISE NETWORKING

CHANGES IN WIDE AREA COMMUNICATIONS

QPSX Communications Ltd which produced the first products supporting DQDB. This Australian proposal, which has been around for more than a decade, was adopted as a US industry standard with no input from European companies.

MANs offer high-speed communications networks providing distributed switching between nodes and supporting speeds ranging from 45Mbit/sec up to 620Mbit/sec in line with the ATM/B-ISDN standards. It is typically implemented on single mode fibre enabling considerable distances to be supported and allowing its use primarily within the boundaries of a city. Some of the first MAN installations in Europe were the cities of Stuttgart and Munich by Deutsche Telekom who were keen to implement them as public networks for large commercial concerns. The cost of silicon for use in the DQDB nodes is at least five to six times that of the cost of silicon for other high-speed technology.

MAN technology as described here needs greater silicon development if it is not to be short lived. Safely into 2001, the MAN is set for a major upgrade as the 10 Gigabit Ethernet Alliance of manufacturers see a commercial opportunity to upgrade these MANs, which were not specifically designed for data, into super-fast, 10GbE using Dense Wave Division Multiplexing (DWDM). This is a technique capable of mixing multiple light sources at different wavelengths down a single fibre cable. There are different implementations known as Dense WDM and Wide WDM. Each wavelength can carry at

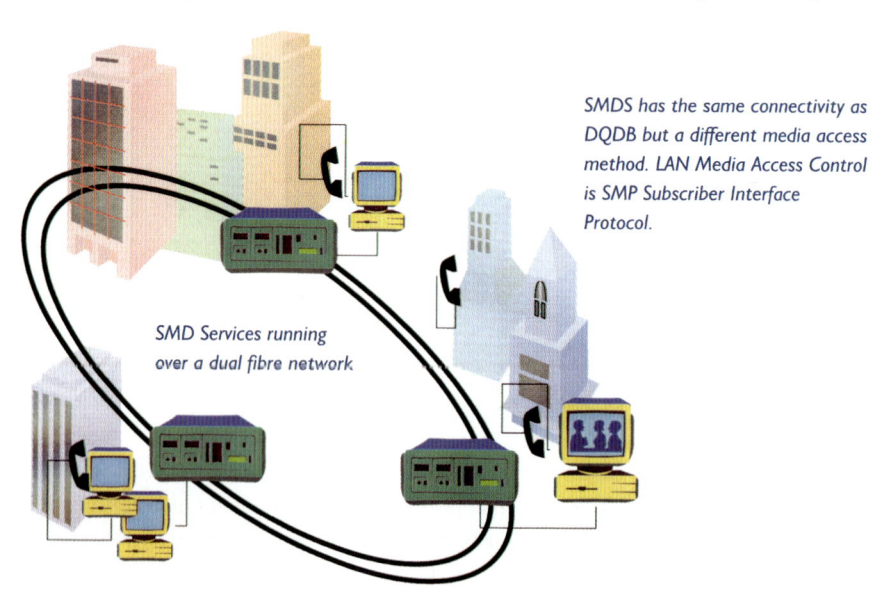

SMDS has the same connectivity as DQDB but a different media access method. LAN Media Access Control is SMP Subscriber Interface Protocol.

SMD Services running over a dual fibre network

ENTERPRISE NETWORKING

CHANGES IN WIDE AREA COMMUNICATIONS

least one signal so multiple signals can be crammed into a single fibre, dramatically increasing its capacity. The IEEE is expected to ratify the 10GbE standard in early 2002 as IEEE802.3ae. The benefit to enterprises is they will get a uniform end-to-end service they understand and already have the skills to support. The promise of company-wide Ethernet is an attractive future.

SMDS

The service that was widely deployed over the physical medium offered by DQDB is that known as Switched Multi-megabit Data Services (SMDS). SMDS uses switching and transmission techniques that evolved out of the technical advances of the LAN industry. It is a high-speed, connectionless, public data networking service using cell and packet switching offering LAN performances with wide area connectivity. SMDS can offer a range of access speeds from as little as 1.54Mbit/sec (T1) to 45Mbit/sec (T3) in the USA and from 2.048Mbit/sec (E1) to 34Mbit/sec (E3) in Europe. This was the first practical step in delivering high-speed communications in the WAN.

Inter-switch trunk speeds are provided by the carriers' core digital networks based on the B-ISDN specifications. Synchronous Optical Network (SONET) services are being established across America with the European equivalent being Synchronous Digital Hierarchy (SDH). SMDS allows the sharing of access to the network to achieve an economy of scale, thus providing a service for multiple customers. Being a connectionless transmission it avoids the overhead of call set-up/teardown routines required to establish connection between end points. Similar to a LAN device, an SMDS cell contains address information within its header, defined by CCITT E.164, which enables the switch to route the cell to its proposed destination. SMDS transports variable length packets up to a maximum of 9,188 bytes, nearly twice that of FDDI. This lends itself to be a useful WAN interface for any LAN technology.

There are two types of SMDS equipment the Subscriber Network Interface (SNI) for the trunk and the Customer Premises Equipment (CPE) for the access point. The only slight drawback with SMDS is that it does have a fair amount of overhead. Every packet received from the LAN side has to be sliced up in a specified but elaborate fashion, into cells the same size as that for DQDB and ATM. Four bytes of the data portion of these cells are required for framing information, adding to the overhead. There is considerable interest in SMDS in the USA and already an interest group has been formed by vendors looking to provide either SNI or CPE product.

ENTERPRISE NETWORKING

CHANGES IN WIDE AREA COMMUNICATIONS

Bellcore was the driving force behind SMDS. The European Technical Standards Institute (ETSI) had standardised CBDS (connectionless broadband data service), which is for all intents and purposes exactly the same as SMDS, for European implementations of DQDB and ATM. SMDS has proved itself to be a valuable stepping stone prior to end-to-end ATM services and with the very long term, deployment of 10Gigabit Ethernet, we will be able to traverse the globe using a common medium.

ASYNCHRONOUS TRANSFER MODE (ATM)

For the full picture see Section 4 but this is a snapshot to complete the section. ATM is an implementation of broadband ISDN in addition it will provide seamless voice, video and data services to the desk at rates from 1.5Mbit/sec up to 622Mbit/sec and beyond using the SONET transport mechanism in a wide area implementation. It can provide both LAN and WAN services of seamless scalable capacity. With one technology providing desk to remote desk, seamless communications the concept of LAN/WAN will cease. The ATM promise is the implementation of 10Gigabit Ethernet in 2002, fulfilled by Ethernet technology which is a salutary lesson to us all. Technical excellence does not guarantee success, it is commercial viability that dominates.

Since ATM supports several types of services it is necessary to adapt the different

AAL Type	Service	Application	Control
1	Constant Bit	Rate Support	Voice Connection Orientated
2	Variable Bit	Rate Support	Video Connection Orientated
3	Variable Bit	Rate Support	Frame Relay Connection Orientated
4	Variable Bit	Rate Support	SMDS Connectionless Orientated
5	Variable Bit Rate Support	Simple and Efficient	Adaption Layer (SEAL) Connection or Connectionless

ENTERPRISE NETWORKING

CHANGES IN WIDE AREA COMMUNICATIONS

characteristics of the application to the ATM layer. This can be one of five types that have been specified.

Network connections for ATM have ranged from 25Mbit/sec to 155Mbit/sec on copper UTP and STP cabling and 155Mbit/sec to 622Mbit/sec on fibre for backbone or server farm connections. These implementations appeared in early 1997. However, during the late 1990s many carriers started implementing 10Gbit/sec links using Dense Wave Division Multiplexing using four light sources to transmit down a single fibre cable. A major Japanese silicon manufacturer around the same time demonstrated 55 colours down the same single fibre cable, this giving a capability of 1,000Gbit/sec. This promises to give close to unlimited bandwidth at reasonable costs at an unspecified delivery date some time in the near future.

Knowing that the PTTs have long test and approval cycles, it was a safe speculating that ATM would be delivered as a LAN technology before wide area services became commonplace. This is exactly how it has panned out. However, ATM failed to dominate the LAN market place and lost ground in favour of Ethernet in all its forms. Ethernet was though not in a position to challenge ATM in the carrier marketplace, being slower to ramp up to the speeds and slower to address the Quality of Service issues. Today we see Ethernet packets dominating all forms of communications, wired, wireless and Internet communications.

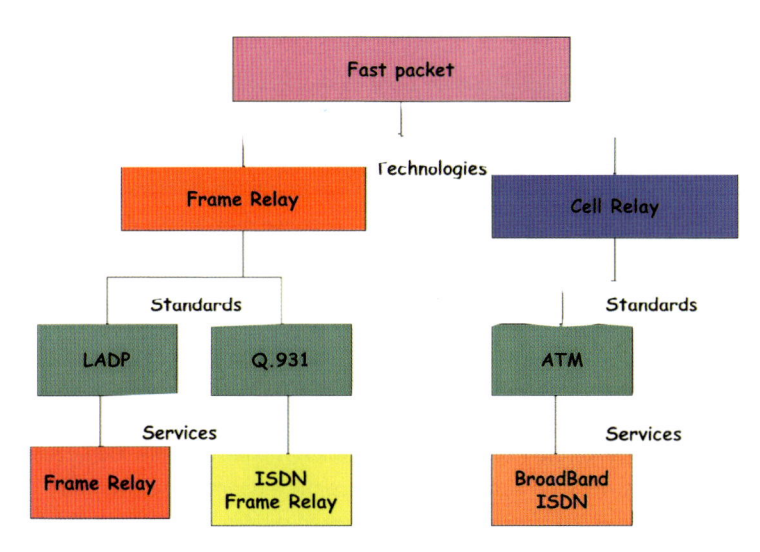

The relationships of some of the Fast Packet technologies

ENTERPRISE NETWORKING

CHANGES IN WIDE AREA COMMUNICATIONS

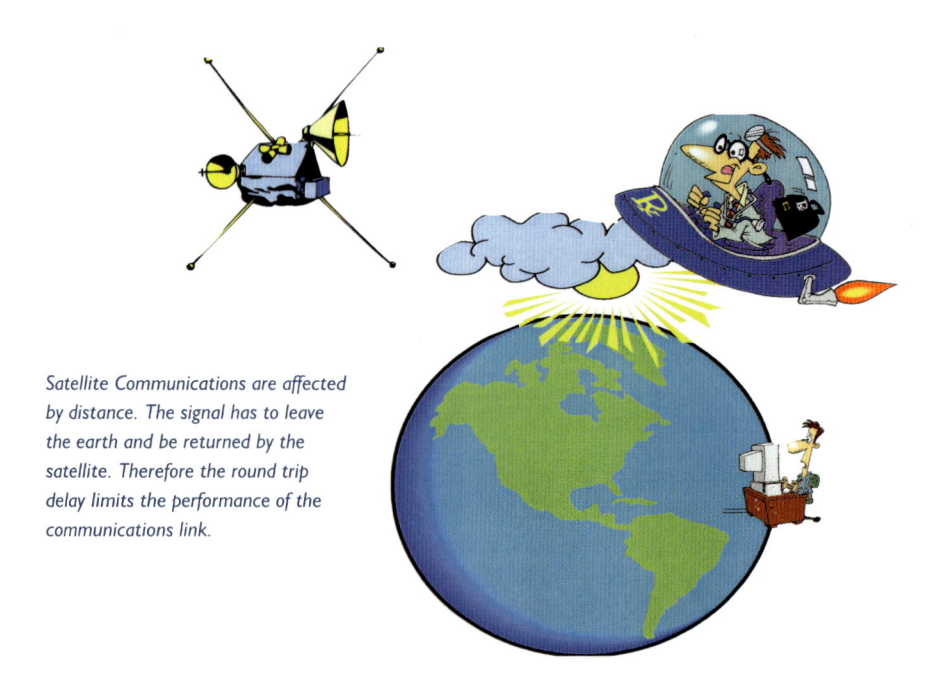

Satellite Communications are affected by distance. The signal has to leave the earth and be returned by the satellite. Therefore the round trip delay limits the performance of the communications link.

The latest Ethernet technology releases have been at 10Gbit/sec. This provides the Ethernet edge connection to the carriers' fibre networks. In Sweden, the PTT has started to install 100Mbit/sec Ethernet over fibre to some homes.

So if it had not been for the carriers building their core networks with ATM today they could very well have decided to use Ethernet and deployed Ethernet everywhere. The goal is that within a reasonable period of time the entire network will appear to be seamless. But it is being driven not by the media access layer but at the transport and network layer. The Internet has shown that it is possible by converging on the IP protocol.

SATELLITE COMMUNICATIONS

Satellite communications have been restricted to voice and low speed data communications because of the time delay in duplex communications. Satellites used for television broadcasting are not so restricted as communication is one-way only. However, a new generation of satellites will soon significantly increase the amount of bandwidth in the sky. The problem to solve is the provision of a high-speed service for data communications when the transport protocol is TCP/IP. TCP/IP was designed to operate

ENTERPRISE NETWORKING

CHANGES IN WIDE AREA COMMUNICATIONS

over any type of network infrastructure with terrestrial distances in mind for turn-round delays. The huge distances created by satellite links and the time delays involved can severely restrict throughput over TCP/IP links, though the less sensitive UDP can achieve greater throughput. New products designed for connecting to satellite links acting as protocol gateways or performance enhancing proxies can overcome the limitations of TCP. The conditions on satellite networks that restrict the speed at which TCP can transmit data include:

Latency: Geosynchronous satellites orbit at an altitude of 22,300 miles, resulting in a round-trip time of approximately 540 milliseconds for a single satellite hop. Without the tuning of TCP parameters, the typical receive window size of 8Kbit/sec sets a throughput limit of only 120Kbit/sec per connection. This would give better Web access to remote users than the traditional modem telephony connection but is insufficient for LAN to LAN connectivity.

Bit errors: TCP assumes that data loss is caused by congestion on the network, making TCP extremely sensitive to the level of packet loss that naturally occurs over satellite and other wireless links.

Asymmetric bandwidth: For economic reasons, satellite nets often combine a large forward channel with a narrow return path, originally designed for television transmissions that have no requirement for interaction with the receiving stations. If the asymmetry is too great, the return path can become a performance bottleneck.

VIRTUAL PRIVATE NETWORK

Geographically dispersed organisations normally operate a WAN to interconnect company departments. A major concern businesses have with the use of WAN technology is the monthly cost of renting the site-to-site connections; they are very visible to finance departments. Cabletron Systems had a leased line running between its factory in Shannon, Ireland, to its headquarters in Rochester, New Hampshire in the USA. The cost of this connection was $38,000 per month. To reduce these costs, in early 2000, they switched to a VPN solution and for the same data transmission rates Cabletron paid $8,000 per month. Therefore it does not take a rocket scientist to calculate that VPN technology offers organisations a cost-effective WAN solution.

A Virtual Private Network (VPN) is a secured network which tunnels through any public or private network providing an encrypted basis for communications, exclusively for the

ENTERPRISE NETWORKING

CHANGES IN WIDE AREA COMMUNICATIONS

organisation's private use. In this section, we are focusing on the biggest public network there is, the Internet. In a VPN, dial-up connections to remote users and leased line or Frame Relay connections to remote sites are replaced with local connections to an Internet service provider or other service provider's point Of Presence (POP). Using the Internet means that an organisation needs pay for local communications only while remote sites cross the Internet for free.

The reach of the Internet is global. No corner of the planet is safe. You are free to stay on-line and doing business even when on vacation VPN providing secure access to your corporate resources as though you were locally connected, means you can take your business with you. Which might make the holiday accomodation crowded!

THREE MAIN TYPES OF VPN

Intranet VPNs allow private networks to be extended across the Internet or other public network service in a secure way. Intranet VPNs are sometimes referred to as site-to-site or LAN-to-LAN VPNs. Remote access VPNs allow individual dial-up users to connect to a central site across the Internet or other public network service in a secure way and are sometimes referred to as dial-up VPNs.

Extranet VPNs allow secure connections with business partners, suppliers and customers for the purpose of e-commerce. These are an extension of intranet VPNs with the

ENTERPRISE NETWORKING

CHANGES IN WIDE AREA COMMUNICATIONS

addition of firewalls to protect the internal network. They aim to provide the reliability, performance, quality of service and security of traditional WAN configurations but at lower cost and with more flexible ISP or other service provider connections.

It is also possible to use VPN technology within an intranet to provide security and controlled access to sensitive information, systems or resources. For example, you might use it to restrict access to financial information or payroll systems to certain users, or to ensure sensitive or confidential information is moved across a network in a secure predictable way. VPN communication requires configuration across existing network infrastructures and there are several ways of implementing them. This next section considers some of the more common solutions so firstly using the Internet and then traditional communications technology to create VPNs.

INTERNET VPN FOR REMOTE USERS.

Basic operation, once software is loaded onto the client PC and the tunnel servers are installed at the corporate HQ, is for a remote user to establish a secure connection to the tunnel server. This usually involves clicking on the VPN icon, firing up the VPN application which in turn uses a modem to dial the HQ site. The client software then identifies itself to the tunnel server using authentication mechanisms such as a password. When the tunnel server is has authenticated the user, the client software and the tunnel server negotiate the authentication, encapsulation, encryption and the keying mechanism to maintain a secure link. The client then establishes the new VPN connection and a secure tunnel now exists between source and destination. The tunnel server encrypts outgoing and de-encrypts incoming messages. The client and the tunnel server periodically re-negotiate the security.

TUNNELLING

Protocol tunnels encapsulate a data packet within a normal packet, which is identified and treated in a special manner. IP tunnels encapsulate a data packet within a normal IP packet for forwarding over an IP-based network. The encapsulated packet does not need to be IP and could be any protocol such as IPX, AppleTalk, SNA or DECnet. However, to create VPNs across the Internet, we need to focus on IP.

IP tunnels encapsulate a data packet within a normal IP packet for forwarding over an IP-based network. The encapsulated packet does not need to be encrypted and authenticated. However, with most IP based VPNs, especially those running over the

ENTERPRISE NETWORKING

CHANGES IN WIDE AREA COMMUNICATIONS

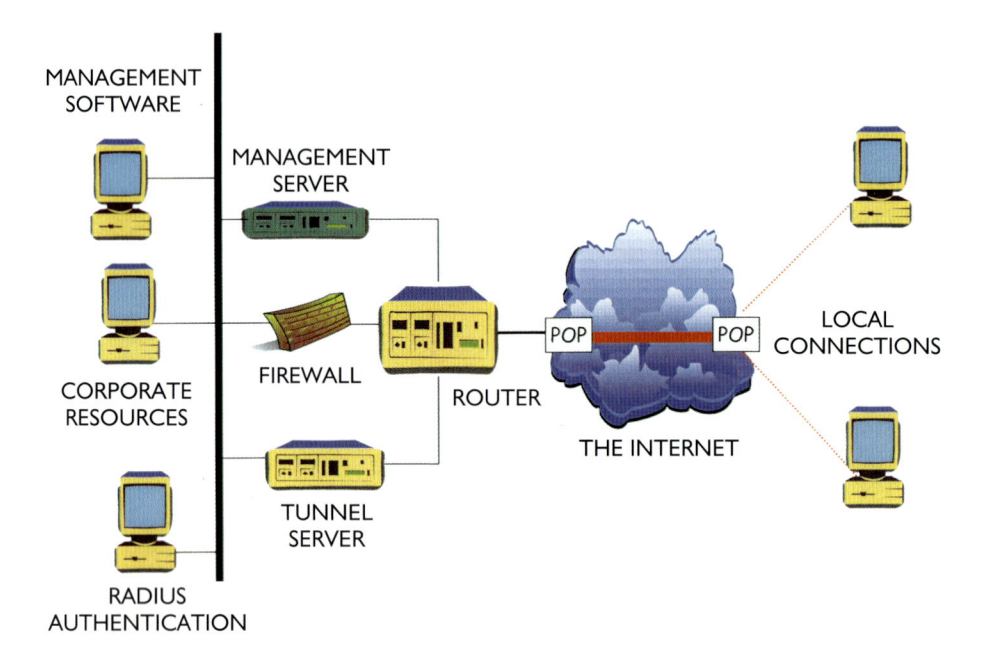

Virtual Private Networks are used by businesses to enable remote workers to log on to the corporate network securely. To do this at very low cost via the Internet. All access to the Internet is via a Point Of Presence owned by an ISP. Therefore all calls are local calls. A remote worker can therefore access his corporate network like a directly connected worker, anywhere around the world and only pay local telephony charges.

public internet, encryption is used to ensure privacy and authentication to ensure integrity of data. The setting up and tearing down of the VPN tunnels can be controlled from many points in the network. For example, IP tunnels can be established between a remote user and a corporate firewall with tunnel creation and deletion controlled by the user's computer and the firewall. Alternatively, with a rented service from an Internet Service Provider (ISP) the IP tunnel is between an ISP and a corporate firewall with tunnel creation and deletion controlled by the ISP. It is also possible to use different transport mechanisms as long as they are configured for IP traffic such as ISDN, Frame Relay or ATM for connections between sites with ISDN B channels, PVCs or SVCs used to separate traffic from other users.

ENTERPRISE NETWORKING

CHANGES IN WIDE AREA COMMUNICATIONS

VPNS BASED ON IP TUNNELS

The main implementation of VPNs using IP tunnelling is by enterprises who need to provide secure but remote and controlled access to the network. Organisations purchase connections from an ISP and install VPN equipment on their own sites, which are configured and managed by the IT staff of that organisation, only relying on the ISP for the physical connection as an access point onto the Internet. However some ISPs have installed VPN technology and offer VPN services based on IP tunnels. These are usually fully managed services with options such as Service Level Agreements (SLAs) to ensure Quality of Service (QoS).

VPNs can bring major benefits to an organisation providing they are manageable. The major issue with them is that you are enabling remote access onto your corporate network and it is this remoteness that causes the problems. How do you maintain the remote users in terms of problem-solving, configuration changes, service provider updates and software upgrades, as well as the really big issue of security? What is mandatory is to manage it centrally and deploy feature-rich end-user applications and robust authentication mechanisms. Many of the end-user applications are known as software shims - very thin applications of about 200K of code. This is not sufficient for central management since a true end-user application is in the tens of megabytes. You will gain all of the benefits of reduced telecommunications costs as dedicated and long-distance connections are replaced with local connections, the main benefit of using the Internet. Other benefits include increased deployment flexibility in provisioning, mobile computing, teleworking and branch office networking; in other words, having your staff where you need them, not where technology says you must have them. Your mobile worker has an easier life as Internet, intranet and extranet access can be provided using a single secure connection.

The main disadvantage of VPNs based on IP tunnels is that QoS levels, provided by the existing Internet, may be erratic and are not yet as good as alternative solutions. Finally - if obviously - VPNs based on the public Internet require higher levels of security such as authentication and data encryption to ensure integrity and security of data.

NOTE

ISP connections used for intranet and remote access VPNs do not necessarily need to be protected by a firewall as data is protected by the use of tunnelling and encryption. You can use separate ISP connections for general Internet access and VPN access, or you can

ENTERPRISE NETWORKING

CHANGES IN WIDE AREA COMMUNICATIONS

use a single connection with a common router with a VPN device and firewall in parallel behind it. In some cases, you can use devices that integrate one or more of these functions. When using extranet VPNs to provide e-commerce connections to business partners, suppliers or customers, it is advisable to use a firewall to protect your internal network.

VPNS BASED ON ISDN, FRAME RELAY OR ATM

VPNs based on public, switched data networks are usually fulfilled by service providers and other carriers, and may or may not provide fully managed services. In most cases, additional services such as QoS options are available. This type of VPN is likely to become popular in Europe where public, switched data networks are widely available and where business use of the Internet is less developed. VPNs based on ISDN, Frame Relay or ATM connections are very different to VPNs based on IP tunnels. This type of VPN uses public switched data network services and uses ISDN B channels, PVCs or SVCs to separate traffic from other users. Single or multiple B channels, PVCs or SVCs may be used between sites with additional features such as backup and bandwidth on demand. Data packets do not need to be IP and do not need to be encrypted. However, due to more widespread awareness about security issues, many users now choose to encrypt their data. The following diagram shows a carrier-based VPN that uses ISDN B channels and Frame Relay PVCs to connect remote clients and devices.

VPN AND SECURITY TERMINOLOGY REFERENCE

VPNs requires organisations to become security-aware because you are enabling remote users to access your corporate resources.

TUNNEL PROTOCOLS

Control of all of the tunnel attributes must be communicated over the Internet. This is the main distinction among the tunnel protocols. Several of the standards (PPTP, L2F, L2TP, and some IPsec implementations) are based on PPP (Point to Point Protocol) and benefit from several years of refinements and interoperability work.

IPsec - IP security architecture, developed in the IETF, this protocol adds security extensions of encryption and message authentication to the IP protocol.

L2F - Layer 2 Forwarding, developed by Cisco, this tunnelling protocol also captures data at layer 2 and uses PPP and UDP to route through the Internet.

ENTERPRISE NETWORKING

CHANGES IN WIDE AREA COMMUNICATIONS

L2TP - Layer 2 Tunnelling Protocol, is the result of IETF efforts to merge PPTP and L2F. It uses IPsec as the security mechanism.

PPTP - Point-To-Point Tunnelling Protocol, developed by Microsoft, 3Com, and others. This tunnelling protocol captures data at layer 2 and uses PPP and GRE to route it through the Internet.

SOCKS - This protocol captures data from layer 5 (under the application and before TCP) and routes it over TCP/IP as a way of tunnelling.

ENCRYPTION ALGORITHMS

To protect communications from eavesdropping, information can be encrypted. Different, well-established encryption algorithms are optimised for software or hardware implementations with little difference in security. Security is most dependent on the length of keys and the way they are assigned and handled. Most attacks centre on breaking the key mechanism.

ARCFOUR - a public domain algorithm that has demonstrated interoperability with RC4 implementations. It behaves like RC4, below.

DES - Data Encryption Standard, a government standard, is a block cipher (meaning data is encrypted in fixed size blocks, packets are padded to become a multiple of the block size) and uses a 56 bit key. DES is optimised for combinatorial hardware.

RC4 - Rivest Cipher 4, is a stream-based cipher (meaning that data packets can be encrypted as it is received) that can use a variable length key. Common key sizes are 40 bits and 128 bits. RC4 is optimised for software execution speed.

Triple DES - a version of DES that consists of a DES encryption with one key, a decryption with a second key and then an encryption with a third key. Even though this uses 168 bits of key, it has the strength of a 112-bit key due to algorithms that can be used in a brute force attack to reduce the number of values that must be tested.

ENCRYPTION AND KEY MANAGEMENT PROTOCOLS

Cryptographic sessions need to be initialised by both parties with a key that is used to start the encryption and decryption process. Like keys to a deadbolt, they must be handled carefully. Key management protocols deal with getting the key to both parties, resetting the key periodically, and protecting the use so that it cannot be stolen.

ENTERPRISE NETWORKING

CHANGES IN WIDE AREA COMMUNICATIONS

Diffie-Hellman - a method to negotiate a key using public messages sent in the clear and result in a key that the listeners don't understand. This is based on large prime number exponentiation of large numbers and the difficulty of factoring such results.

ECP - Encryption Control Protocol is a subset of the PPP suite for negotiation of encryption within a PPP connection. As a result it can be used in PPTP and L2TP tunnels.

Hashing - Hashing is an algorithm that takes plain text and converts it into a fixed length encrypted 'message digest'. This message digest is sent along with the file and is used to check the integrity of the file when it reaches its destination.

IKE - Internet Key Exchange, a protocol using part of Oakley in conjunction with ISAKMP to obtain authenticated keys for use with ISAKMP, and for other security associations such as AH and ESP.

ISAKMP - Internet Security Association and Key Management Protocol, used by IPsec to provide a framework for authentication and key exchange but does not define them. ISAKMP is designed to be key exchange independent; that is, it is designed to support many different key exchanges like IKE or Oakley.

KMI - Key Management Infrastructure refers to schemes used for providing key escrow or on-demand key recovery for an encrypted message. This is usually put in place to satisfy US government restrictions on export of encryption products. The US government prohibits export of encryption products using a key greater than 40 bits unless the product has an approved KMI.

MPPE - Microsoft Point-to-Point Encryption, generates a key based on a hash of the user's password and invokes RC4 encryption. Current MPPE has flaws in the way keys are assigned and re-keyed. With these flaws MPPE is still very difficult and time consuming to attack. Microsoft claims to be addressing these concerns in coming releases.

Oakley - describes a series of key exchanges, called 'modes', and details the services provided by each (e.g. perfect forward secrecy for keys, identity protection, and authentication). Used with ISAKMP to negotiate keys for an encryption session.

AUTHENTICATION SCHEMES

Users must be authenticated to verify they are who they claim to be and whether they are permitted access to the destination network. The authentication scheme must offer a secure, easy to manage method for transferring user credentials to the tunnel server.

ENTERPRISE NETWORKING

CHANGES IN WIDE AREA COMMUNICATIONS

CHAP and MS-CHAP encrypt passwords over the connection so that they cannot be intercepted, whereas tokens generate a new password for every connection so that an intercepted password is useless. Certificates provide a way to encrypt log-on information with a private/public key pair and have a set of components all of their own.

Certificates - a private key is kept by the user (in a file, smart card, floppy, or other) and used to sign a request to the other party. The other party can look up the public key of the requester to verify the signature on the request thus verifying the authenticity of the request.

CHAP - Challenge Handshake Authentication Protocol, rather than send the password in the clear, a random number is sent to the client as a challenge. The challenge is one-way hashed with the password and the result is sent back to the server. The server does the same with its copy of the password and verifies that it gets the same result to authenticate the user.

MS-CHAP - Microsoft CHAP, a version of CHAP used by Microsoft that uses a different hash of the password.

PAP - Password Authentication Protocol, the traditional send the username and password in the clear method used for logins in the days before eavesdropping security concerns. It is still the most common method of remote access and ISP login.

Tokens - by using a device carried by the user (usually a credit card sized card with a display) a password is retrieved from the token, which is based on the time and date or a random number sent by the server and entered by the user. The result is sent via PAP or CHAP to the server for authentication.

PPPoE - PPP over Ethernet, an authentication method for Cable/DSL users to 'log in' to get Ethernet connectivity. PPPoE can provide a dynamic address via IPCP.

AUTHENTICATION SERVERS

The authentication server protocol allows the user to be validated against a user list with other servers and functions. The most common protocol is RADIUS and it is support by nearly all user database systems. LDAP is showing promise for a more flexible successor to RADIUS as it becomes accepted. NT and NDS can be accessed by RADIUS and some tunnel servers can access them directly, eliminating some configuration effort.

LDAP - Lightweight Directory Access Protocol, is a protocol for retrieving information from a common database. For user authentication, this can be certificate information,

ENTERPRISE NETWORKING

CHANGES IN WIDE AREA COMMUNICATIONS

access control information or other operational criteria.

RADIUS - a protocol for communicating to a server that maintains a user directory to verify a user's identity. RADIUS can support most of the authentication schemes above. The schemes supported vary among implementations.

RADIUS Proxy - networks of RADIUS servers can be built where a RADIUS server can forward an authentication request to another radius server for verification. For example, an ISP's RADIUS server could act as a RADIUS proxy and send login requests to an enterprise's own RADIUS server to authenticate a user. In this way the enterprise can add and delete users without the ISP's involvement.

NDS - NetWare Directory Services, Novell's method for user authentication and access rights retrieval for a network.

NT Domains - Microsoft's method for user authentication for a network.

AD - Active Directory, Microsoft's new directory service released with Windows 2000, not yet widely implemented. Microsoft's IAS (internet Authentication Service) provides a RADIUS interface to AD.

Token Servers - Manufacturers of tokens (see above) generally provide a server that can verify that the output of the token is correct, thus authenticating the user. Products supporting tokens can usually talk to these servers using a native protocol or via RADIUS.

CERTIFICATE TECHNOLOGY

Certificates provide an ability to present a data packet that states who you are and which allows another trusted party to vouch for the authenticity of the packet. They are based on asymmetric keys and the ability to hash the packet with these keys for a CA (see below) to sign the certificates. Issues surrounding certificates are reliable distribution, expiration, renewal, and revocation.

Asymmetric keys - allow a different key to be used for encryption from the decryption. The public key can be used to encrypt something that only the key owner can decrypt with the private key. The key owner can encrypt with the private key something anyone can decrypt with the public key but could have only come from the key owner.

CA - Certificate Authority, is an internal entity or trusted third party that issues, signs, revokes, and manages digital certificates.

CRL - Certificate Revocation List, after a certificate has been issued, the employee may

ENTERPRISE NETWORKING

CHANGES IN WIDE AREA COMMUNICATIONS

leave the enterprise or other action, which requires revoking the certificate. The CRL is like a credit card hot list, used to verify that a certificate is still valid once it has been issued. A secure certificate implementation must check all certificates against the CRL to guard against certificates that have been revoked.

PKI - Public Key Infrastructure, certificates are based on

Public Key - In a two-part key scheme, this key is made public and signed by a CA to attest to the owner. It can then be used to encode information to the owner of the key and to decode information from the owner. The public key cannot be used to decode information encoded with it.

Private Key - The other part of the two-part key scheme, it functions like the public key but for the key owner to decode messages to them and encode messages from the owner.

RA - Registration Authority, an optional system to which a CA delegates certain management functions for example a RA can sign up users in a PKI and arrange to have their certificates signed by the CA. It can also be responsible for maintaining the CRL.

X.509 - The most common standard for organising the information stored in a certificate. Certificates contain validity dates, the issuer, the owner, a serial number, the public key and signatures of this.

COMPRESSION

Since encrypted data is not compressible by the modems outside of the tunnel, compression should be performed in the tunnel prior to the encryption. Additionally, compression is improved if history is kept over the duration of a session so that the codes for expanded data can be learned and reused for larger quantities of data.

CCP - Compression Control Protocol, is a subset of the PPP suite for negotiation of compression within a PPP connection. As a result it can be used in PPTP and L2TP tunnels. Note: Microsoft also uses CCP to negotiate MPPE encryption in its implementation of PPP.

Compression History - When compressing a data stream, reoccurring strings of data are placed in a dictionary and replaced with a code representing the string. When this dictionary is stored and remembered from one packet to the next the compression is said to maintain history. This results in better compression after initial packets load the dictionary with the likely patterns. Also called stateful compression (stateless compression is compression without history).

ENTERPRISE NETWORKING

CHANGES IN WIDE AREA COMMUNICATIONS

MPPC - Microsoft Point to Point Compression, is a LZS based stream compression protocol that can be invoked by Microsoft clients for dial-up connections. It is currently history-based, although there has been discussion about eliminating the history in tunnelling applications.

STAC LZS - STAC Lempel-Ziv Standard is the compression algorithm adopted for default PPP connections. It can be used with or without history depending on the application. Most PPP implementations use a Stac LZS with history.

ADDRESS NEGOTIATION

An address for the client to must be assigned or negotiated for all traffic originating from the client. This forms the basis for a user's identity on the enterprise network. Addresses must be selected that allow transparent operation and do not clutter network routing tables. DHCP is simple and works in small networks. Larger networks need to assign subnets to tunnel servers for efficient routing and extranets can create the need for NAT to compensate for overlapping addresses among partners. PPP based tunnel protocols assign the address to the client using IPCP and IPXCP.

DHCP - Dynamic Host Configuration Protocol is a method of assigning IP addresses to hosts and clients on a LAN. When a host or client is initialised, it broadcasts a request for an address that is responded to by a DHCP server with an IP address for the requester.

IPCP - IP Control Protocol is part of the PPP suite of protocols. Among other functions, the server IPCP will assign an IP address to clients of the PPP link for use during the connection.

IPXCP - IPX Control Protocol is part of the PPP suite of protocols. Among other functions, the server IPCP will assign an IPX address to clients of the PPP link for use during the connection.

NAT - Network Address Translation is used to convert an address of a client to a different address to be used on a different network. This allows a client to select its address and, when connected to a tunnel server, have that address converted in all packets to a different address on the server's network. This is typically used to reconcile conflicting addresses on multiple networks.

Subnet Assignment - Using a dedicated address subnet range for tunnel servers. This improves routing table efficiency by setting the tunnel server up as a peer router in the network.

ENTERPRISE NETWORKING

CHANGES IN WIDE AREA COMMUNICATIONS

CLIENT TECHNOLOGY

Each solution must find a way to process the data as it goes from the client to the VPN server. There are several ways for this to happen.

Shims - refers to a communications software module that is placed between two other communication protocols to perform an extra function. For example a shim to perform a specific tunnel protocol could be placed between an application and the TCP/IP stack.

Stack replacement - a method of adding a protocol by replacing an existing implementation with a new version. For example, TCP/IP could be replaced with a vendor's own version that implements IPsec.

VxD - Virtual Device Drivers - a method of adding a communication protocol module into Windows '95 and '98 as if it were a new device. For example, an IPsec VXD can be added that accepts IP data and encapsulates it in ESP and sends it back to IP.

ENCAPSULATION PROTOCOLS

All of the data transmitted may need to be encapsulated for transportation over the Internet. This selection can impact firewall traversal and packet overhead. UDP is more firewall-friendly, GRE has lower overhead for slightly better performance.

AH - Authentication Header is an IP header defined by IPsec for signing a packet to validate that it has not been altered and is as it was sent.

ESP - Encrypted Security Payload is the IP protocol header defined by IPsec and used for an IPsec packet to enclose the encrypted packet and corresponding control information.

GRE - Generic Routing Encapsulation, an IP protocol for encapsulating any other type of data and maintain order of arrival.

PPP - Point-to-Point Protocol, the standard protocol for dial-up networking. The family of standards covers many aspects including authentication, encryption, compression, addressing, multi-protocols, and so on.

Tunnel Mode - An ESP mode that encapsulates the entire IP packet within the ESP payload and encrypts the entire packet. Tunnel mode is typically used in site-to-site or client-to-site connections where the internal (tunnelled) packet is going to be routed on the destination network.

Transport Mode - An ESP mode that keeps the original IP header and encrypts the

ENTERPRISE NETWORKING

CHANGES IN WIDE AREA COMMUNICATIONS

payload of the IP packet within the ESP payload. Transport mode is typically used in point to point transfers where the internal payload is not an IP packet and is destined to the end points of the ESP connection. This mode is used for security of L2TP tunnels.

Edge to Edge tunnel - A tunnel which begins and ends at the ISP POPs

End to End tunnel - A tunnel which begins at the client, travels through the Internet and terminates at the enterprise tunnel server.

Table 1 illustrates which technologies can be used together in each of the common tunnelling protocols. Table 2 shows how the protocols are stacked in each of the implementations and where each of the functions is performed.

Tunnel Protocol	PPTP*	L2TP	IPsec	SOCKS
Layer	2	2	3	5
Authentication	PAP, CHAP, or **MS-CHAP**	PAP, **CHAP**, or MS-CHAP	**Shared secret**, Certificate	PAP, CHAP, Certificate
Encryption negotiation	ECP or **CCP**	**IPsec**, ECP or CCP	ISAKMP	
Encryption	**RC4**, DES, 3DES	**IPsec**	DES, RC4, 3DES	SSL, IPsec, PPTP, L2TP
Key Management	**MPPE**	ISAKMP	IKE	
Compression	**MPPC**	**LZS**, MPPC	none	none
Address Assignment	IPCP, IPXCP	IPCP, IPXCP	none	none
Tunnel Encapsulation	**GRE**	**UDP** or GRE	ESP Tunnel Mode	SOCKS
Multi-protocol	IP, IPX, NetBEUI	IP, IPX, NetBEUI	IP	TCP/IP

Table 1 - Tunnel Protocols
Minimum interoperability shown in BOLD, although the PPTP protocol implementation supports the options shown, Microsoft only supports the defaults, so most

ENTERPRISE NETWORKING

CHANGES IN WIDE AREA COMMUNICATIONS

implementations are likewise restricted.

Table 2 - VPN Protocol Stacks

PPTP	L2TP	IPsec	SOCKS		
IP, IPX, etc.	IP, IPX, etc.	IP	App		The protocol used by the user's applications
PPP	PPP		SOCKS		multi-protocol, compression, authentication, address assignment, and optional encryption
GRE	GRE or UDP		TCP		Wraps user's data into an ordered stream over IP
	IP				IPsec tunnel mode IP header (TBD - IETF discussion)
	ESP	ESP			IPsec encryption
IP	IP	IP	IP		Internet connection between VPN client and gateway
PPP	PPP	PPP	PPP		Connects client to Internet POP (for dial up users).

section ten

Wireless Technology - an Overview

Section 10: Wireless LANs

Networking without any cabling is now possible. Recent improvements have increased bandwidth and so widened the scope of wireless LAN application. As standards bodies focus on ever higher speeds, applications will become more widespread. The industry once said that twisted-pair copper wire had reached its limit at 112 Kbit/sec but today products that deliver 1000Mbit/sec are available from several manufacturers. Wireless has moved from the 1Mbit/sec to the very latest 802.11a standard for 54Mbit/sec.

ENTERPRISE NETWORKING

WIRELESS LANS

INTRODUCTION

Local Area Networking has established itself as the viable means to provide company-wide connectivity, the sharing of expensive resources and the seamless integration of business applications. The initial drawback of LANs, having to install a specialist cabling system, which was not easily extended or changeable, has been solved by structured wiring schemes. Now organisations pre-wire each user location with a connection, anticipating future requirements and enabling mobility of the workforce around the organisation. Two factors now strain even as flexible a system as this, the popularity of laptops and palmtops, and the frequency of the organisational changes occurring in today's modern business.

Casual workgroups can be set up with no effort in any location within the range of the wireless technology used. Wireless LANs can be deployed for temporary departments and re-deployed when the network is no longer required.

Employees who now rely on laptop computers leave their organisers at home and do not attend any meetings without first consulting their portable PCs. This new breed of computer users is demands mobility, to be able to wander freely around departments accompanied by their laptop, while having continual access to the corporate data.

The second problem is to deal with organisational changes without effecting employees' productivity. Many such changes are temporary, for example while building work is carried out or the finance department is moved to another location to enable a new computer system to be installed.

ENTERPRISE NETWORKING

WIRELESS LANS

The clear solution to this demand for ever-greater flexibility and mobility of IT resources is wireless networking. Wireless LANs are ideal for conference room locations, no wires required. Employees can wander in and out with laptops and do not have to worry about finding a free connection. Any temporary accommodation problem can benefit from networking services without incurring investment on fixed assets because there's no cabling to be installed. Note that wireless LANs don't replace the fixed infrastructure but rather they complement it by extending the services available. Consider them an overlay network to the fixed installation that can extend the reach of network services not just for the mobile user but from building to building without incurring carrier tariffs for the external service. They offer a unique solution to modern business requirements for employee mobility and installation flexibility.

WIRELESS TECHNOLOGY

There are three basic techniques used by wireless network products, which can make use of either radio frequencies or infrared light to transmit data. The technologies differ in usage, communications distances and configuration with each displaying strengths and weaknesses depending on the application.

SPREAD SPECTRUM TECHNOLOGY

Spread spectrum is the most widely used technology for wireless LANs. Originally developed in the 1950s by the US Government, spread spectrum provided secure and reliable communications in the battlefield. Security is achieved by including a 'separate code' within the data stream. Anyone without the spreading code will be unable to tap into the network. By using a unique code for each Spread Spectrum network, it is possible to use multiple spread spectrum systems within the same area or region. Units that receive data from different networks will not have the correct code so these data transmissions look to the system like noise.

There will be the possibility of performance degradation if more than one spread spectrum network is in the same area. this is because each network competes for the same range of frequencies for transmitting the data. When the FCC approved Spread Spectrum for commercial use in 1985, it allocated three bands of frequencies 902 to 928MHz, 2400 to 2483.5MHz and 5725MHz to 5850MHz for commercial use. This are the Industrial, Scientific and Medical (ISM) bands as designated by the Federal

ENTERPRISE NETWORKING

WIRELESS LANS

Communications Commission. Use of the ISM bands does not require a licence from the FCC, but their use is regulated to prevent interface problems. End-user licensing is not a requirement of the FCC and users can move from area to area without fear of interfering with other devices operating at the same frequency. In Europe the freeing and approving of higher frequencies for the technology has delayed the widespread installations but these regulatory services are catching up.

NARROW BAND HIGH FREQUENCY RADIO (RF)

Narrow band high frequency radio uses low power at 18GHz. This kind of high frequency radio requires each device to use the same frequency when transmitting and, as narrow band requires a clear channel uninterrupted by other devices, each user of a narrow band product must register and obtain a licence before operating the device. There are different licensing authorities for different geographical regions making global solutions a problem. Since each transmitter/receiver pair of devices transmits using its own unique frequency, it is unlikely to interfere with other RF devices in the same licensing area. However, if a device is moved to another area where other devices are in operation it is possible to interfere with a device operating on the same frequency. Security on an RF network is maintained and enforced by including network IDs as part of the data system. Without the correct network ID, the data cannot be decoded.

INFRARED

Most people are familiar with infrared devices such as the TV remote control. Infrared is light, although not visible to the human eye. Light, naturally enough, will not penetrate solid objects but, with a frequency of over 1000GHz, infrared has the bandwidth available to carry hundreds of megabytes of data. You may recall that this is how data is transmitted down fibre cables - see Section 4 on FDDI. No government bodies control light frequencies so there are no licensing requirements which means infrared technology has globally unlimited use.

Each infrared device has a transmitter and a receiving unit which sends and receives; the light is then converted to electrical signals. Using mirrors to focus the signal down to a fine beam would be one way of implementing infrared and would allow for high-speed transmission because most of the light beam is focused to a particular spot. It's a technique that is typically used when transmitting the beam across buildings or for long distances. This method requires that the devices be positioned so they have a clear line of

ENTERPRISE NETWORKING

WIRELESS LANS

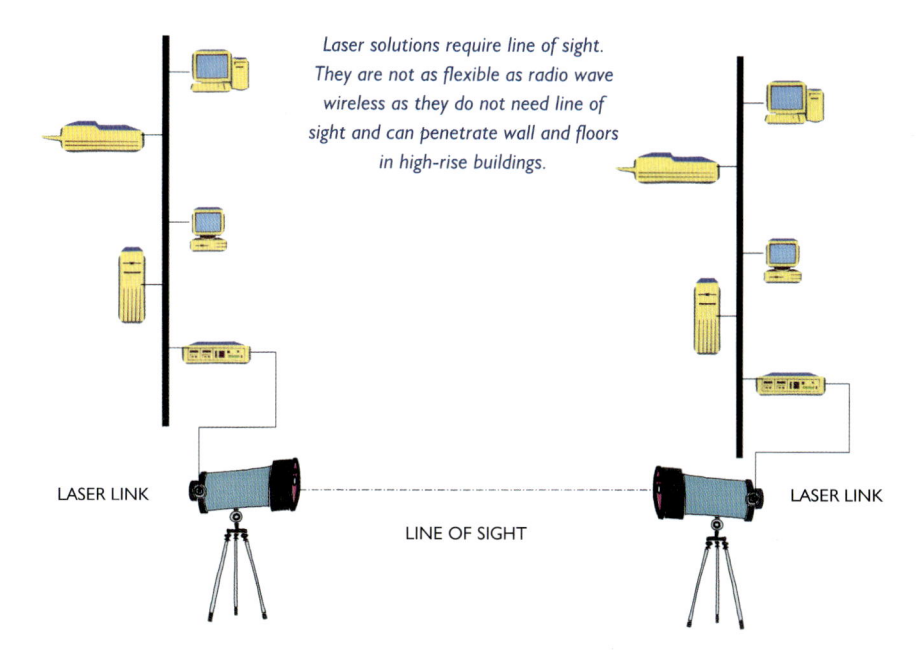

Laser solutions require line of sight. They are not as flexible as radio wave wireless as they do not need line of sight and can penetrate wall and floors in high-rise buildings.

LASER LINK

LINE OF SIGHT

LASER LINK

sight. Another approach is to flood a room with the signal by not focusing the beam as much, much like a standard tungsten light bulb. The advantage is that a transmitter can communicate with multiple receivers. The disadvantage is that the distance and data rates are reduced as a result of the lost energy so, typically, infrared operates between devices between devices are no more than 25 metres apart.

Security in an infrared system is achieved in the same manner as a high frequency radio system. Network IDs are inserted into the data stream. Without the network ID the data cannot be decoded. As infrared signals are not part of the radio spectrum, they are not regulated.

WIRELESS ARCHITECTURE

There are two approaches that can be used when implementing a wireless network, namely peer-to-peer and hierarchical. The latter is based on a base station controller concept.

ENTERPRISE NETWORKING

WIRELESS LANS

PEER LEVEL ARCHITECTURE

In a peer level architecture, each device has the same level of priority. Any device can communicate with any other device on the network directly without going through a mediator. A peer level architecture is less expensive to implement because it does not require a central controller for inter-device communication. When communicating at peer level, users can experience a problem known as the 'near-far' problem. The problem occurs when devices close to each other communicate among themselves and are unable to communicate with devices located further away from the original group. This is because the receivers adjust themselves to the incoming signal, so once they have adjusted to a near station the far station's signal is below the threshold now acceptable to the receiving station.

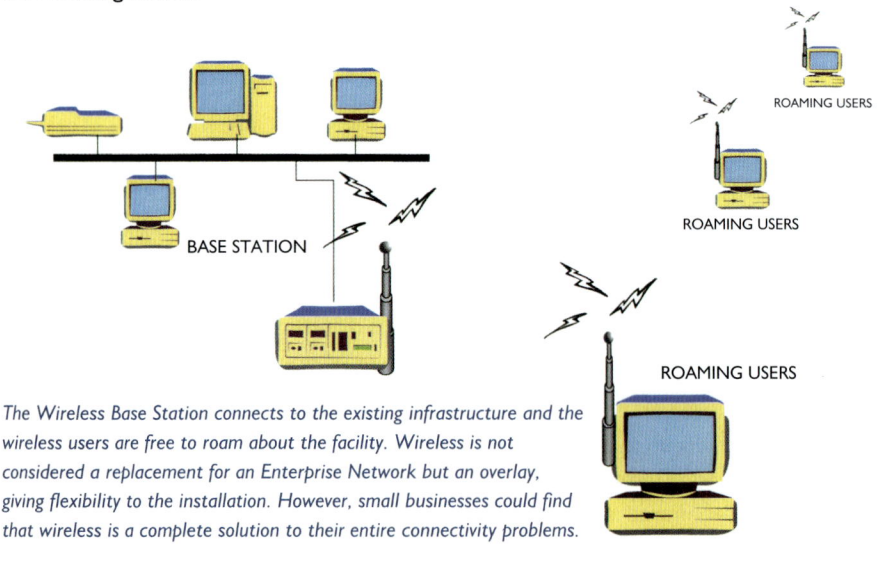

The Wireless Base Station connects to the existing infrastructure and the wireless users are free to roam about the facility. Wireless is not considered a replacement for an Enterprise Network but an overlay, giving flexibility to the installation. However, small businesses could find that wireless is a complete solution to their entire connectivity problems.

Networks based on peer level architecture provide a way for small workgroups to form ad hoc networks wherever convenient. Typical examples include groups of people getting together for a meeting or conference without the convenience of having a central hub available. They generally have less need for large amounts of bandwidth, requiring only the ability to transfer small files or to co-ordinate organisers etc.

Using this type of architecture throughput speeds are typically 1-2Mbit/sec and distance is limited to around 40 metres. In addition, a peer-level architecture does not lend itself to providing network management capabilities.

ENTERPRISE NETWORKING

WIRELESS LANS

BASE STATION ARCHITECTURE

As the name implies, this architecture uses a centralised base unit that controls access and communications between the devices on the network. The near-far problem, which is prevalent in peer level architectures, does not affect hub based architectures because each device uses the central controller for communicating. The base station is a convenient location for integrating wireless LAN devices into existing networks and provides a convenient way to allow network managers to control the wireless network. These architectures provide wireless LAN devices with high data throughput rates - as much as ten times the 1-2Mbit/sec that is currently available for peer-to-peer implementations. These higher performance implementations provide larger coverage between the wireless LAN devices and the base station.

Standards bodies have not been slow in responding to market demands for wireless technology. Today IEEE802.11 committee has ratified specifications for 11Mbit/sec IEEE802.11b and 54Mbit/sec IEEE802.11a. These standards specify Ethernet packet framing across a wireless transport mechanism. There is an added element for security not needed in wireless solutions. The WEP (Wireless Equivalent Privacy), which is part of the 802.11 specification, protects wireless connections against eavesdropping and assisting with unauthorised access. WEP relies on a secret key that is used for encryption between the wireless devices and the base station. The encryption specified is RC4 encryption algorithm which is known as a stream cipher and covers 40-128 bit encryptions.

802.11 WIRELESS AND BLUETOOTH

Recent interest in wireless has been fuelled by three factors. The first has been the publication of the IEEE802.11a standard for 54Mbit/sec enterprise performance wireless, and the fact that many networking vendors cooperated in achieving the earlier specification of IEEE802.11b 11Mbit/sec standard. They achieved this by participation in interoperability testing at the independent lab at the University of New Hampshire, and the Wi-Fi certification process of the Wireless Ethernet Compatibility Alliance. The third has been the hype surrounding personal area networking (PAN) using Bluetooth-compliant products.

Bluetooth has been developed and marketed by an industry consortium of communications vendors including Intel, Motorola, Siemens, 3Com, Toshiba and others. Microsoft also supports it. Bluetooth operates in the same 2.4GHz band as the Wi-Fi

ENTERPRISE NETWORKING

WIRELESS LANS

products and there is the possibility of radio interference between Wi-Fi and Bluetooth. Initially, Bluetooth supports bandwidths of under 1Mbit/sec with a range of approximately 10 metres but this will improve as the standard evolves.

Bluetooth-enabled products will include PCs, printers, keyboards, PDAs, cell phones, pagers, and any personal product. Underlying it is the concept of a PAN that, by replacing incompatible and messy cabling systems with wireless links, can synchronise all the IT tools a user might need. In contrast to Bluetooth's personal networking approach, wireless LANs based on 802.11 are designed as a high-performance networking systems. However, Bluetooth promises to scale to both wide area and local area network applications, potentially offering a greater degree of mobility but with reduced performance and security. Wireless LANs, specifically IEEE802.11-based products, are already on the move; there is already a specification for 22Mbit/sec and 54Mbit/sec products based on IEEE802.11a standards are becoming available.

Home RF is another wireless industry consortium using frequency hopping (FH) technology and which also operates in the 2.4GHz band. Aimed at home users, companies supporting this technology have decided not to transition their wireless products to the new 802.11 specifications. Specifically the change to Direct Sequence- (DS) based products. The Home RF technology is 1.6Mbit/sec shared Wireless Access Protocol, however the FCC ruled on allowing 10Mbit/sec rates for this technology so the future could be a confusing range of choices.

However, the issue for businesses are clear: performance, standards and high security with control over access to the network.

USES FOR WIRELESS CONNECTIVITY

Businesses today are implementing wireless LAN technology to meet the needs of both mobile users and temporary re-organisations. Environments suitable for wireless devices typically require wiring flexibility and mobility of employees. It's also useful in environments that cannot accommodate standard cabling transmissions, such as electrical noisy factory environments or listed buildings that for architectural reasons cannot be wired.

WIRELESS APPLICATIONS PROTOCOL (WAP)

The WAP Forum was founded in 1997 by Ericsson, Motorola, Nokia and Unwired Planet Inc. to create a specification for wireless devices to gain access to information on the

ENTERPRISE NETWORKING

WIRELESS LANS

Internet. The idea being that smart phones, personal assistance and palmtops could gain access to the multimedia available on the Web. WAP 2.0 provides support for TCP and HTTP giving WAP devices access to the exciting internet content. The WAP specification covers the use of GPRS (General Packet Radio Service) and third generation (3G) wireless cellular transport mechanisms to support TCP and HTTP sessions.

EXAMPLE APPLICATIONS

- Retail point of sale systems with several cash registers. These environments are continually being reorganised to present a fresh look to the shopping public.

- Factory floors where a number of people walk around inputting information to the central computing resource. This makes it difficult to make a direct cable connection to a network.

- Company environments where the employees are mobile and changing stations extensively or environments that only require temporary or occasional network connections.

- Buildings that cannot be modified or altered because of their historical significance.

ISSUES TO CONSIDER BEFORE IMPLEMENTING

Before wireless connectivity can become a standardised, widespread solution in most companies, there are several issues to be considered, not least security. The common perception is that on a wired LAN the data stays on the wire. Likewise if one is using a wireless LAN, the bits and bytes are flying all through the air, available to all. The reality of the situation is that wire, particularly unshielded twisted pair (UTP), is an unintentionally designed radio LAN as much as wireless is an intentionally designed wireless radio LAN. UTP also acts as an antenna that is susceptible to noise and signal distortions that degrade a LAN's performance. For the real answer to security issues one must look to the next level in the network layer and examine how the data is encoded on the wireless LAN, the power and coverage area of the signal, and what security features that particular wireless LAN architecture possesses.

Security is also needed for products using spread spectrum radio transmission techniques. Since the US Army used this radio technology in the 1950s for secure battlefield communications, it has been used since 1967 by the Israeli military for voice and

ENTERPRISE NETWORKING

WIRELESS LANS

Wireless technology is ideal for installations where a fixed infrastructure is difficult or not desirable. Point of Sale is an ideal application, giving the retail outlet full flexibility in designing the customers' retail experience.

telemetry communications. the overriding reason for the military's extensive use of spread spectrum is because of its inherent security characteristics. A spread spectrum signal is extremely difficult to detect. Once detected it is difficult to decode, and also very difficult to interfere with or jam its transmission. It has only been in the last few years that spread spectrum radios have become both small and cheap enough for commercial applications. Extending wire-based security to wireless installations helps allay security concerns. Several manufacturers have added RADIUS user authentication and one manufacturer has even added IEEE802.1x user authentication to the wireless base station.

Most of the wireless products that are available today exhibit lower performance rates than their traditional wire-based counterparts. However, the introduction of IEEE802.11a 54Mbit/sec solution is set to change this low performance perception. The reason for wired solutions racing ahead of wireless performance has been a lack of mass manufactured, wireless components accurate enough to achieve LAN data rates. Today the trend is changing. With the proliferation of wireless voice products, such as cellular telephones and the newer generation of digital cellular telephones, semi-conductor manufacturers are producing in high volumes parts suited to data applications. Vendors have also perfected more accurate design techniques so as to achieve high data rates. As

ENTERPRISE NETWORKING

WIRELESS LANS

new applications for wireless continue to evolve, volumes and performance will be driven to even higher levels while costs will fall further.

Some manufacturers are looking to the mobile telephony services of the main carriers based on GSM technology as a solution for mobile computing. My issue with this approach is that a LAN-based wireless once installed provides the communication services for free. On the other hand using telephony wireless would mean that all business communications in the enterprise would incur a carrier tariff. It is the cost to the enterprise that makes me sceptical of this approach ever gaining acceptance.

section eleven

Network Management

Section 11: Network Management

We provide a complete overview of the problems facing network administrators along with some technology recommendations as potential solutions. Developments in networking hardware have helped make management features more useable especially with respect to policy-based management. We also look at attempts to establish network management standards.

ENTERPRISE NETWORKING

NETWORK MANAGEMENT

The 1980s will go down in IT history as the decade of networking, both in the wide and local areas, despite the decade starting with two industries having clearly defined market areas and differing product sets. There was never any hint of encroachment by the telephony industry. Yet the 1990s saw LAN and WAN merge into one communications industry, forced into it by the invention of switching. In this new millennium, the prospect is that communications and telephony will merge into a multi-service industry.

This is fine in terms of communications products but management applications are needed to maintain services at acceptable levels. After a decade of installing and supporting LAN technology, network manufacturers have the advantage of understanding the problem. With this understanding and the clear mandate from the purchasers of products that only standards-based solutions are acceptable, manufacturers can and are starting to deliver real corporate network management products.

Network management is a long-term strategy. The biggest investment you will make as an organisation is the training and skills set which are developed around the network management platform. To select a network management platform, you must understand

The Network Manager and his trusty MIS team have developed specialist skills for dealing with the unexpected. The bonus of network management applications is they know that this is where men are men and disasters happen! Only wimps read manuals in this department, they live on their nerve endings.

ENTERPRISE NETWORKING

NETWORK MANAGEMENT

the problems. If you have had a network for some time you will recognise them instantly but, if you are just making your initial foray into networking, you cannot possibly know what you need until you have suffered without it.

The management problem covers three main areas each of which has been addressed by the manufacturers to some degree, but to date not collectively. To ensure that an enterprise network is adequately administered, the three mandatory elements are network product management, fix assist configuration and location, and cable management.

The first area to consider is the traditional network management problem that the OSI network management forum has defined in considerable detail. The forum has split this problem area into five discrete requirements which are helpful in understanding and describe exactly this first problem of network management:

Configuration management is the monitoring and control of your whole network from anywhere on the network. An example problem is the disabling of a port on a terminal server in a remote office. You would not want to employ an engineer in a remote office for a few devices, on the other hand you do not want to drive four or five hours to the remote office for such a trivial task.

Fault management is obviously a requirement. If your business is committed to a network and the network fails, your company could suffer financially from lost business or from dissatisfied customers who did not receive the timely response they were expecting from you. Inherent in fault management must be a degree of automation. You cannot watch everything or make a split-second decision on actions to take when an alarm goes off, not given the million and one things that could have caused it. So automation must be present to isolate the problem and provide alternative connection, but must preserve the network's integrity at all costs.

Performance management may not initially grab you as a vital problem that has to be addressed but I can assure you that if on your network you are adding PC users, inter-networking products, bridging, routing and other devices, or going for distributed computing or implementing a client server architecture, then performance is a big problem. To be able to measure, record, analyse and simulate, traffic load levels are essential in fine tuning your network and gaining the maximum performance from a resource that you already own. It will also give you the statistics you will need to purchase further LAN products.

ENTERPRISE NETWORKING

NETWORK MANAGEMENT

Account management tells you who is connected to what and for how long. Why do you need it? Going to the financial controller and asking for a new printer could receive a sharp negative response but, if you can show documented evidence that work is being slowed down by excessive queuing, you could be on to a winner.

Security management controls whether, for example, a user with a password may access a service on a particular host on the network from a particular port today between two and five pm. It is arguable that making these kinds of checks each time data communication takes place could affect the performance of your system. Some feel that security is more geared to internal company procedures and policies than pure communications facilities. However, security can be controlled by the communications infrastructure so by default becomes a network management responsibility.

To sum up, the first problem area that needs to be addressed is network product management, which enables in-band (across the network) and out-band (a separate communications path outside of the network) control of configuration, fault and performance issues from a central location. It must also provide accountability and security that mesh with your organisation's specific procedural requirements. You must not however, measure these functions by the features they offer. Supplier A offers 100

Network Managers need to know physical information about the installation. When an icon goes red, the fault cannot be repaired or replaced if you cannot locate its position. Similarly, the configuration of a workstation needs to be known from the management station. To reduce the mean time to repair the MTTR, an engineer needs to have the correct diagnosis, correct parts and the correct location.

ENTERPRISE NETWORKING

NETWORK MANAGEMENT

features, supplier B offers 70 features, therefore supplier A must have the superior product. The critical questions to ask yourself after you have identified that the main areas are covered are: *"can I use this product every day?"* and *"can I then understand information that is being presented to me?"* Never lose sight of the fact that a live network will have problems and each PC brings problems not only for the network but also for the expert user.

You will have to use the network management product every day. If the manufacturer has not spent equal amounts of development time getting the right standard of network management control and agent programmes, along with the user interface, you are just asking for a difficult life.

The second problem area is a practical issue indirectly associated with the technology. LANs enable the distribution of resources such as placing printers near the users or putting host resources in the computer room away from the users. This, historically, has resulted in the distribution of LAN products such as terminal servers, repeaters, or even the bridges, while the wide area products traditionally remained in the communications room safely out of reach of the users. The problem to be addressed is *"where is this product physically?"*. A broken networking component could be disabling the whole network but it is not useful to know that terminal server seven has an inoperative port, if you cannot then physically locate the unit in a timely manner.

Then there are the dreaded PC users. Out of necessity, the department responsible for the LAN installation is usually responsible for connecting PCs to the network too. This involves installing a network card and configuring the driver. As this responsibility lies in the domain of the networking team then so does the fixed asset problem that goes with it.

For the day-to-day maintenance of any network, the network manager needs to know what equipment is connected to the network, where it is physically located in terms of the user devices, who the user is, what their phone number is so you can to let them know beforehand that you are disabling the machine. You also need to know the configuration of the PC itself, what applications it is running and what services are available.

This type of information is generally relegated to a paper filing system so the information is often only available after some physical difficulty locating it. Some forward-thinking network managers attempt to address the problem by keeping a site plan, but this is subject to the self-discipline of the individuals' department to keep the physical record up to date.

ENTERPRISE NETWORKING

NETWORK MANAGEMENT

The third problem area - cable management - has always been a LAN manager's burden but, with structured wiring schemes, it has raised its potential for mayhem considerably. Though viewed as a low level task you will probably have the cable plant accurately planned and documented, each run defined, each connector, and each possible cable path available. This has been well automated onto PCs with several packages providing planning, managing and cable inventory services.

If the equipment checks out OK, then you plainly have a cable problem. Finding a cable fault requires keeping accurate documentation on the cable layout which means the spare cables as well. If the patching has been changed on any punch down block, these changes need to be recorded. Software tools can help manage the cable plant but they still rely on the engineer being conscientious about recording additions and changes.

However, cable management packages are often not integrated into the network management package and is infrequently used compared to network management. Yet in a modern structured wiring environment, a service can be changed by the simple movement of a jumper cable on the punch down blocks. This small alteration, along with the normal changes or removing cables and adding new ones, if not recorded, can escalate the simplest problem into a complete disaster. A simple scenario would be a PC that is auto-segmented, (isolated by the network management) for exceeding an error

ENTERPRISE NETWORKING

NETWORK MANAGEMENT

threshold. Network management shows the hub to be functioning correctly so it is the transmit side of the PC that seems to be at fault. The networking card in the PC is changed and even the software configuration checked but excessive errors are still occurring. There is nothing wrong with the ends of the links, it must be the link itself that is at fault.

If no record has been kept of the cable location once the cable from the PC reaches the wall, there is no telling where the cable runs, since it's now one of many in a bundle.

The solution would be to have an engineer sit down and check all the physical connections until he found the broken cable. Meanwhile the business has had its information flow distributed for a significant time. We need a solution that provides understanding, not from hours of technical training but from simplicity at being shown the relevant information in an understandable format.

The generic market for network management products began in the late 1980s with the introduction of the Simple Network Management Protocol (SNMP), which evolved out of the Internet Engineering Task Force (IETF). This quickly became a de facto standard enabling the management of a fast increasing range of LAN and WAN devices by an equally increasing number of platforms that emerge to take advantage of the situation, such as SunNet Manager, HP OpenView and SPECTRUM from Cabletron.

SNMP is described in the next section but the idea is that each device records its own status and reports this to a central data collection point the management platform. These platforms have a range of applications that can do a simple task like turn a port on or off to a more complex task like record the traffic over several hours on a link and produce graphs to enable analysis of the traffic.

Today, a wide and diverse variety of offerings, ranging from comprehensive 'do-it-all' enterprise applications, like SPECTRUM that manage heterogeneous environments, to NetMetrix whose products focus on providing Remote Monitoring (RMON) solutions. Towards the lower, commodity end of the market, a whole range of tools or point solutions are available which can provide element management or perform specific single tasks. They are often low-cost, easy to use, and use Java-based Web technology.

Over the last two years, a new and exciting market has emerged from the requirement to manage both IT systems, as well as the underlying network communications infrastructure upon which they are so dependent to deliver their intrinsic value. Several companies have focused on this demand by providing very comprehensive systems

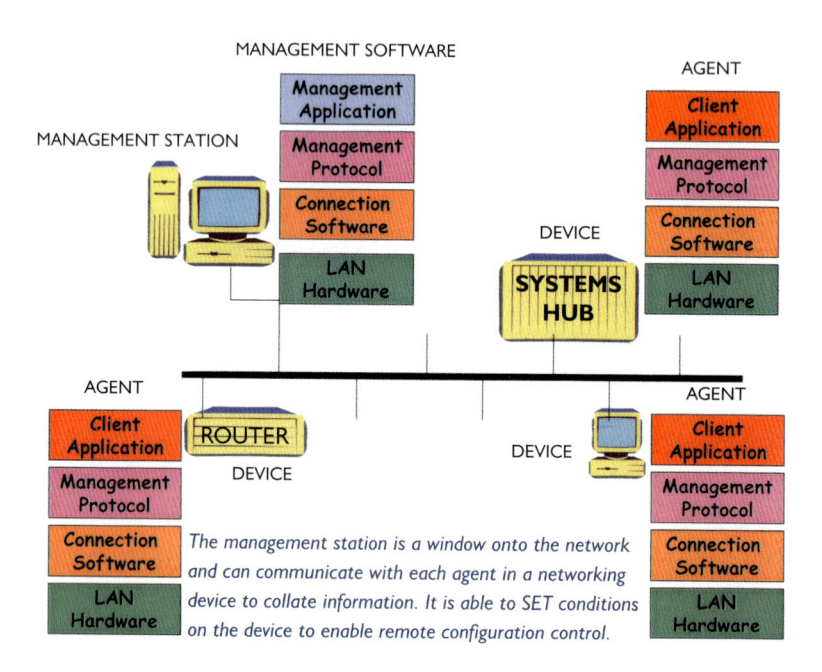

ENTERPRISE NETWORKING

NETWORK MANAGEMENT

MANAGEMENT STATION — **MANAGEMENT SOFTWARE**: Management Application, Management Protocol, Connection Software, LAN Hardware

DEVICE — SYSTEMS HUB

AGENT: Client Application, Management Protocol, Connection Software, LAN Hardware

DEVICE — ROUTER

AGENT: Client Application, Management Protocol, Connection Software, LAN Hardware

DEVICE

AGENT: Client Application, Management Protocol, Connection Software, LAN Hardware

The management station is a window onto the network and can communicate with each agent in a networking device to collate information. It is able to SET conditions on the device to enable remote configuration control.

orientated management frameworks. They are Computer Associates with Unicenter, TNG & Tivoli Systems with TME 10 now part of IBM and SPECTRUM Enterprise from Aprisma. These frameworks are a significant investment for companies and are systems-orientated in their approach.

DIRECTORY SERVICES IMPROVE MANAGEABILITY

One of the most significant enabling technologies for delivering advanced networking solutions is directory services. In the early 1990s, network technology and devices were building enterprise networks that had no common services. Each device operated individually and as such the network did not function as a co-ordinated system. This lack of system level interaction made deployment of advanced services almost impossible. In fact many valuable services available on network devices were not being utilised because they failed to operate at the system level.

A prime example is the use of alarm limits on switch and hub ports. This technology, found in most vendors' products, allows the network devices to monitor the activity at the edge of the network. If traffic levels increase above the specified thresholds, the device can notify the management system or even take corrective action such as disabling

ENTERPRISE NETWORKING

NETWORK MANAGEMENT

ports. While this service seems to be an ideal way to enhance the network's pro-active monitoring capabilities, these features are almost never used. The reason is an average network might include hundreds of switches or hubs and thousands of ports. Since these services are configured individually, not at the system level, the time involved in doing the needed per port configuration would be so overwhelming that the service is simply not viewed as a viable option in most networks. This is unfortunate in that such services, when properly enabled, will almost certainly offer the customer a significant return on investment as possible network failures can be pro-actively avoided through automated actions within the network.

Cabletron Systems recognised that this need for system level configuration and management required more than just a better configuration tool using the same management paradigms. It required a model of network device interaction that made each device aware that it was an element in a system and that its knowledge should be aggregated into a central service point at which common management could occur. The ideal mechanism for this type of service would be one based on directory architecture. Cabletron being an engineering company installed the first directory-enabled network in 1994. However the world never knew because they called it SecureFast.

In this model, each network device (switch, router, hub and so on) can gather local information about the network's operation - devices attached, protocols, user, statistics seen and so on - and that data is combined in a common database/directory server that provides a system-wide view of the network's operation.

But this directory is not just for monitoring the network. It can now become an interactive part of the communication infrastructure. System wide actions can now be initiated through the directory server rather than interacting directly with each network element. Tasks such as tracking users' locations can be facilitated by simply asking the directory where a device was. Since network switches are adding real-time information about the location and actions of devices in the infrastructure to the directory, when asked for data on a particular device, the directory can quickly provide the location, addresses, and activities of any device in the infrastructure. Without a directory, the same task is been much more difficult and time-consuming as the requester would have had to use the management tool to integrate every switch or network device in the communications path for the information individually.

Extending this example, the directory can then be used to map policy onto the device. Since the policy exists in the directory, a device will always receive the same common

ENTERPRISE NETWORKING

NETWORK MANAGEMENT

policy rules regardless of the switch it attaches to. When a switch sees the device, the switch asks the directory for the policy relating to the device and applies it. Using a common directory to store policy means the switches themselves can be simpler because they need not store persistent policy information about every device that might ever attach to them. In fact, the centralisation of policy management makes it far more scalable and significantly simpler to implement. The actual policy types stored in the directory are not subject to restrictions and can include such rules as VLAN membership, access rights, class of service, Quality of Service rules and auditing services or combinations of rules to define a specific policy.

Complete Managed Services Profile

Operational Command and Control		
Policy Administration	Decision Support Services	Infrastructure Services
Directory Services		
Protocol Control / Security Service / SLA/QoS Service / Configuration Policy	Metering / SLM/Auditing / Network Engineering / Asset/Inventory Management	Topology Services / IP Multicast / Dynamic Mapping / Address Management
Information Transport		

POLICY BASED MANAGEMENT

According to recent reports from IDC, there is a growing demand among enterprise customers for policy-based management solutions and directory services that better control network systems. As one observer put it:

"Network management is breaking free of the equipment markets. Stabilisation among network equipment vendors is opening the door to unprecedented levels of activity in network management."

ENTERPRISE NETWORKING

NETWORK MANAGEMENT

What this quote refers to is that the initial requirements of network management have been met by manufacturers putting enough intelligence into their hardware to meet the needs of MIS staff. With networks moving towards centre stage in most organisations there is now pressure from business managers that the infrastructure should provision services in line with business requirements. In other words, the company has policies and procedures on how employees perform their functions and as these functions are automated across the network, the network should be capable of enforcing company policies. This puts another layer of capability into the hardware and a bigger demand on the network management platform.

A simple company policy might be that only marketing staff have access to the Internet during normal working hours. Management platforms have to be able to accept this command and implement it. So an understanding of people and business function is required and the networking products have to understand what networking traffic this function will generate so it can be monitored and controlled.

The understanding of a person by function is the very purpose of Directory Enabled Networking (DEN). A database is maintained in the network operating system to log an individual on and record information about them. Examples are, DNS (Directory Network Services) from Novell and Active Directory from Microsoft. Information is collated from networking and computer resources so that the directory can record all attributes of the individual. When the individual tries to perform a network function like accessing the Web, the individual is checked against the profile for what resources should be made available and at what service level. From the profile stored, the management platform needs to be able to configure the underlying hardware to enable or restrict different traffic types and applications depending on this profile.

This is how policy-based networking works. It requires a high degree of intelligence and control in the hardware as well as some sophistication in the management software because policies are business not engineering requirements.

There are a couple of important standards that enable a multi-vendor solution to be configured and that is IEEE802.1p and IEEE802.1Q. The former enables priorities to be set by identifying traffic types and classes of service, while the latter enables VLANs to be configured and controlled. Products supporting them have the ability to recognise protocol types and to understand priority therefore traffic control across multiple vendors is viable given a management package that also understands IEEE802.1p/Q.

ENTERPRISE NETWORKING

NETWORK MANAGEMENT

The opportunity for network managers to select the most cost effective products to a given requirement is limited by their staff's ability to install and maintain it. Uniformity in network management means that similar types of products from different manufacturers have common configuration and diagnostic capability.

HIGH-PROFILE MIS FUNCTION

The increased visibility of the network within the enterprise has significantly changed the role of network management, forcing IS and corporate management to think differently about managing the IT infrastructure, including the use of advanced management platform products. Control from the desktop through the communications infrastructure to the application revision levels of all business functions is now expected.

Today almost all sites use hardware from multiple vendors. Not only is computer equipment multi-vendor, but so are the network products that provide the connectivity. Therefore, networks have become highly complex, multi-vendor, multi-protocol, multi-media, multi-technology global resources for many major organisations. This complexity of networking solutions has only been achieved by the conformance to the many standards available for communications. The way to manage these networks from one integrated central console without the need for an army of expensive experts must also lie in the hands of the standards committees.

So the object of the next section is to review how these are doing. Taking it from the

ENTERPRISE NETWORKING

NETWORK MANAGEMENT

top, let's understand how the International Standards Organisation (ISO) is tackling the problem. Those with some history in the networking field will have discovered that the ISO's ability to rectify a standard and get it accepted is as effective as 'swimming the butterfly in treacle'. ISO has contributed a conceptual model by defining not seven but five functional areas for management. These areas cover configuration management, fault management, performance management, account management and security management. In an effort to get out of the treacle, an industry pressure group was formed with over 100 contributory members, the Network Management Forum.

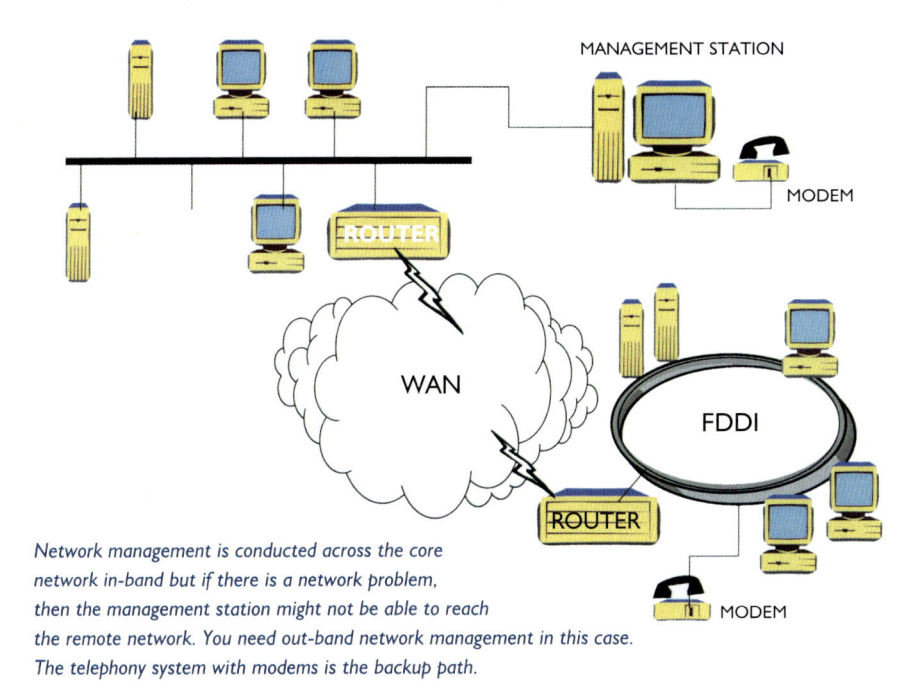

Network management is conducted across the core network in-band but if there is a network problem, then the management station might not be able to reach the remote network. You need out-band network management in this case. The telephony system with modems is the backup path.

The objective of this forum was to speed up the standards process to make ISO network management deliverable in our lifetimes. The first piece of this work is to enable specifications to be agreed for the implementation of CMIP (Common Management Information) Protocol. The mechanism for transferring information and control between the management station and the management agents, which monitors and controls its host device, is defined by CMIP. CMIS (Common Management Information Service) is the application layer programme that will do something meaningful with this exchanged management information and control. Many manufacturers set up development teams

ENTERPRISE NETWORKING

NETWORK MANAGEMENT

throughout the nineties to work on CMIS/CMIP and a major issue was the amount of memory and processing power required by networking hardware to process the code. Many products installed do not have the spare capacity for any other function than their primary networking function.

The reality today is that if anyone delivered it to a real network it wouldn't be able to manage anything. Standards bodies can lose sight of the fact that nothing in life is free. You may run a 3,000 node network but do the networking devices have the memory and processing power to run an ISO management agent for this new management platform, and can you afford the software upgrade for 3,000 devices? Ponder on how you are going to persuade your financial controller to sign the purchase order?

"You want to buy ISO management? What extra connectivity does it give the company? What application does it run to help the business?"

Your only defence is to say it will make your job easier and I doubt this would carry much weight.

So what is the state of the products you can buy today while waiting for CMIS/CMIP? The answer is Simple Network Management Protocol (SNMP) which came out of the TCP/IP development work. Manufacturers want to sell network management, and SNMP is here and not stuck in the treacle. All of the LAN/WAN vendors already supply SNMP so it is a practical solution to an existing problem and has been available for at least ten years. Only half of our theoretical 3,000 node network might to be upgraded to take SNMP-and it will use half the memory and half the processing power, so you probably won't need cardiac resuscitation for the financial controller!

All LAN/WAN vendors support SNMP for the exchange of management information between the management station and the managed agents. The manageable elements that are accessible within any devices are described in the Management Information Base (MIB), defined by the Internet Activities Board in a set of RFCs (Requests For Comment). This means all SNMP format devices can be managed to a defined level of a defined set of functions while leaving manufacturers with the flexibility to add differentiating extensions for their own products.

Changes are afoot though and we are about to get a major enhancement SNMP version 3. Network management is an application and, just as using word processing has progressed from being a complex, highly skilled task to an intuitive, Windows-based, mouse click with online help, so has network management advanced. An end user might

ENTERPRISE NETWORKING

NETWORK MANAGEMENT

ISO promised to be all things to all people but it is never the technical excellence that wins the decision, it's the practical cost effective fix. The computer industry is full of examples for 'the best technology' but they rarely achieve market dominance. ISO required networking hardware to run too much software and the existing equipment did not have the memory or spare processing capacity to run the ISO protocol stacks. This was especially the case with CMIP the ISO based Network Management protocol. SNMP was simple, less code by a factor of ten and gave a wide spread practical solution.

need help with initial setup and configuration but, with tools like auto discovery, topology mapping and fault isolation all bringing an intuitive, easy-to-use approach, things are easier for the hard pressed network manager.

Reporting tools like Iview from Opticom help by mining the huge amount of data known about the network and hence the business process, presenting the information in a fashion that line managers can understand and make decisions with. These tools bring the business and the network into line and both parties - MIS and business staff - can manage the resources in line with the company's goals.

If you feel like you want more in-depth technical information along with a more detailed overview of SNMP, the next section awaits.

section twelve

SNMP, RMON and SMON

Section 12: SNMP, RMON and SMON

Not a very exciting subject. You either have Management or you don't. However, there must be some people who have time on their hands, who want to know the details. So, for those few readers, here is a more detailed overview of Simple Network Management Protocol SNMP, the Remote Monitor standard RMON and Switch Monitor SMON.

ENTERPRISE NETWORKING

SNMP, RMON AND SMON

SIMPLE NETWORK MANAGEMENT PROTOCOL BACKGROUND

In 1986, the Internet Activities Board (IAB) which governs the strategic direction of the Internet, realised that the size and scope of the Internet was growing very rapidly because of the addition of low-cost LANs, PCs and workstations. So the IAB directed the Internet Engineering Task Force (IETF) to form various network management working groups that would start to develop a framework for managing the Internet, both for the short term and the long term.

The IETF in response to the number of connections to the Internet, started several working groups to solve the problem of multi vendor network management.

Three major groups eventually emerged as the opinion leaders in this area. The first group proposed the High Level Management System (HEMS), described in RFC's 1021-1024, and has the responsibility for managing the daily operations of the Internet backbone network. This group eventually withdrew its proposal in order to focus more resources on the other network management proposals. However, the HEMS group made a very important contribution to the process. It developed an extensive and well-defined Management Information Base (MIB) of network objects which could be monitored and controlled, and the HEMS MIB became the foundation for the Internet-standard MIB.

ENTERPRISE NETWORKING

SNMP, RMON AND SMON

The second group proposed the predecessor of SNMP, the simple gateway monitoring protocol (SGMP), described in RFC 1028. This group was responsible for managing university networks in New York state in the South Eastern conference. Its primary interest was to develop network management tools as quickly as possible and have the prototypes ready by 1988. Because of its success, the SGMP was used as the foundation for the SNMP proposal, which was specified by the same group. SNMP was then chosen by the IAB as the short-term solution for managing TCP/IP based components in the Internet and TCP/IP products with SNMP functionality were demonstrated at the Interop '89 conference in October 1989.

The third and final group proposed an OSI approach to network management based upon the ISO Common Management Information Services /Common Management Information Protocol (CMIS/CMIP). The CMIS/CMIP approach has been chosen by the IAB as the long-term solution for managing the Internet. Though no implementations of CMIS/CMIP have emerged yet, a path has been set by RFC 1095. This is the common management information services and protocol over TCP/IP (CMOT) and provided a feasible framework for initial testing and further development.

It has been decided by the IAB that both SNMP and CMOT work with the same Internet standard, MIB, therefore making the transition between the two approaches more manageable.

SNMP ARCHITECTURE

SNMP is designed with three primary goals in mind:

- Minimise the complexity of the management functions
- The protocol should be sufficiently extensible
- The architecture should be as independent as possible from any constraints imposed by any network device.

SNMP follows a very simple model. A network consists of network management stations and network elements. Network management stations execute applications which monitor and control network elements. Network elements are devices such as hosts, routers, switches and terminal servers, which have management agents that perform

ENTERPRISE NETWORKING

SNMP, RMON AND SMON

management functions on behalf of the management stations. SNMP is used to communicate information between management stations and management agents.

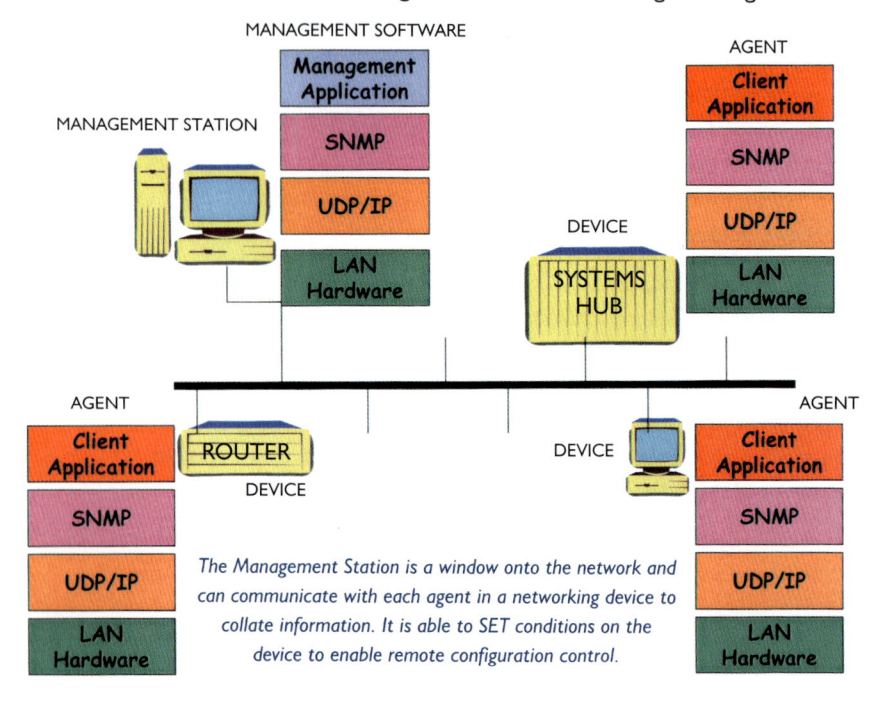

The Management Station is a window onto the network and can communicate with each agent in a networking device to collate information. It is able to SET conditions on the device to enable remote configuration control.

SNMP's architecture provides a framework with respect to the following areas:

Scope of management information, representation of management information, operations supported on management information, form and meaning of protocol exchanges, definition of administrative relationships and the form and meaning of references to managed objects.

The scope of the information communicated by SNMP between management entities will be object types as defined in either the Internet-standard MIB, or defined elsewhere according to the Internet-standard structure of management information (SMI). The MIB application object types currently supported are the network address, physical address, counter, gauge, time ticks, opaque, generic types such as tables, table entries and table indices are also supported as aggregate objects.

ENTERPRISE NETWORKING

SNMP, RMON AND SMON

SNMP's architecture uses a subset of the Abstract Syntax Notation One (ASN.1) data representation language. ASN.1 is also used by the SMI and the MIB. SNMP supports access to non-aggregate object types, definite-length encoding, and non-constructor encoding. The ASN.1 language is flexible enough so that network objects can be added to the MIB as needed. ASN.1 was created within the ISO framework and was therefore chosen for the SNMP, SMI and MIB in order to ease the eventual migration to the CMIS/CMIP. For the sake of simplicity, a management station may request that a network element management agent either retrieve (GET) or alter (SET) management-related variables in the network element. This limitation to GET and SET means that the management agent has only to perform two functions. Another constraint is that it inhibits the introduction of application-specific commands into the architecture. For example, instead of specifying a re-boot command, this action might be accomplished by setting a parameter indicating the number of seconds until the system re-boots. A managed device may also notify the central management station of an event by issuing a TRAP to the management station.

Minimising the complexity of the management agent, the exchange of SNMP messages requires only an unreliable datagram service such as UDP or TPO and every message can be entirely and independently represented by a single datagram.

The Internet's influence on SNMP's architecture becomes very clear in the area of administrative relationships. With a large set of autonomous networks sharing critical resources within the Internet, the basic issue becomes who controls what resource on the Internet.

SNMP application entities are management stations and network elements which communicate with one another. An SNMP community is the pairing of an SNMP agent with an arbitrary set of application entities. A SNMP MIB view is a subset of objects in the MIB that pertains to some network element. An element of the set (read-only, write-only) is called an SNMP Access Mode. The pairing of the access mode and the MIB view is called SNMP Community Profile.

This community profile is used by the management agent at a particular network element to either execute or reject an operation on a variable in that network element's MIB view. The pairing of a community and the community profile is called SNMP access policy. This represents the access privileges associated with a MIB view that a management agent can grant to other members of that community. This essentially allows the definition of various communities of interest. All administrative relationships are

ENTERPRISE NETWORKING

SNMP, RMON AND SMON

architecturally defined by these access policies.

The SNMP architecture also allows proxy access policies and proxy agents. All this means is that it provides a mechanism for SNMP agents to manage attached devices that are not TCP/IP network elements such as modems, multiplexers and even redundant power supplies.

IDENTIFICATION OF OBJECT INSTANCES

SNMP deals with the small set of objects identified and defined in extensive detail in RFC 1066, 'Management Information Base for Network Management of TCP/IP based Internetworks'. It identifies six major object instances from the MIB that it needs to monitor and control.

These object instances are:

- Subnetwork Interfaces
- Address Translation Mappings
- IP Addresses
- IP Routes
- TCP Connections
- Exterior Gateway Protocol (EGP) Neighbours.

SNMP would be interested in the type of sub-network - for example, Ethernet, Token Ring or X 25-that is attached to a particular interface port. The protocol would also want to find the physical address of a network element as identified by its IP address, and an interface port in an address translation table, such as an address resolution protocol cache. Given an IP address, the SNMP can alter or retrieve the IP attributes of the network element associated with that address. The SNMP also needs to monitor to control the attributes of an IP route destination, identified by an IP address, such as the address of the next hop.

The state and attributes of TCP connections are important to monitor and control. The SNMP can access this information by identifying the [local address, local port][remote

ENTERPRISE NETWORKING

SNMP, RMON AND SMON

address, remote port] pairs which represent the connection.

The last major object instance is EGP Neighbours. SNMP will inquire about the state of a network element's neighbour by using the IP address of the network elements. This will be useful in managing logical networks or routers.

SNMP VERSION 3

The IETF Network Management Area has been working to resolve a number of deficiencies of SNMP Version1 protocol. The new specification should be ratified this year and product available in 2001. These changes are to accommodate support for the new bigger and more complex networks being deployed today. Areas improved are the basic management feature set, scalability features allow for better management of very large networks, security and access control for remote configuration and security of the management platform preventing unauthorised personal disrupting the network.

RMON - AN SNMP MANAGEMENT EXTENSION

Network managers would probably assume that they are using maybe one or two protocols on their network. When a major problem occurs and swapping hardware does not fix the problem, the network manager resorts to a protocol analyser. These products are portable tape recorders which can be moved to network trouble spots in order to record network traffic, displaying it in a variety of pie charts and histograms. Such network probes are tools to help fix problems thown up by communications software. As today's networking is based mainly on intelligent hubs, it is reasonable to expect these hubs to be able to record and display network traffic information. This is precisely what happened with the standards bodies approving the RMON (Remote Monitor) specification.

RMON defines the standard network monitoring functions and interfaces for communications between SNMP-based network management platforms, the remote monitors such as probes and agents which form part of the intelligence of networking products. The way RMON works is to view all packets on the network and then either save, count or trap them into specific categories. RMON has nine functional groups, each with a specific function and network managers should be able to achieve an objective by using one or more of each of the nine.

ENTERPRISE NETWORKING

SNMP, RMON AND SMON

THE NINE GROUPS OF RMON

The Nine Groups of RMON

1. **Statistics:** maintains low level utilisation and error statistics such as the number of packets sent, packet sizes, broadcasts, multicasts, network errors and collisions.

2. **History:** provides user definable trend analysis based on information in the statistics group. It creates a set of counters for a specific time interval for each data from which trend information can be obtained.

3. **Alarms:** allows a user to configure an alarm for any managed object. A sampling interval and alarm threshold can be set for any counter or integer recorded by the RMON agent.

4. **Events:** logs three types of events: rising threshold, falling threshold, and packet match. This group can generate traps for each event.

5. **Host:** a table of statistics based on MAC addresses. There are counters for broadcast packets, multicast packets, error packets, and a number of bytes which includes data for both transmitted and received data for each host.

6. **Top N Hosts:** contains sorted host statistics. It can be configured to keep a table of activity for the ten busiest nodes communicating to each host. Rather than the management station receiving lots of data from the management module, the management module processes the data and sends a list of only the busiest nodes across the network to the management station. This keeps traffic low and performance high.

7. **Packet Capture:** allows the operator to define buffers for packet capture, change buffer sizes, and specify conditions for starting and stopping packet capture.

8. **Traffic Matrix:** shows error and utilisation in matrix form based on address pairs, so the operator can retrieve information for any pair of network addresses. It allows the management station to view the network traffic conversations; who is talking to whom and how often?

9. **Filter:** includes a buffer for incoming packets as well as any number of user definable filters. Filters can be set to look at a special address, group of addresses, a certain protocol, or any combination desired.

It should be noted that RMON, as defined in FRC 1757, was specified to work on a single

ENTERPRISE NETWORKING

SNMP, RMON AND SMON

networking segment. So in router-based networks, RMON cannot view the whole network as the objective is to build separate subnets or segments. RMON I supports up to 10 groups and RMON II, as defined in RFC 2021, is an extension to RMON I and includes the control and manipulation of remote probes by the network management protocol without human intervention. It also extends the monitoring capabilities which includes the monitoring of traffic flow. Monitoring is made harder by switching because each switched port becomes an individual network.

Monitoring a switched network demands a new specification, moving from RMON to Switch MONitor (SMON). The ATM forum has taken this on board for switched ATM networks by specifying AMON.

SWITCH MONITOR

The Internet Engineering Task Force's (IETF) time-tested RMON and RMON II standards monitor single network segments but RMON was developed for shared media networks and is not appropriate for current implementations. The move to a switched infrastructure where each port becomes a separate network requires a new monitoring application. The SMON standard as defined in RFC 2613 extends RMON to switched networks.

SMON provides performance information on virtual LANs, priority levels, quality of service (QoS), Differentiated Services flows or layer 3 switching. The SMON module can monitor all traffic moving through the switch, not just the port being copied as is the case with RMON. The SMON application is independent from the switch and can monitor the classification of packets in the virtual LANs and priority level setting without hindering performance. The SMON MIB enhances RMON to enable the definition of physical entities and logical entities such as VLANs as valid RMON data sources. The SMON MIB allows the monitoring of utilisation for different priority levels according to the IEEE802.1D tags. Although it dramatically extends the RMON standard, SMON deals exclusively with monitoring Layer 2. Managers still need to monitor switched networks at Layer 3 and higher. SMON enables network managers to monitor from the top down large campus networks consisting of hundreds of switches and thousands of LAN segments. This enterprise SMON capability aggregates individual switch statistics into a consolidated view of switch statistics for the entire enterprise network.

ENTERPRISE NETWORKING

SNMP, RMON AND SMON

TERMS

Agents: Entities that perform the network management functions requested by the network management Station.

MIB: The Management Information Base (RFC 1066) defines variables needed by the SNMP to monitor and control various components in a network.

Network Management Elements: Entities that run management applications that monitor and control network elements.

Network Elements: Devices such as hosts, gateways and terminal servers that have management agents.

RMON: Defines standard network monitoring functions and interfaces for communications between SNMP-based management stations and remote monitors or probes.

RMON II: Extends the capabilities of RMON.

SNMP: Simple Network Management Protocol (RFC 1098) used to communicate management information between network management stations and agents in network elements.

SNMP 3 updates SNMP to accommodate current trends in networking.

section thirteen

Network Management based on Artificial Intelligence

Section 13: Network management with Artificial Intelligence

There is a major move to introduce Artificial Intelligence (AI) into managing a network. This section discusses the options of rules-based AI against inductive modelling-based AI.

ENTERPRISE NETWORKING

NETWORK MANAGEMENT BASED ON ARTIFICIAL INTELLIGENCE

Over the last decade, network management products have been developed as a means to configure product attributes and perform remote diagnostics from a central location. This involved developing an architecture for network management that is still valid today. In the network device a software module is required to accept commands from the network management platform to control and configure the device. The same piece of software has been extended to store information about the devices itself. This software is known as a network management agent. When each device contains an agent, it means network management time is not related to the size of a network. In other words, as networks get bigger and more complex, the devices that build the network contain their own management, increasing proportionately the management compatibility.

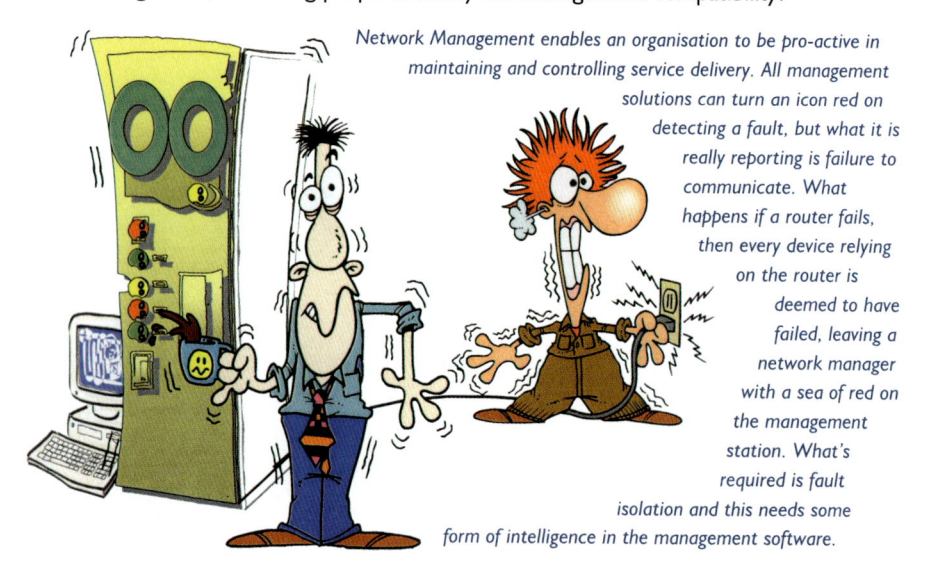

Network Management enables an organisation to be pro-active in maintaining and controlling service delivery. All management solutions can turn an icon red on detecting a fault, but what it is really reporting is failure to communicate. What happens if a router fails, then every device relying on the router is deemed to have failed, leaving a network manager with a sea of red on the management station. What's required is fault isolation and this needs some form of intelligence in the management software.

NETWORK MANAGEMENT ARCHITECTURE.

Distributed management agents are accessed from a central management station which provides the window onto the network, interrogating network devices when instructed to do so, or in a sequential polling scheme looking for errors and certain specified network events. Communicating with distributed agents requires a protocol that can both traverse the whole network and, in the case of a network malfunction, still communicate. Standard, error-correcting communications protocols which are resilient are inappropriate. The network management stations themselves provide the ability to

ENTERPRISE NETWORKING

NETWORK MANAGEMENT BASED ON ARTIFICIAL INTELLIGENCE

configure the network device, enabling and disabling ports, setting speeds, identifying control characters for pre-defined actions and so on. The management stations also provide a window to view statistics such as send and receive packet counts, error counts and even a breakdown of specific errors. The more advanced management stations provide alerts when specific network errors are encountered and the selection and filtering of certain error conditions enable a priority system to be developed.

With the advent of graphical capabilities, vendors began to add a graphical layer on top of the remote console facilities in order to give the user a picture in which the various devices could be recognised and their status's understood at a glance. Standards such as SNMP and CMIP have allowed these systems to embrace more than a single vendor's equipment, providing the possibility of integrated network management. Many vendors have rallied around this banner and have produced a generation of multi-vendor device management systems. Some have even opened some of their internal interfaces to provide application interfaces or APIs. These APIs allow MIS staff to write their own applications.

ARCHITECTURE WITH SMNP AGENT OR CMIS AGENT

Network management architecture is, therefore, clearly defined as the management station, the communications protocol and the device-specific management agent. The standards map onto this SNMP or CMIS for the management station, UDP or CMIP for the communications and a SNMP or CMIS agent. These systems however, are still based on the original network management paradigm, which is remote monitoring of device information.

The current generation of management systems places a tremendous burden on the network administrator. First, he must be a networking expert in order to understand the implications of a particular attribute in a management information base of a device.

Second, he must understand the topology of each section of the network in order to understand what may have caused the change. Third, he must sift through reams of information and false alarms in order to get to the root cause of a problem. Fourth, he must keep track of endless administrative details in order to utilise effectively the large human and capital resources for which he is given responsibility. In short, he must not only be an expert in networking technology, but have had a substantial tenure with the particular organisation in order to understand the current configuration and procedures,

ENTERPRISE NETWORKING

NETWORK MANAGEMENT BASED ON ARTIFICIAL INTELLIGENCE

let alone plan for future growth. All this while being bombarded by reams of management information and many unhappy users!

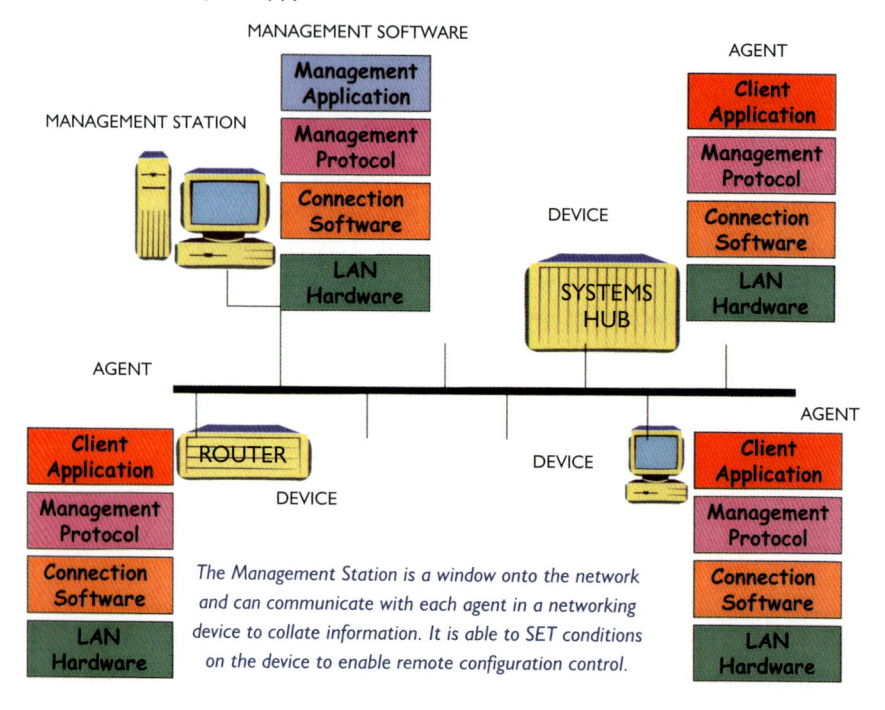

The Management Station is a window onto the network and can communicate with each agent in a networking device to collate information. It is able to SET conditions on the device to enable remote configuration control.

This creates problems of shortage of resources - people and time - and of reliability. Networking technology is complex and diverse, moves fast and is always changing. As a result, expertise in this area can only be built over time so there are relatively few experts, while those that there are have long since been absorbed in this quickly growing industry and can command a hefty salary.

Time is the second problem. Networks provide a competitive advantage in the sharing and processing of information. They must be deployed quickly in order to compete, which brings us to the third problem, reliability, which encompasses up-time, security and performance. As a business uses its network so it comes to depend on it. In some cases a network outage can cost a company millions of dollars, all of which rests on the head of the elusive networking expert.

The solution to these problems is not to replace or eliminate these experts. They will become increasingly important to the success of the enterprise. The solution is to

ENTERPRISE NETWORKING

NETWORK MANAGEMENT BASED ON ARTIFICIAL INTELLIGENCE

unburden these experts from the mundane tasks and details so they can have the time and energy to focus on the critical tasks of planning, deployment and solving the thorniest technical problems. This can be accomplished through a new generation of management systems that can synthesise the knowledge of the networking experts such as that most common problems can be detected, isolated, and repaired either automatically or with the involvement of less skilled personnel.

Artificial Intelligence (AI) based network management systems are the obvious solutions to unburden the expert. Two fundamental AI techniques, expert systems and inductive modelling, could be employed to solve the problem.

The expert systems approach is to create a set of rules that can be applied to a situation.

The problem with networks is that they never stand still. New technology is continually being added. Users constantly want faster services so the design is tweaked every time a new application is added. Herein lies the fundamental flaw with a rules-based management system. It would need an engineer to amend the rules in step with the ever changing environment. Networks always get bigger, therefore the rules-based system would have to scale in line with changes. This is a non-trivial task.

The action is to check the events against the list of rules and make decisions accordingly. The problem with this approach is that no two networks are the same either in topology or the protocols and applications running across them, so to make this viable, an AI expert system would have to be configurable by the user to define the system.

Could you come up with five rules that would apply to your network in all given circumstances? If you cannot think of five, how are you going to think of the hundreds you would need for all eventualities?

ENTERPRISE NETWORKING

NETWORK MANAGEMENT BASED ON ARTIFICIAL INTELLIGENCE

Even if you could magically create a set of rules, how would it be maintained, because each new device and application interaction would require new rules and one crossed rule could upset all the previous rules. Other considerations are the practical implications of running the software. As you add devices you will add new rules, therefore the ability to check all conditions, to make a decision, is getting slower as the network get bigger.

The alternative solution for AI is to use inductive modelling. Firstly, we have to break the task into many small pieces. Each piece of the system will be modelled individually because the complexity at any one point is dramatically lower. Each piece of the system is represented by data structures and a code that mimics the function of that element. Each of the elements now interact with the other elements passing data and signals. These individual elements fit together to form the 'landscape' of the entire collection of models and the system they represent.

The data elements modelling individual devices such as cables, connectors, bridges and routers require a database technology specifically designed to manipulate data as a group and that is object-oriented. Object-oriented systems allow programmes to deal with another order of magnitude of data organisation and programme complexity than

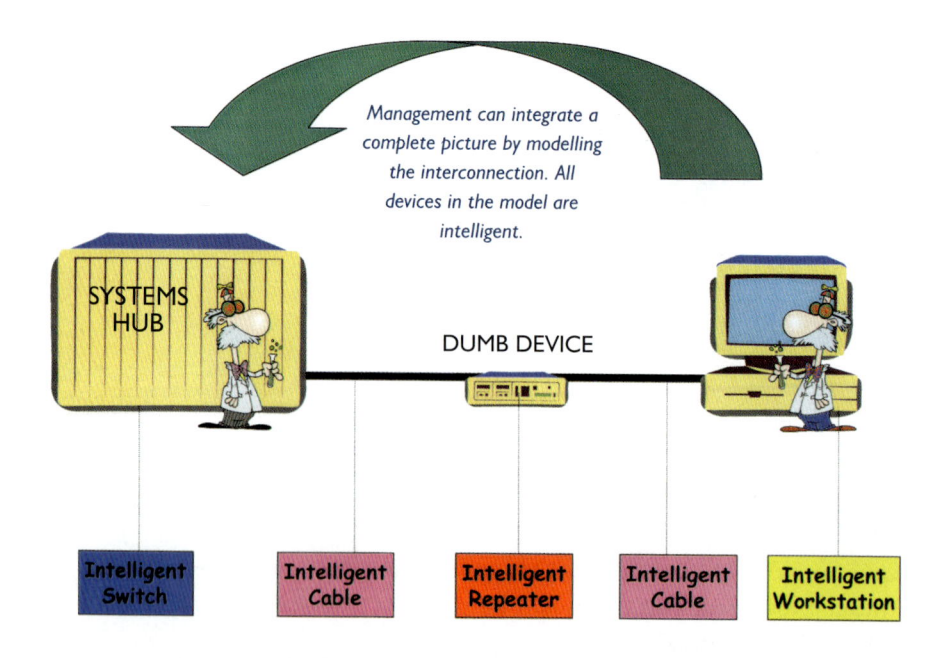

Management can integrate a complete picture by modelling the interconnection. All devices in the model are intelligent.

SYSTEMS HUB

DUMB DEVICE

| Intelligent Switch | Intelligent Cable | Intelligent Repeater | Intelligent Cable | Intelligent Workstation |

ENTERPRISE NETWORKING

NETWORK MANAGEMENT BASED ON ARTIFICIAL INTELLIGENCE

traditional software architectures. Rather than separating the code and the data portions of a program, the information and operations are combined together into software objects. This technique reinforces the use of well-defined interfaces between sections of a programme. It is, in fact, much like a modelling system where each component is individually represented and has its own data base and capable of independent actions.

The next important feature lies in a process known as derivation. Derivation allows for the creation of new objects on the basis of existing objects.

Once we have developed our objects representing the elements of the network we have to establish a way of using them to perform the network management task for us. Software programs have, until now, been task-driven. A certain task is to be completed and we are to use procedures and data to accomplish the task. The brain, on the other hand, is very much reaction-driven. Input from our senses drives much of our perception and thought processes. We too have tasks and goals to accomplish but these are as a result of information previously gathered; for example, the room has gone dark, implying that someone turned out the lights. This idea can be incorporated into the modelling system by changing the fundamental operational principles of the programme. Rather than being results-driven, the programme can be set to respond to changes. The direction of the change, magnitude and rate can all produce inferences which can be set up to trigger on specific changes in the data. The difference is subtle but far-reaching. Programmes have always had functions to manipulate data, now data manipulation can trigger functions. This means we can have huge sets of inferences attached to various pieces of data and an inference will fire only when the data attached is caused to change.

Therefore, instead of having a myriad of rules to compare events against as in an expert system, inductive modelling allows an event to create an inference that reacts with models of the networking elements, creating other inferences with the new state of the network. Therefore, as long as the models exist for the different elements that make up the network, a network management station does not have to know all the possible events and all the possible conclusions from those events but responds by inferences to each new set of conditions. The inferences create their own path between objects they are associated with. Therefore we have a dynamic and interactive system to manage a dynamic and interactive system.

This simple description understates the complexity and the effort required to produce such a system, however it gives a overview of an inductive modelling system. The processing effort is not proportional to network size, so the largest, most complex

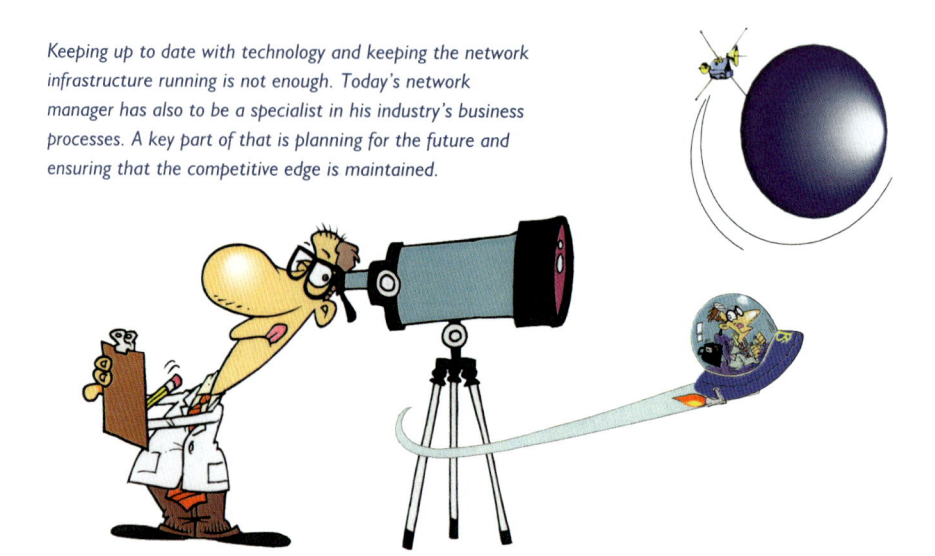

ENTERPRISE NETWORKING

NETWORK MANAGEMENT BASED ON ARTIFICIAL INTELLIGENCE

Keeping up to date with technology and keeping the network infrastructure running is not enough. Today's network manager has also to be a specialist in his industry's business processes. A key part of that is planning for the future and ensuring that the competitive edge is maintained.

networks can be managed on an affordable platform. To make the solution complete the inductive modelling technique needs to be integrated with a user-friendly front end, enabling inexpert users to understand the information and perform any activity the station recommends.

Aprisma, a software company owned by Enterasys Networks, markets an inductive modelling platform called Spectrum. It uses the technology to isolate faults in massive networks, saving engineering resource and reducing drastically the MTTR (Mean Time To Repair). It currently provides the management platforms for an installation in Germany which manages the delivery of telephony services to nine million locations. This is 1,200 integrated management platforms scaling to probably the largest management platform in the world today.

The modelling pre-processes all of the raw data into useful information. There is data available in these models that is simply unobtainable from the raw system such as histories, rates, standard deviations, states of devices and more, which are all calculated and maintained as part of the model. Now, when you lay graphics on top of your models the result is a complete, detailed animation system able not only to display but also control virtually every aspect of the system. The result is a display which has highly detailed graphics capable of showing connections, data flows, critical paths, dynamic threshold of traffic, failures, and any other aspect of real-time network information.

ENTERPRISE NETWORKING

NETWORK MANAGEMENT BASED ON ARTIFICIAL INTELLIGENCE

Visualisation and inductive modelling has important ramifications for design of complex systems. Once real systems have been effectively modelled, the building blocks can be reused to create and test totally new systems. Today, the technology is coming together to enable a network management system to be developed which actually manages a network the way a traditionally trained engineer would. Therefore, an organisation gains an expert without the risks associated with investing all the skills and knowledge into one or a group of individuals who are at risk at leaving for a higher paid job at a competitor.

section fourteen

Risk Management

Panel of Experts

Section 14: Risk Management

Networks today are built on technology that has many thousands of hours between failures. The more that is pushed into silicon the better the MTBF figures are. But hardware fails, so manufacturers have devised features to overcome the inevitable link failure. Recently the standards committee has defined a minimum set of standards that provides some degree of failsafe. It is now possible to build networks with 100% service delivery guaranteed.

ENTERPRISE NETWORKING

RISK MANAGEMENT

INTRODUCTION

Your choice of networking technology has less impact than the cabling infrastructure, which is the most significant investment an organisation makes. Companies new to networking are usually shocked to discover that the LAN technology rarely accounts for more that 30% of the costs. Instead, the design, procurement, project management and installation of the cabling infrastructure will account for the lion's share of the project's budget. Once this major investment is undertaken, corporate purchasers historically consider the cable infrastructure as a 10-15 year investment. This makes the cabling decision critical in any long-term technology planning process. The decision is not an easy one. Can you live for 10 years on copper to the desk, or where do you place fibre, and what type of fibre? Technologies can change, indigenous host suppliers can be usurped by new competitive start-ups, but all modifications to the IT solution must live with the cable infrastructure.

Companies on the whole, are in business to make money and grow to make more money. Any IT solution is therefore destined to grow in parallel. It is vital in any organisation investing in information technology, that it should have a network strategy and this strategy should account for the risk network failure would have on the business. The technology that has evolved to make best use of structured cabling schemes is the modular hub. A modular hub is a network concentrator providing connectivity for 8-500 devices from a central location which makes this type of product ideal for star wired systems. Modular hubs have made massive strides in connectivity and performance today they are the platforms that house the layer 3 and layer 4 switches.

Hardware can fail. The more functions that can be embedded within the silicon, the greater the MTBF (Mean Time Between Failures). Today it is possible to build communications infrastructures with 100% availability of service. This means that a unit can fail and the system can re-route to re-establish the service without the user being affected. These features in communications products are nearly all ratified as standards by the IEEE. The only issue is the value of that redundancy to the business.

ENTERPRISE NETWORKING

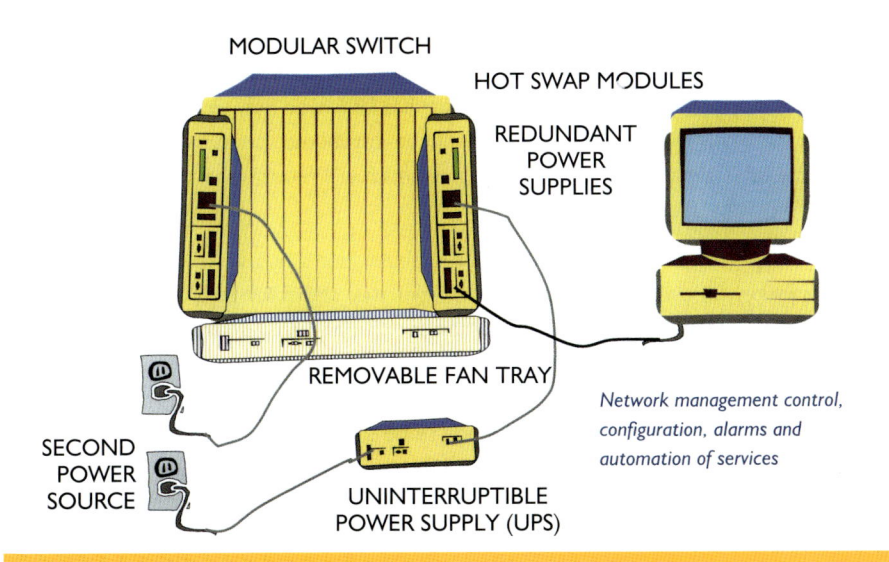

RISK MANAGEMENT

MODULAR HUB/SWITCH RESILIENT FEATURES

These types of products were initially designed to take advantage of the structured cabling schemes. But they entered the market place ten years after the first commercial LANs were installed. Therefore these hubs had to support existing as well as future technologies. Because they support the cabling scheme, they were intended to have the same 10-15 year capabilities, not the shorter replacement cycle of processor technology.

This causes significant differentiation of product in the market place. Some manufacturers periodically completely replace their hub with a new design with new capabilities. Other manufacturers continually provide backplane upgrades which entail taking down the network, disassembling the hub and reassembling it with a new backplane module. One manufacturer had seven backplane upgrades over a span of three years, which is a record in this industry. The best implementation strategy is to provide a completely passive backplane design, which has bandwidth capacity at least a factor of ten above the current full capacity of the available network interface modules. The interface modules must be the mechanism that enables new features, new technology and new performance to be added to the hub so, as you change or grow the network, you can insert the desired technology on a network interface module. The hub being totally passive can be considered an integral part of the cable plant. These features form the foundation of today's modular switching technologies.

ENTERPRISE NETWORKING

RISK MANAGEMENT

To protect the network against failure we must consider the resilience features that are supported by modular hubs, starting with the power supply. There's a need to support load-sharing power supplies and uninterruptible power supplies which maintain power after failure, while an orderly shutdown is undertaken to prevent corruption of any data. Redundant load sharing power supplies have the ability to withstand a power unit failure without affecting the network because a spare has automatically taken over.

The hub should have the ability to monitor the environment including the temperature and humidity, as well as allowing fans and filters to be swapped while the system is live. Hardware does fail therefore the repair of one segment should not impinge on the entire network. Therefore the ability to 'hot swap' modules and reload configurations without interrupting the network is mandatory for risk management.

Intelligent hubs and switches are those devices that can be monitored and configured from a management station. This implies that there is a processor and memory with a monitoring application actually running in the hub. In terms of management it is not enough just to be able to monitor the hub and modules but each port must be monitored and configurable. There should be a degree of automation available to ensure problems are isolated from the remainder of the network because automated responses are more efficient than providing information for human intervention and interpretation before any action is taken.

Distributed management and distributed network functions will add dramatically to the resilience of any configuration. This means that the network interface modules themselves carry management instead of a single management module, which could become a single point of failure. The use of switching has improved networking performance a thousand-fold but the function should be distributed across the network interface modules and not a central switching engine which will remove the risk inherent in such a single point of failure.

One of today's major concerns is the bandwidth available within a hub/switch. Manufacturers jockey for prominence with their exaggerated claims for their internal back-plane speeds, quoting figures from 10,000Mbit/sec to 100,000Mbit/sec. But you have to be careful whether these are meaningful figures. A hub supporting 100 users each capable of 10Mbit/sec of data throughput would instinctively need a 1,000Mbit/sec hub. This could not be further from the truth. Common sense should tell you that these 100 users do not talk to the hub but to a server and each other. So if they could, 50 devices would talk to the other 50 that would be 500Mbit/sec. In reality the bandwidth used by

ENTERPRISE NETWORKING

RISK MANAGEMENT

50 connections depends on the types of application they are using. Performance problems usually show themselves first thing in the morning, just after lunch and going home time because office workers collectively access network servers at these times to load their applications from the office server.

A final trivial point to consider is where the cables plug into the hub, the front or the back. If cables plug in the back and the unit is mounted into 19in. racking which itself is mounted against a wall, how do you change a connection or add a new adapter. The hub is part of the cable plant, which is the foundation of the network. Any networking activity that takes time and is complex is against the very reason you have selected a hub solution.

MINIMISING RISK

Many organisations have been through downsizing exercises, where an organisation moves away from host-centric business applications to a PC server-based system. This would be fine if a company could start from scratch. The reality is that most large corporates have 15-20 years of business data stored on a mainframe so the real downsizing exercise is to integrate this mainframe-based storage on to the PC-based business systems. Key to this is networking. Organisations who make the change to a networked information system expect the same levels of performance and security the mainframe systems provide. Networks are designed to give everyone access to everything which is alien to host-centric systems. Like all good businesses that survive you have to manage the risk. In this distributed environment of networking, the risks are the integration and reliability of the communications paths and the security of the data that traverses these paths.

Networking with the correct modular hub technology can still suffers equipment failure. However, redundancy is available to minimise this risk. This means accepting that things will go wrong and monitor for the events. On detecting an event, the system must allow the automation of an immediate recovery irrespective of the particular component that has failed. Many of the management features built into today's networking products free will perform the required functions. However, it is up to the network administrator to enable the features and it is up to the financial controller to sanction risk management. Cable redundancy is all well and good as a free feature but only if you have installed the spare cable properly.

ENTERPRISE NETWORKING

RISK MANAGEMENT

This means that risk management is not an afterthought but a key part of an overall networking strategy. The areas to be considered are environmental redundancy, hardware redundancy and cable redundancy. Should the network span other geographically remote sites then wide area communications path redundancy is a further consideration.

Environmental redundancy means protecting network resources. Here the hub-based architecture - specifically intelligent hubs and switches - can provide features that once implemented can reduce the risk of failure dramatically. These features start with the monitoring of power supplies, temperature of the unit and humidity. By using redundant power supplies and fans, any alarm indicating a failure of these parameters enables a redundant unit to take over without taking the network down. A further enhancement would be to use load-sharing power supplies. These balance the load so they provide both redundancy and better reliability because the components are more lightly stressed. You can also provide separate power feeds for greater protection, extending these features by using a Uninterruptible Power Supply (UPS). These units provide power after the mains supply has failed allowing an orderly shut down without data loss.

Hardware and cable redundancy are the next elements to be considered in our risk management strategy. The idea is to smoothly replace network hardware without disrupting the rest of the system. This is where cable redundancy comes in. You need dual hardware connected in parallel with spare cable so that if there is a cable failure or hardware failure the standby connection can be used. Many of today's intelligent hubs can monitor these primary connections and switch over to the secondary connection automatically on a range of preset failure conditions. FDDI had a feature known as dual homing. The dual connection normally used to connect to the dual backbone ring, which is the main feature of FDDI, is used to connect to two different locations. If a dual connection is placed in a server then the server can be connected to two different hubs. This gives the server complete connection redundancy in both hardware and cabling.

Instead of using one connection, several connections can be made. Known as a trunk, today's technology can use all links in a trunk, load balancing across all connections and, if a failure occurs, automatic re-routing of traffic occurs.

Hardware and cable redundancy are interdependent so, while planning and budgeting for one feature, the second feature must be included. These network infrastructure features are mirrored by features provided by the network operating system software supplier. Today file servers can be configured from mirrored disks right up to fully fault tolerant,

ENTERPRISE NETWORKING

RISK MANAGEMENT

totally mirrored systems.

Network to network redundancy used to be provided by bridges and routers but, today, these features are embedded into silicon, switches performing the same tasks but at much higher speeds. Bridges provide the ability to link networks together at the media access level. Redundant connections can be supported provided the bridges support the IEEE802.1d spanning tree algorithm. This puts the bridges that are providing the backup connections into 'hot standby'. The algorithm enables the insertion of the backup path transparent to the users. a disadvantage is that bridges not in the primary path are not being used unless there is a failure. Routers on the other hand are extremely sophisticated devices and have a full understanding of the network topology. This enables them to route connections around problem links. They can be configured to select the cheapest route or the fastest or the shortest path. To further add to router redundancy VRRP (Virtual Router Redundancy Protocol) has been specified. This allows connections not to a fixed router but to a virtual router and the virtual router then picks the most appropriate router to accomplish the task. Therefore a group of routers can look like one logical router and this will mask any router failing as the load will be passed to the next best fit.

Over the past 20 years the networking industry has been striving to offer five nines availability that is 99.999% uptime. Today, it is possible to build networks that can deliver 100% availability of service. Hardware will fail but enough redundancy has been standardised to provide for fail safe configurations and the service delivery can be guaranteed.

Core components to deliver the full risk management are:

Equipment hardware resiliency features

- Distributed switching
- Power resilience
- Cable redundancy
- IEEE standard communications features for layer 2/3

ENTERPRISE NETWORKING

RISK MANAGEMENT

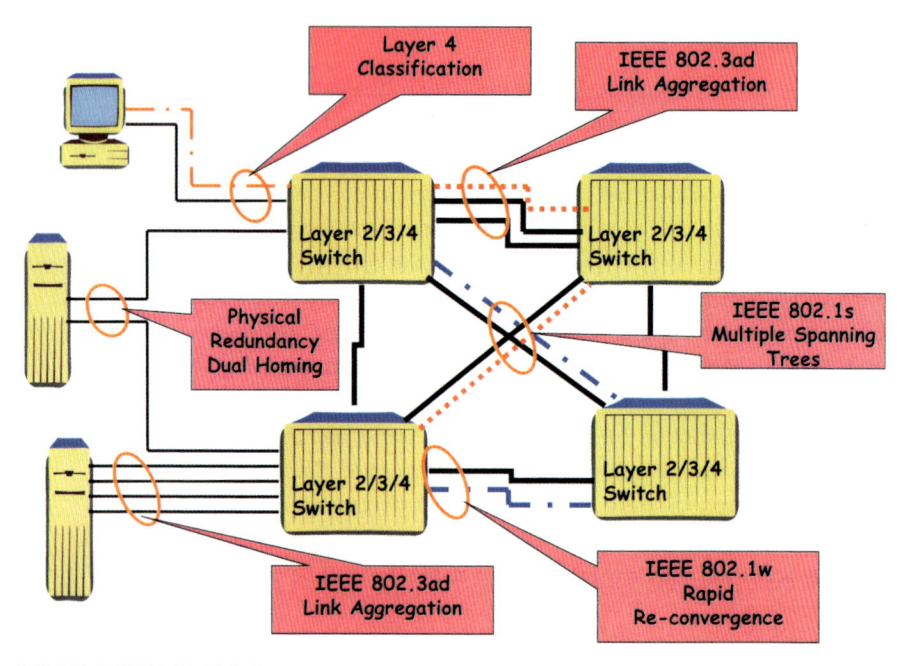

LAYER 2 STANDARDS

802.3ad: (Trunk) Link Aggregation for resilient and high capacity connectivity for switch to switch and switch to server connectivity.

802.1d: Spanning Tree for bridges.

802.1s: Multiple Spanning Tree – ability to support per VLAN spanning tree, to increase efficiency of traffic distribution and to allow for multiple data paths within a single infrastructure.

802.1w: Rapid Re-convergence the automatic re-routing of data paths around link or component failure.

LAYER 3 STANDARDS

Multi-path OSPF: enables the selection of multiple data paths across a layer 3 infrastructure.

OSPF: Rapid Re-convergence layer 3 re-routing of data paths upon failure

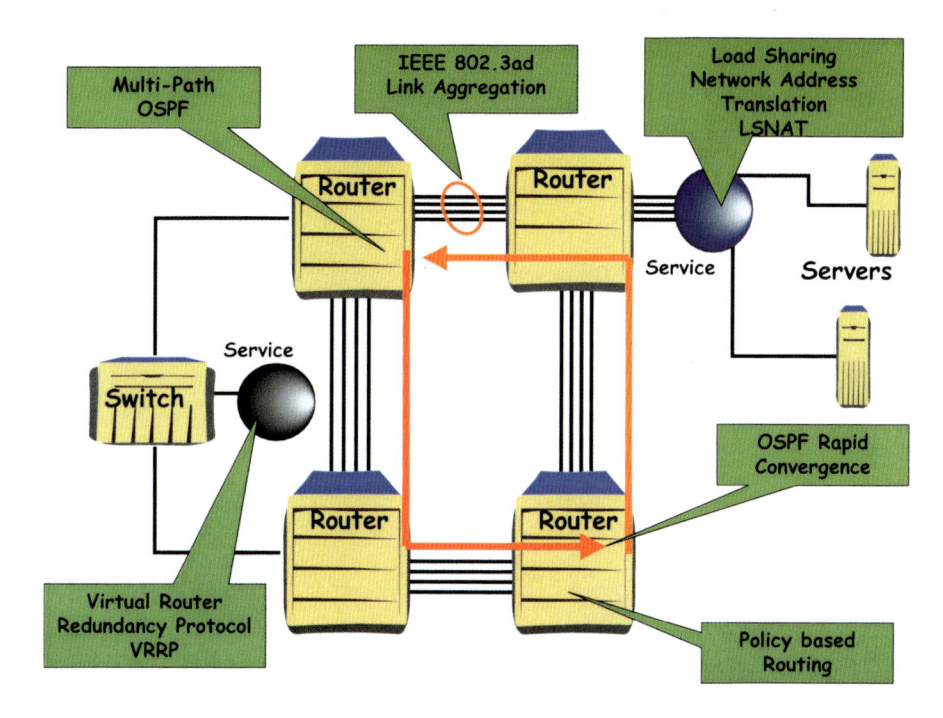

ENTERPRISE NETWORKING

RISK MANAGEMENT

Diagram showing a redundant network topology with callouts:
- Multi-Path OSPF
- IEEE 802.3ad Link Aggregation
- Load Sharing Network Address Translation LSNAT
- OSPF Rapid Convergence
- Policy based Routing
- Virtual Router Redundancy Protocol VRRP

Components: four Routers interconnected, a Switch, Service nodes, and Servers.

VRRP: Virtual Router Redundancy ensures hot-standby connectivity for ingress and egress routes to servers and to WAN/Internet connectivity

LSNAT: Load Sharing Network Address Translation ensures resilience of content but also balances load across multiple servers in a high availability server farm or e-commerce Web site.

All of these areas of risk management features are generally available in many of today's products. Organisations should plan upfront for risk management and install the backup systems as part of the overall networking strategy. Going back and implementing risk management features as an afterthought can be done but there will be a price premium. So that the automatic nature of these features are made visible and controllable by an organisation, I highly recommend that a network management platform should form an integral part of any risk management strategy.

section fifteen

Security - Information Access is an issue for today

Section 15: Security - Information Access is an issue for today

The Internet has changed the dynamics of networking. We now have the freedom to surf the Internet, we have intranets to service our own employees and we have extranets to service business partners. This opening up of company resources puts a business at risk from hackers within and without. This is a summary of today's defences.

SECTION FIFTEEN

ENTERPRISE NETWORKING

SECURITY - INFORMATION ACCESS IS AN ISSUE FOR TODAY

There was a time when organisations had data. The acceptance of PCs meant we all could have our own data. This happy state of affairs was bound to change when the software companies discovered how to display the data so that mere mortals could understand it. Then it became information. Managers discovering that they had access to information started to use it as a means not only to run their businesses but to give their organisations the competitive edge. Once managers have access to something then they worry about 'who else' has access. This is where security raises its many faceted head. This section does not explain how to achieve security. I believe that security isn't strictly a technology issue but a company procedural issue. It is far too easy for the rogue employee to ask an innocent question of the wages clerk, observe the log in and wait unitl that person is sick. With a vacant desk they are free to use the real machine with the right access point at the right time with the right pass word from the right location. If you want 100% security go back to data. What this section will try to do is suggest where technology can minimise the risks. However, to succeed, a security regime has to be implemented across the whole organisation and is only assisted by technology. If users are permitted to use their phone number or nickname or worse still 'SECRET' as their password into any given service then nothing you do with technology will protect confidential information.

An organisation might have security applications and technology to assist in protecting the business but if there are no security policies and procedures that employees are required to follow, then you might as well give your corporate secrets away. That way at least you know who has them!

ENTERPRISE NETWORKING

SECURITY - INFORMATION ACCESS IS AN ISSUE FOR TODAY

The early computer systems, both mainframe and mini computer relied on a centralised resource providing all services and information storage a business required. The information housed on this single resource enables security to be implemented by controlling the access into the host. Today, host systems have name and password restriction schemes originally in the application but currently embedded in the actual operating system. These schemes controlled not only access, but also the capabilities of the users once they were logged into the system. The explosion of PC users and the wide acceptance of LAN technology and the opening up of these systems to the internet the whole emphasis is open access. Network users can access any resource, any service and share data that is distributed in various locations around the network. Terminal users were only a minor threat because they could view and alter information but PC users have the ability to remove information to local storage, in effect to steal the information. The security risks is not only restricting to output, PCs with their in built intelligence are capable of down loading information in the other direction - to the host. Potentially putting the whole organisation at risk. Opening the door for unauthorised software to be placed onto a shared resource maybe with a virus and the potential for mayhem is all too well understood. Events like the St. Valentine's day virus, ILOVEYOU email has focused attention on restricting this open access. As security has become an issue in these open systems it is reasonable to expect that the International Standards Organisation for Open Systems Interconnect should try and address the problem.

SECURITY LEVELS DEFINED

There was a time when only the organisation had data but the acceptance of PCs meant we could all have our own data. This happy state of affairs was bound to change when the software companies discovered how to display the data so that mere mortals could understand it. Then it became information. Managers discovering that they had access to information started to use it as a means not only to run their businesses but to give their organisations the competitive edge. Once managers have access to something then they worry about who else has access. This is where security raises its many-faceted head.

This section does not explain how to achieve security. I believe that security isn't strictly a technology issue but a company procedural issue. It is far too easy for the rogue employee to ask an innocent question of the wages clerk, observe the log in and wait until that person is sick. With a vacant desk they are free to use the real machine with the right access point at the right time with the right password from the right location. If you

ENTERPRISE NETWORKING

SECURITY - INFORMATION ACCESS IS AN ISSUE FOR TODAY

want 100% security go back to data. What this section will try to do is suggest where technology can minimise the risks. However, to succeed, a security regime has to be implemented across the whole organisation and is only assisted by technology. If users are permitted to use their phone number or nickname or worse still 'SECRET' as their password into any given service then nothing you do with technology will protect confidential information.

1	Security Policy of your organisation
2	Host Security System
3	Auditing
4	Network Security
5	Firewalls
6	Intrusion Detection Systems
7	Incident Response Plan

Security is more a mind set than a set of products. This list shows products and company requirements. Items 1 and 7 are the most important points to address first.

Early computer systems, both mainframe and mini computer relied on a centralised resource providing all services and information storage a business required. Information housed on this single resource could be secured by controlling access to the host. Today, host systems have name and password restriction schemes originally in the application but currently embedded in the actual operating system. These schemes controlled not only access, but also the capabilities of users logged into the system. But with the explosion of PC users and the wide acceptance of LAN technology and the opening up of these systems to the Internet, the whole emphasis is open access. Network users can access any resource, any service and share data that is distributed in various locations around the network. Terminal users were only a minor threat because they could view and alter information but PC users have the ability to remove information to local storage, in effect to steal the information. The security risk is not restricted to output because PCs with

ENTERPRISE NETWORKING

SECURITY - INFORMATION ACCESS IS AN ISSUE FOR TODAY

their inbuilt intelligence are capable of downloading information to the host, potentially putting the whole organisation at risk. Opening the door for unauthorised software to be placed onto a shared resource maybe with a virus and the potential for mayhem is well understood. Events like the St. Valentine's day virus and ILOVEYOU email have focused attention on restricting this open access. As security has become an issue in these open systems it is reasonable to expect that the International Standards Organisation for Open Systems Interconnect should try and address the problem.

SECURITY LEVELS DEFINED

The following list shows the area of responsibility of the communications paths in assisting with the minimising of the security risk. The numbers relate to the layer in the ISO communications model where the functions take place. The ISO model is described in section 18.

Data Origin Authentication	3, 4, 7
Access Control	3, 4, 7
Confidentiality, which covers Encryption and Access control	1, 2, 3, 4, 5, 6, 7
Selective Field Confidentiality	6, 7
Integrity	3, 4
Selective field integrity	6, 7
Non Repudiation of Origin	7
Non Repudiation of Delivery	7

This breaks down responsibilities so that layers 1, 2 and 3 are the responsibility of the networking infrastructure, 4, 5, 6 are the networking operating system and 6, 7 are the host operating system. As we are focused on communications the IEEE802.10 committee has come up with a technique that can mark or tag frames of information being passed on a network to enable secure data exchange. There is also some work being done by the IEEE802.2 committee around the link layer protocols to assist in security. IEEE802.10

ENTERPRISE NETWORKING

SECURITY - INFORMATION ACCESS IS AN ISSUE FOR TODAY

security has been co-opted for identification of virtual networking groups. Hence implementation of VLANs will assist in controlling access and hence security.

The latest improvements in security are being initiated by the IEEE802.1x standards working group which has produced a specification for user authentication. This is targeted at providing an extra layer of network security before you reach the server. When you log on a network today you have already made a connection across the network to a server, which is where the login is taking place. User authentication pushes this out to the workstations at the network edge so the unauthorised may never get access to the underlying network.

OPERATING SYSTEM SECURITY

PC networking is based around a central networked file server, which stores the applications and data. There are two risks to consider - the hacker and the failure. Improvements in file server network operating systems (NOS) have gone some way to resolving the problems of unauthorised file access and systems failure. Fail-safe processes are now available in the operating system to support parallel disk systems, mirrored disk systems and total server mirroring. One example would be Novels System Fault Tolerant (SFT) NOS. SFT provides passwords and access rights and restricts unauthorised users from logging onto the server. The files holding these passwords are hidden and encrypted. However, SFT does not attempt to detect unauthorised users on the network unless they are trying to access the file server and, in a network where every user receives every packet, there is still a high security risk through illegal receipt of data.

An example would be a disgruntled engineer using a network analyser which can read data, like a tape recorder, straight off the network. Furthermore, since the NOS does not sense a new user, unless that user is attempting to connect to a file server there is no security against unauthorised connections to the file server. Individual PC operating systems today offer no security features at all beyond keyboard/password locks. IEE802.1x however is targeted directly at the NOS and is key to the delivery of this new level of security management.

Server-based security software is an obvious requirement and a variety of third party software applications are now available for access-control providing ID and password protection. This will work across a variety of networks providing there is a corporate strategy in place to ensure uniformity and adherence to the procedures. Further security

ENTERPRISE NETWORKING

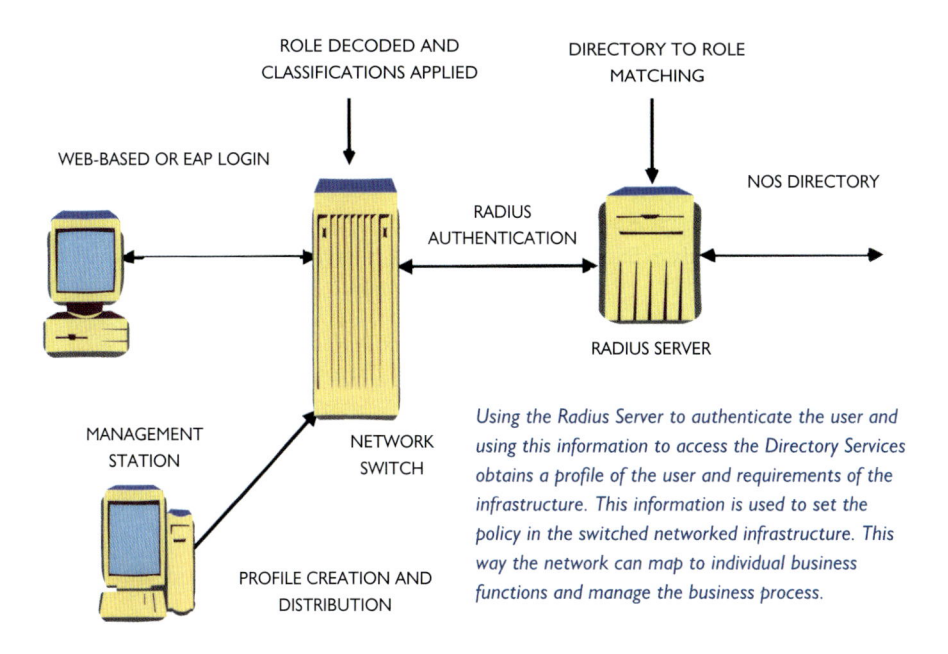

SECURITY - INFORMATION ACCESS IS AN ISSUE FOR TODAY

Using the Radius Server to authenticate the user and using this information to access the Directory Services obtains a profile of the user and requirements of the infrastructure. This information is used to set the policy in the switched networked infrastructure. This way the network can map to individual business functions and manage the business process.

can be achieved by adding physical locks and swipe card pin access to restrict use of the devices that are network enabled.

SECURITY WITHIN APPLICATION SOFTWARE

Operational features embedded in applications have gone a long way to addressing the requirements for increased security. Applications can restrict access to data, restrict changes to data, forbid the loading of unauthorised software and the associated risk of virus and prevent unintentional deleting of files. Application programmers may strive to add these security layers into their code but they are software programmes. Software manufacturers are required by their customers to publish known problems in their code and technically competent hackers can exploit the known bugs in software to their advantage. They have the ability to append their own code to facilitate easy access for the hacker to extract and change data controlled by the application. Hackers who produce these back door subroutines give them exotic names and post them on the Web for other hackers a recent infamous one is known as Back Orifice. These subroutines are

ENTERPRISE NETWORKING

SECURITY - INFORMATION ACCESS IS AN ISSUE FOR TODAY

difficult to detect and many organisations are leaking information all over the Web.

Applications have limited ability to protect themselves so there is the need to implement security software in a structured way. The security solution needs to be constantly updated with the new threats as they are discovered. However, the problem of authorised users of the network reading packets on the network, which they are unauthorised to receive remains. A solution to this unauthorised data browsing is to implement encryption of all data. Encryption techniques are overviewed in this section's glossary.

CONNECTION SECURITY

Originally networks shared the physical media but the move to today's switched infrastructure has greatly enhanced security. Centralising the wiring concentrators in one cabinet and placing these in secure wiring closet provides better hardware security against interfering idle hands on a physical level.

HUB-BASED SECURITY

With advances in integrated circuit technology, manufacturers have been able to incorporate more functionality into single chips. This allows for more efficient design and requires fewer components, reducing production costs, power consumption and heat dissipation. It also provides an opportunity to integrate data security into chipsets, saving on present software overheads. Hub-based security is dependent on a secure repeater chip which tackles the problem of eavesdropping by delivering clear data to identified users and scrambling data to unauthorised sources; eavesdroppers will also see only scrambled and unreadable data. Provide a random encryption technique is used the scrambled data follows no logical pattern and therefore cannot be decoded. This can be further enhanced by access security whereby the chip learns, or is taught, the identity of authorised users on the network on a per port basis and any unauthorised connections to the network are recognised and disconnected this is using user authentication IEEE802.1x in conjunction with Directory Services. The additional management overhead and cost to the network is negligible, limiting overhead in terms of network bandwidth requirements and in terms of processing overhead at the workstations.

Switching technology further assist the security issue. When you use your telephone you actually get a single 'point to point' connection between you and person you are calling.

ENTERPRISE NETWORKING

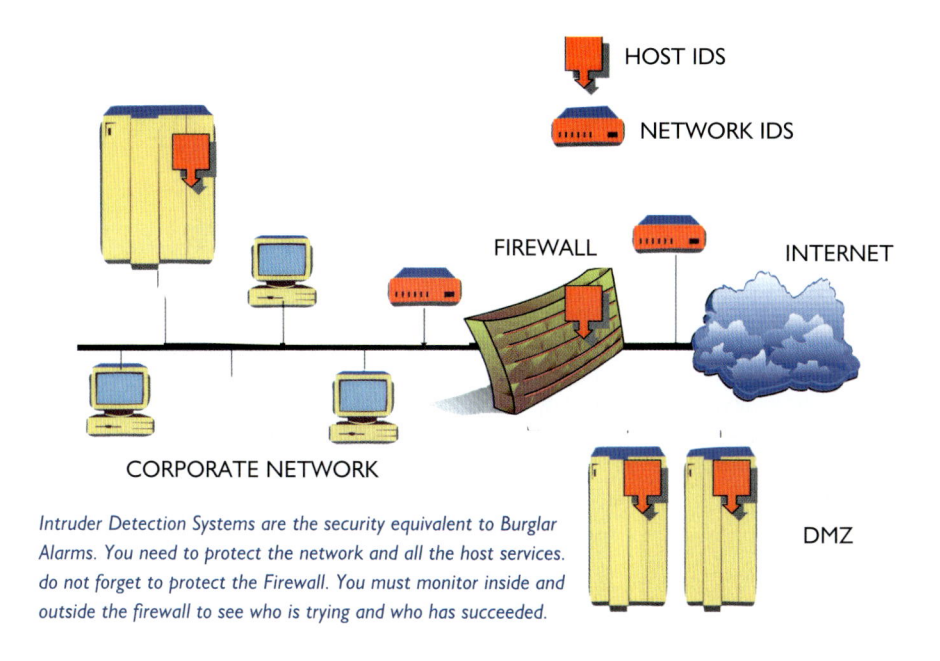

SECURITY - INFORMATION ACCESS IS AN ISSUE FOR TODAY

Intruder Detection Systems are the security equivalent to Burglar Alarms. You need to protect the network and all the host services. do not forget to protect the Firewall. You must monitor inside and outside the firewall to see who is trying and who has succeeded.

There is no sharing of the media. This is inherently secure. Therefore the new switching systems that are replacing the older shared media networks are removing most if not all of the connection risks.

NETWORK SWITCHES ASSISTING SECURITY

Today's network modular switches operating at layers 2, 3 and 4 have embedded features that increase the level and capabilities of network security. Embedded features such as Inbound Rate Limiting can control and limit the amount of bandwidth a specified protocol can consume on an inbound port. This helps protect against intruders trying to interfere with a service by using up all available access to that service - a Denial of Service (DoS) attack. During such attacks, authorised users find that the access ports are constantly busy. Hackers do this to Web sites to prevent customers gaining entry into the company the hacker is attacking. DoS attacks were not mounted against telephony systems perhaps because there wasn't the equipment on the market place that would facilitate the access to the telephony core network. However, IEEE803.1q VLAN technology enables segmentation by protocol, MAC address and IP address and it is the

ENTERPRISE NETWORKING

SECURITY - INFORMATION ACCESS IS AN ISSUE FOR TODAY

You're in bed knowing that you have locked all the doors and nailed all the windows shut. But a burglar takes the tiles off the roof and drops inside. He has got through your defences. What you need is a burglar alarm. This is an example of an Intrusion Detection System. Fido is quite effective provided the robber doesn't have chocolate biscuits.

switch's ability to constantly monitor for these parameters that it can identify anomalies and place them into null VLANs and alert the Network Manager. The processing capabilities of these devices also enables them to support firewall features such as access control lists which implement and automate user login and password checks.

What is required is the ability to extend this to authentication which is now addressed by the IEEE802.1X specifications. Only when a user logs on and passes the authentication test do they receive authorisation to access the network. This can now be done by the access device on the very edge of the network.

INTERNET-INSPIRED SECURITY

Businesses that expose themselves to the Internet see themselves as at risk from anyone with spare time and a PC to hack with. This is a perceived risk, though, since an FBI

ENTERPRISE NETWORKING

SECURITY - INFORMATION ACCESS IS AN ISSUE FOR TODAY

security report in 2000 showed that the lone student hacker accounted for only 2% of security breaches doing it for an intellectual challenge or out of boredom. The biggest threat comes from within the organisation - 74% of security breaches - your own employees, only 24% from outsiders with malicious intent. To address these issues, a range of products has reached the marketplace, some with the ability to be used to take preventative action, others to work as an alarm system monitoring events, generating alarms and collating the forensic evidence for later use.

FIREWALLS

Firewalls are barriers to restrict communications to sensitive resources or data. They use access control lists and a range of techniques to ensure only authorised users reach any protected resource. Firewalls provide a secure Internet entry point by monitoring incoming traffic against attack signatures and monitors outgoing traffic for approvals. Therefore, once a security breach has occurred, then a profile of the data packets can be configured as a signature and any further attempts can be recognised by the firewall and stopped. This relies on those that are attacked informing the Internet community about the attack, so limiting the effect. This failed to stop the ILOVEYOU email doing damage. It is passive, not pro-active: if you do not have a signature, you cannot stop the security breach.

The ACL can be configured both ways. One way to identify users who enter, the other to identify users who cannot leave and therefore prevent access to certain destinations within the Web. Many networking devices have the ability to monitor IP or MAC addresses or can read HTTP scripts, thereby using their traffic filtering algorithms to extend to security restrictions.

VULNERABILITY ASSESSMENT SCANNERS

This is a useful tool to determine how much at risk you are. Effectively it's a hacker in a box designed to penetrate your network and quantify your vulnerability to attack.

HOST INTRUDER DETECTION SYSTEM

This is software residing on a host using processing cycles to monitor for attacks. The host-based agent records a snapshot of a correct profile of all the tables in use and then monitors for changes. When a change is detected it can generate alarms. This can also

ENTERPRISE NETWORKING

SECURITY - INFORMATION ACCESS IS AN ISSUE FOR TODAY

monitor repeated login attempts. However, once again the security breach is happening or has happened; what is required is pro-active solutions.

NETWORK INTRUSION DETECTION SYSTEM

This provides an extra layer before the host system is at risk. Network intruder detection systems monitor all traffic on a segment, continually comparing current traffic patterns with stored attack signatures. They can also monitor for network protocol violations, stored the results for later analysis and generating reports along with alarms for all violations. A key feature of these types of products is the range of signatures they can monitor. A security system that lets the end user create and control the signature generation is putting that company in charge of its own risk management. Early we saw that 74% of the risk is from internal employees.

HR department staff will know that Fred did not get his pay rise and is thinking of leaving so he might try and copy the customer data to take with him to his new company, which is guaranteed to be a competitor. So a manufacturer cannot supply you with a signature to watch Fred, only your HR can do that. These systems are known as open signature systems. Another key feature to look for is anomaly tracking. This is where I work in sales and I use only sales and marketing resources. Then, one day I try to access the finance server. This is an anomaly and MIS should be informed and put a trace on me to see what I am up to.

Forensics is an important feature to ask for from any type of detection system. To be alarmed that someone is trying to do damage an organisation needs an audit trail both to see how they got through the defences and how to block the hole. Also if they succeed then the audit trail can backtrack to the origin and be used in courts of law to prosecute offenders.

Everyone has information and reputation to protect. Many of the security breaches that have occurred over the last 12 months have been high profile and damaging to the organisation that has experienced the breach.

"Failing to implement the security essentials exposes an organisation to the unnecessary risk of potential loss of income or customer loyalty, costly legal challenges, or, at worst, major business disruption."

Source: META Group, 'Enterprise Security: The Bare Essentials', March 1999.

ENTERPRISE NETWORKING

SECURITY - INFORMATION ACCESS IS AN ISSUE FOR TODAY

SECURITY TERMS GLOSSARY

DATA ENCRYPTION

Encrypting data is becoming more common in various applications. These applications rely on a password to decode the encryption and hence gain access to the data. Encryption techniques are based on specific algorithms, and the level of security offered depends on the complexity of the algorithm. The more complex, the harder the unauthorised decoding of the data. Encryption causes extra overhead at the user's workstation as data is encrypted and a further overhead at the receiving workstation or host as the data is decoded. Data encryption is normally installed on a per workstation basis and is typically expensive. It still depends on a password and therefore the confidentiality of that password.

Hashing schemes are a type of encryption. A file to be sent is passed through a hashing algorithm and this produces a unique key known as a 'message digest'. The hashed file is sent with the 'message digest'. When it is received, it is passed through the same hashing algorithm to produce another key. If the keys match, the new data is clean, if there is a mismatch, the data has been corrupted.

ENCRYPTION ALGORITHMS

Encryption algorithms are used to protect communications from eavesdropping. Different encryption algorithms are optimised for software or hardware implementations with little difference in the security level achieved. Security is a function of the length of keys and the way they are assigned and handled. Most attacks centre on breaking the key mechanism.

ARCFOUR - a public domain algorithm that has demonstrated interoperability with RC4 implementations. It behaves like RC4, below.

DES - Data Encryption Standard, a US Government standard, is a block cipher meaning data is encrypted in fixed size blocks, packets are padded to become a multiple of the block size. Using a 56 bit key, DES is optimised for combinatorial hardware.

RC4 - Rivest Cipher 4, is a stream-based cipher meaning that data packets can be encrypted as it is received using a variable length key. Common key sizes are 40 bits and 128 bits. RC4 is optimised for software execution speed.

ENTERPRISE NETWORKING

SECURITY - INFORMATION ACCESS IS AN ISSUE FOR TODAY

Triple DES - a version of DES that consists of a DES encryption with one key, a decryption with a second key and then an encryption with a third key effectively a 168 bits of key.

ENCRYPTION AND KEY MANAGEMENT PROTOCOLS

Cryptographic sessions need to be initialised by both parties with a key that is used to start the encryption and decryption process. Key management protocols deal with getting the key to both parties, resetting the key periodically, and protecting the use so that it cannot be stolen

Diffie-Hellman: a method to negotiate a key using public messages sent in the clear and result in a key that unwanted listeners don't understand.

ECP: Encryption Control Protocol is a subset of the PPP suite for negotiation of encryption within a PPP connection. As a result it can be used in PPTP and L2TP tunnels.

IKE: Internet Key Exchange, a protocol using part of Oakley in conjunction with ISAKMP to obtain authenticated keys for use with ISAKMP, and for other security associations such as AH and ESP

ISAKMP: Internet Security Association and Key Management Protocol, used by IPsec to provide a framework for authentication and key exchange but does not define them. ISAKMP is designed to be key exchange independent; that is, it is designed to support many different key exchanges like IKE or Oakley

KMI: Key Management Infrastructure refers to schemes used for providing key escrow or on demand key recovery for an encrypted message. This is usually put in place to satisfy US government restrictions on export of encryption products. The US government prohibits export of encryption products using a key greater than 40 bits unless the product has an approved KMI.

MPPE: Microsoft Point to Point Encryption, generates a key based on a hash of the user's password and invokes RC4 encryption. Current MPPE has flaws in the way keys are assigned and re-keyed. With these flaws, MPPE is still very difficult and time-consuming to attack. Microsoft claims to be addressing these concerns in coming releases.

Oakley: describes a series of key exchanges, called 'modes', and details the services provided by each (such as perfect forward secrecy for keys, identity protection, and authentication). Used with ISAKMP to negotiate keys for an encryption session.

ENTERPRISE NETWORKING

SECURITY - INFORMATION ACCESS IS AN ISSUE FOR TODAY

AUTHENTICATION SCHEMES

To increase the level of security, a mechanism for only allowing certified users access to resources is needed. User authentication means verifying they are who they claim to be and that they are permitted access to the destination network; there is shortly to be an IEEE standard for this type of mechanism. The authentication scheme must offer a secure, easy to manage method for transferring user credentials such as handshaking techniques such as CHAP and MS-CHAP. Passwords must be encrypted over the connection so that they cannot be intercepted; tokens can generate a new password for every connection so that an intercepted password is useless. Certificates provide a way to encrypt login information with a private/public key pair and have a set of components all of their own.

Certificates: a private key is kept by the user (in a file, smart card, floppy, or other) and used to sign a request to the other party. The other party can look up the public key of the requester to verify the signature on the request thus verifying the authenticity of the request.

CHAP: Challenge Handshake Authentication Protocol. Rather than send the password in the clear, a random number is sent to the client as a challenge. The challenge is one-way hashed with the password and the result is sent back to the server. The server does the same with its copy of the password and verifies that it gets the same result to authenticate the user.

MS-CHAP: Microsoft CHAP, a version of CHAP used by Microsoft that uses a different hash of the password.

PAP: Password Authentication Protocol, the traditional send the username and password in the clear method used for logins in the days before eavesdropping security concerns. It is still the most common method of remote access and ISP login.

Tokens: by using a device carried by the user (usually a credit card sized card with a display) a password is retrieved from the token, which is based on the time and date or a random number sent by the server and entered by the user. The result is sent via PAP or CHAP to the server for authentication.

PPPoE: PPP over Ethernet, an authentication method for Cable/DSL users to login to get Ethernet connectivity. PPPoE can provide a dynamic address via IPCP.

ENTERPRISE NETWORKING

SECURITY - INFORMATION ACCESS IS AN ISSUE FOR TODAY

AUTHENTICATION SERVERS

The most common protocol in use is RADIUS as the authentication server protocol. RADIUS is supported by nearly all user database systems allowing the user to be validated against a user list, servers and functions. Lightweight Directory Access Protocol (LDAP) is showing promise for a more flexible successor to RADIUS as more manufacturers provide implementations. NT and NDS can be accessed by RADIUS and some tunnel servers can access them directly, eliminating some configuration effort.

LDAP: Lightweight Directory Access Protocol is a protocol for retrieving information from a common database. For user authentication, this can be certificate information, access control information or other operational criteria.

RADIUS: a protocol for communicating to a server that maintains a user directory to verify a user's identity. RADIUS can support most of the authentication schemes above. The schemes supported vary among implementations.

RADIUS Proxy: networks of RADIUS servers can be built where a RADIUS server can forward an authentication request to another radius server for verification. For example, an ISP's RADIUS server could act as a RADIUS proxy and send login requests to an enterprise's own RADIUS server to authenticate a user. In this way the enterprise can add and delete users without the ISP's involvement.

NDS: Novell Directory Services, Novell's method for user authentication and access rights retrieval for a network.

NT Domains: Microsoft's method for user authentication for a network.

AD: Active Directory. Microsoft's new directory service released with Windows 2000 and not yet widely implemented. Microsoft's Internet Authentication Service (IAS) provides a RADIUS interface to AD.

Token Servers: Manufacturers of tokens (see above) generally provide a server that can verify that the output of the token is correct, thus authenticating the user. Products supporting tokens can usually talk to these servers using a native protocol or via RADIUS.

CERTIFICATE TECHNOLOGY

Certificates provide an ability to present a data packet that can state who you are and allow another trusted party to vouch for the authenticity of the packet. They are based

ENTERPRISE NETWORKING

SECURITY - INFORMATION ACCESS IS AN ISSUE FOR TODAY

on asymmetric keys and the ability to hash the packet with these keys for a CA to sign the certificates. Issues surrounding certificates are reliable distribution, expiration, renewal, and revocation.

Asymmetric keys: allow a different key to be used for encryption from the decryption. The public key can be used to encrypt something that only the key owner can decrypt with the private key. The key owner can encrypt with the private key something anyone can decrypt with the public key but could have only come from the key owner.

CA: Certificate Authority, is an internal entity or trusted third party that issues, signs, revokes, and manages digital certificates.

CRL: Certificate Revocation List, after a certificate has been issued, the employee may leave the enterprise or other action, which requires revocation of the certificate. The CRL is like a credit card hot list, used to verify that a certificate is still valid once it has been issued. A secure certificate implementation must check all certificates against the CRL to guard against certificates that have been revoked.

PKI: Public Key Infrastructure, certificates are based on

Public Key: In a two part key scheme, this key is made public and signed by a CA to attest to the owner. It can then be used to encode information to the owner of the key and to decode information from the owner. The public key cannot be used to decode information encoded with it. Public and private keys

Private Key: the other part of the two part key scheme, it functions like the public key but for the key owner to decode messages to them and encode messages from the owner.

RA: Registration Authority, an optional system to which a CA delegates certain management functions. For example, an RA can sign up users in a PKI and arrange to have their certificates signed by the CA. It can also be responsible for maintaining the CRL.

X.509: the most common standard for organizing the information stored in a certificate. Certificates contain validity dates, the issuer, the owner, a serial number, the public key and signatures of this.

section sixteen

SNA in an open Multi-Protocol Network

Section 16: SNA in an Open Multi-Protocol Network

SNA is IBM's proprietory networking specification and being old is well established. Users have been moving their SNA networks to open multi-vendor solutions based on IP for the last ten years. This section gives an overview of the environment and the issues to be considered when migrating to standards based LAN solutions.

ENTERPRISE NETWORKING

SNA IN AN OPEN MULTI PROTOCOL NETWORK

I decided to keep this section in the re-write of this book, because it was an interesting challenge at the time. Now that we're firmly entrenched in the third millennium, I do not know how many of these technology challenges survive but, if you come across any, I hope this section gives you some pointers. The current generation of SNA devices support TCP/IP and both Ethernet and Token Ring are fully supported. The hope is that life is easier today.

The early years of computing were dominated by the mainframe. The only way to get information in and results out was to hand your work to the guy with the white coat and special security pass. The major breakthrough came when dumb terminals were invented to access the mainframe directly. This required communications protocols to allow data transfers to take place. In 1974, IBM introduced System Networking Architecture (SNA), the ultimate communications specification for connecting to its mainframes. SNA served the industry with a robust and reliable communications service until LANs took over in the late 1980s.

SNA (System Networking Architecture) was created by IBM in 1974 as a communications architecture for predominantly mainframe networks. As with everything involved with mainframe technology, nothing changes overnight but by the mid-1980s, SNA had become the dominant networking solution for the IBM mainframe environment. The position during the early 1990s was that SNA accounted for 50% of all networks installed. However, throughout the 1990s, a migration took place to convert as much as possible to an IP network based infrastructure. SNA was complex but well understood

ENTERPRISE NETWORKING

SNA IN AN OPEN MULTI PROTOCOL NETWORK

and, although very expensive to implement, it was reliable, manageable, predictable and secure.

In the SNA world, there was a range of jargon that had evolved to describe the elements making up the network. The first was 3270, the generic term for terminal devices making up an SNA network, a 3278 display unit was generally known as a 3270 terminal and a 3287 printer would have been known as a 3270 printer. In the SNA world a device's functionality was defined by two categories or types: a physical unit type (PU) and a logical unit type (LU). In general the physical unit type defined the intelligence of a particular device, with a large number indicating a more intelligent device, while the logical unit type defined an addressable (software) entity within a device and its ability to communicate with other devices.

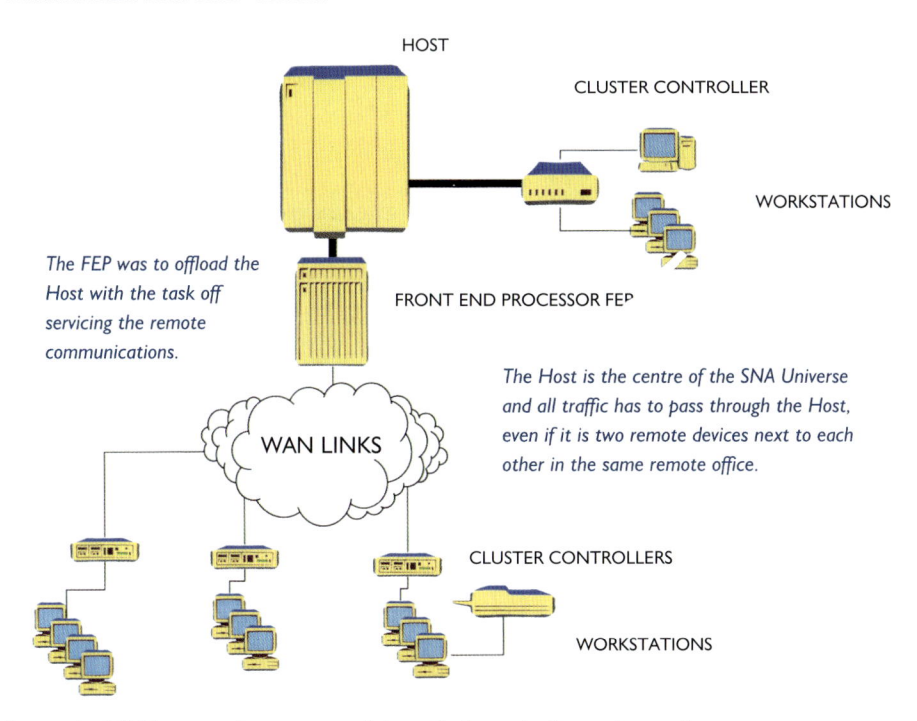

HOST

CLUSTER CONTROLLER

WORKSTATIONS

The FEP was to offload the Host with the task off servicing the remote communications.

FRONT END PROCESSOR FEP

The Host is the centre of the SNA Universe and all traffic has to pass through the Host, even if it is two remote devices next to each other in the same remote office.

WAN LINKS

CLUSTER CONTROLLERS

WORKSTATIONS

In a typical SNA network a group or 'cluster' of terminals, made up of screens or printers, was connected by co-ax cable to a controller, often referred to as a cluster controller. The cluster controller can connect either directly to the host (mainframe) or over a WAN link to a Front End Processor, or FEP. The FEP front end supports multiple

ENTERPRISE NETWORKING

SNA IN AN OPEN MULTI PROTOCOL NETWORK

WAN links arriving at the computer room from remote locations and connects them to the host. The cluster controller ran software to allow it to establish 'sessions' or connections with the host, via the FEP if necessary. A 3270 terminal would then use such a session for sending keyboard entries to the host and the host would send screen refreshers back. The protocol used for this communication in all SNA networks was known as SDLC (Synchronous Data Link Control). This was a data link layer type protocol, equivalent to layer two of the OSI stack and was used by all serial devices on an SNA network.

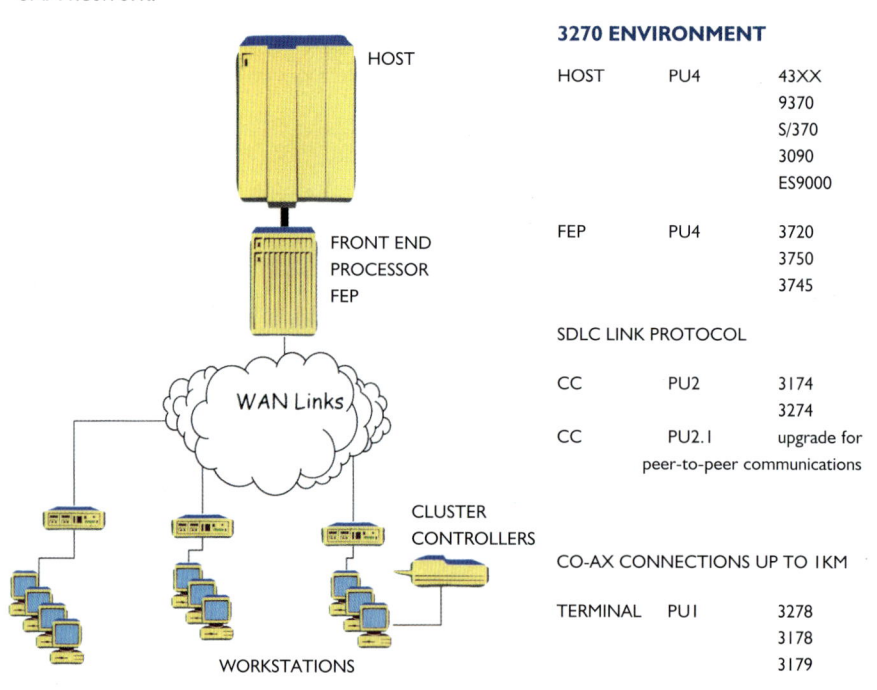

3270 ENVIRONMENT

HOST	PU4	43XX
		9370
		S/370
		3090
		ES9000
FEP	PU4	3720
		3750
		3745

SDLC LINK PROTOCOL

CC	PU2	3174
		3274
CC	PU2.1	upgrade for peer-to-peer communications

CO-AX CONNECTIONS UP TO 1KM

TERMINAL	PU1	3278
		3178
		3179

The traditional SNA network was hierarchical, which means that any device wishing to communicate with any other device has to do so via the mainframe. The mainframe was the central focal point of a SNA network, with all devices below it acting as slaves to its control. In practice this means that two users wishing to exchange information, can do so via a session linked through the host, even if that host is many miles away and the two users are sitting next to each other. This concept received a rude awakening during the mid 1980s as the PC exploded into the business environment. Business people found that communications with other PC users was easy and did not require any involvement from

ENTERPRISE NETWORKING

SNA IN AN OPEN MULTI PROTOCOL NETWORK

a central mainframe. At the same time a range of solutions evolved to connect PCs to the mainframe, so that they could take part in the SNA environment.

These solutions were devices such as the IRMA card that provided the connection, a co-ax port and the emulation software for the PC to act like a 3270 terminal. However, the PCs still acted as slaves to the mainframe, just as the terminals they emulated. The future direction of SNA was to provide device communication on a peer to peer basis, without having to transfer information via the host.

You will already be aware that during the mid 1980s IBM adopted Token Ring as its preferred networking technology for PCs. Since then all of IBM's strategic products have been enhanced with Token Ring capabilities. This resulted in a fragmentation of the SNA environment. The older, well established applications ran on the traditional hierarchical SNA networked solution, while the newer PC-based client-server solutions were being installed in separate, often multi-protocol, Token Ring networks. This resulted in many organisations running parallel networks to meet all of their communications needs, with multiple WAN links carrying the SDLC traffic cluster controllers to FEP and separate

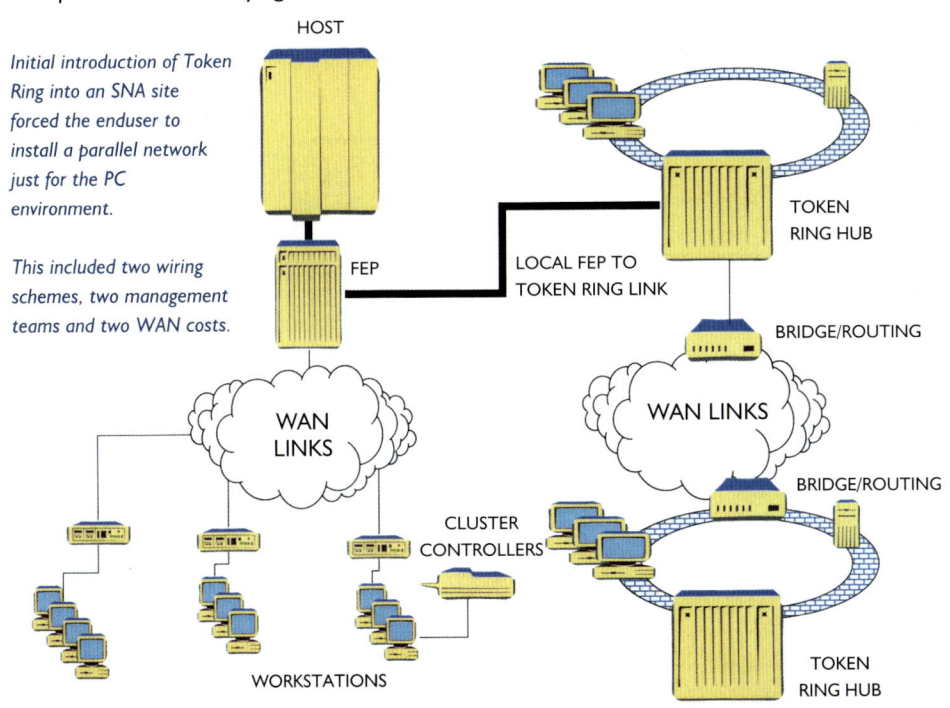

Initial introduction of Token Ring into an SNA site forced the enduser to install a parallel network just for the PC environment.

This included two wiring schemes, two management teams and two WAN costs.

ENTERPRISE NETWORKING

SNA IN AN OPEN MULTI PROTOCOL NETWORK

WAN links to connect the bridged or routed LAN topologies we are familiar with. The situation became more complicated when IBM expanded support to include Ethernet solutions. Duplication of communication links was not only very inefficient but difficult to manage. What was needed was to pull the differing solutions together to reduce communication costs and enhance the connectivity capabilities. The first step in the integration of the differing environments was to migrate the older SNA devices onto Token Ring networks cost-effectively, including, in this integration, the even older devices, which could not be upgraded with Token Ring technology.

Intelligent hubs were the logical location for an interconnectivity device, which could integrate the old SDLC-based devices into the emerging Token Ring networks. This was based on the fact that intelligent hubs were already an excepted part of modern multi-protocol networking architectures and were capable of supporting multiple technologies in the same managed and fault tolerance chassis. To add yet another technology to a hub was a relatively simple process and this in turn opened up the full range of hub-based internetworking solutions to the SNA networking environment. Higher performance

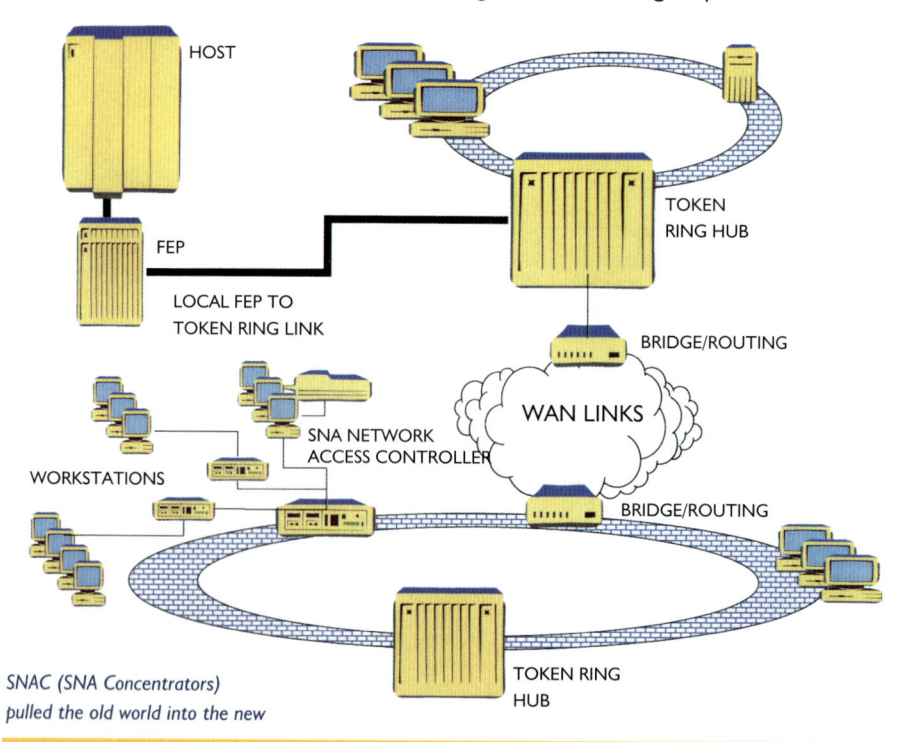

SNAC (SNA Concentrators) pulled the old world into the new

ENTERPRISE NETWORKING

SNA IN AN OPEN MULTI PROTOCOL NETWORK

integrated LAN to LAN connectivity solutions, such as those offered by bridges and routers. SNA itself was a non-routable protocol, which means only flat bridged networks can be constructed until IBM had implemented IP upgrades for key communication controllers.

SNA was evolving to fit the new networking paradigm. There were two main camps providing solutions in this area. IBM itself defined Advanced Peer to Peer Networking (APPN), which allowed the SNA protocol to be routed by certain SNA devices, without the intervention of a central host. IBM licensed this technology to third party manufacturers who wish to incorporate APPN capabilities. The second camp consisted of a consortium of third party manufacturers, who had approached the problem from a non-IBM perspective. The alternative Advanced Peer to Peer Internetworking (APPI).

This approach took the SNA protocol and encapsulated it in IP packets, which can be routed in the normal manner over a TCP/IP network. The eventual aim of APPI was to understand SNA sessions and route them over IP networks without the overhead associated with full encapsulation. This was proposed as the open solution as opposed to the IBM-controlled APPN. It also had the advantage that no proprietary protocols were required. Any solution which attempts to translate SNA into a native router protocol and reverse the process at the destination, would limit the internetwork to a single vendor and hence proprietary solution. Once the hardware was integrated, the second step was to ensure network services were kept at maximum availability. The only way to achieve this was through the use of network management.

In the IBM SNA world, network management was NetView. NetView was IBM's proprietary network management product that ran on the mainframe and provided management facilities for all SNA devices. To allow NetView to manage non-SNA devices a service point had to be used. A service point was IBM-speak for software that acts as an interface between NetView and a downstream non SNA network. At this point in the architecture, a gateway product could be placed, either on the same or different platform to the service point itself. The gateway passed management information between NetView and the third party system, which could be using SNMP management for example. The problem however, was that NetView promoted the old hierarchical structure of master/slave inhibiting automation of fault recovery. When a fault was detected it had to be reported to the NetView console, then remedial action was instigated via the host. Hub technology provided such independent features as automatic segmentation of Ethernet and beacon recovery for Token Ring networks. These features isolate faults from the rest of the network before they cause major problems, reporting

ENTERPRISE NETWORKING

SNA IN AN OPEN MULTI PROTOCOL NETWORK

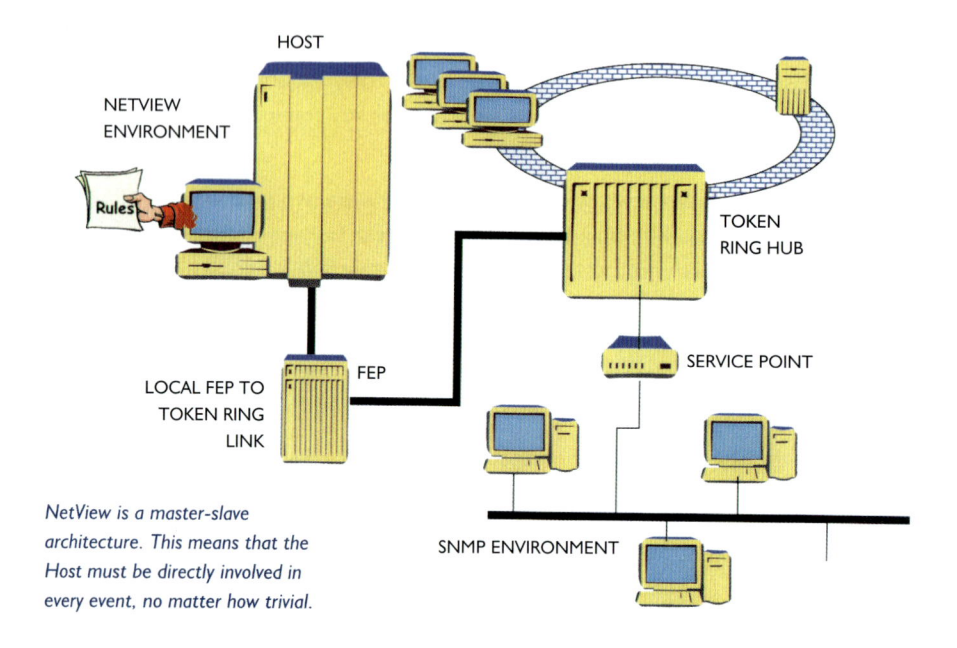

NetView is a master-slave architecture. This means that the Host must be directly involved in every event, no matter how trivial.

to the host for action requests could only serve to delay their instant automatic response and thus remove their benefit.

A REVIEW OF MANAGEMENT IN A SNA NETWORK ENVIRONMENT

NetView was announced in 1986 as an umbrella product for IBM's network management offerings. IBM had many independent applications and management tools, and NetView was nothing more than a packaging of five such independent products: NCCF (Network Command and Control Facility), NPDA (Network Problem Determination Application), NLDM (Network Logical Data Manager), VNCA (VTAM Node Control Application) and NMPF (Network Management Productivity Facility). NetView presented a front end menu for these five products and allowed the user to move from one to another and return to the spot where he/she left. Since then, NetView evolved and expanded in architecture as well as features and functions. IBM had long held the belief that he who controls the network, controls the account. In that vein IBM announced their Open Network Management Architecture (ONMA) in 1987, which positioned NetView running on a mainframe as the network's central control point or focal point. NetView was the management station within the ONMA and was positioned as the network control centre

ENTERPRISE NETWORKING

SNA IN AN OPEN MULTI PROTOCOL NETWORK

(NCC) to manage SNA devices as well as non-SNA devices.

NetView is a mainframe-based, VTAM (Virtual Telecommunications Access Method) application that manages SNA devices and, with the aid of vendor-supplied applications, manages non-SNA devices through service point products. These were NetView/PC and AIX NetView which were the NetView gateway products that enable developers to write applications to pass events up to NetView and receive commands back. NetView/PC and AIX NetView service points did not manage devices but were pass-through products that allow non-SNA devices to be managed from NetView. Users of NetView/PC or AIX NetView service point wrote the applications that converted events from their native formats into NetView's protocol, NMVT (Network Management Vector Transport), loosely the SNMP of the SNA world. The user had also to provide applications that passed and processed the commands from NetView. Many vendors offered these types of gateways, some used NetView/PC and/or AIX NetView Service Point, others were bespoke.

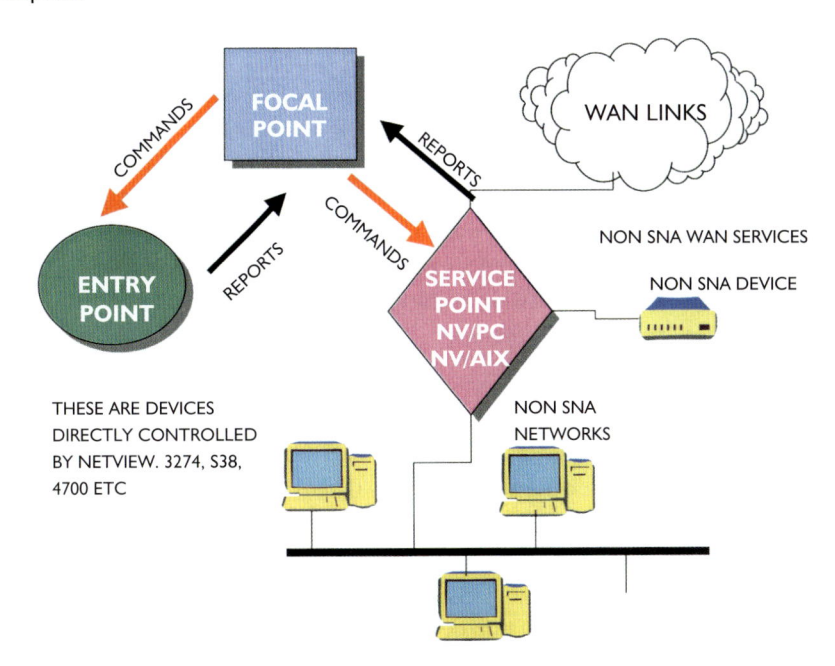

Service Points are the translators of non NetView environments into a limited subset of NetView alarms. They then take the NetView demand and translate into an SNMP set command.

ENTERPRISE NETWORKING

SNA IN AN OPEN MULTI PROTOCOL NETWORK

There were three major pieces to IBM's Network Management Architecture:

1. ENTRY POINT

Quoting IBM manuals, an entry point was *"an SNA node that provides distributed network management support. It may be a PU type 2.0,2.1,4.0, or 5.0 (physical unit - a product that controls resources, like a 3274 controls terminals and printers, the 3274 is a PU types 2.0, the terminals and printers are LUs, 3278 terminals are LU types 2). It sends SNA formatted network management data about itself and the resources it controls to a focal point for centralised processing, and it receives and executes focal point initiated commands to manage and control its resources."* Entry points are SNA products that report into NetView and take commands from NetView. Examples of entry points are 3274s, 4700s, AS/400s, S/36, S/38s, 37x5s etc. The most typical discussion of an entry point refers to the 3270 cluster controller-class products, the 3274 and 3174.

2. FOCAL POINT

"An entry point that provides centralised management and control for other entry points for one or more management categories. In the NetView programme, the focal point domain is the central host domain. It is the central control point for any management services element containing control of the network management data." Focal points were SNA-addressable products that managed other nodes in the network. Originally a focal point was the centralised management station NetView. IBM improved the architecture by the inclusion of PU 2.1 sessions, and peer-to-peer NetView interaction. This slightly altered the definition of focal point to accommodate this need.

Prior to PU 2.1, every SNA session had to go through the host control point to be established. So NetView was aware of all nodes and all node communications. With the introduction of the AS/400 a PU 2.1 device and the ability hold sessions without host control, that is, AS/400 to AS/400 without a mainframe, without VTAM, IBM was faced with the problem of incorporating network management data from these devices. PU 2.1 existed before NetView, so followers of IBM's management architecture had recognised that something was going to have to change. The SNA definition of domain was the set of nodes that were configured subservient to a particular mainframe or SSCP System Services Control Point. An SSCP was distinguished as a type 5 PU. It could start, stop, and display for example, those devices via NetView, the focal point. This was the function of NCCF before NetView arrived.

ENTERPRISE NETWORKING

SNA IN AN OPEN MULTI PROTOCOL NETWORK

3. SERVICE POINT

"A product or set of products that provides network management support for itself and attached products. It provides a connection through which network management data can be converted to SNA formats and transmitted to the focal point for processing. The service point must be in the same SNA domain as the focal point, but the products it supports do not need to be in the same SNA domain as the focal point or service point." NetView/PC and AIX NetView service points accepted network management data in SNA formats, Network Management Vector Transport - NMVT, verified the protocol and forwarded it to the host running NetView. The user's application was responsible for constructing the NMTV from the protocol they were implementing either standard or proprietary. The service points also received commands from the host and present them to a user application for processing. The 'attached products' referred to were typically non-SNA devices such as T1 multiplexers, SNMP devices and OSI stacks.

NETVIEW IN THE MARKETPLACE

NetView became a de facto standard in the network management arena. Well over half of the Fortune 1000 used NetView by the mid-1990s. There were at least 4,000 NetView installations in the USA, and 10,000 licences worldwide. Systems Centre Inc. marketed a product called Net/Master, another VTAM mainframe based SNA management product that competed directly with NetView. They achieved a 5%-10% share of the SNA management market around that time. Almost every SNA enterprise required some amount of NetView compatibility from its selected vendors although few actually used NetView to its fullest or seriously managed non-SNA devices from it. This was largely due to the fact that an administrator of a network eventually needs to know something about the configuration, status and diagnostics of the devices he/she is managing in order to be effective. The service point approach relying on NetView Gateway products was limited to providing alerts to the mainframe and the receipt of commands in the form of the NCCF RUNCMD. Furthermore, once a service point was implemented, the administrators had a problem with terminology. Just as SNMP administrators didn't know what 'PCTD1' meant, NetView administrators did not recognise 'pingable'. The most successful integrations with NetView were those that would be the most non-threatening to the NetView administrator who was used to being the centre of every action and using terms he/she would have been familiar with.

ENTERPRISE NETWORKING

SNA IN AN OPEN MULTI PROTOCOL NETWORK

The reason for NetView not gaining full utilisation was the complexity of the service points and the NetView product itself. Netview/PC and AIX NetView service points were difficult to implement and NetView's user interface was textual for most of its existence. IBM did offer NetCentre, a DOS-based product developed by US West that could front end NetView and GMF (Graphics Management Facility) an OS/2 based NetView front end. Artificial intelligence was rudimentary in NetView amounting to little more than automated operations and rules based reactions to events in the network. Even in the mid-1990s the number of installations wanting to manage non-SNA devices from NetView remained strong, though host based applications still dominated the industry. A significant number of these applications were unlikely to be re-written as distributed applications. Many are 10-20 years old, written in COBOL and 370 Assembler. Therefore there will still be SNA networks around well into the 21st century.

As for NetView, it has completely changed. In 1989, a bunch of IBM employees formed their own company to focus on systems management. This company was Tivoli. They managed to gain significant market penetration of their enterprise management framework solution TME 10. So successful were they that IBM bought Tivoli in 1996 and gave it responsibility for IBM's management solutions and, with the release of Tivoli Netview 5.1 in 1998, a solution was available to provide interactive end to end systems management for an IBM installation.

section seventeen

Multi-Service Networking

Panel of Experts

Section 17: Multi-Service Technology

The new drive for businesses is to rationalise technology spending and in networking, this means moving to a Multi-Service Network. This is voice, video and data running over a common communications infrastructure. Networks have grown organically over the past decade. Some are complex technology nightmares but it is possible to plan a strategy and move to it without scrapping your existing investment and starting again. Planning is required to ensure that the service levels required by voice and video are acceptable to an organisation's user community.

SECTION SEVENTEEN

ENTERPRISE NETWORKING

MULTI-SERVICE NETWORKING

INTRODUCTION

A multi-service network is a single network infrastructure that can provide the transportation and delivery of voice, video and data with the correct service level for the specific traffic type. There have been several business drivers over the last decade for moving in this direction. Enterprises need this unification for cost savings in implementing, managing and evolving their networks. Retail businesses have discovered they need it to properly conduct business over the Internet. Educational institutions have discovered they need it to facilitate the delivery of distance learning.

And because this idea is not an especially new one, even though its realisation is, out of interest I have included descriptions of several early solutions to fixing variable path delay, which was a major inhibitor to integrating voice traffic, caused by routing that got into mainstream use.

Multi-Service Networking is the integration of voice, video and data across a common communications infrastructure. The industry is a-buzz with convergence and Voice over IP. The underlying driver is to deliver full-motion video so that Service Providers can send movies on demand. They will then add this to other services such as telephony, Internet access and VPNs to enable you to work from home. The benefits of multi-service networking is that only one set of cabling and technology is required which provides a cost-effective solution.

ENTERPRISE NETWORKING

MULTI-SERVICE NETWORKING

GENERAL BUSINESS REQUIREMENTS

Most enterprises today use technology to run their businesses. The desktops of employees whose job functions are core to the running and development of the business are equipped with productivity tools to gain efficiency and assist the business in gaining a competitive advantage. These tools consist of the personal computer, the telephone handset and, for the very advanced organisations, video-conferencing equipment. These devices are equipped with three entirely separate kinds of network connection with each network providing the level of performance required by the differing services.

The PC is usually connected to a LAN that supports bursty traffic with a best-effort, no guarantee of communications or performance connection. The phone is connected to a PABX providing a dedicated connection with some guarantees on performance provided the connection is not busy. Video systems tend towards separate ISDN connections wired to the specific user's desk or to specified meeting rooms.

This organic growth of technology into different directions does not match the business requirements of increased efficiency at lower cost. It is easy to see that an organisation which has to install a data network, a telephone network and a video network is going to pay for three cabling schemes, three sets of equipment, three support groups and has to negotiate three maintenance contracts. The current buzzword is convergence which describes the solution, which is to install one multi-service network that can run data, voice and video over a single network infrastructure. To understand how this is now possible, the latest developments in the three services and how the standards have evolved to integrate them into a single solution need to be examined.

INTERNET AND INTRANET BUSINESS DRIVERS

The Internet is a router-based network of remote file servers. These file servers carry information and services from the organisation that provided the server and is now the IT industry's preferred way of disseminating information. The benefit to the IT industry is the savings in producing printed material and savings in postal costs. If you need information you pay to connect to their server, download the brochure and pay for the printing locally. Because there are so many file servers connected to the global router-based network they are collectively known as the worldwide Web. The access points into the router based network are known as portals and access to these provided by your local Internet Service Provider (ISP). Once you have signed up and have TCP/IP installed,

ENTERPRISE NETWORKING

MULTI-SERVICE NETWORKING

a Web browser, and the correct hardware - usually a low cost modem - you can make a local modem call to the ISP router and then have access to the world. The Internet is an IP-based network and this protocol is similar to posting a letter. You don't need prior agreement from the destination, you just randomly initiate communications.

Today the Internet is a data distribution system and interactive communications is limited to typing to a person whom you have contacted across the Internet. There are many solutions for providing video and voice across the Internet and they all use clever software techniques to overcome the lack of QoS (Quality of Service) on the network. E-commerce, basically a seller displaying a catalogue over the Web and a consumer placing orders, is driving Web-based voice and video.

The current buzzword is 'click to talk'. A consumer looking at a retail product can access the retailer's call centre directly from the Web page which means that the Internet infrastructure has to become a multi-service network. To understand the issues here we have to review how we build networks.

This is relevant to you, even if you find using the Web slow, because its success in disseminating information means that commercial organisations are looking to use this technology inside their own networks. This has been termed intranets which entails using company

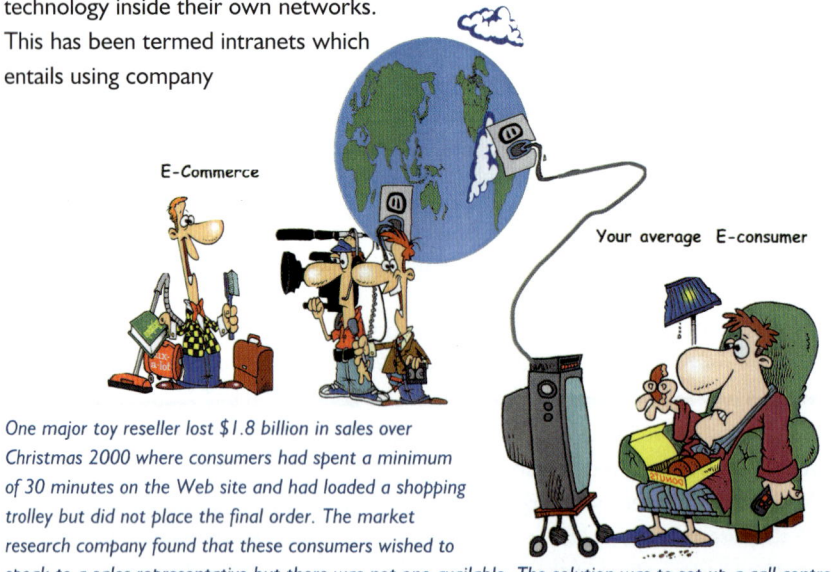

One major toy reseller lost $1.8 billion in sales over Christmas 2000 where consumers had spent a minimum of 30 minutes on the Web site and had loaded a shopping trolley but did not place the final order. The market research company found that these consumers wished to speak to a sales representative but there was not one available. The solution was to set up a call centre manned 24 hours a day while the Web site needs to support voice interaction. The consumer end requires a 'click to talk' application.

ENTERPRISE NETWORKING

MULTI-SERVICE NETWORKING

Web servers for their own employees, extending it as an information and business processing resource for business partners.

DEVELOPMENTS IN VIDEO CONFERENCING

Businesses are slowly beginning to discover that video-conferencing can help to reduce travel costs and improve international subsidiary incorporation into their overall business. Universities are finding they can extend their reach if the embrace the technology and offer distance learning facilities to remote students. Up till now, however, solutions have been based on a conference room system approach, where a meeting room is equipped with video facilities and meeting schedules are set out. This does not blend well with the dynamics and spontaneity of real working practices.

What is required is the ability to deliver to the desktop real-time video that's as freely accessible as the telephone. The standards bodies have responded to this with a specification H.323 (video on the LAN) and H.321 (video over ATM), both published by the ITU (International Telecommunications Union). These describe the distribution of real-time video to desktop systems. Networking manufacturers have had to solve the problem of multicast communications across a switched infrastructure. It is not only the delivery of multicast, one source to many recipients, but the prevention of broadcast situations reducing the risk of interfering with normal business traffic. The PC manufacturers are assisting in this by providing video compression hardware as a standard PC feature and the PC operating system providers are bundling decompression software as a standard feature.

DEVELOPMENTS IN TELEPHONY

It would appear that the PC revolution, which brought distributed computing power to every desktop and reduced the dependence on the corporate mainframe, is about to repeat itself in the telephony market place. The PABX is the telephone equivalent of yesterday's mainframe computer, having the same cost model and support overhead. So changing a business application when running a call centre requires long development cycles and expensive software. The telephony handset has changed very little over recent years and there have been very few visible developments to enhance user productivity. Most workers, even with a fully featured phone, still use only the most basic functions. Meanwhile, over the past five years, the PC user interface has evolved dramatically. The move to a client/server PABX will bring the benefit of the PC cost model, that is,

ENTERPRISE NETWORKING

MULTI-SERVICE NETWORKING

application availability, local supportability and the PC's graphical interface directly to telephony by improving productivity.

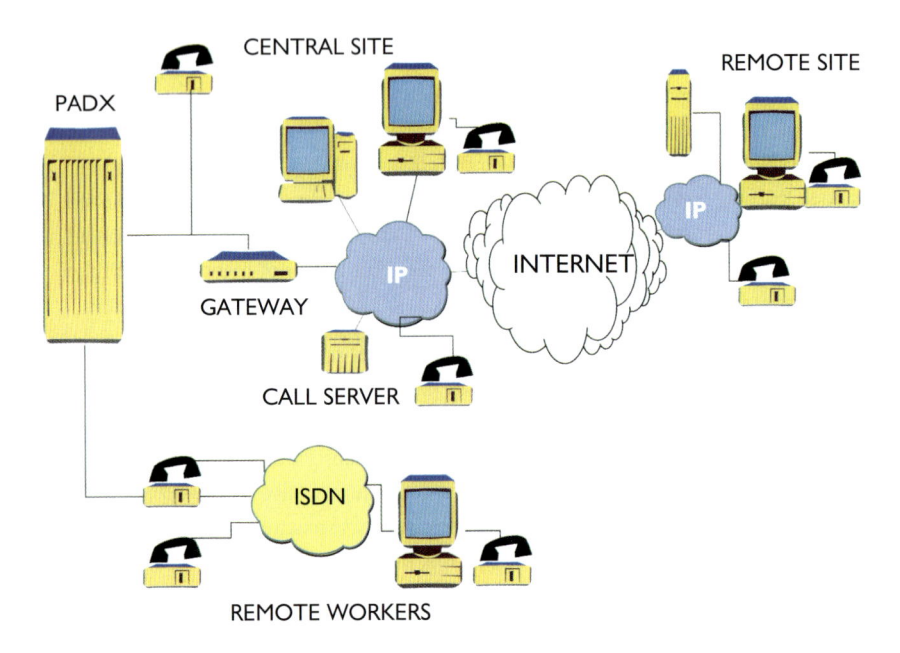

Convergence is the integration of voice services onto the data infrastructure but it is not commercially viable to replace the existing telephony system. Therefore, the two systems must co-exist and interoperate.

The ATM forum has responded to these advances with Voice Telephony over ATM (VToA) standard for supporting real-time voice calls over ATM technology. The WAN industry's answer was Voice over Frame Relay (VoFR) and the network industry came back with specifications for VoIP (Voice over IP) networks. These are usually described in a company's convergence strategy.

BACKGROUND

Packet voice technology emerged in the 1980s as Data Over Voice (DOVe) a viable way to combine voice and data traffic over private, packet-switched data networks. Concern over voice quality limited its market penetration and restricted it to Virtual Private Networks based on traditional Public Switched Telephone Network (PSTN) services. As

ENTERPRISE NETWORKING

MULTI-SERVICE NETWORKING

the carriers moved to digital infrastructures with the more reliable Public Data Networks (PDNs) in the 1990s, a range of technologies attempted voice integration with data. These included Frame Relay VoFR access devices and switches and similar ATM products (VoAT).

Wide area communications costs are driving the integration of voice and data services. This is particularly true for long distance and international voice traffic where great savings can be achieved by avoiding public, long-distance voice services. In 1994, several companies began to experiment with passing voice over IP networks. The attraction was the possibility to pass voice traffic over the Internet almost for free. IP as a telephony protocol clearly paves the way for data and voice integration.

Unlike VoFR or VoAT, VoIP suffers from the consequences of IP's connectionless character. Frame Relay and ATM networks are designed to establish end-to-end connectivity and, during communication, they are connection-oriented. This allows data/voice packets to pass through network switches with very low latencies or delay. For voice calls to be successful the total end-to-end (ear-to-ear) should not exceed about 180 milliseconds because anything longer leads to the perception of lower than PSTN quality. Traditional routed networks on the other hand inject significantly more delay, primarily because of the need to do router look ups at each router in the path. Additionally, IP packets are typically larger than Frame Relay frames or ATM cells. This leads to longer queuing delays even for prioritised voice packets which must wait while already exiting and larger data packets are transmitted out of buffers and onto relatively slow, wide area, interconnecting circuits.

WHAT ABOUT MY CURRENT NETWORK?

The major issue facing router manufacturers today is moving the installed base to a technical level that would enable support of multi-service networking. The technical task is to support voice with an acceptable quality of service that makes it usable.

If we look at the basics of today's networking and understand the problems that these cause to voice traffic then the solution becomes clearer. The first issue is the variable nature of the data that is transported across the networks. We can produce packets of data from as small as 64 bytes up to 17,000 bytes. If we were to process these packet extremes with a processor working at 10Mbit/sec then a 64 byte packet would be processed in microseconds while the 17,000 byte packet would be processed in tens of

ENTERPRISE NETWORKING

MULTI-SERVICE NETWORKING

milliseconds. Because we cannot predict how many and what size packets will be on a working network then we will randomly be processing in microsecond and millisecond intervals, which causes variable delays. Also, when sharing a communications link, a 64-byte packet will take a lot less time to be sent out across the link than a 17,000-byte packet, causing further variable delay.

And variable delay is the voice killer. Just try holding a satellite-routed, transatlantic call. The delay means that both parties start talking at the same time, so you make a real effort to compensate and ensure you are speaking in small bursts. If this delay became variable you would not know if the other end has finished speaking or not. The speakers would constantly interrupt each other and not be able to complete a single sentence.

We have to eliminate variable delay. One way would be to take the ATM approach by restricting packets to a fixed length. To get a good feel for the effectiveness of this let's fix IP packets to the ATM size. The problem here is a commercial problem. With ATM the addressing information is 10% of the cell, so 10% of the communications that you are paying for is not used for data. IP with a fixed packet size the same ATM cells - 53 bytes - results in 52% of the communications you pay for being wasted on moving the protocol. This is a worst-case scenario but it illustrates the problem of messing with packet size when we have to support the existing IP traffic. As this is not feasible the only

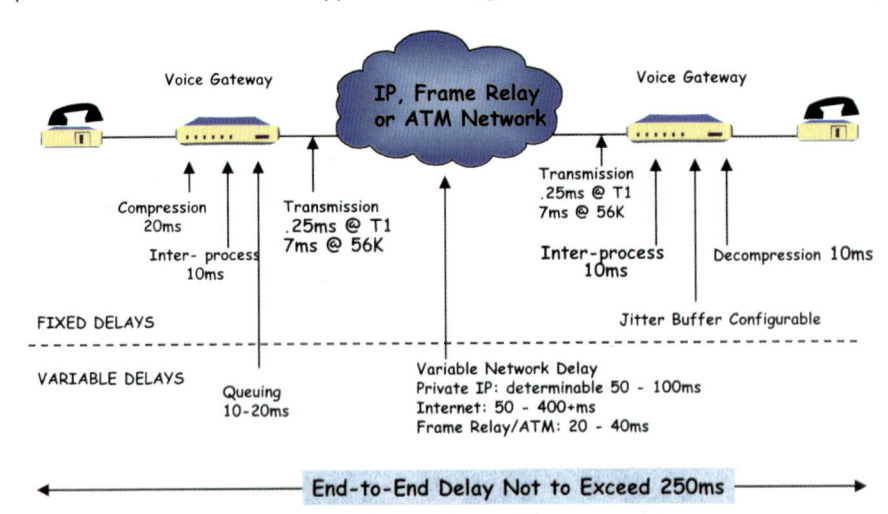

The delays that affect voice services using a data infrastructure. If the voice gateway is also dealing with data packets which are of random length, this would introduce unacceptable variable delays into the voice stream.

ENTERPRISE NETWORKING

MULTI-SERVICE NETWORKING

alternative is to prevent the nodes processing the packets therefore not introducing these variable delays in the first place.

Layer 4 switches and the use of RSVP software solves this problem today. If you want to know what has been tried as a solution read the appendix to this section.

DEVELOPMENTS IN LOCAL AREA NETWORKING

MIS is usually the first to be aware of data networks running out of bandwidth. More users are connected, using client-server computing and the applications running are more graphic with bigger files. The solution to this bandwidth problem has been to segment the network into smaller workgroups. This way fewer users compete for available bandwidth. The interconnection of larger numbers of segments has been achieved through switching technology. This accounts for the growth of both Ethernet switching and Token Ring switching.

Ethernet and Token Ring LAN technologies are a legacy from the infancy of networking, when the big issue of the day was having many users sharing a single cable. Today's problem is different. Business applications have moved from a batch-processing model to an interactive model. The batch-processing model is well supported by the bursty data support provided by Ethernet and Token Ring but, to support interactive communications, a connection-oriented system is required. The solution for networking interactively is Asynchronous Transfer Mode (ATM) technology.

ATM can provide real-time communications and at the same time provide better use of existing bandwidth due to embedded features collectively known as the Quality of Service (QoS) capability. QoS enables business managers to identify which applications are mission-critical and which require real-time response. The available bandwidth is then automatically managed and allocated to match these business requirements. The reality is that ATM has not dislodged Ethernet from its installed base so network manufacturers have had to invent mechanisms to offer the ATM-style QoS features for Ethernet and Token Ring networks. The solution has been to embed extra buffers on the switches to enable different types of traffic to be separated so different priorities can be set and different levels of service can be implemented. TCP/IP protocols have also been extended to enable service levels to be requested and bandwidth reserved for time-critical applications. The hardware manufacturers implemented IEEE802.1p at layer 2 Traffic Classification and Prioritisation and Diffserv/TOS byte mapping at layer 3, enabling wire-

ENTERPRISE NETWORKING

MULTI-SERVICE NETWORKING

speed differentiated services. At each queuing point in the system, the hardware uses this policy-based classification to make buffering and forwarding decisions. To prevent low-priority traffic from waiting indefinitely as higher-priority traffic is serviced a 'Weighted Fair Queuing' mechanism (WFQ) provides adjustable minimum bandwidth guarantees thereby ensuring that some traffic from each priority class always gets through. Random Early Detection (RED) can also be applied to keep congestion under control when traffic is predominantly TCP based. Another technique to give even greater control over bandwidth utilisation is 'rate limiting'. This enables the user to set up a Committed Access Rate (CAR) on traffic that has been classified. Each IP flow can be rate limited at the input. Bandwidth is allocated on a per flow basis. If the IP flow exceeds the bandwidth limit, then the arriving packet is either dropped or assigned to a lower priority.

WHY MULTISERVICE NETWORKING NOW?

After two decades of installing data networks and a decade of enhancements to PC networking, virtually all businesses now run on a network. Every desk is automatically wired with telephony support. Video support, although somewhat a late starter, will be virtually free on all new PCs. These trends mean that these services will be provided by default, albeit across separate networks. The business requirement is for increased productivity as a direct result of these technologies, without incurring the operational costs of running three systems. Multi-service networking is now possible because the underlying technical problem of ensuring QoS over data networks has been solved. Data communications can match business requirements as well as enabling real-time voice and video streams to be prioritised and provided with the correct QoS. It has not been possible to go out and purchase real-time network applications until the release of Winsock 2.0 by Microsoft in 1997. This was the first programmer interface where programmers could demand a QoS of the underlying network for the application they were writing.

HOW TO MAKE THE MOVE

The first step is to use the lack of bandwidth availability to justify the cost of the move to a layer 4 switched backbone. Then the normal adds, moves and changes budget can be used to introduce LAN switching into the workgroups. Where there is a business case for high performance business functions, layer 3 switching can be introduced, ensuring that these users are provided with the latest PCs. Any secondary group will still be able to

ENTERPRISE NETWORKING

MULTI-SERVICE NETWORKING

benefit, provided that the numbers on their segment are reduced to three or four devices. Although ATM is QoS-ready, not all LAN switches are. Therefore, it will be necessary to get the manufacturers to explain how they intend to support QoS on legacy systems. There are several standards and protocols to consider such as IEEE802.1p, 'Real Time Protocol' (RTP) and 'Resource Reservation Protocol' (RSVP).

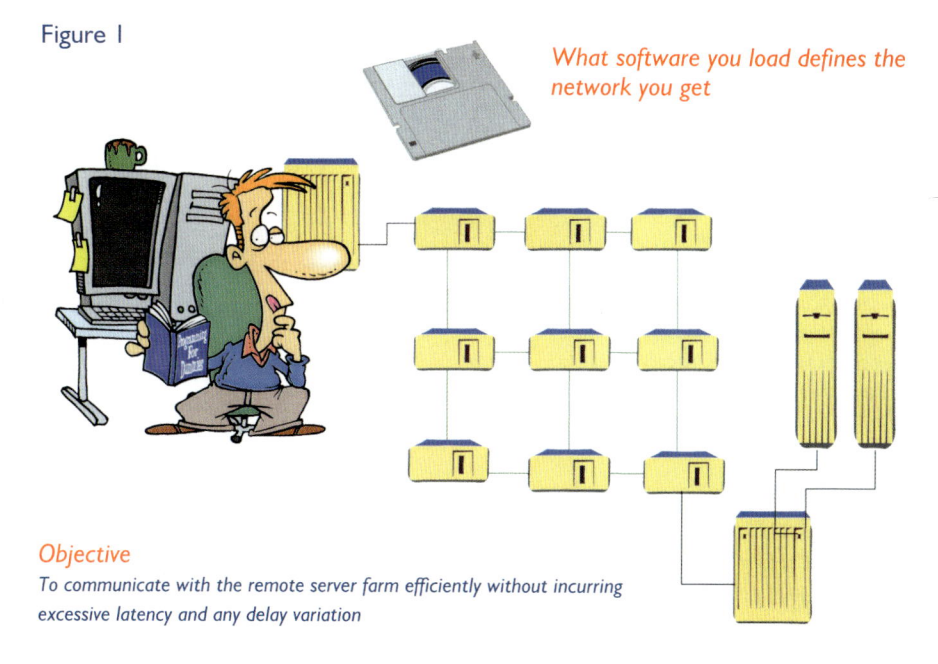

Figure 1

What software you load defines the network you get

Objective
To communicate with the remote server farm efficiently without incurring excessive latency and any delay variation

APPENDIX

A PATH TO A SOLUTION

To better understand the issues with legacy networks when dealing with multiservice networking we need to understand how networks behave when we construct them with bridges, routers or switches. We will start with a generic network and the idea is that we will load different software to provide one of the functions bridging, routing or switching.

Figure 1 shows a generic network made out of communications boxes that have no software loaded; we have removed the sub-networks to show just one user and two servers.

ENTERPRISE NETWORKING

MULTI-SERVICE NETWORKING

Figure 2

Load Bridging Software

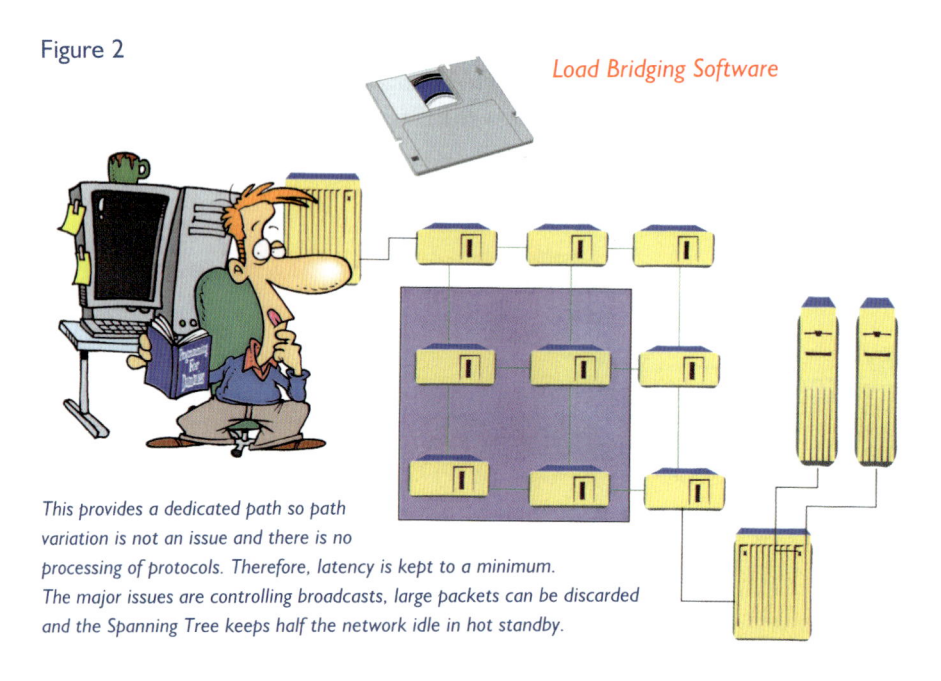

This provides a dedicated path so path variation is not an issue and there is no processing of protocols. Therefore, latency is kept to a minimum. The major issues are controlling broadcasts, large packets can be discarded and the Spanning Tree keeps half the network idle in hot standby.

Figure 2 shows what happens when we load bridging software and the boxes behave as layer 2 bridges. The shaded area shows all the communications products and links you have paid for that are in 'hot standby' because of the Spanning Tree algorithm. This is the standard way bridges prevent closed loops. The shaded area will only operate if there is a failure in the primary path. The advantage of this bridged network however is that there is no packet processing so they run at wire speed with no processing-induced variable delay. Also, there is a fixed path length between the user and the server hence there is no variable delay added by packets taking a different route through the network.

Figure 3 shows the main advantage if we now load routing software and change our boxes to routers. We can use all our communications paths we do not have to wait for a failure to use the spare paths. The way routers work is to receive a packet from the user network and use its internal tables to decide on which port to forward the outgoing packet. In doing this task the router actually removes the current MAC layer destination addresses, the physical address, and adds the physical address of the next port on the chosen path. Then the packet is sent on its way and forgotten about. The next router receives the packet and goes through the same processing cycle. Therefore every node between the source and destination processes the packet, creating plenty of opportunity

ENTERPRISE NETWORKING

MULTI-SERVICE NETWORKING

Figure 3

Load Routing Software

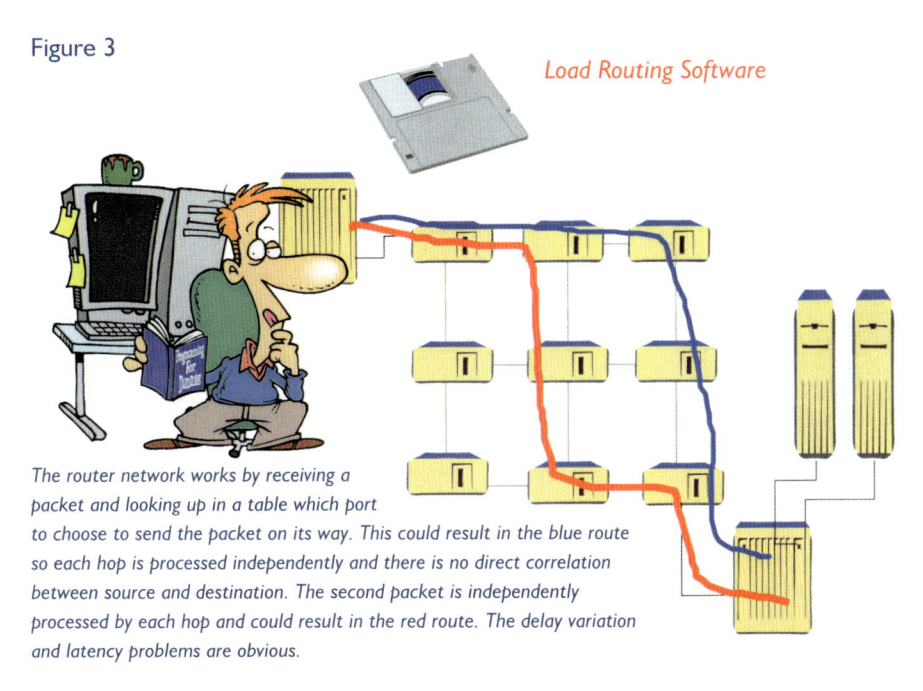

The router network works by receiving a packet and looking up in a table which port to choose to send the packet on its way. This could result in the blue route so each hop is processed independently and there is no direct correlation between source and destination. The second packet is independently processed by each hop and could result in the red route. The delay variation and latency problems are obvious.

to introduce variable delay. As each router goes through its process it can change the path that a packet takes through the network depending on the available bandwidth of the upstream link. So the way that routers work can add huge amounts of variable delay by taking different paths through the network. So if we want to harness the router advantage of using the whole network that we have paid for then, when we have real-time traffic, we must both prevent routers processing and fix the path for the duration of the call.

Figure 4 shows these two features added in other words, turn the boxes into switches. Here, when the user wishes to communicate with the server there is a mechanism for finding the best path through the whole network and once this is established it is fixed. There is no path variable delay. Through this fixed path there is no need to process at each node therefore we can perform at wire speed and not introduce any processing variable delay. The issue is determining the correct mechanism for finding and fixing the path through the network, remembering that most manufacturers believe IP is the only protocol that will survive in the future. In 1997, there were about 17 proposals for that mechanism which could be categorised into five groups. All used basically the same process but with different manufacturers' protocols pushed forward as the only way to do it.

ENTERPRISE NETWORKING

MULTI-SERVICE NETWORKING

Figure 4

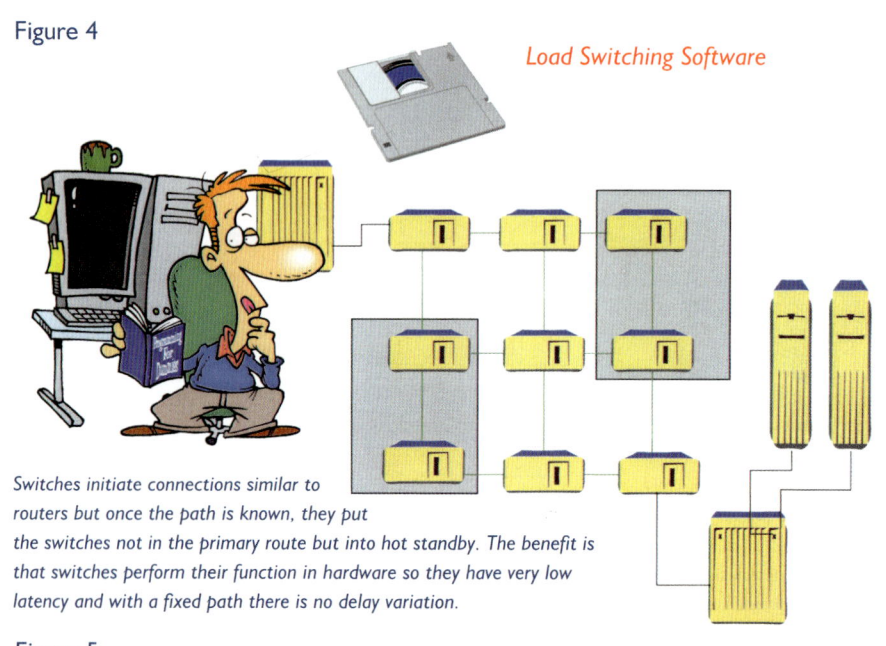

Load Switching Software

Switches initiate connections similar to routers but once the path is known, they put the switches not in the primary route but into hot standby. The benefit is that switches perform their function in hardware so they have very low latency and with a fixed path there is no delay variation.

Figure 5

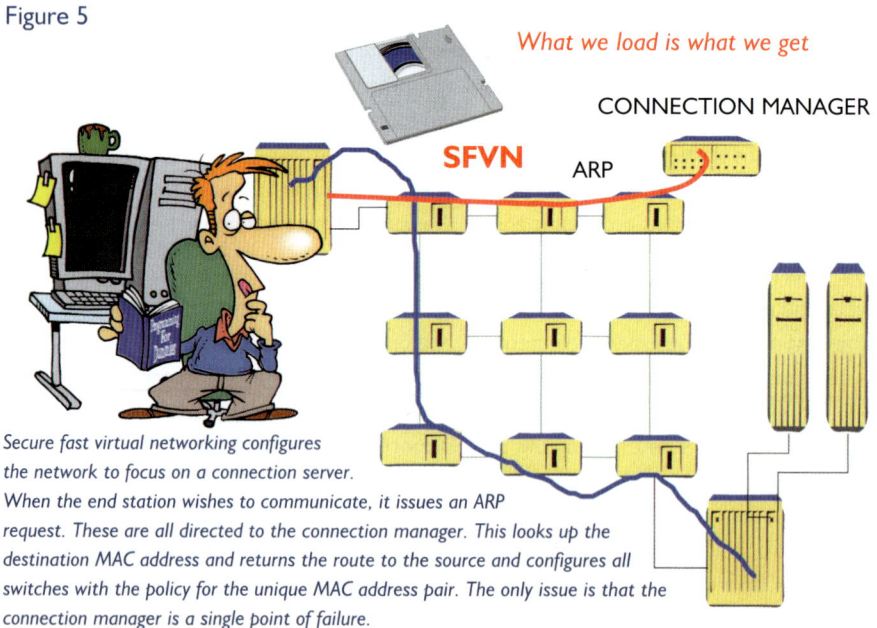

What we load is what we get

CONNECTION MANAGER

SFVN   ARP

Secure fast virtual networking configures the network to focus on a connection server. When the end station wishes to communicate, it issues an ARP request. These are all directed to the connection manager. This looks up the destination MAC address and returns the route to the source and configures all switches with the policy for the unique MAC address pair. The only issue is that the connection manager is a single point of failure.

ENTERPRISE NETWORKING

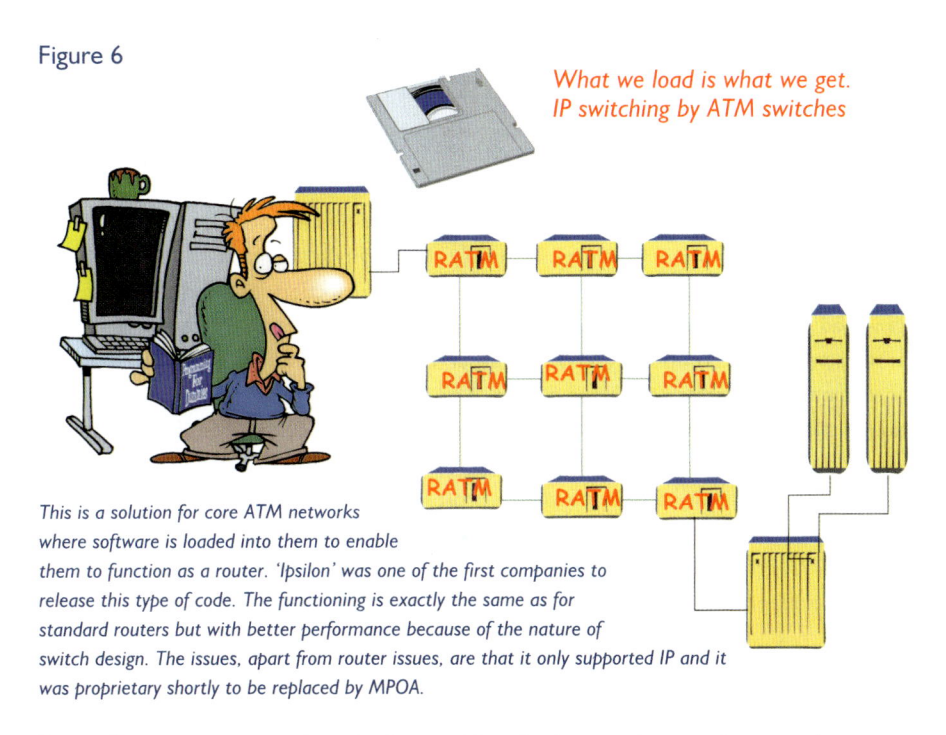

MULTI-SERVICE NETWORKING

Figure 6

*What we load is what we get.
IP switching by ATM switches*

This is a solution for core ATM networks where software is loaded into them to enable them to function as a router. 'Ipsilon' was one of the first companies to release this type of code. The functioning is exactly the same as for standard routers but with better performance because of the nature of switch design. The issues, apart from router issues, are that it only supported IP and it was proprietary shortly to be replaced by MPOA.

Figure 5 shows the server-based solutions. The idea here is that any device wishing to communicate will make its first connection to the server. Configuring all the end stations to be on the same subnet and the default address (address of the nearest router is also on the same subnet) causes all workstations to initiate a communications with an ARP (Address Resolution Protocol) request. All ARPs are forwarded to one point in the network the communications server. On receiving the ARP, the server sends the destination MAC address to the requesting workstation. Therefore, the source workstation has the physical address of where it has to go. This is now a unique combination the source and destination address pair. This is used by the communications server to programme the path through the network and fix it for the duration of the call. Each node on reading the unique address pair will just forward without processing the packet. The disadvantage is the administration to set up the IP addressing required and to program the communications server, which could be a single point of failure. The major advantage is that each communication session is enabled by the communications server. This enables what's known as policy management. Network managers can make the server run the company communication policy - *"Can this user, from this location, at this*

ENTERPRISE NETWORKING

MULTI-SERVICE NETWORKING

time of day, with this bandwidth requirement, communicate with the required device over which external services?"

Figure 6 shows a network that is required to support proprietary IP switching. Note this is not an existing router network but an ATM switched network on which the proprietary code is loaded. This code is a modified routing engine. The process is that when a workstation wishes to communicate it uses its default MAC address that is its nearest router engine. Here, the router engine does its normal routing function. The packet is then segmented, passed to the ATM hardware and passed on to the next ATM node. The packet is reassembled, the router engine performs its routing task and once again the packet is segmented and passed to the next node. This is carried on until it reaches the destination. If this is a continuous communication the proprietary code can identify the source destination address pair and fix the virtual circuit which is passed to all nodes in the path with their proprietary flow management protocols. The problem with this approach is that it's using ATM switches as IP-only routers and is proprietary. The ATM forum ratified Multi-Protocol over ATM (MPOA) in 1997, a standard router engine for ATM switches to support all protocols, making this solution short lived.

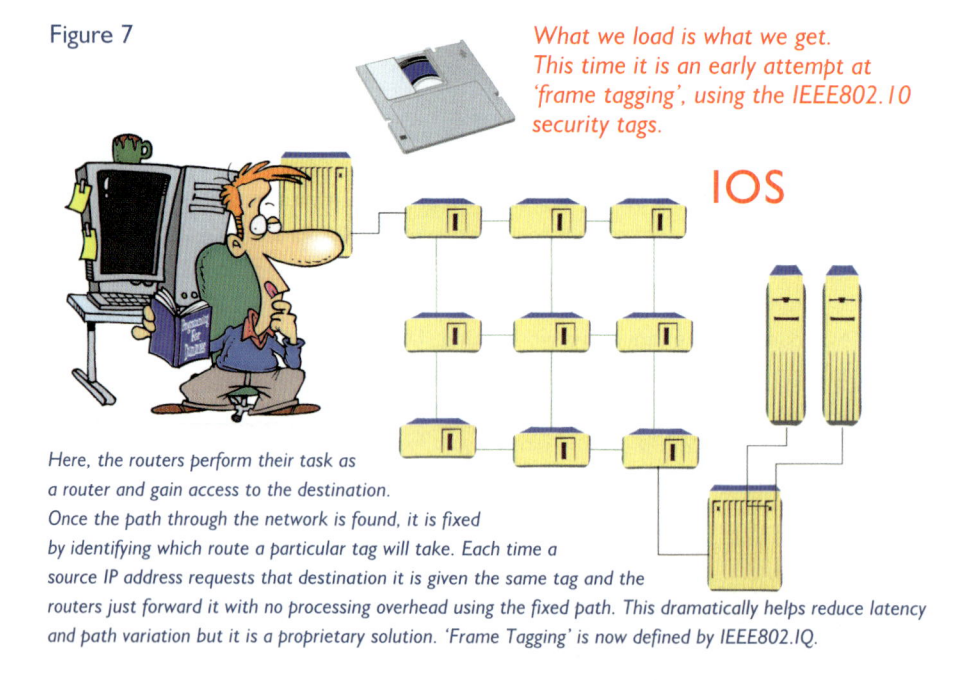

Figure 7

What we load is what we get. This time it is an early attempt at 'frame tagging', using the IEEE802.10 security tags.

Here, the routers perform their task as a router and gain access to the destination. Once the path through the network is found, it is fixed by identifying which route a particular tag will take. Each time a source IP address requests that destination it is given the same tag and the routers just forward it with no processing overhead using the fixed path. This dramatically helps reduce latency and path variation but it is a proprietary solution. 'Frame Tagging' is now defined by IEEE802.1Q.

ENTERPRISE NETWORKING

MULTI-SERVICE NETWORKING

Figure 7 shows an existing, software router-based network such as the Internet. Here the task is the same: fix the path and reduce the processing. When the workstation wants to communicate with the distant server it uses as its default MAC address the nearest router. The normal routing function gets the information across the network to the destination MAC address. If this is a continuous communication then a proprietary tag update protocol marks the IP source destination address pair with a frame tag number. Then each node in the path is informed of the tagging. Any time the workstation wants the same destination it is tagged by the edge router and the tag carries it across the network. The major advantage is that any other member of the subnet that wishes to use the same resource can use the same tag to bypass the routing function. So tagging gains more efficiency from an existing network of routers. The tagging scheme was based on IEEE802.10, the standards sub-committee working on tagging to identify IP traffic for setting security levels.

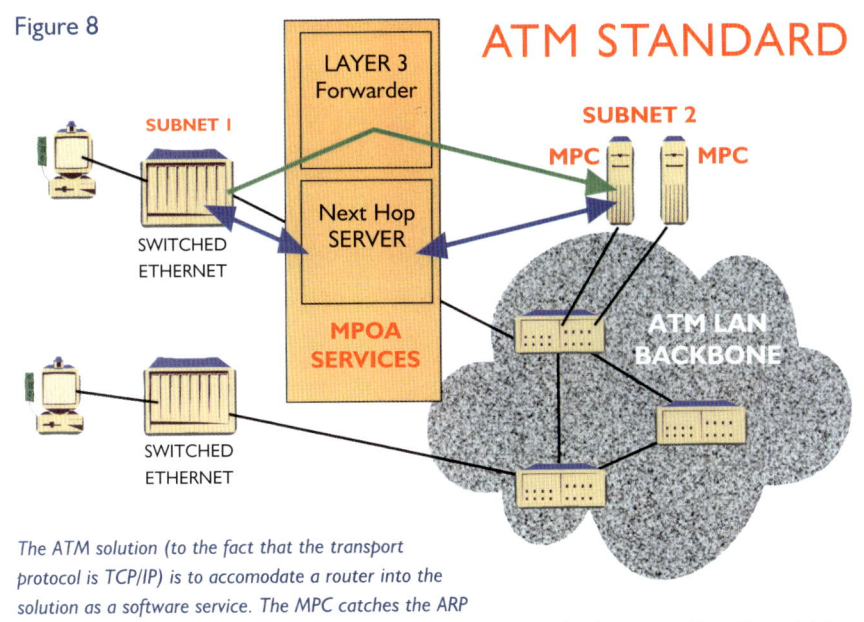

Figure 8

ATM STANDARD

The ATM solution (to the fact that the transport protocol is TCP/IP) is to accomodate a router into the solution as a software service. The MPC catches the ARP requests and uses the layer 3 forwarder to route the information to the destination. Once the path is known, the MPOA service uses the next hop server to set up virtual curcuits from source to destination, thereby fixing the path and allowing pure switching to take place. This is the standards-based solution for ATM switches in a packet world.

ENTERPRISE NETWORKING

MULTI-SERVICE NETWORKING

Figure 8 shows the ATM solution to supporting existing protocols across the ATM switched network MPoA (MultiProtocol over ATM). Here, like the proprietary model, there is a routing engine on the ATM switches but this time it's standards-based. The difference here is that the edge switch has an MPOA client that requests from the routing engine the ATM address and virtual circuit to use. Once the connection is made it can be taken over by the end node client enabling end-node to end-node communications without passing through the routing engine. The issues that network managers had to consider have since been superseded by the introduction of hardware-based routers that provide performance and support priority and QoS mechanisms to run voice applications.

Businesses today are free to upgrade their networks to standards-based switching solutions and write off the software routers. Or, if funding is short, these same routers can be redeployed onto the edge of the network and provide WAN services. The bigger issue is the Internet. There is such a vast number of software-based routers installed that it is going to take years to replace them all with hardware-based switching. While this happens, mechanisms will be deployed to gain that extra gram of performance and skim a fraction from the latency.

section eighteen

Introduction to Standards

Section 18: Introduction to Standards

This explains the OSI seven-layer communications model, which is mandatory in any communications publication. Hopefully, this explanation is short and sweet. There is no denying that the OSI protocols didn't make it but the TCP/IP protocol did.

ENTERPRISE NETWORKING

INTRODUCTION TO STANDARDS

Open Systems Interconnect originated from the International Standards Organisation. In plain English and to make it very clear, we have OSI from ISO - no wonder we all get confused.

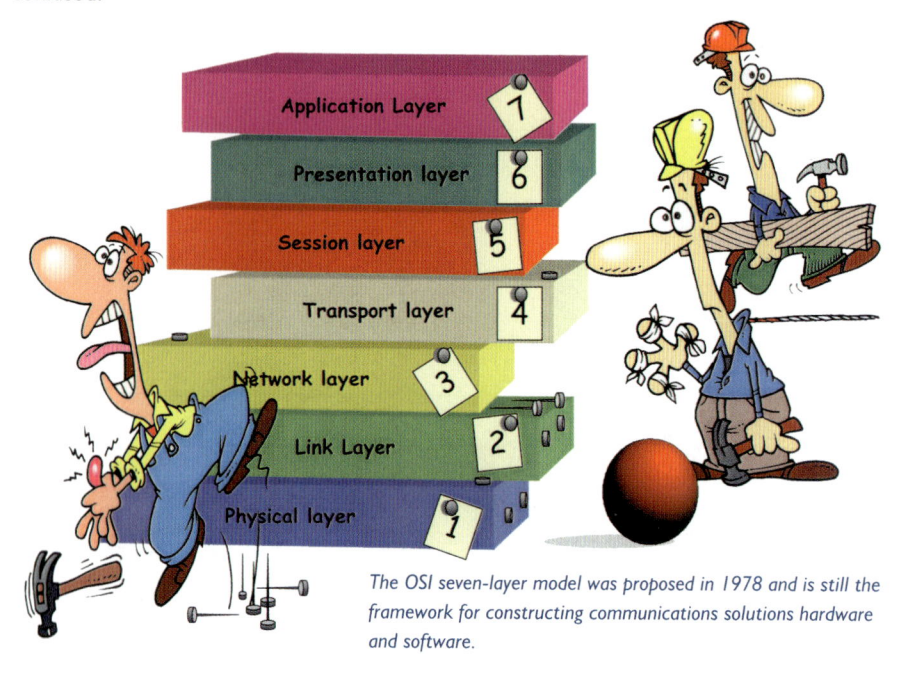

The OSI seven-layer model was proposed in 1978 and is still the framework for constructing communications solutions hardware and software.

In this section we will have a more formal look at the official standards. But, first the overall idea of OSI and the seven-layer communications model is covered. You need only to appreciate that OSI is all about one machine transferring information to another, so when data gets to the new machine it is correct and useable. The OSI model is a quick, easy way to understand the rules covering this communication. What we have to consider is the steps we have to take to ensure that two dissimilar machines can connect together and transfer meaningful data.

LAYERS 1 AND 2

The first step is to ensure that two machines wishing to communicate are connected physically together using the same wire, same plugs and sockets, and the same signal levels. So layer one is simple, consisting of the wire or fibre that is used to string the

ENTERPRISE NETWORKING

INTRODUCTION TO STANDARDS

Layer 1
The first layer of the OSI model is about the physical connection. For two machines to communicate they must be plugged into one another with the correct pin-out and signal levels.

Layer 2
This is about the use of the connected wire and is known as the Media Access Control (MAC) layer. First, a station checks the wire to make sure it's OK to communicate, Above it is the link layer which is responsible for passing the electrical signals from one machine to the other.

machines together. We also have to agree on whether we use +5 volts electricity or +12 volts electricity to indicate a signal. Or in fibre terms, do we use a green or a red light. All of these physical things are included in layer one, so you can ignore layer one.

Layer two concerns the chipsets. Chipsets contain the rules for sharing the wire, so 802.3 is the set of Ethernet rules for sharing the wire. 802.5 is another set of rules for using Token passing techniques for sharing wire. FDDI is yet another set of rules for sharing wire. An additional responsibility is to ensure that each device has a unique address, the MAC address. This is so that on the shared media, stations know what information they should be picking up or ignoring. Also, the chipsets are responsible for knowing that they sent information (six ones and ten zeros) to station number 57. Station 57 has to acknowledge that it did receive (six ones and ten zeros) and if it didn't please send it again without user intervention, this is the link layer protocol. Therefore we can view layer one and two as the hardware specifications that gets embedded in the networking products. These products are selected to interface into the cabling installation that is chosen for reasons of economics or distance or performance. Layer 1 and 2 implemented together define the communications infrastructure of an organisation.

ENTERPRISE NETWORKING

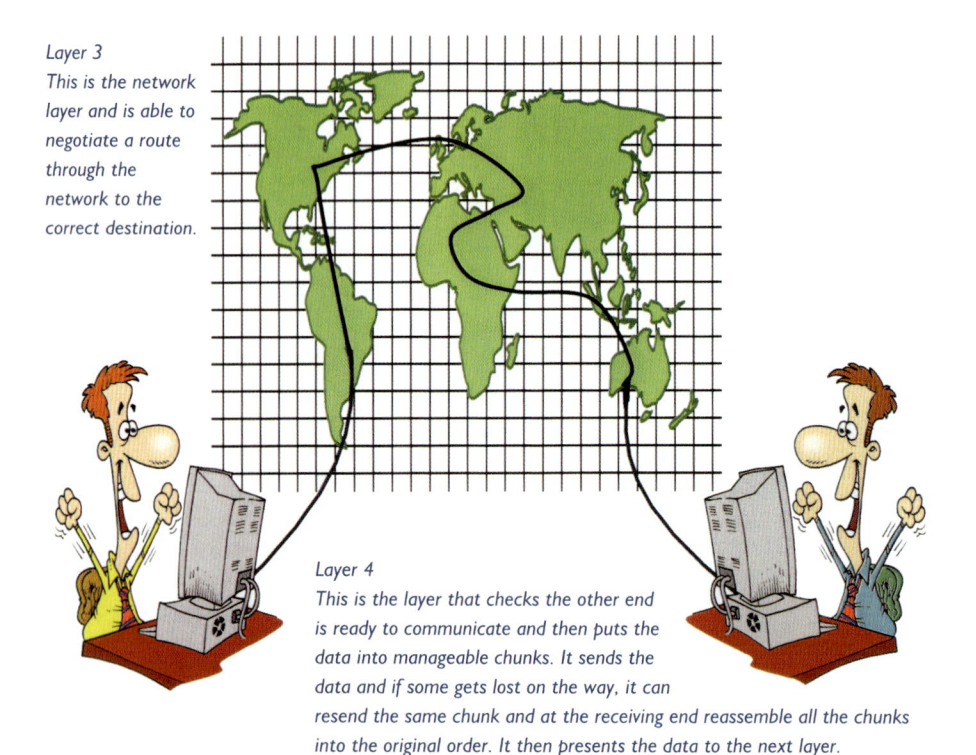

INTRODUCTION TO STANDARDS

Layer 3
This is the network layer and is able to negotiate a route through the network to the correct destination.

Layer 4
This is the layer that checks the other end is ready to communicate and then puts the data into manageable chunks. It sends the data and if some gets lost on the way, it can resend the same chunk and at the receiving end reassemble all the chunks into the original order. It then presents the data to the next layer.

LAYERS 3 AND 4

Layers 3 and 4 are pieces of software whose task is to understand the underlying communications infrastructure and ensure that connections made across it are secure and reliable. They have to provide extra addressing to get across more than the cable and they have to control the sending of information in manageable chunks. They have to talk to the software at the same level 3 and 4, on the receiving station and check they are receiving data OK or retransmission requests.

And if the connection is too slow, maybe it needs a different route is needed to get to the destination. That is why layer 3 is protocol-aware because it's the protocol's job to make such choices. In simple terms this software makes the connections. For example, if I pick up the phone and ring Hong Kong and that guy picks up the phone, that is equivalent to what I get from layers 3 and 4. When I say *"hello"* in English and then don't understand the response, we cannot communicate so we need another piece of software.

ENTERPRISE NETWORKING

INTRODUCTION TO STANDARDS

So far, layer 1 through to layer 4 is about making a connection, like picking up the phone and dialling China. The system is clever enough to make a connection ring the other end.

Communications cannot take place because the two end systems talk different languages, have different rules for protocol and different priorities. This is where the software of layers 5,6 and 7 come into play. These layers allow true communications, logging to hosts, file transfers and running remote applications.

LAYERS 5, 6 AND 7

The requirement of this second piece of software is to allow us to log onto a host, transfer a file and do simple electronic mail. This is the function of layers 5, 6 and 7, to provide meaningful communications. These layers are usually placed in the host computer or, in PC networking terms, in the network operating system. So, looking at the OSI model, layers 1 and 2 are the physical communications foundation on which are built layers 3 to 7.

CHOICES

For your cabling requirements, you can use copper in the form of co-ax, unshielded twisted pair, shielded twisted pair, fibre single mode or multimode or wireless using the radio waves. At layers 1 to 2, you can deploy various chipsets, giving you different technology. The choices you have are 802.3 Ethernet, 802.5 Token Ring, FDDI the 100Mbit/sec fibre distributed data interface networking standard, or ATM.

There are many choices for layers 3 and 4. If you had bought an old DEC system, they would have provided you with DECNet (old 3Com installations which tend to be XNS). Today, globally, TCP/IP is an accepted de facto standard. The advantage TCP/IP has over

ENTERPRISE NETWORKING

INTRODUCTION TO STANDARDS

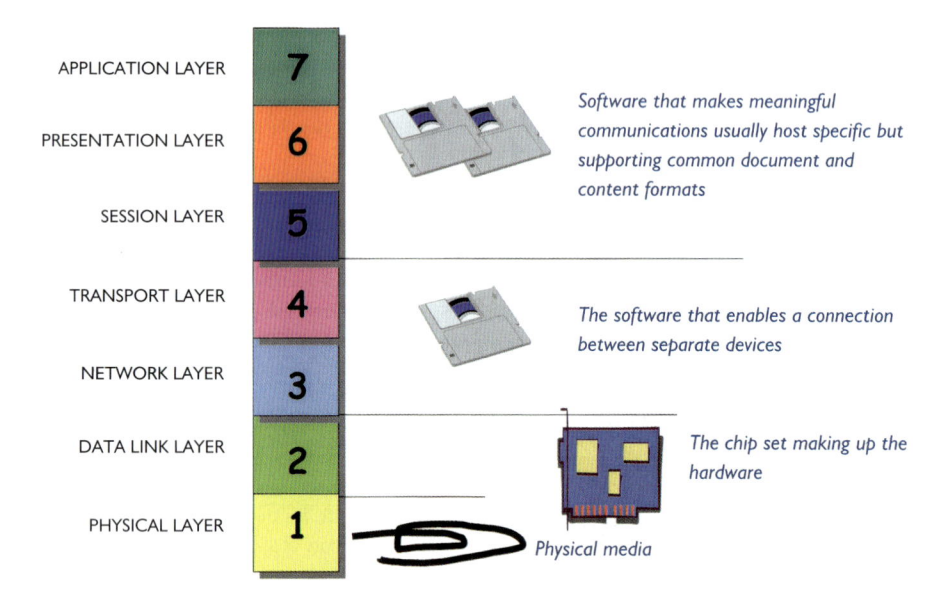

APPLICATION LAYER	7	
PRESENTATION LAYER	6	*Software that makes meaningful communications usually host specific but supporting common document and content formats*
SESSION LAYER	5	
TRANSPORT LAYER	4	*The software that enables a connection between separate devices*
NETWORK LAYER	3	
DATA LINK LAYER	2	*The chip set making up the hardware*
PHYSICAL LAYER	1	*Physical media*

XNS is that with top layers 5, 6 and 7, the communications piece of software is specified. So, you have telnet to actually make a connection to a host, virtual terminal that allows you to log on and be a terminal, File Transfer Protocol (FTP) which allows you to move files around and Simple Mail Transfer Protocol (SMTP), the protocol for sending e-mail. Programmers can access the network directly by using the TCP/IP-defined application interfaces of plugs and sockets.

So, TCP/IP is widely accepted and widely supported. In the IBM arena, if you bought an IBM Token Ring, your PC you would probably be running NetBEUI. This is just SNA on the Token Ring while IBM's way of doing communications is with an APPC LU6.2 interface. There were some companies that were selling layer three and four OSI protocol stacks, usually called OSI four. At the top end FTAM (File Transfer Access Method) accomplishes the same as FTP and virtual terminal is equivalent to the virtual terminal in telnet.

The problem with the OSI implementation is that there is no conformance testing, so if you brought someone's OSI seven-layer stack, then that is what you have bought. You have not bought someone's international standard, you have bought someone's interpretation of it. So communication software is definitely vendor-dependent and depends on the host. True standards come with conformance testing. All the suppliers

ENTERPRISE NETWORKING

INTRODUCTION TO STANDARDS

OSI SEVEN LAYER MODEL

Layer					
7	PROPRIETARY	TELNET VT FTP HTTP	APPC LU6.2	FTAM VT	M A N A G E M E N T
6					
5					
4	XNS	TCP/IP	SNA	OSI	
3					
2	802.3	802.5	FDDI	802.11	
1	CO-AX STP UTP FIBRE				

and all these protocols are available today, and if you want freedom of choice of host, then you have to support all these protocols. If you do have a LAN, the average number of protocols running across it is five. To compound things even more, the seven-layer model has approximately 257 specifications. Of this, approximately 70 - 100 have been ratified and are therefore real standards. To enable two machines to communicate they have to select the same specification for each of the seven layers. This has resulted in customer-driven selection of the specifications to make the implementation easier. These selections are known as profiles, a few are described later.

A MORE FORMAL APPROACH TO STANDARDS

No single vendor supplies the total solution. This being the case we should expect to see a range of dissimilar equipment in a computer installation. However, the company that owns the equipment must to be able to access the information on these dissimilar products. Therefore, if communications are to be established, a common language is

ENTERPRISE NETWORKING

INTRODUCTION TO STANDARDS

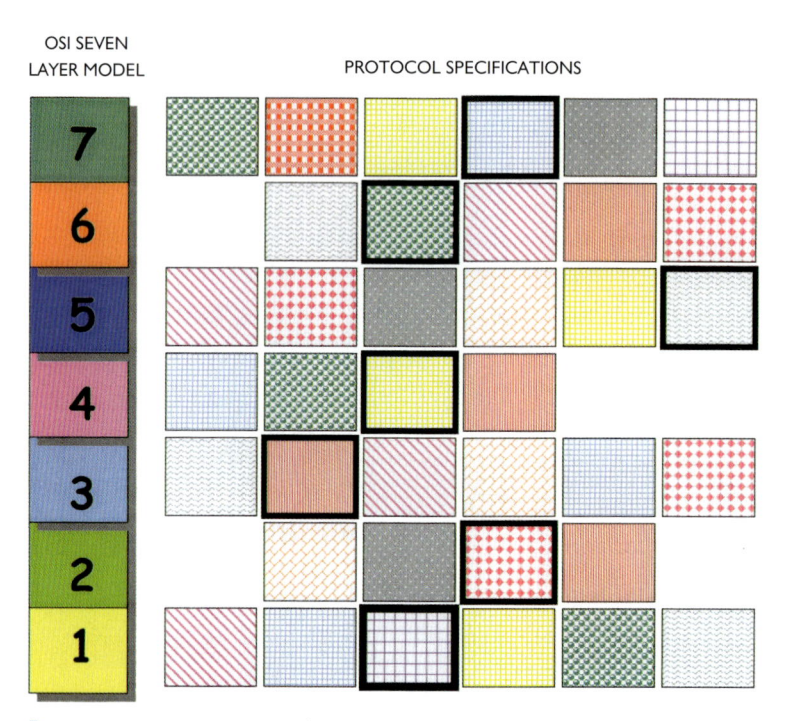

For two systems to communicate, they must support the same profile. A profile is a selection of the available layer specifications to provide a full seven-layer implementation. The most well known profiles are MAP and TOP.

required which all players understand. The International Standards Organisation (ISO) in 1978 addressed this communications problem, publishing a proposal for Open Systems Interconnect (OSI) commonly referred to as the seven-layer model. This proposal considers several pieces of equipment and the problem involved in establishing two-way secure communications, covering aspects such as the wiring between machines, addressing, and the presentation of information.

Huge progress has been achieved by the CCITT, now the International Telecommunications Union (ITU) which has ratified recommendations for level 1. These are covered in the V24/28 and X24/X21 specifications, to name a few. So far, recommendations have reached all the way to layer 7. Commonly understood standards such as X.25 provide levels 2 and 3.

For LAN standards conforming to the model, we have to look to the IEEE (Institute of Electrical and Electronics Engineers) and its 802 committees. The networking standards

ENTERPRISE NETWORKING

INTRODUCTION TO STANDARDS

published are: 802.3 (Ethernet), 802.4 (Token Bus), 802.5 (Token Ring), and even 802.11 (Wireless Networking). The American National Standards Institute (ANSI) has also been very active and its X3T9.5 committee is responsible for the FDDI (Fibre Distributed Data Interface) standard. Today, we have more standards than you can shake a stick at.

THE STANDARD SETTERS

INTERNATIONAL

CCITT - Geneva	Comité Consultatif International now the ITU
ITU - Geneva	International Telecommunications Union
ISO - Geneva	International Standards Commission
IEC - Geneva	International Electrotechnical Commission
IEEE - USA	Institute of Electronic and Electrical Engineers
IETF	Internet Engineering Task Force

REGIONAL

CEPT - Bern	Conference Europeane des Administrations des Institute of Electrical Administrations des Postes et Telecommunications and Electronics Engineers
CEN - Brussels	Comité European de Normalisation
CENELEC - Brussels	Comité European de Normalisation Electronique
ECMA - Geneva	European Computer Manufacturers Association

NATIONAL

BSI - Britain	British Standards Institute
DIN - Germany	Deutsches Institute fur Normung
ANSI - U.S.	American National Standards Committee
JISC - Japan	Japanese Industrial Standards Committee

ENTERPRISE NETWORKING

INTRODUCTION TO STANDARDS

AFNOR - France   Association Francaise de Normalisation

UNI - Italy   Ente Nazionale Italiano de Normalisation

NBS - U.S.   National Bureau of Standards

The whole computer manufacturing fraternity is announcing its commitment to standards, driven by purchasers asking the question, *"What about standards?"* So, when buying computer products you will be looking to standards, so you should be aware of the standards machinery.

Standards Committees are made up of suppliers, regulation bodies, and in some cases major users. The ITU has a four year cycle between publishing standards. A major influence is the European PTP (Public Telecommunications Operators). ECMA has 32 members studying distributed office systems, and has an average two years between agreed recommendations. The ISO committees liaises continually with both ITU and ECMA. The committee procedure results in conflicts but these are resolved by compromise. Therefore, in the standards recommendations for level four of the model, which is the transport mechanism, there are five options for implementing this level. Vendors are committed to those standards slowly being introduced. The message is that all vendors are committed to standards. The standards are being produced, but it is a slow process.

THE ISO REFERENCE MODEL

The major advantage of this layered implementation is to simplify the management of change in a networking system: each layer may be changed independently, as long as interfacing standards between layers are obeyed.

ENTERPRISE NETWORKING

INTRODUCTION TO STANDARDS

THE ISO REFERENCE MODEL

LAYER	FUNCTION
Application 7	Ensures that the application running in the enduser system has access to the underlying services and these are directly comprehensible to the applications programmes.
Presentation 6	This layer is capable of understanding the information presented by this system and on receiving remote data can ensure it conforms to the local requirements. This is achieved by restrictions data to and from a standard format used within the network.
Session 5	Ensures that both ends are capable of communicating and synchronises and manages end to end information exchange. A device that can multitask can have multiple session active simultaneously.
Transport 4	Provide transparent, reliable data transfer from end node to end node. Breaks the data into manageable packet sizes dependant on the transmission scheme. Manages the reception and correct sequencing of packets at the received end. Can resend any error packets even though they may be out of sequence.
Network 3	Adds an address layer to the packet stream and understands the concept of multiple networks. Performs the packet routing for data transfer between nodes.
Data Link 2	Provides the media access mechanism to determine when the media is available and the data link protocol improves error rate for frames moved between nodes also controls information flow between nodes.
Physical 1	Provides the physical interface onto the communications media copper cable, fibre or wireless. Then provides the bit level encoding and physically bit transfers bit between nodes.

ENTERPRISE NETWORKING

INTRODUCTION TO STANDARDS

THE SEVEN LAYERS EXPLAINED

1: Physical Layer
This provides the means to interface to the physical medium (wire, fibre, etc.) and the way to control its use, e.g. V24 RS232, V11, X21, 802.3 10Base 2, 802.3 10Base 5, 802.11a etc.

2: Data Link Layer
In recognising that physical transmission media are subject to random faults and noises, data link protocols are introduced in the data link layer to enable transmission errors to be detected and corrected. Flow control (known as logical link control) can also be implemented at this layer to prevent a fast transmitter from drowning a slow receiver. This is also the layer where the arbitration takes place for devices sharing a common cabling scheme known as the MAC layer, Media Access control.

3: Network Layer
This layer provides the functionality to route, switch and maintain communications between various networks. It is, therefore, capable of using routes provided by the Data Link Layer between or over networks.

4: Transport Layer
This layer specifies to the network layer which routes should be used for a communication, (parallel routes to obtain bandwidth if necessary), to optimise the utilisation of the network. The transport layer is the pivot of the model, in that it negotiates between the capability of the network below it, and the requirement of the processes (applications) above it.

5: The Session Layer
This is the lowest of the high level protocols. It specifies the type of transmission that is required, for example, full/half duplex and wire speed. Additionally, it communicates with the corresponding session layer in the receiving equipment to synchronise and manage the data communicated.

6: The Presentation Layer
The presentation layer performs the two-way function of taking information from applications and converting it into a form suitable for common understanding (that is, machine dependent), and also presenting the data exchange between systems to the applications in a form they can understand. Data can also be modified without changing its meaning (for example, it can change data characters from ASCII to EBCDIC).

ENTERPRISE NETWORKING

INTRODUCTION TO STANDARDS

7: The Application Layer
The highest layer defined by the ISO reference model is concerned with supporting the applications that exchange information with others. Many different types of applications are relevant to OSI, from terminal to computer transaction processing, to interconnected real time process control programmes.

OTHER STANDARDS

A number of the relevant standards have already been mentioned. It is, however, worthwhile to review these standards to indicate their relative position and importance.

The **IEEE802.1** working group is chartered to develop standards and recommended practices in 802 LAN/MAN architecture, internetworking, network management and protocol layers above the MAC & LLC layers.

The **IEEE802.2** working group develops standards for Logical Link Control.

The **IEEE802.3** working group develops standards for CSMA/CD (Ethernet) based LANs. Active projects include IEEE802.3ae, 10Gbit/s Ethernet and IEEE802.3af DTE Power via MDI. CSMA/CD was the first fully ratified standard by the IEEE committee. It describes the physical and link layer specifications of the OSI model, and provides a carrier sense multiple access protocol with collision detection (CSMA/CD). This means that all devices have equal access rights to the network. Devices listen to the network and if no traffic is detected, then a device can use the network for connection and transfer of data. If a device listens and data traffic is on the network, the device will wait until the transfer of information is complete. If two or more devices use the network at exactly the same time, there is a collision. When this happens, the devices recognise the symptoms and stop using the network for a small random period of time, thus they will not all access the network together a second time. Generally known as Ethernet, it operates at 10Mbit/sec, 100Mbit/sec, 1Gbit/sec and, from 2002 onwards at 10Gbit/sec, it is the most widely installed technology.

The **IEEE802.4** working group develops standards for Token Bus. Token Passing Bus standard is fully ratified by the IEEE, and used within the MAP protocol in the lower two layers. It provides a token passing scheme between nodes on a bus co-axial cable network. The access method can be modulated in three ways, broadband modulation being most popular. Packets are transmitted on the network at a bit rate of 10Mbit/sec, however, several channels can be modulated onto a single physical carrier to provide additional bandwidth. Current work being completed by the IEEE802.4 committee covers

ENTERPRISE NETWORKING

INTRODUCTION TO STANDARDS

the operation of carrier band, a low cost alternative, using optical fibre to support the access method and modulation technique, conformance testing, redundant media, and through-the-air media. IEEE802.4 was never as popular as IEEE802.3 and IEEE802.5

The **IEEE802.5** committee took responsibility to ratify the Token Passing Ring standard which was brought to prominence by IBM in the mid-1980s. It describes the the OSI model's physical and MAC layers, and provides a token passing access method for up to 250 nodes. Any one node on the system may take system management responsibility on a priority basis. The speed of transmission on the LAN initially was limited to 4Mbit/sec or 16Mbit/sec. Today, an industry group has collaborated to bring 100Mbit/sec and 1000Mbit/sec token passing.

The **IEEE802.6** working group develops standards for Metropolitan Area Networks (MANs). This standard describes a MAN which interconnects nodes within a 50Km diameter using optical fibre cable. The intention is to operate at 100Mbit/sec connecting nodes over a 2Km distance. The standard exists in a draft form but does not have extensive approvals, as it is considered inadequate to support voice traffic.

The **IEEE802.7** Broadband Technical Advisory Group (TAG) develops recommended practice for broadband LANs. The group is inactive but is supported by 802.14.

The **IEEE802.8** Technical Advisory Group (TAG) develops recommended practices for fibre optics.

The **IEEE802.9** working group develops standards for Isochronous LANs, this was seen as a LAN solution for integrated voice and data communications over a common infrastructure.

The **IEEE802.10** working group is ratifying standards for interoperable LAN/MAN Security (SILS). This defines a 48-byte packet extension to enable the packet content to be security tagged. This standard was used by a group of manufacturers to produce frame tagging to enable virtual networks to be configured. This implementation was superseded by IEEE802.1q.

The **IEEE802.11** working group develops standards for wireless communications. The two significant standards are IEEE802.11b 11Mbit/sec and IEEE802.11a, the 54Mbit/sec standard.

The **IEEE802.12** working froup develops standards for Demand Priority.

The **IEEE802.15** working group develops Personal Area Network consensus standards

ENTERPRISE NETWORKING

INTRODUCTION TO STANDARDS

for short distance wireless networks the most visible of which is Bluetooth supported by the computer manufacturers.

The **IEEE802.16** Wireless MANTM Standard for Broadband Wireless Metropolitan Area Networks.

The **IEEE802.17** Resilient Packet Ring Working Group

FIBRE DISTRIBUTED INTERFACE (FDDI)

There are four FDDI standards developed by the X3T9.5 committee of the American National Standards Institute (ANSI). ANSI is a member of the ISO, and is responsible for developing the seven-layer OSI reference model. The FDDI standards are in accordance with layers one and two of the OSI reference model.

TYPES OF FDDI DEVICES

FDDI supports the interconnection of four types of devices. These devices are categorised by their connection to the FDDI network. The four types are as follows:

Dual Attach Stations (DAS) - an FDDI device that connects directly to both dual pairs of counter rotating rings (four fibre connections) in the back bone or back end.

Single Attach Stations (SAS) - an FDDI device that connects to a single pair (two fibre) link coming from an FDDI concentrator (DAC or SAC). An SAS is typically a workstation (or network management station), however, could also be a bridge or router.

Dual Attach Concentrator (DAC) - a DAS with multiple single attach ports for access to multiple SASs.

Single Attach Concentrator (SAC) - an SAS with multiple single attach 'M' ports for access to multiple SASs.

IMPLEMENTED PROFILES

There are many standards ratified by the standards bodies and the nature of the OSI seven layer model is that any layer 4 code will interface into any layer 3 code. For two computers to communicate with each other successfully they must have compatible selections for all seven layers. A selection of specific specifications is known as a profile. There are some very famous profiles that are listed below.

ENTERPRISE NETWORKING

INTRODUCTION TO STANDARDS

MAP AND MANUFACTURING

Common communications standards are needed for both equipment and programmes, so that all automation equipment can communicate via existing and planned networks. MAP stands for Manufacturing Automation Protocol, and was originated by General Motors to enable the interconnection of various proprietary manufacturing computer sub-systems which existed in their plants. The standard has now become internationally supported, in Europe and the US. MAP has declined in prominence because of the costs of implementing the broadband infrastructure.

TOP

TOP stands for Technical and Office protocol, and is similar to the MAP structure. It enables computer-aided workstations to be linked into manufacturing networks. Pioneered by the Boeing Corporation, the TOP specification release 3.0 is very similar to MAP release 3.1, except for the application layer and physical layers being based on Ethernet. In TOP, only FTAM (File Transfer, Access and Management) and Limited File Management have been specified for the application layer - IEEE802.3 is specified rather than the IEEE802.4 Token Ring bus which is used in MAP.

GOSIP

GOSIP is an acronym of the OSI profile specified by government procurement departments (Government Open Systems Interconnection Profile). This is a selection of the OSI protocols that a supplier must provide to gain any governmental business. The problem with GOSIP is that there are two flavours, European GOSIP and US GOSIP. They are different specifications so there are two OSI standard profiles for suppliers to support.

POSIT.

In 1994, GOSIP changed to POSIT the Profile for Open Systems Interconnect with TCP/IP. This enabled goverment procurement departments to purchase TCP/IP solutions instead of demanding OSI protocols from suppliers. The Internet's reliance on and world governments' specification of IP signed the death warrant of other networking protocols.

section nineteen

Network Industry History

Panel of Experts

Section 19: The History of this Industry

If you are reading this and have got this far, you must be working in or with, communications products. Having lived through all the changes within this industry, I can remember many of the significant milestones. However, if you remember them differently to me, let me know.

SECTION NINETEEN

ENTERPRISE NETWORKING

NETWORK INDUSTRY HISTORY

INTRODUCTION

This is a biased view of the history of the networking industry. It has to be. The only history I know is the one I lived. I started life as a radar technician in the British Army and worked on computers that had more valves in them than transistors. The introduction of large scale integration (LSI) technology was a great relief. Work became fun. Problem solving was more like figuring out a crossword puzzle, where as the valve systems problem solving was more like brain surgery. I joined the computer industry with Wordplex, a word processing company, where we thought 8K of RAM and a 1MHz processor was as good as it gets. In 1981 Wordplex's headquarters in the UK decided to implement a local area network (LAN). The quote for the cable installation was $30,000. I was the training manager and volunteered my team of five guys to do the networking task over a weekend for $1,000 each and all the beer and pizza we could eat. We went for it and installed all the networking (including the active components) and configured the system by Monday morning, users could log in and go. This was exciting and a revolution in how we connected up our systems. From this installation, local area networking was my chosen path.

This is a limited view and if you know better, you may be able to fill in the gaps. Email them to me and we will include the update in the next re-write. I would only ask you

ENTERPRISE NETWORKING

NETWORK INDUSTRY HISTORY

focus on the effects to the LAN industry. I will leave computers, storage and wide area communications to others who most probably had just as much fun as I have had in this industry.

1956: Bell Labs scientists receive the Nobel Prize for inventing the transistor in 1947, without it we would not have our industry and the world would be a duller place.

1969: the founding of the ARPAnet, the US DoD networking project to create a connectionless method of defence and, later, academic computer users to connect to each other, enabling the sharing of data and research information. This also started the process known as RFCs (Request For Comments). This is where the members of the ARPAnet could develop a solution to a communications problem and circulate it to all other members. Once all contributions are collated the RFC is eventual acceptance as a specification for widespread implementation. This is still the process today and is driven by the IETF (Internet Engineering Task Force). This process led to the development of TCP/IP in 1982.

The other major communications event was the release of the RS232 serial interface specifications for the physical level connections of computer and communications equipment. This was created and published under the EIA (Electronics Industry Association). Apollo 11 lands on the Moon and Neil Armstrong becomes the first man on the Moon.

1971: the enabling technology that would drive the communications industry for the foreseeable future was released the Intel 4004 chip. This took the integrated circuit to a whole new level by integrating all the components of a computer from the central processing unit, memory, and input and output controls onto a single chip. This microprocessor could be mass manufactured and then programmed to perform any and all the tasks required by networking manufacturers. This has been partly sidelined today with the greater emphasis on Application Specific Integrated Circuit (ASIC) technology.

1973: Robert Metcalfe publishes a description of what will become Ethernet as part of his Harvard PhD thesis. Metcalfe and David Boggs would later create the first Ethernet network at Xerox in Palo Alto, California. Metcalfe would later start 3Com Corporation in June 1979.

1974 was also the year that IBM created System Networking Architecture (SNA) as an architecture for communications, predominantly mainframe networks. As with everything involved with mainframe technology, nothing changes overnight but, by the mid-1980s,

ENTERPRISE NETWORKING

NETWORK INDUSTRY HISTORY

SNA had become the dominant networking solution for the IBM mainframe environment. The position during the early 1990s was that the SNA accounted for 50% of all networks installed. However, throughout that decade a migration grew in the direction of IP until by the end of that decade, it was clearly unstoppable. SNA was complex and very expensive to implement but well understood, reliable, manageable, predictable and secure.

1976: X.25 is specified to provide a pay as you go packet-based communications service with speeds from 9600 baud to 48Kbit/sec.

1976: the CCITT, now the ITU, defines the X.25 protocol for public, packet-switched networks, causing a huge problem for LAN manufacturers building gateways.

1977: Digital Equipment Corporation (DEC) becomes the first computer company to create its own Internet site.

1977: Xerox Corporation patents Ethernet. NASA launches the spacecrafts of Voyager I and Voyager II to explore and eventually leave our solar system. Both crafts are now heading out of the solar system. In 1998, Voyager I became the most distant man-made object in space when it passed Pioneer 10.

1978: in Sydney, Australia, the International Standards Organisation (ISO), a working group of the Consultative Committee for International Telephone and Telegraphy (CCITT), published a specification for Open Systems Interconnect which became known as the OSI seven-layer model. It specified the rules covering all physical, electrical and process signalling needed to ensure two dissimilar communications devices could connect and transfer meaningful data.

The layers have defined interfaces so that any layer can be changed for a different module without having to change all seven layers. This enables easier product development and has been used to demarcate manufacturer responsibilities. Today the seven-layer model is still used to construct communications equipment and solutions. Different groups have adopted one specific standard for each of the seven layers. This is known as a profile, notable ones were MAP, TOP and POSIT.

In **1979** Ungermann-Bass is incorporated and, using co-ax line drivers, manufactures a 4Mbit/sec shared media LAN. As far as I can remember, this is the first commercial available LAN product designed to simplify and introduce flexibility into cabling into a host computer. Somewhere, there is the development of the Cambridge Ring based on a ring topology and used slotted ring, that is, a fixed number of packets on the ring. This never

ENTERPRISE NETWORKING

NETWORK INDUSTRY HISTORY

really arrives so is not noticed when it goes.

1980: Intel, DEC and Xerox jointly release the Ethernet specification, which becomes the de facto networking standard and forms the bases of the IEEE802.3 CSMA/CD standard. Ungermann-Bass is one of the first manufacturers to release a commercial Ethernet standard based product in the NetOne product range. IBM announces the IBM PC and created a new industry: cloning.

1981: The Institute of Electrical and Electronic Engineers (IEEE) meets to discuss independent standards for the new industry of networking. The first meeting is in room 802 so they became the IEEE802.xxx where the xxx became the standard for any ratified specifications providing networking services. They start work on defining the access method and link layer protocol for CSMA/CD Ethernet and publish the first Ethernet standard in 1983. They maintain physical compatibility with the de facto Ethernet V2 specification from the original gang of three. IBM releases its IBM PC and more than 65,000 are sold in the first four months.

1982: The TCP/IP protocol specification was published. Bob Metcalf (Mr Ethernet), left DEC to found 3Com and focus on PC networking. IBM releases its first PC networking product, which works using broadband token passing. Racal Milgo releases the Planet LAN that used token passing on a dual co-ax cable. Racal doesn't pursue the IEEE standards so the technology is never widely supported and after achieving 25% of LANs in Europe by 1984 disappeared by 1987. Coincidentally, the FDDI standard that's yet to come has all of the Planet features but is based on dual fibre.

1983: Internet Activities Board (IAB) is founded and a number of task forces created, including the Internet Engineering Task Force (IETF), with the aim of handling specific technological issues. TCP/IP is officially adopted as the protocol for use on the Internet. Cabletron Systems is incorporated and starts life as a cable company. 3Com outships IBM in the PC networking market place. ChipCom is incorporated and manufactures modem products becoming one of the first manufacturers to support the later released IEEE802.3 10Base36 specification: Ethernet over broadband cabling. Novell is out looking for venture capital as PC networking is seen as a niche solution because IBM is providing a limited and expensive solution. TCP/IP addressing is seen as complicated and not user friendly so the University of Wisconsin gives the world Domain Name Server (DNS). This allows humans to type in user-friendly names while the client looks up the IP address at the nearest DNS. TCP/IP and DNS dominate the Unix computer marketplace.

1984: BICC (a British networking company) which makes Ethernet transceivers and

ENTERPRISE NETWORKING

NETWORK INDUSTRY HISTORY

repeaters signs up Cabletron as its American distribution partner. IEEE802.4 committee ratifies the Token Bus standard for broadband networking, which is then adopted by General Motors as its de facto standard. GM goes on to specify a complete OSI profile Manufacturing Automation Protocol (MAP). Two companies incorporate to address this market place, Concorde Data Systems and INI Industrial Networking Inc. The IEEE802.3 10Base36 subcommittee specifies a broadband version of Ethernet. This used industry standard co-ax at the physical layer and radio frequencies as a carrier signals down the cable plant. Bridge Communications is a player in this market place before being purchased by 3Com. Ungermann-Bass does not use the IEEE standard but uses the CCTV (Closed Circuit Television) standard believing that while broadband is too expensive to use just for networking, deploying multiple services makes it commercially viable. The ARPAnet is extended from the American military to cover academic requirements. ISDN is specified by the CCITT as a subscriber service at speeds from 64Kbit/sec to 2Mbit/sec.

1985: Cabletron introduces the first networking test equipment and becomes the first installation company that can certify a cable installation. Key Xerox communications staff resign and take a licence to manufacture and develop Xerox networking products. Thus, Synoptics enters the market with a flying start. Novell hosts its very first NetWorld conference and exhibition in Dallas underlining its newfound dominance in Network Operating System market place. TOP, the technical office protocol, is specified by Boeing which adopts the specifications supported by MAP but uses Ethernet as the MAC layer. Racal Milgo becomes the European distributor for Concorde MAP products. IBM releases Token Ring networking close to the IEEE802.5 standard for 4Mbit/sec token passing networking - but it is not quite the same. IBM suffers a major problem because its network is supposed to support 256 workstations but fails above 22 workstations because of jitter. It takes a year to fix by reducing the rings to 72 devices. This all helps to reduce the market share of Proteon Networks which have established itself as the pioneer of token passing networks with a proprietary 10Mbit/sec product. The most significant change the young LAN industry has experienced occurs as AT&T announce sits structured wiring scheme. IBM and others have similar structured wiring schemes but none has the same impact as the unshielded twisted pair solution from AT&T.

1986: the U.S. National Science Foundation (NSF) initiates the development of the NSFNET which provided 45Mbit/sec backbone communications services for the Internet. DEC having been the first manufacturer to register its domain on the Internet creates the first defences against unauthorised access by building the world's first firewall. Cabletron

ENTERPRISE NETWORKING

NETWORK INDUSTRY HISTORY

releases the first communications product with diagnostic indicators, the ST500 transceiver. From this release onwards, diagnostic lights become a standard feature on all communications products. This innovation launches Cabletron and, within two years, an IDC report gives Cabletron 81% of all transceivers installed worldwide. 3Com increases its offering for PC networking by introducing diskless workstations and support for a version of Microsoft's MS-Net networking operating system in competition with Novell. IBM, in order to maintain account control, releases Netview, its proprietary network management product for SNA networks. IBM follows up this announcement a year later with its ONMA (Open Network Management Architecture) for third party vendors to fall in line with how IBM sees the world from its dominant position.

1987: The Simple Gateway Monitoring Protocol (SGMP) is demonstrated to monitor products connecting to the Internet. This protocol is later to evolve into SNMP. The MAP standards committee releases MAP 2.1 in April and announces that MAP 3.0 will be released in October, requiring a hardware upgrade. At the time of the announcement, Concord has 16% market share and INI owned by Ungermann-Bass has 75% market share, IBM, DEC and Ferranti sharing 9%. From the announcement in April, customers stop buying MAP product, waiting for the completion of MAP 3.0. This results in salespeople not achieving targets and hence not getting paid and MAP engineers not installing networks and having to be redeployed. With no revenue coming from MAP products by October, Ungermann-Bass discontinues its MAP range and closes down INI. Users of MAP have no upgrade and no future products from the dominant player in the market place. Today, MAP based on broadband is dead. Structured wiring is taking off for telephony installations but uptake is slow for data services until Gartner compares telephony ownership costs against data terminal ownership costs, since both resources lived on employees' desks. In a seminal report, Gartner showed that telephony devices had an annual cost of ownership of $300 but computer devices was $1,500. This is a result of the churn rate, the adds, moves and changes that occur in an organisation every year, the average being 22.5% of all employees who will change location. In the finance industry this proves to be 75% of employees over the next five years. The savings in telephony are attributed to the support of saturation wiring making the churn rate easier to implement and manage.

1988: the network industry responds big time with Cabletron and the MMAC chassis, Ungermann Bass with the Access One and Synoptics with its 1000 chassis. These are all modular hub devices that support structured wiring schemes with different technologies: Ethernet, Token Ring, FDDI, Terminal Servers; Ungermann Bass even has 3270 cluster

ENTERPRISE NETWORKING

NETWORK INDUSTRY HISTORY

controller networking devices. 3Com withdraws from the Microsoft alliance and admits defeat in trying to take on Novell with its version of MS-Net. 3Com moves into mainstream networking, purchasing bridge communications giving it a bridge and router range of products.

Tandem Computers purchases Ungermann Bass but never really figures out how to benefit from being able to provide a complete solution. ETSI rewrites the ISDN specification and tries to unify the different interpretations across Europe known as Euro-ISDN. The ANSI standards body ratified the HIPPI specifications for 800Mbit/sec simplex and 1.6Gbit/sec full duplex. This solution is focused on the supercomputer market place and is supported by only a handful of manufacturers. The first transatlantic fibre-optic cable linking North America and Europe is completed and can handle 40,000 telephone calls simultaneously. It's nothing to do with networking but it is really cool. Voyager 1 passes Pioneer 10 to become the most distant manmade object in existence and will continue to send information back to earth until 2020.

1989: IBM finally figures out that PC networking is the way of the future and that its unique, proprietary implementation is inhibiting the success of Token Ring, which is being outsold by Ethernet by a ratio of ten to one. Madge Networks, a UK Token Ring company, is outshipping IBM in the adaptor marketplace, using these funds to develop a whole range of networking products that compete directly with IBM in its own customer base. Synoptics sets its stall in the marketplace by dropping its 1000 chassis and replacing it with a new chassis the 3000 with no buy-back, upgrade or compensation for customers of the 1000 who found they had no future. Another significant event is a bunch of IBM Netview developers who leave IBM and set up Tivolli to build true Open Systems management based on the ideas created by the Network Management Forum supported by the ISO. They will become one of the dominant systems management framework products in the market by the late 1990s. The first specification for Point to Point Protocol (PPP) is released in RFC 1134, a protocol used by almost all dial-up Internet users today.

1990: The year when network management becomes a significant tool in the network marketplace. There are several vendor specific implementations of SNMP management regimes and a computer company Sun has released SUNNet Manager, a generic management platform for hardware manufacturers to customise and sell, so they have only to develop hardware agents. Sun even goes through a phase of giving it away to gain significant market share. HP from the diagnostics point of view comes up with a similar idea for HP OpenView, another generic platform for launching vendor-specific modules

ENTERPRISE NETWORKING

NETWORK INDUSTRY HISTORY

using a common database of information about the networking infrastructure. The major achievement of the year is the release of Spectrum by Cabletron Systems. A network management product with a difference, it is based on Artificial Intelligence. The technology is cutting edge, using C++ and object oriented programming, with inductive modelling at its core. It leverages a new technique called inference handlers which is revolutionary for a hardware vendor which only started manufacturing transceivers five years earlier. The competition reacts to the launch by announcing that it will have C++ product by 1995, thus enhancing the amazing achievement of Cabletron. A scientist, Tim Berners-Lee, at CERN releases the specification for HTML, the Hypertext Mark-up Language that makes page information the way to share information on the Internet and HyperText Links that enable hopping from page to page without worrying about location. This opens up the Internet for use by non-technical users. Mr Bereners-Lee is the first to coin the phrase worldwide Web.

1991: Chipcom joins the hub club with its release of the Online Ethernet segmenting hub. Bytech enters the Token Ring market with a hub that supported Port Assignment. This means that once devices are connected, rings can be configured by any combinations of ports whereas the competition has to assign whole interface cards to specific rings. These startups are outmanoeuvred by the vastly more resourced big three: Cabletron, Synoptics and 3Com. 3Com purchased BICC which gives them a chassis product line. All three companies responded with multi-segmenting hub releases.

An 'up-start' router company with shed-loads of software and the most expensive hardware you could imagine IPO's and onto the scene steps Cisco Systems. Focusing on WAN interoffice networks, Cisco isn't seen as significant networking player, a huge mistake by marketing strategists. They argue that a LAN might need two to three hundred hubs in each building but you only need one router at each end of the link. Cisco is dismissed as a niche player.

1992: the big move in the marketplace is IBM's SNA network architecture recognising that TCP/IP dominates the world of communications and that its customer base wants more open systems that allowed the use of open platforms. Cabletron moves into the SNA marketplace with TCP/IP to SNA encapsulating products so that both protocols can securely transition the others infrastructure. Ungermann-Bass always had solutions for this marketplace and Synotics solved the problem with development partnerships. The oddball is 3Com which decides this was the moment to discontinue its 3174 and 5250 networking solutions. IBM puts resources into network management to lock the competition out with Netview and its master-slave architecture, only IBM can be a

ENTERPRISE NETWORKING

NETWORK INDUSTRY HISTORY

master of this. Cabletron responds by integrating into the architecture a release of Blue Vision that puts its Spectrum AI product into IBM accounts, enabling the SNA world and the IP world to be managed and controlled from the same platform. It will take till 1996 when IBM purchased Tivoli for it to solve the same problem. During the 1992 US Presidential election, Vice-Presidential candidate Al Gore promises to make the development of the information superhighway an administrative priority. This fuels investment into the Internet on a global basis. Countries who have not been taking this communications revolution seriously finally see the light.

1993: The year of ATM, a solution without a problem. Fore Systems launches serious products and the big three all go along for the ride. The premise is that you no longer need to purchase and support multiple technologies, Ethernet, Token Ring, FDDI and a whole set of WAN products. Instead, ATM can be deployed end to end and will support all service requirements of voice, video and data. This turned out to be a big mistake. What the manufacturers' marketing departments did not do was check the economics. If a corporation had 3,000 nodes of Ethernet working well why would it change out the technology for ATM, when there are no specific ATM-dependent applications. Three thousand nodes at $1,500 per node is $4,500,000 and you then must swap out all of your networking hubs for ATM switches. This is not an economically viable proposition. Ungermann-Bass tries to reinvent itself with a new name and rationalised product range as UB Networks. The first Web graphics browser, Mosaic is released.

1994: Wellfleet buys Synoptics. Although announced as a merger the senior management team around the world is predominantly Wellfleet staff. They rename the company Bay Networks. Wellfleet was Cisco's major router competitor with well-engineered products but not the protocol support. 3Com releases its stackable product range to challenge the modular hub in the SME marketplace. Kalpana releases the first Ethernet switch. A cut-through switch, it ushers in a new era to the networking industry of switching. Cabletron launches SecureFast, a router-free network that can implement routing and bandwidth control per MAC address. This was the first implementation of the future directory-enabled networks (DEN). This work pioneered Virtual Networking. Wireless LANs become the new thing but only deliver low speeds of around about 1-2Mbit/sec, so they don't become mainstream. The core backbone of the Internet is upgraded to ATM. Not an easy task as the traffic is based on TCP/IP packets, so these units have to support routing services with some of the early implementations described in section 17. The final specification for IPv6 is released by the IAB recommending 128-bit addresses (RFC 1883), enough to address everyone in the world several times over. Also this year the leading

ENTERPRISE NETWORKING

NETWORK INDUSTRY HISTORY

Token-Ring manufacturers form the Alliance for Strategic Token-Ring Advancement and Leadership (ASTRAL). ASTRAL's mission is to promote Token-Ring technology in the face of increasing popularity of Ethernet. A strange interest group, as most are Ethernet suppliers benefiting from its popularity.

1995: Cisco realises that LAN suppliers dominate corporate directions because they control all the desktops. Cisco's response is to start an acquisition trail that eventually builds the largest company in the industry, at one time topping Microsoft. It acquires Kalpana the switching manufacturer, Lightstream, an Ungermann-Bass company focused on ATM solutions both LAN and WAN, and this is just the start of a whole raft more. Xylan starts up and is first to develop a modular switch that can support Ethernet, Token Ring, FDDI and ATM in one cross-connected chassis.

1996: Xylan starts its marketing campaign to be known as the Virtual Networking Company and does a reasonable job because Alcatel takes a 10% equity stake and signs up as a worldwide partner. Most of the manufacturers are pushing switching as the new paradigm. The whole industry is promoting LAN switching in the core of the network and the router is relegated to a software service on the edge of the network. 3Com purchases Research Machines which manufactures a range of consumer and modem products, giving the impression that it is heading to the retail marketplace away from the SME market where it has been dominant. WorldCom acquires MFS Communications, a fibre optic network builder, for $14bn and signals the start of major consolidation of the communications industry that will continue into the new millennium. AT&T restructures into separate companies: Lucent Technologies, NCR, and a new focused AT&T. AT&T Labs is formed from Bell Laboratories in the same restructuring.

1997: ATM struggles to make any headway in the enterprise market place. It has some success competing with FDDI as a backbone technology but all the issues of deployment involving LANE and MPOA mean it fails to gain any real traction on the desktop. The use of 25Mbit/sec was not helping as the industry views this as IBM using its Token Ring chipset to wind down the inventory. Madge Networks comes out with a neat piece of technology cell in frame; an American university has specified a way of putting ATM cells into Ethernet and Token Ring frames so you can write an ATM application and run the same exact code on an Ethernet workstation or a Token Ring workstation. This has the promise of getting some ATM applications developed for the huge Ethernet market but running native on an ATM network. Madge develops a voice application. In its development labs in the UK they has 200-odd ATM users with a few Token Ring users using exactly the same application and no PABX. The engineers could make and receive

ENTERPRISE NETWORKING

NETWORK INDUSTRY HISTORY

phone calls, watch television, listen to local radio and run applications in different windows on the PC. Although this is proof that network convergence involving ATM, Ethernet and Token Ring, Madge never releases the product.

1998: The year of Storage Area Networking, this year sees Fibre Channel announcements from a range of companies. Analysts report that storage requirements will double every 12 months. If your archive required eight hours to complete, it would be taking 16 hours by the end of the year. Cabletron purchases DEC's networking division: DPNG and Compaq purchases the rest; who would ever have thought that there could be a networking industry with no Digital in it? Olicom and IBM are the first companies to ship 100Mbit/sec Token Ring, a standard that only supports dedicated connections which means a switched or point to point connection. The ANSI standards body ratifies the HIPPI-6400 specification for 6.4Gbit/sec simplex and 12.8Gbit/sec full duplex connections for high performance networking.

1999: Integrated voice and data move closer to realisation with Siemens launching its Hi-path IP voice solution onto the market. Cisco has released its AVVID solution so the market is being primed to a round of Voice over IP. Governments across European auction the next generation wireless licences to European telecom suppliers raising $127bn, crippling the telecom industry and the major manufacturers who supply them with infrastructure products. It will be at least another four years before any products are available to use these new services. The telcos stop installing new infrastructure products. Across the globe, 140 million kilometres of fibre is installed to build the new communications infrastructure. It's enough fibre to reach the sun but only 5% is lit. JDS Uniphase, a Canadian laser manufacturer which makes components for driving light down the communications fibres acquires SDL, a company no one has heard of for $41bn, the largest acquisition in the communications industry. In a sign the world has gone mad over the next 12 months the company's value will fall to $6bn.

The most significant event of this year was that scientists, after five years research using the Hubble telescope, announced that the universe, as we know it, was formed 12 billion years ago: on a Saturday.

2000: The event of the year is the NASDAC falling to 50% of its value during the first quarter which affects our industry massively. Cisco, the dominant player in the market, has honed its strategy of development by acquisition using its share price but virtually overnight its business strategy is left up the creek without a paddle. This is attributed to the dotcoms but the whole industry is topsy-turvy.

ENTERPRISE NETWORKING

NETWORK INDUSTRY HISTORY

I live in the Boston area during 2000 and get into the habit of watching the NASDAQ every day just like the rest of my company. I open an e-trade account to play the game. On opening this account with $6,000 they offered me a loan of $6,000, which I decline. Had I been an American, who do not see the stock market as gambling, I would have been trading with $12,000. Some even take an extra mortgage out on their home to buy more shares. As a European, I find this astonishing. When the first dip in the stock market happens and accounts fall below the loan value, the loan is automatically called in. The system is designed to collapse massively. If the shares have halved, all you have is what you borrowed. That money is then demanded back. Where do you get the money to pay it? Sell more shares at a loss, and with no money left what do you do? I assume they obtained traditional bank loans if they had any collateral left. All happens in the first half of 2000, so it's no surprise that the American consumers have no money to spend for the rest of the year. 3Com discontinues its CoreBuilder range of products. My information was that this product line accounted for the lion's share of the development budget but contributed only a fraction of the revenue stream.

Enterasys Networks releases the first commercial 10Gigabit Ethernet product. The serious but amusing event of the year happens to Microsoft. The IEEE802.1x committee, chaired by Microsoft, is developing a new security standard for user authentication. This is embedded in to the next generation of OS from Microsoft, code named 'Whistler'. In November, a hacker steals the source code to Whistler.

Also in this year, Cabletron Systems announces that it is reforming its business and spins off four independent operations; Riverstone, focusing on ISP/ASP markets, GNTS an independent consultancy group, software management company Aprisma and Enterasys Networks, an enterprise focused solutions manufacturer.

Shortly after the announcement, Lucent Technologies announces its enterprise division. At the same time, Microsoft is fighting to stay as one company.

2001: Cisco announces it is reducing its work force by 25%, a major blow to the networking industry. If the largest player in our industry is seen to be failing what chance has the rest? Nortel and Lucent fair no better, Lucent Technologies are in talks with BT, which is trying to reduce its $30billion dept, talks that are seen as a major threat to the new, focused Marconi Systems. Who in turn, is rumoured to be an acquisition target of Cisco. And Alcatel is rumoured to be interested in Lucent, so 2001 looks like it is going to be an interesting year. but that is where my story has to end.

section twenty

Glossary

Section 20: Glossary of LAN Terms

This is supplemented by cable specification at the end of section two, LAN standards in section 3 and redundancy specifications at the end of section fourteen.

ENTERPRISE NETWORKING

GLOSSARY

Access Control Method

This is the main distinguishing feature between different LAN technologies. It regulates each workstation's physical access to the cable or other transmission medium, directs traffic around the network and determines the order in which nodes gain access so that each user gets an efficient service. Access methods include Token Ring's token passing, ARCnet, FDDI, and carrier sense multiple access collision detection (CSMA/CD), employed by Ethernet.

ACL

Access Control List is a secrecy feature to control and authenticate users of networks or resources or information. They require a user name and password to gain access to the resource or information. The current implementation of ACLs includes the rights and privileges that a user with respect to a resource once access is granted.

Address

One of a group of characters that specifies the recipient or originator of transmitted data. Alternatively, an address may denote the position of a piece of data in computer memory or the packet of data while traversing the network. IEEE802.3 and 802.5 recommended unique address for each and every device worldwide. IP has its own 32-bit addressing scheme and, with 128-bit IP V6, there's enough addresses to give everyone on the planet a unique number.

Adjusted Ring Length

When a segment of trunk cable fails in a Token Ring network, the wrap feature connects the main path to the back up path (Token Ring is a dual ring). The worst case (that is, the longest path) would be brought about by the failure of the shortest trunk cable segment. To compensate for the worst case, the Adjusted Ring Length (ARL) is calculated during network design to ensure the system will always work.

Alert on LAN

Alert on LAN was developed jointly by IBM and Intel and consists of special 'wake on LAN' adapter to enable Token Ring adapters to send an alert across the network even when the PC itself is powered off.

Algorithm

An Algorithm is a process or set of rules necessary for a computer to perform a task.

ENTERPRISE NETWORKING

GLOSSARY

Analogue

An Analogue signal is electrical and varies constantly in voltage, unlike a digital signal that varies between two constant values usually denoted as 0 and 1. The value of the analogue signal varies all the time during transmission whereas a digital signal only ever changes between two set values without intermediate variations.

APPC

Advanced Programme to Programme Communications (APPC) developed by IBM was a communications protocol that enabled peer to peer communications and was implemented on LU6.2-compliant products.

AppleTalk

A stack of OSI-compliant, media-independent protocols that can run on Ethernet, Token Ring and LocalTalk. LocalTalk is Apple Computer's proprietary cabling system for connecting PCs, Apple Macintosh and peripherals and using a Carrier Sense Multiple Access with Collision Avoidance (CSMA/CA) access method.

Applet

This is a small program that performs a specific function on your computer commonly used when accessing the Internet. These are downloaded from a host computer to accomplish a given task such as display an image, search a file or run an animation.

Application Layer

This is the seventh of the seven-layer OSI data communications model, drawn up by the ISO. Layer 7 provides the interface between the end users application and the communication system. Its function is to present the end user application with the various available services, including file transfer and electronic mail. (see OSI and ISO, below).

Application Software

Software that carries out a task which is both of use to the user and with which the user interacts, as opposed to the network operating system or system software, which is transparent to the user. Applications programmes include spreadsheets, databases, graphics, word processing and communications packages.

Application Programming Interface (API)

API makes a computer's facilities accessible to an application programme; all operating

ENTERPRISE NETWORKING

GLOSSARY

systems and network operating systems have APIs. In a networking environment it is essential that various machines' APIs are compatible otherwise programs would be exclusive to the machines they reside in. As networking has developed, some APIs have become *de facto* standards, including NetBIOS and DOS 3.1.

Architecture

Normally used to describe how a piece of hardware or software is constructed and which protocols and interfaces are required for communications. Network architecture specifies the functions and data transmission formats needed to convey information across a network from user to user.

ARP

Address Resolution Protocol is used by an IP network device to broadcast to everyone to find the destination's MAC address. The device matching the IP request sends its MAC address. If the MAC address is on a different network, the router responds with its own MAC address.

ARQ

Automatic Repeat reQuest is a type of error correction that ensures a Transmission device automatically resends any data that contains errors when received.

ASCII

The American Standard Code for Information Interchange or ASCII is a means of encoding characters into bits. It is the US version of the International Standards Organisation's 7-bit character set, used in data communications and processing on smaller machines. It often contains an eighth or parity bit. 128 different characters can be represented in ASCII. HTML documents are sent as ASCII files with tags that are interpreted by Web browsers to display the content.

ASIC

Application Specific Integrated Circuit is the term used to describe the new paradigm in network hardware design. Instead of running a process in memory controlled by a processor and software much like a PC, ASICs have replaced this by putting the function into silicon. This means that the operations are carried out directly in the hardware which greatly improves the speed.

ENTERPRISE NETWORKING

GLOSSARY

ASTRAL

A group of like-minded manufacturers forming the Alliance for Strategic Token Ring Advancement. There are other groups like HSTRA High-Speed Token Ring Alliance. The intention is to develop new high speed Token Ring standards for the existing token ring user community.

Asynchronous

A way of transmitting data where each bit is sent separately. This means each of those bits has to be labelled so the recipient machine can recognise the character. This is achieved by adding other bits to the beginning and end of each character, known as the start and stop bits. Asynchronous transmission is the most rudimentary type of communication, as the originating and recipient machines do not have to be in step. It is generally regarded as a cheap, reliable method of communication, commonly used by PCs and minicomputers. The disadvantage of asynchronous communication is all the extra bits necessary for the information to be interpreted which consumes bandwidth. It is also known as start/stop transmission.

ATM

Asynchronous Transfer Mode, a high-speed switching technology that uses 53-byte cells (5 byte heater, 48 byte payload) to transmit different types of traffic simultaneously, including voice, video and data.

ATM adaptation layer (AAL)

These are standard protocols to translate user traffic from the higher layers of the protocol stack into cells.

AAL 1 addresses CBR (constant bit rate) traffic such as digital voice and video and is used for applications that are sensitive.

AAL 2 is used with time-sensitive, VBR (Variable Bit Rate) traffic such as packet voice.

AAL 3/4 handles bursty connection-oriented traffic, like error messages, or variable-rate connectionless traffic, like LAN file transfers.

AAL 5 accommodates bursty LAN data traffic with less over-head than AAL 3/4. Also known as the Simple and Efficient Adaptation Layer (SEAL).

ENTERPRISE NETWORKING

GLOSSARY

Attenuation

When signals are being transmitted, they naturally become weaker or attenuated the further they travel from their point of origin. Amplifiers are used to recharge the signal. Attenuation is a major factor in LAN design, and the lengths that cables can be run to.

Audit Trail

A network audit trial is a record of a network's activity and is a useful network management tool because it shows how resources are being used and who is using them, which can help identify where problems lie.

Authentication

Users must be authenticated, checked and approved, to verify they are who they claim to be and that they are permitted access to the destination network. Authentication schemes must offer a secure, easy to manage method for transferring user credentials to the Security server. IEEE802.1x is a standard for user authentication for access to networks. The authentication server protocol allows the user to be validated against a user list with other servers and functions. The most common protocol is RADIUS and it is support by nearly all user database systems. NT and NDS can be accessed by RADIUS.

Available Bit Rate

ABR defines a class of service in which the ATM network makes a 'best effort' to meet the traffic's bit-rate requirements.

Backbone

Generic term for a LAN or WAN connectivity between sub-networks across the enterprise. The sub-networks are connected to the backbone via bridges and/or routers, and the backbone acts as a communications trunk.

Balun

Baluns are used to connect different cable types together. A transformer for levelling out impedance differences so that a signal generated onto a co-axial cable can transfer onto twisted pair if necessary. Baluns are often used so that IBM 3270 can run off the cheaper twisted pair, but the use of a Balun usually results in some level of degradation.

Bandwidth

This is the range of signal frequencies that can be carried on a communications channel.

ENTERPRISE NETWORKING

GLOSSARY

The capacity of a channel is measured in cycles per second, or Hertz (Hz), between the highest and the lowest frequencies. While this indicates the channel's information bearing capacity, it is more commonly expressed as bits per second (bit/sec). Bandwidth varies according to the sort and method of transmission.

Baseband

A technique whereby the digital input is applied directly to the transmission media, without the intervention of a modulating device. This works well where there is a wide bandwidth and the information only needs to travel a short distance, no further than a few hundred metres. It is commonly used by LANs and by limited distance modems. The other technique for LANs is broadband. Baseband is the simple and most cost effective solution, with the whole of the bandwidth being used to transmit a single digital signal. See Broadband.

BGP-4

Border Gateway Protocol is a standard inter-router communications protocol (defined in RFC 1654 and updated for the Internet in RFC 1771) and is used to interface into the public network domain between ISPs and the Internet domain. It is used to connect and manage large numbers of remote router locations in an efficient manner. BGP prevents routing loops and determines the best route through the network of large numbers of routers.

Bit Error Rate

The percentage of received bits that cannot be interpreted properly on their first transmission. Usually expressed to a power of ten.

Bits per second

This is expressed in a variety of ways such as bit(s) and bit/sec, and is a description of transmission speeds. However, bit(s) can be measured in a variety of ways and many factors affect it including how quickly data is taken from a disk and how great the error rate is. 1,024bit/sec = 1Kbit/sec; 1,024,000bit/sec = 1Mbit/sec; 1,073,741,824bit/sec = 1Gbit/sec.

Block

A collection of transmitted data that is treated as a complete and separate identity, typically having its own address, control routing and error checking data. (See packet and packet switching).

ENTERPRISE NETWORKING

GLOSSARY

Booting

The process of loading a computer's memory with the information it needs to operate. Remote booting usually refers to loading software over the network.

Bridge

Bridges are used to connect networks using dissimilar protocols and operate at the data link level or layer two of the OSI model. They are often described as media access control level or MAC level bridges. They do not carry out any interpretation of the information they are carrying. When two LANs are successfully bridged together, they become one effective LAN. Various load balancing techniques have been developed to combat the problems of bandwidth limitations and the failure of any element on the network. Bridges are increasingly used to control network traffic and security. They can filter the transmitted data to contain local traffic so that the rest of the network is not involved. This boosts network performance and is also useful for security purposes. (See router and gateway).

Broadband

This term has a number of meanings. It was coined originally to describe a channel with more bandwidth than a standard voice grade channel that is usually a 48kHz link, equivalent to 12 voice grade channels. These voice grade channels have being superseded by digital circuits. Broadband is also one of the two prevalent ways of conveying information round a LAN, the other, simpler one being baseband. Baseband puts the digital signals straight onto the cable from the data communications device without any form of modulation whereas broadband needs modems. Baseband can only carry one data signal at once but broadband has multiple frequency channels, operating independently of each other, that can carry voice, data and video. This is usually achieve by Frequency Division Multiplexing (FDM) which modulates each channel to a particular frequency level in the cable.

Broadband Inter-Carrier Interface (BICI)

BICI is a carrier-to-carrier interface similar to PNNI (private network-to-network interface).

Broadcast

When a user sends a message from one terminal that is received by all the other people on the network. Broadcasts are a common way network devices locate network

ENTERPRISE NETWORKING

GLOSSARY

resources. Many poorly designed network broadcasts, known as broadcast storms, can bring a network to a standstill.

Browser

Originally a programme for viewing pages and navigating around the world wide Web. Examples include Netscape Navigator, Opera and Microsoft Internet Explorer. These have evolved with more complex functions including reading and creating Internet mail and the ability to display complex multi-media animations. Manufacturers now design their applications to support a browser user interface to increase user ability and reduce the training requirement.

Buffer

A buffer can be a software programme, a storage facility or a box whose function it is to compensate for differing speeds of data transmission on a network. Whatever its guise, a buffer is there to make sure data always has somewhere to go, even if it has to be held up for a while in the buffer until it can be transmitted to its intended destination.

Bus Network

This is a LAN where all the workstations are connected to a single cable. This means all the workstations hear all the transmissions but are able to identify the data intended for them and ignore the rest.

Cable Loss

The amount of radio frequency lost by a signal as it travels along a cable.

Cable Modem

An interface that lets a cable TV system serve as a data communications link. Most cable TV systems use co-axial cable or fibre-optic lines for their links, and both these types of wiring can carry data at far higher rates than the twisted-pair wires used for local telephone connections.

Category 5e

Cable specifications for networking are defined in categories and the 100Mbit/sec networking technologies are covered up to category 5. The category 5e extends this to 100MHz for the higher speeds of Gigabit Ethernet but also increases the number of pairs of cables used and limits the distances supported. There are more amendments on the way with proposed standard for Category 6 at 250MHz, and the proposed standard for

ENTERPRISE NETWORKING

GLOSSARY

Category 7 at 600MHz.

Cell Relay

Protocol based on small fixed packet sizes known as a cell. This technique is capable of supporting voice, video and data at very high speeds.

Circuit Switching

A switched circuit is only maintained while the sender and recipient are communicating, as opposed to a dedicated circuit which is held open regardless of whether data is being sent or not.

Classical IP and ARP over ATM

An adaptation of TCP/IP and its Address Resolution Protocol (ARP) for ATM defined by the IETF (Internet Engineering Task Force) in RFCs (Requests for Comment).

Client-Server Computing

This describes the division of an application into two parts, with one part running on the server and the other running on a PC or workstation. The rationale behind client-server computing is to exploit the superior processing power of the server to govern and process the centrally held information. The client or PC is carrying out the application's front-end talk. The expectation was that client servers would reduce network traffic but in reality it dramatically increases the overall network traffic.

Clustering

A technique where multiple processors providing a single computing resource allowing lower performance machines to provide services of higher performance and therefore higher cost machines. The cluster consists of several processors usually connected to a switched network that provides communication among the processors and access to the cluster as a single resource (see LSNAT definition). Digital Equipment Corporation (DEC) pioneered clustering in the mid-1980s.

CMIP

Common Management Information Protocol is an evolving OSI standard for network management that should enable different network management systems to exchange information.

ENTERPRISE NETWORKING

GLOSSARY

CMOL

CMOL (Common Management Information Protocol) for use over LLC the layer 2 low-level protocol. It could also be run over the OSI layer 3 Management Protocol CMIP. This was predominantly a 3Com/IBM protocol for managing Ethernet and Token Ring networks. It was before CMIP platforms were available and CMIP agents in networking devices. This appeared originally in LAN Network Manager for OS/2, and many sites are still operating today. The related CMOT (CMIP over TCP/IP) standard was aimed at allowing information to be transported using layer 3 IP packets but this never made the mainstream.

Co-axial Cable

A TV aerial type of cable which has a long history of use in the IBM environment particularly for connecting terminals and other devices that need high speed links. Co-ax is used in Ethernet as 'thick' and 'thin (cheaper)' cable. Co-ax is also widely used and can carry voice data and video simultaneously. However, it has several disadvantages. It is difficult to add or remove devices from a co-axial LAN as the cable itself is unwieldy and thick. It has now been displaced by twisted pair which is cheaper and can cope with the transmissions of up to 10Mbit/s and with four pais of cables, 100Mbit/sec.

Collision

Collisions happen when two workstations are trying to use the same cable and the electrical signals carrying information run into each other. This renders both lots of data useless so they have to be sent again. A random delay mechanism used by both senders drastically reduces the chances of another collision happening.

Collision Detection

The devices at each of the links are designed to detect collisions instantaneously and simply try to send the signal again. This is the principle on which CSMA/CD is based and is the control access method used by Ethernet. An alternative form of collision detection is that the originator of the signal does not receive an acknowledgement of receipt from the remote device.

Communications Server

Often one machine on a LAN will act as communications server or gateway for all the other nodes. The server machine provides connections to mini-computers, main-frames, modems and other non LAN devices that all the workstations on the LAN can access.

ENTERPRISE NETWORKING

GLOSSARY

Converter

Converter is a repeater that also converts from one media type to another, for example, from fibre to copper or vice versa. Sometimes referred to as Media Adapter.

Congestion control

Mechanisms that control traffic flow so switches and networking devices are not overwhelmed with the volume of traffic and reduces the risk of packet or cells lost.

Constant bit rate (CBR)

CBR is a communications service that enables digital information, such as video and digitised voice, to communicate effectively must be represented by a continuous stream of bits.

CSMA/CD

Carrier Sense Multiple Access with Collision Detection (CSMA/CD) is a control access method through which several nodes can transmit over one cable (multiple access) although not simultaneously. Any device that wishes to send data firstly has to check that no-one else is currently using the LAN. It listens for (senses) any signals on the LAN, known as a carrier. If no carrier signal exists, it means no-one else is using the LAN. The device can now transmit its data, but while doing so checks the signal to make sure it has not collided with data from other devices further down the LAN. If no collision occurs it assumes the data has been sent successfully.

If a collision does occur it knows two things:

1. The data has been lost and must be resent.
2. Someone else is trying to use the LAN. Thus it waits for a short time, measured in microseconds, in the hope that the other party will finish its transmission, and then resends the data. This CSMA/CD process is repeated until the data is successfully sent.

CSMA/CD is used by Ethernet and IEEE802.3 specifications. Devices transmit only after finding the data channel clear for some period of time. When two devices transmit simultaneously, a collision occurs and the colliding devices delay their retransmissions for a random length of time.

ENTERPRISE NETWORKING

GLOSSARY

CSU/DSU

Channel Service Unit/Data Service Unit is a digital interface unit that connects end user equipment to the local digital telephone loop.

Cyclical Redundancy Check (CRC)

A way of checking for errors in a message by doing mathematical calculations on the number of bits in the message, which are then sent along with the data to the recipient. The recipient checks what it has received and repeats the calculation. If there are any discrepancies in the two calculations, the recipient requests the originator to send the data again.

Data Compression

This describes a way of reducing the amount of data to be transmitted by applying an algorithm to the basic data at source. A decompression algorithm expands the data back to its original state at the other end of the link. Digital video requires up to 45Mbit/sec for reasonable performances but with compression can achieve the same in 1-3Mbit/sec.

Datagram

A means of sending data by which parts of the message are sent in a random order and the recipient machine has the task of reassembling the parts in the correct order.

Data Link Layer

The second layer of the seven layer OSI model, it is responsible for moving information across a particular link. Across that link, it ensures good transmission and correct delivery by checking errors, re-transmitting as necessary and attaching appropriate addresses to the data sent. The connection access methods (such as CSMA/CD, Token Passing) are regarded as Layer 2 activities.

DCE

Data Communications Equipment, the hardware that provides connection to the network in wide area networks, modems, multiplexers and packed assembler/disassemble (PAD) are all examples. In a LAN, a transceiver (IEEE802.3) or multi-station access unit (IEEE802.5) are examples.

Device Driver

Software to extend DOS's ability to operate with peripherals or that improves DOS's

ENTERPRISE NETWORKING

GLOSSARY

own facilities. Examples of device drivers include those that support printers, disks, mice and so on. Sometimes they are individual programmes, but more usually they are an integral part of an application. Some network operating systems act as device drivers loading before anything else and so having first claim on memory space. This means they also control DOS's use of peripherals.

DHCP

Dynamic Host Configuration Protocol is a method of assigning IP addresses to hosts and clients on a LAN. When a host is initialised, it broadcasts a request for an address that is responded to by a DHCP server with an IP address for the host.

Diagnostics

A programme test procedure used to test a piece of equipment, a link or network for faults.

DiffServ

Today's networks need to carry a variety of traffic with different expectations of service for different applications. This is commonly called a differentiated service (DiffServ) Quality of Service (QoS) Strategy. The standards body has ratified IEEE802.1q to enable an in-packet service level request to be passed across an entire network. In the past, all data applications used a QoS strategy called best effort.

Digital Signal

A signal that only has two values, normally 0 and 1, during transmission, as opposed to analogue signal whose values vary all the time.

Directory

The term directory is used to describe many existing services both inside the computer communication field and out. Some common directories we use daily include the telephone directories such as the Yellow Pages, company directories listing employees and phone numbers, and email directories listing the addresses of persons within an enterprise. These directories all serve similar purposes, allowing information to be centralised, stored, indexed and accessed. While the type of information may be different and their format, organisation and access methods are dissimilar, they are all considered directories of some sort or another.

ENTERPRISE NETWORKING

GLOSSARY

Directory Enabled Networking

Directory Enabled Networking correlates all LAN directories and integrates them into a single centralised logical entity. It also provides automatic-mapping mechanisms to switch back and forth between different data formats. While the term directory enabled networking is a recent addition, the concept and practice have been present in many forms over the past decade. A prime example of the use of a directory is seen within Novell NetWare, a network operating system that has always maintained some form of understanding of end systems and users in a directory structure. Known as Novell Directory Services (NDS), the directory contains user login identities and other information about user identities, their network access rights and their other network-related activities. Microsoft's version is known as Active Directory. The understanding a NetWare system has about its users is not shared with other directories such as the cc:MAIL email directory or Microsoft NT. Therefore what is required is one directory structure that all elements of a system shares and uses to allocate resources by named individuals by location and job function.

DMI

The Desktop Management Interface standard covers the monitoring and retrieval of status and error information from workstations. It serves much the same purpose as SNMP but applies to user workstations themselves rather than the building blocks of the network.

DNS

The Internet needed to find and interconnect millions of servers. The solution was a simplified directory services protocol called the Domain Name Service (DNS) that quickly locates IP server locations. It also substitutes user-friendly names for IP addresses.

DOS

The widely used abbreviation for disk operating system, which comprises a programme or suite of programmes that manages a disk-based computer system. It schedules and supervises work and allocates computer resources and the operation of peripherals. There are a number of versions of DOS from different vendors, some of which have several updated versions. The most common forms for PCs are Microsoft's MS-DOS which is derived from the Microsoft version. DOS 3.1 was the first version of MS and PC-DOS able to support LAN functions. One of its most important innovations was record and file locking, now standard on any multi-user system.

ENTERPRISE NETWORKING

GLOSSARY

DOS LAN Manager

A DOS version of Microsoft's Network Operating System, LAN Manager. This gives named pipes support to DOS machines enabling them to use the client/server environment.

Drop Cable

A cable that allows connection and access to the trunk cable in a a network. It is also called AUI (Attachment Unit Interface) cable, and sometimes transceiver cable.

DCE

Data Communications Equipment or Data Circuit-terminating Equipment is a device that establishes, maintains and terminates a session on a network. It may also convert signals for transmission. It is typically the modem. Contrast with DTE.

DES

Data Encryption Standard is a government standard where data is encrypted in fixed size blocks and a key is used of varying length depending on the sensitivity of the data. Encryption keys can be from 40 to 128Mbit/sec. The original DES used a 56-bit key but the newer Triple DES (3DES) uses three separate keys but has the security of an 168-bit key.

DS1/DS3 See T1 and T3

DMI

The Distributed Management Interface DMI was developed under the Distributed Management Task Force DMTF. DMI defines a standard framework for managing and tracking components in a computer.

DSL

Digital Subscriber Line, a technology that adds high-speed data comunications to a standard phone line using frequencies above the voice telephone spectrum. New equipment must be installed on both ends of the copper wire, a DSL modem in the end-user's premises home and, at the telephone company's exchange, a DSL Access Multiplexer (DSLAM) which is effectively a connection concentrator . DSL users must be closer than six kilometres from the telephone company's exchange. Flavours of DSL include:

ENTERPRISE NETWORKING

GLOSSARY

ADSL: Asymmetric DSL provides speeds of up to 8Mbit/sec downstream from the Internet to your computer and up to 1.5Mbit/sec upstream from your computer to the Internet.

G.lite: A new, cheaper form of ADSL (mainly used in the USA) that delivers simultaneous high-speed connection and telephone service over the same line. This is intended for the residential and small business users for speeds of up to 1.5Mbit/sec downstream and 512Kbit/sec upstream.

SDSL: Symmetric DSL supports connections at the same speed upstream and downstream at 160Kbit/sec to 2.3Mbit/sec. SDSL does not support telephone service on the same line and is more suited to business use.

HDSL: High-bit-rate DSL supports symmetric connections at 1.54Mbit/sec, but does not allow simultaneous use of telephone service. HDSL uses 4 wires (2 pairs) as opposed to the 2 wires used by the other types of DSL. Often used as the basis for newer T1 lines from the telephone company.

VDSL: Very high-bit-rate DSL is intended for consumers within short distances of the telephone company's exchange, up to 1Km. It supports connections up to 51Mbit/sec and can be used simultaneously with telephone service.

DTE

Data Terminal Equipment, a generic term applied to devices that use the network, such as computers, printers and plotters.

Dynamic Address

A network address assigned to a particular user for the duration of a particular session rather than on a permanent basis. There is a limited number of Internet addresses available to any domain so most Internet providers and large organisations maintain a pool of addresses that they assign to active sessions only for the period of the session.

Dynamic Routing

A procedure for sending messages across a network with a resiliency feature for line failures or overloading. The system will automatically reroute the message. Packet switching operates on this principle, with the system always poised to react to ever changing conditions, as opposed to static routing where data is sent along pre-programmed paths and is delayed if that path becomes blocked.

ENTERPRISE NETWORKING

GLOSSARY

E1

European standard for digital transmission service at 2.048Mbit/s

E3

European standard for digital transmission service at 34.368Mbit/s (transports 16 E1 circuits)

Early Token Release

Early Token Release allows a station to release the token before its message has come back thus there will be two tokens on the ring at the same time.

EGP

External Gateway protocol is used by gateways that interconnect different autonomous systems. EGP allows gateways to share routing information through advertisements of their connection services.

Emulation

Hardware or software, or a combination of the two, that behaves like another device or programme. Examples of this include PCs emulating dumb terminals.

Encapsulation

This is a technique used to place information inside a coded packet for transmission over a medium not normally supported. An example could be carrying voice traffic over the Internet. The voice once digitised is placed inside an IP packet so that it appears to forwarding equipment on the Internet to be normal data.

Encryption

This is the process of converting data or plain text into a form that cannot be understood without a matching decryption process. In communications it makes it impossible to read messages without the required key.

Ethernet

Ethernet, one of the oldest and most successful LAN technologies, was originally developed by Xerox, Intel and DEC. It was developed to run over co-axial cable although it can now run over twisted pair. It uses CMSA/CD and is similar to the IEEE802.3 standards in that they share the same cable specification and can communicate with each

ENTERPRISE NETWORKING

GLOSSARY

other. LAN-based Ethernet currently runs at up to 100Mbit/s although other, mainly fibre-based, versions extend this to 10Gbit/sec.

Fault Tolerance

See Redundancy

Fast Packet

Fast Packet is a general term for various streamlined packet technologies including Frame Relay, BISDN and ATM. Compared to X.25 packet switching a Fast Packet system contains a much reduced protocol set relying more on the underlying infrastructure for its resilience features. The lower protocol overheads means that fast packet systems can operate at higher communications rates at the same processing cost.

FasTR

FasTR is the name for a special implementation of Token Ring for high-speed operations. It describes token ring implemented using ATM adapters that encapsulates the token ring frames using ATM AAL5. This means that the end devices think they are Token Ring at 4/16Mbit/sec but the communications is actually ATM at 155Mbit/sec.

FDDI

Fibre Distributed Data Interface is an ANSI standard for use of fibre optics to provide networks up to 100Mbit/sec. Incorporates token passing and packaged data.

Fibre Channel

Fibre Channel was developed under the ANSI X3T11 committee in 1998. It was a designed to overcome the limitations of SCSI in connecting storage devices by networking these devices and so is the foundation of Storage Area Networking. Fibre Channel adopted the same media specifications as Gigabit Ethernet, therefore giving manufacturers wider use of the media chipsets and enabling Fibre Channel to get to market more quickly. Fibre Channel specifies four data rates, three kinds of media, four transmitter types, three distance categories, three classes of service, and three possible fabrics.

Fibre Channel-based SANs can be configured in several ways as Fibre Channel Arbitrated Loops (FCAL) or switched fabric networks. They can be local or remote, spanning campuses and using wide-area connections.

ENTERPRISE NETWORKING

GLOSSARY

FireWall

Firewalls are electronic barriers to protect information resources, providing secure Internet entry points by monitoring incoming traffic against attack signatures while checking outgoing traffic for approvals. Firewalls are used to protect an enterprise network against unauthorised access and malicious attacks. They can check and source information and content contained in a data flow which can help guard against virus attacks. With the increase in remote users using RAS or VPN technology to gain direct access to the network, malicious attacks sometimes target remote users, tunnelling through the remote access mechanism to avoid the firewall. Personal firewalls have been the technology response to this phenomenon. The first firewall was implemented by Digital Equipment Corporation (DEC).

FireWire

Pioneered by Apple Computer and developed within the IEEE1394 working group, FireWire is designed to integrate personal computers with the world of consumer electronics. FireWire is a digital peer-to-peer interface enabling multiple computers to share a given peripheral without any special support in the peripheral or the computers. FireWire supports data rates of 100, 200, and 400Mbit/sec, interconnecting up to 63 devices with a maximum cable length of 4.5 meters between devices. The maximum number of hops in a chain is 16 for a total maximum end-to-end distance of 72 meters.

Flow Control

This is a routine for controlling the transfer of data between two points in a network; for example, between a protocol converter and a printer. This avoids data loss when a recipient device's buffer is full. Buffers play an essential role in overall flow control on a network.

Frame

A group of bits sent over a link that contains its own control information, such as address and error detection. The size and composition of the frame varies according to the protocol. The terms frame and packet tend to be used synonymously, although strictly speaking in OSI terms a frame is made at layer two, a packet at layer three or above.

FRAD

Frame Relay Assembler/Dissassembler is used to format outgoing data into the format required by a Frame Relay network and control the access to the network. These devices

ENTERPRISE NETWORKING

GLOSSARY

can function as a network router.

Frame Relay

An interface spawned from ISDN (CCITT recommendation 1.122) designed to provide high-speed frame or packet transmission with minimum delay and efficient use of bandwidth. The interface can be used on LANs, Time Division Multiplexed (TDM) links and on packet and non-packet switched networks. It operates at level 2, the data link layer in the OSI seven-layer model. Using Frame Relay, the network delivers the frame to a destination indicated by a layer 2 address field in the frame. Frame Relay does not acknowledge or request re-transmission and although it can detect errors in the frame, they are simply disregarded. Eventually, Frame Relay switches will be implemented.

Frame Relay is effectively the next generation of X.25, the robust packet-based protocol designed to send packet data across old, unreliable telephony circuits. With the installation of digital carrier services X.25 was no longer needed and Frame Relay with its lighter protocol requirements has taken over. Today routers support the routing of IP traffic over Frame Relay networks as specified in RFC 1490.

FTP

File transfer protocol is a general purpose file transfer protocol for TCP/IP systems.

Full Duplex

This is the ability of a communications device to transmit and receive information simultaneously.

Full-duplex Dedicated Token Ring

When Token Ring is used as a point to point connection this is known as a DTR connection (Dedicated Token Ring). Normal Token Ring implementation between a device and a hub/switch is made with two twisted pairs of wires. One pair is used for the receipt of data and the other used for the transmission of data while the standard Token Passing Protocol (TKP) ensures these will never happen simultaneously. Rather, a frame will be received first by the station and then a frame will be transmitted around the ring. DTR provides a dedicated connection between end station and switch, and both devices can transmit and receive concurrently.

G.703

This is a CCITT standard for the physical and logical attributes of transmission over digital

ENTERPRISE NETWORKING

GLOSSARY

circuits. It now includes specifications for the US-based 1.544Mbit/s as well as the European 2.048Mbit/sec, and the circuits with larger bandwidths on both continents. G.703 is generally used to refer to the standard for 2.048Mbit/sec.

Gateway

A combination of hardware and software that interconnects otherwise incompatible networks or networking devices. Examples of gateways include Packet Assembler/Disassembles (PADS) and protocol converters. Gateways operate at levels 5, 6 and 7 in the seven-layer OSI model; they are the session, presentation and application layers respectively. An example of a gateway would be a device to link Ethernet to X25.

Graphics User Interface

GUI (goo-ee) is an interface that enables the user to select a menu by using a mouse to point to a graphical icon. This is an alternative to the more traditional character-based interface where an alpha-numeric keyboard is used to convey instructions. GUIs make computers/applications easier to be used by human beings.

Hashing

This is a security facility for ensuring files are not tampered with. A file is passed through a hashing algorithm to produce a unique number and the file sent with the number. At the receiving end, the file is re-hashed and a new number is produced. If the new number and the sent numbers are different, the file has been tampered with. The hashed number is known as a message digest.

HDLC

High-level Data Link Control, always referred to as HDLC, is an international standard set by the International Standards Organisation (ISO). HDLC procedure is a set of protocols defined by the ISO for carrying data over a link with error and flow control. HDLC is similar to IBM's SDLC and, is in fact, a superset of SDLC. Versions of HDLC are being developed for multi-port lines. The name is a misnomer as HDLC is not a High Level protocol.

Head-end

A central point or hub in broadband networks that receives signals on one set frequency band and re-transmits them on another. Every transmission from one workstation to another has to go through the Head-end in a broadband network. The Head-end is the piece of hardware that enables a network to send and receive on the same piece of cable.

ENTERPRISE NETWORKING

GLOSSARY

Header

The control information added to the beginning of a transmitted message containing essential information such as the packet or block address, destination, message number and routing instructions.

HIPPI

High-Performance Parallel Interface was an early high-speed connection standard developed by ANSI (American National Standard Institute) in 1988. It was originally developed to allow mainframes and supercomputers to communicate with one another, and with directly attached storage devices, at gigabit speeds. Speeds 800Mbit/sec and 1.6Gbit/sec; cabling: 50-pair STP, single-mode and multimode fibre; distance: 50m point to point over copper. Cascaded switches can be extended 200m over copper; 300m over multimode fibre, 10Km over single-mode fibre.

HIPPI-6400

In 1998, ANSI ratified a new HIPPI standard specifying a physical-level, point-to-point, full duplex link layer interface for reliable, flow-controlled, transmissions at 6400Mbit/sec each way. Supporting distances of up to 1Km. A parallel copper cable of 46 shielded twisted pairs for distances of up to 40m is specified. Fibre is specified for longer distances.

HNF

The High Performance Networking Forum was organised to promote Gigabyte System Network. This includes IEEE1355 the high-speed simple serial link protocol, a high-speed RS232 serial connection, and High Performance Parallel Interface (HIPPI) networking. This industry initiative is committed to providing open and interoperable GB/sec solutions.

Host Intruder Detection System

Relies on a host-based agent to keep a snapshot of a correct profile. Any changes can generate alarms. Such systems can also monitor repeat failed log-in attempts. See Intruder Detection Systems.

HTML

The English-like computer language used to express the source statements creating pages for the World Wide Web. HTML statements are then interpreted by a browser

ENTERPRISE NETWORKING

GLOSSARY

programme to provide actual on-screen formatting and images.

HTTP

The protocol used for requesting and supplying Web pages and other information. It precedes a standard Web address, as in 'http://,' to indicate to a browser programme to use this protocol when retrieving a Web page.

HSSG

This is the High Speed Study Group that instigated the IEEE802.3ae 10Gigabit Ethernet task force which hopes to ratify the standard early 2002.

Hub

The hub is the central networking device of a star topology network or cabling system. The network nodes do not usually directly interconnect but communicate via the central point. LAN hubs had become popular with the growth of twisted pair and fibre optics and the need for network management. Today, these hubs are being replaced by switches.

IEEE

The Institute of Electrical and Electronic Engineers is a publishing and standards organisation, responsible for many of the standards governing LANs. The 802 series is the best known.

IEEE802.2

A data link communication standard for use with the IEEE802.3, 802.4 and 802.5 standards. It specifies how the basic data connection over the cable should be set up.

IEEE802.3

A physical cabling standard for LANs as well as a method of transmitting data and controlling access to the cable. It uses the CSMA/CD access method on a bus topology LAN and is operationally similar to Ethernet.

IEEE802.4

A physical layer standard which uses the token-passing access method on a bus topology LAN. Used by LANs implementing Manufacturing Automation Protocol (MAP). ARCnet operates in a similar way but does not follow the 802.4 standard, which it predates; ARCnet supporters have been trying to get the technology ratified as an IEEE standard

ENTERPRISE NETWORKING

GLOSSARY

for some time without success.

IEEE802.5

A LAN physical layer standard that uses the token-passing access method on a ring topology LAN. Used by IBM on its Token Ring Systems.

IETF

Internet Engineering Task Force, the public organisation that creates the standards, called RFCs request for comments. These are draft standards proposals that are sent to manufacturers for comment and form the basis of the communications standards that have built the Internet.

In-band Signalling

A technique by which a signal bearing control information is sent over the LAN it is controlling. See Out of Band Signalling.

Interim Interswitch Signalling Protocol

Formerly known as PNNI Phase 0, ISSP is a temporary routing scheme requires network managers to establish PVCs between switches from different vendors.

Interface

In networking terms this is a connector or piece of equipment, which interconnects between two systems or processes. Probably the most common interface is the RS232-C port, and on LANs the attachment unit interface (AUI) between computer and transceiver.

Internet

A communications network started by the US epartment of Defense in 1969 to enable remote computers to communicate with each other without having fixed connections. This was known as ARPANet, was opened up to the universities in 1970 and to the world in 1982 at which point it invoked the invention of TCP/IP and became known as the Internet. To make the use of the Internet easier for non-technical people, a paged-based protocol (HTTP) that supported hypertext links in the page was invented. This enabled the transparent linking of information sites spawned massive usage and the term World Wide Web was used to describe the vast array of HTTP-based0 information sources.

ENTERPRISE NETWORKING

GLOSSARY

Internet2

Internet2 is a research and development project with a goal of advancing Internet technology and applications vital to the research and education missions of higher education. Over 170 US universities, working together with partners in industry and government, are leading the Internet2 project. Internet2 is working to enable applications such as telemedicine, digital libraries and virtual laboratories that are not possible with the technology underlying today's Internet.

Internet Packet Exchange

IPX is a Novell NetWare communications protocol used to route messages from one node to another. IPX had an advantage over XNS because it included network addresses so could support multiple networks. IPX does not guarantee delivery of a complete message so lost out to TCP/IP.

Internet Protocol IP

A portion of the TCP/IP protocol suite that specifies how the information is addressed, sent, and received between systems.

Inter-Process Communications (IPC)

Communications between several programs, either all based on one computer or across several machines. There are several approaches to achieving this end. The most common in networking circles are probably APIs like APPC and NetBIOS.

Intruder Detection Systems

IDS's come in two basic forms; Network (NIDS) and Host-based (HIDS). Their task is to monitor, record and alarm any malicious or specified activity. They can look at content and find attachments or specific illegal codes and can monitor for protocol activity where someone is trying to discover a network resource. The really sophisticated NIDS can monitor for anomalies. These are events that do not normally happen, such as the salesperson who uses the marketing and sales servers suddenly trying to gain access to finance. This is an anomaly and good systems will alarm MIS and start recording an audit log of this person's network activity. See also Host Intruder Detection System and Network Intruder Detection System.

IP Address

A unique 32-bit number assigned to each host computer on an IP network such as the

ENTERPRISE NETWORKING

GLOSSARY

Internet. The addresses are structured to specify the class of network, network address and the sub-network that specifies a particular machine or group of machines. To make life easier for users and administrators, a Domain Name Server (DNS) is used to names to be substituted, the DNS server translating them into IP addresses for message routing and delivery. To make it easier to understand IP address are written in 'dotted decimal notation' showing four decimal numbers between 0 and 255 separated by full stops.

IPSec

IPSec is short for IP Security Protocol provides confidentiality with encryption, integrity with one-way-hashing, origin authentication, replay protection by sequence number checks and traffic-flow confidentiality by encrypting the origin addresses. These services are provided at the IP layer, offering protection for IP and upper layer protocols.

ISDN

Integrated Service Digital Network (ISDN) is a CCITT standard that covers a range of voice, data and image services. It provides end to end, simultaneous, digitised voice and data traffic on the same links via the same exchanges. Access channels include basic (144Kbit/sec) and primary rate (1.544 and 2.048Mbit/sec, depending on which side of the Atlantic you live). ISDN is described in the CCITT's I-Series of recommendations in the 1990 'pink book'. Most video conferencing systems use ISDN as the transmission medium.

ISO

The International Standards Organisation, based in Geneva and responsible for many data communications standards, the best known of all being the seven-layer Open System Interconnection (OSI) model.

Jabber

To continuously send random data. A device that does this on a LAN prevents other devices using the LAN, so transceiver hardware provides a jabber lock. by which it can disconnect the offending device.

Java

A programming language developed by Sun Microsystems to add dynamic features to World Wide Web pages. Web pages that include Java send the browser an applet which then invokes a Java interpreter. Only the interpreter has to be customised to the specific type of computer, not the applet, which can remain the whether the interprter is a PC, Mac or a other type of workstation. The specifications also include security features to

ENTERPRISE NETWORKING

GLOSSARY

prevent an applet from corrupting files on the target computer. Microsoft promotes a competing technology called ActiveX.

LAN

See Local Area Network.

LAN emulation

A way for legacy, Ethernet and Token Ring to access work transparently across an ATM network.

LAN Manager

A Network Operating System developed by Microsoft and IBM for PCs based on Intel's 80286 and 80386 CPUs running IBM's OS/2.

LAN Network Manager

IBM's proprietary network management software for Token Ring networks.

Latency

This is the time taken to service a request or deliver a message. In a communications network, latency is a problem to be overcome. Different networking technology introduces differing amounts of latency. Software routers add significantly more latency to a communications path than a Layer 4 switch. The more devices in a given communications path, the greater the latency experienced by the traffic passing over that path. In packet networks where packet sizes change and paths through the network change, latency can cause serious problems with time-sensitive information like voice.

Layer

Describes a way of dividing specifications such as OSI, SNA and other communications protocols. The idea is to group functions that together comprise one step in the hierarchy essential for successful data communications.

LDAP

Lightweight Directory Access Protocol is a protocol for retrieving information from a common database. For user authentication, this can be certificate information, access control information or other operational criteria. LDAPv3 (RFC 2251) is the latest version of the standard. In addition to defining a basic access protocol it also defines a hierarchical information schema for common standard values such as people, organisations and

ENTERPRISE NETWORKING

GLOSSARY

countries. LDAP is fully compatible with X.500 standards and has been adopted by all major directory vendors, forming the infrastructure for true directory interoperability.

LFAP

Lightweight Flow Accounting Protocol (LFAP, RFC 2124) is a protocol that provides reliable, TCP-based, resilient flow accounting measuring total time length of conversations between end stations in addition to total bandwidth consumed. LFAP complements RMON by providing detailed flow data collection such as source and destination socket identifiers for UDP and TCP protocols.

Load balancing

The use of multiple, connected devices across which the load imposed by demands for data are shared so that they appear to the end user as a single device. The advantages are that there is no single point of failure and that a greater number of requests can be handled simultaneously. The mechanism for implementing this can be at layer 2 using IEEE802.3s or at layer 3 using load balancing techniques such as OSPF.

Lobe

A cable between a Token Ring station and the Trunk Coupling Unit to which it is connected. In practice the lobe length will consist of a patch cable from the TCU to the main wiring panel, the length of the main wiring to the station's location, and then a patch cable from a floor/desk socket to the station. Lobe cabling can receive wires and is straight through with no crossovers.

Local Area Network

LAN describes a data communications network that can cover a limited area of up to about six miles in radius, with moderate to high data speeds. The machines linked by a LAN may all be in the same building or a group of buildings in relatively close proximity. It is user-owned and does not run over leased lines, although it might have gateways to the PSTN or other private networks.

Logical Link Control (LLC)

A data link protocol-based HDLC, developed for LANs by the IEEE802 committee and consequently common to all LAN standards for data link (level 2) transmission.

Logical Unit (LU)

A term normally associated with IBM's SNA to describe a unit that relays user requests to

ENTERPRISE NETWORKING

GLOSSARY

the network. This is done through a suite of interface programs. IBM's LU6.2 is used to implement programme-to-programme connections in conjunction with Advanced Programme to Programme Communications (APPC).

LSNAT

Load Sharing and Network Address Translation is a server load balancing technology. This allows a server farm made up of several servers to appear as one big server. LSNAT runs on a switch connected to all servers. It passes requests to the least loaded server and, if a server should fail, then this would no be noticed by the users as the switch would reconnect them to other servers in the farm with spare processing cycles. The address translation is to allow the farm to be seen as one device. This is seen as a critical requirement for businesses running on server-based applications such as ERP, CRM or an e-commerce site.

MAC

Media Access Control: the way that nodes gain access to transmission media. Most widely used in reference to LANs.

MAC-based VLANs

This uses the unique workstation layer 2 address, the MAC address to identify a user and provide services based on this address. This would enable an employee to unplug their workstation move to a new location and plug back into the network from this new location and receive the same services.

MAN

See Metropolitan Area Network

MAP

Manufacturing Automation Protocol is a token passing, bus topology LAN designed by General Motors for factory environments similar to the IEEE802.4 standard.

MSAU - Multi Station Access Unit

This is a Token Ring device of a multiple group (normally eight) or Trunking Coupling units with ring in/ring out ports. Also known as a concentrator, many people drop the 'S', causing confusion with the Ethernet MAU.

ENTERPRISE NETWORKING

GLOSSARY

Mean Time Between Failure

MTBF describes the reliability of equipment. Manufacturers do all sorts of gruelling tests on machines before they ship them to establish the MTBF as a selling point. Useful guide in a limited way but laboratory and office environments do not have a great deal in common.

Medium

The physical matter or method used for transmission so it applies equally to a piece of fibre optic cable or a satellite link.

Medium Interface Connector

The medium interface connector (MIC) is a hermaphrodite connector used on IBM patch panels and specified in the IEEE802.5 standards. The MIC provides a mechanical (spring) wrap on both the lobe connector and the multi station access unit connector, the positive transmit pins shorting the positive receive pins.

Metropolitan Area Network

MAN describes a network spanning a geographical area greater than a LAN but less than a WAN (Wide Area Network). IEEE802.6 specifies the protocols and cabling for a MAN using DQDB technology though this has been superseded by networks using ATM technology. 10Gigabit Ethernet (IEEE802.3ae) is widely seen as the foundation for next-generation MANs.

MIB

Management Information Base a generic term for the database of the objects managed in a network.

Modem

Abbreviation of MODulation/DEModulation, the modem converts digital computer signals into analogue form for transmission over analogue telephone systems. Modems work in pairs, so at the other end of the channel the signal is returned to digital form. Remember, traditional telephone networks were designed for the human voice, which is analogue, not digital computers.

Multi-mode Fibre

Fibre with a core diameter of 62.5 microns or the older European favourite of 50 microns.

ENTERPRISE NETWORKING

GLOSSARY

These cables can transmit light delivered by inexpensive LED technology. The distances supported are in the 1-2Km range, where as single mode fibre can extend to 50km.

Multi-Protocol Label Switching

The Internet Engineering Task Force IETF has defined MPLS as a standard for tagging packet flows with labels with the aim of providing better bandwidth management. The switched infrastructure switches on the information associated with the label which provides higher performance and lower latency operation from devices that have to look up the full destination address field.

Multi-tasking

This describes the concurrent execution of two or more tasks or the concurrent use of a single program that can carry out many duties.

Multi-user

This describes a program (usually an operating system) that supports several users with little detriment to any of them.

Named Pipes

An application interface from Microsoft for the interprocessing communications and distributed applications; part of LAN manager. It is an alternative to NetBIOS and is designed to extend the interprocess interfaces of OS/2 across a network, offering easier programming and use. Distributed applications should become easier to create because of the improved programme-to-programme communications on different machines.

NAT

Network Address Translation is used to convert the address of a client into a different address to be used on a different network. This is typically used to reconcile conflicting addresses on multiple networks.

NDIS

See Network Driver Interface Specification

NDS

Novell Directory Services, Novell's method for storing and retrieving information relating to network user authentication and access rights.

ENTERPRISE NETWORKING

GLOSSARY

NT Domains

Microsoft's method for user authentication for a network implementation, uses a RADIUS interface into Active Directory, Microsoft's new directory service released with Windows 2000.

Name Resolution

Defines the process for translating an Internet address name from the symbolic form used by people to the numeric address used by the machines, such as Server 7 to 123.45.211.37. It is the function of the Domain Name Server (DNS).

NetBEUI

NetBIOS Extended User Interface is an IBM network transport protocol for transferring data round a network. It is an extended network version of the NetBIOS protocol used by network operating systems such as Windows NT for peer to peer networking that formalises the transport frame and adds specific network functions.

NetBIOS

Network basic input/output system (NetBIOS) developed by IBM. It is an interface used by IBM PCs to access a LAN and its resources. This network operating protocol has two modes of operation datagram and session. The datagram service is the faster but less reliable of the two, using a self-contained packet with send and receive addressing and limited to 512 bytes. The session establishes a two-way communications mode of guaranteed delivery up to 64KB of data. Unlike IP and IPX, NetBIOS is not routable and is only used on a single network segment.

NetView

NetView is IBM's SNA network management product announced mid-1986. Although it started off life as a rather half-hearted bundling of various network management products including NCCF, NLDM, MPDA, VTAM node control application and NMPF.

NetWare

Novell's family of LAN networking products including an operating system that has the largest installed base of the LAN server sector.

Network Driver Interface Specifications

NDIS is a standard interface specification developed by Microsoft to separate

ENTERPRISE NETWORKING

GLOSSARY

communications protocol from the PC networking hardware. The driver has the added feature of being able to run multiple stacks concurrently.

Network Interface Card/Controller

The circuitry that connects a node to the network, usually in the form of a card fitted into one of the expansion slots in the back of the machine. It works with the network software and operating system to transmit and receive messages on the network.

Network Intruder Detection System

Monitors all traffic on a segment and compares with stored attack signatures, network protocol violation monitoring stores and reports and alarms at all violations.

Network Layer

The third layer in the OSI stack that is responsible for the necessary routing and relaying through one or more networks in multiple link or wide area environments.

Network Management

The ability to configure monitor and control resources on a network. As networks become larger and more complex, efficient management of them becomes vital to a company's well-being. As yet there are few complete solutions available: a patchwork of network management systems covers a variety of different areas of the subject. Basically, vendors of systems fall into one of two main camps, concerned either with the physical (hardware) elements or the logical side of the network (control and management on inter-process communication).

Network Operating System

A NOS connects all the devices on network so that resources can be shared efficiently and files can be transferred. The software handles administration of all network functions and is usually in two parts; server and client/requester. The requester puts the workstation onto the network and reroutes data over the network when necessary. The server software runs on the server machine and makes disks, software, ports and other facilities available to a node on request. Each device offering services can be requested by a PC and are accessed by the requester software.

Network-to-network interface

The NNI is the interface between ATM network nodes (switches) defined in the ATM Forum's UNI (User Network Interface).

ENTERPRISE NETWORKING

GLOSSARY

NFS

Network File System. A set of Unix protocols (originally developed by Sun Microsystems) for file sharing across a LAN.

Nodes

Devices on a network that demand or supply services or where transmission paths are connected. Node is often used instead of workstation, or to describe any device connected to a network.

ODI

A similar specification to Microsoft's NDIS, the Open Data link Interface from Novell enables PC adapter cards to support ODI and so run multiple protocols to access various implementations of NetWare.

OPERATIONS, ADMINISTRATION, AND MAINTENANCE (OAM)

A range of network management functions performed by dedicated ATM cells.

OSPF

Open Shortest Path First is a routing protocol to allow routers to negotiate fast convergence of paths through a network. It allows load balancing across links, path configuration across multiple technologies and high performance routing across large infrastructures. OSPF is recommended where large scale deployment is the requirement.

Out of Band Signalling

This describes a technique that uses a separate channel to the LAN to allow LAN management and control information to be sent. It allows network management devices to access LAN devices, even when the LAN itself is not functioning, thus providing an extra degree of resilience. See In-band Signalling.

Packet Switching

Is a method of switching data in a network where individual packets of a set size and format are accepted by the network and delivered to specified network destinations. The sequence of the packets is maintained and the destination established by the exchange of control information (also contained in the packets) between the sending terminal and the network before the transmission starts. The network is open to all users, all the time, with packets from the various nodes being interleaved throughout the network. The

ENTERPRISE NETWORKING

GLOSSARY

packets can be sent in any order, as the control information sent at the beginning of the transmission ensures they are interpreted in the correct order at the receiving end. Because each packet carries its own control instructions, it can use any route to reach its destination. The link only lasts as long as the transmission. A CCITT standard for a packet switched network's interfaces was drawn up in 1980, known as recommendation X.25. Hence packet-switched networks are often referred to as X.25. This has being superseded by Frame Relay and eventually by ATM.

PDS

Premises Distribution System is an unshielded twisted pair wiring scheme that supports data and voice communications developed by AT&T and renamed Systimax. Fibre structured wiring is also supported within PDS.

Peer to Peer

Describes communications between two devices on an equal footing, as opposed to host-terminal, client-server or master-slave. In peer to peer communications, both machines have to use processing power.

Permanent virtual circuit (PVA)

A virtual link with fixed end-points that are defined by the network manager. A single virtual path may support multiple PVC's.

Phantom Current

A phantom current is a DC voltage applied by a Token Ring station that wishes to join the ring. The current opens the by-pass relay in the Trunk Coupling unit allowing the station access. The voltage is transparent to the data signal, hence the name phantom. If a cable failure causes the phantom current to drop, the relay will close thus bypassing the faulty lobe, offering protection to the whole ring against one faulty cable.

Policy-based Routing

Routers traditionally route depending on the connectivity tables in the router's memory. Policy-based routing enables an external application to dynamically control these tables according to company procedures and business functions. This requires a higher order of sophistication in the router. Layer 3 switches that are replacing software-based routers include this as a major feature.

ENTERPRISE NETWORKING

GLOSSARY

Polling

A way of controlling terminals on a multi-point line by which a computer acting as master calls or polls each of the terminals in turn to find out if they have any data to send. This access method is used in star topology networks but is generally being superseded by the preferred interrupt method. However network management requires a polling scheme to gather network statistics.

PoP

Point of Presence refers to a location where routing or switching equipment is directly connected to the Internet. The new developments on the Internet refer to GigaPoP, which must have high capacity of at least 622Mbit/sec, high reliability, and availability. Each GigaPoP must use the Internet Protocol (IP) as a bearer service, and must be able to support emerging protocols and applications.

Port

The exit and entrance point for information going out of and into a computer or other data communications device.

PPP

Point-to-Point Protocol is the standard protocol when using a dial-up line to establish a connection between two computers. The standard covers all communications aspects including addressing, error recovery, authentication, encryption, compression and multiple protocol support. Routers can use their Frame Relay interfaces to supports IP traffic over PPP via an encapsulation technique. ARP correctly resolves MAC addresses, while Inverse ARP maps the Frame Relay DLCI to the IP address, as defined in RFC 1293.

Presentation Layer

The sixth of seven layers in the OSI model whose job it is to ensure that two computers wanting to communicate establish the ground rules for how they can interoperate.

Priority and Class of Service

To deliver differing levels of service to different applications such as voice or video a priority scheme is required to identify which traffic has to get special treatment at possible points of congestion and identify what is the service to be provided. IEEE802.1Q describes how user priority information shall be included as part of the MAC frame, thus preserving packet priority values across the entire network. IEEE802.1p is a standard for

ENTERPRISE NETWORKING

GLOSSARY

implementing multiple transmission queues to enable higher priority to be given to time sensitive or business critical traffic.

Private Network-to-Network Interface

PNNI is a routing information protocol that allows different vendors' ATM switches to be integrated in the same network. PNNI automatically and dynamically distributes routing information, enabling any switch to determine a path to any other switch.

Protocol

A set of rules governing the setup and control of information flow within a communications infrastructure. Protocols control format, timing, error correction, and running order. They are essential for a device to be able to interpret incoming information. Suites of protocols are often used in networks, with each protocol responsible for one part of a communication function.

Protocol Independent Multicast (PIM)

Protocol Independent Multicast (PIM) is an IP multicast routing protocol, much like MOSPF and DVMRP. PIM extends the LAN multicast functionality to the network layer, allowing a sender to send a single packet to multiple receivers. The protocol discovers the receivers, also known as group members, through the IGMP protocol and then builds a path between any sender and all the receivers in the group. The routing software supports both PIM Sparse-Mode (PIM-SM) and PIM Dense-Mode (PIM-DM) protocols. PIM Sparse-Mode is used in networks where the sources and receivers of multicast traffic are sparsely distributed. The members must explicitly join to participate in PIM. PIM Dense-Mode is used in networks where the sources and receivers of multicast traffic are densely distributed through the network. The Query Interval and Join Interval timers control the number of PIM protocol messages sent across the network.

Proxy Server

Proxy Servers are is used to re-direct connections to a private resource. For example when a company uses an ISP to host its Web services but does not want to give the ISP the ability to enable or disable user access rights, the ISP provides a RADIUS Proxy Server that re-directs connections to the enterprise, where the real access lists are managed. This puts a second layer of protection with anyone trying to gain access to the RADIUS Server for unauthorised use. See RADIUS Proxy.

ENTERPRISE NETWORKING

GLOSSARY

PVST

Per VLAN Spanning Tree is a standard to enhance VLAN deployment, making VLAN to VLAN communications more efficient especially useful for Broadcast and Multicast applications. PVST enables multiple paths across a single physical infrastructure that enhances the ability to provide resilience across a network.

QLLC (Qualified Logical Link Control)

QLLC routines are to provide Synchronous Data Link Control (SDLC).

Quality of Service Classes

There are five categories specified by the ATM Forum's UNI 3.0.

Class 1 specifies performance requirements comparable with the service offered by standard digital connections. Class 2 specifies necessary service levels for packet video and voice. Class 3 defines interoperability with other connection-oriented protocols, particularly frame relay. Class 4 specifies interoperability for connectionless protocols, including IP, IPX, and SMDs. Class 5 is effectively a best-effort at delivery.

RADIUS

Radius is a protocol for communicating to a server that maintains a user directory to verify a user's identity. RADIUS can support most of the security authentication schemes available.

RADIUS Proxy

Networks of RADIUS servers can be built where a RADIUS server can forward an authentication request to another radius server for verification. For example, an ISP's RADIUS server could act as a RADIUS proxy and send login requests to an enterprise's own RADIUS server to authenticate a user. In this way the enterprise can add and delete users without the ISP's involvement.

Reconfiguration

Is the process of physically changing around the various elements that compromise a network or system. However, the term is increasingly used with the word automatic to describe how more sophisticated networks are able to reconfigure themselves and continue working in the event of a link or device going down.

ENTERPRISE NETWORKING

GLOSSARY

Redirect

A packet switching function that routes a call to an alternative network address if the link to the original address is not working. It function is carried out by end point switches.

Redundancy

In data transmission, this refers to those characters and bits that can be removed from a transmission without affecting the message. In data processing and data communications, it means providing backup for the major components should one of them fail, so that the system continues to operate without interruption. There are several approaches to this, but complete redundancy for every element is very hard to achieve. Organisations such as banks and other financial institutions are keen on building in as much redundancy as they can because they lose money hand over first minute their system is down. Also described as fault tolerance.

Repeater

Within a LAN, this is a device that repeats a signal from one cable to the next, thereby increasing the reach of a LAN connection. In fibre optics, a repeater is an opto-electrical module that receives an optical signal and converts it into an electrical form of optical signal.

RFC

Request For Comment, although the name sounds different, these are the standards that drive the Internet. They cover all aspects of interoperability and protocols for communicating via the Internet.

Ring

One of the early LAN topologies where every workstation is connected to two others, one each side. All data is passed from node to node, in one direction only, with each node acting as a repeater for the next one in the loop. The response time is a ring is determined by the number of workstations on it; the more there are, the slower it is. One of the dangers of ring topology is that if one PC goes down, then the loop is broken. Most rings now have a self-healing capacity so that, if a node fails, the loop is automatically reconfigured. With IBM's Token Ring, the problem workstation is simply removed so that its neighbours are directly linked.

ENTERPRISE NETWORKING

GLOSSARY

Ring In and Ring Out

Ring in and Ring Out are the Token Ring connectors on the MSAU that connect the unit to the trunk cabling. The wrap feature is implemented at these interfaces.

Routing Information Protocol (RIP)

RIP is a protocol that automatically creates and maintains network routes among routers that support RIP. When a router, in a network, learns about changes in its routes from one of its next step connections, this router passes this information to other adjacent routers. This way all routers in a network keep their routing tables up to date. RIP also gives a degree of resilience into the network by routing around any failure. When the faulty is cleared, the network changes back to the previous configuration.

RMON

Remote Network Monitoring (RMON) is concerned with the implementation of probes, either as standalone or embedded in networking device firmware. RMON is an SNMP specification for statistics gathering across equipment from multiple vendors. The information gathered can be used to troubleshoot and monitoring remote LANs. RMON probes are typically accessed across the network using IP protocols and allow the retrieval of status information, percentage utilisation, and traffic levels complementing SNMP applications, which controls configuration information and the retrieval of error information. The devices that support RMON must support the collection of networking statistics needed by a central manager. This data is defined in the Remote Network Monitoring Management Information Base (RMON MIB) and can facilitate network fault diagnosis, trend analysis, planning and performance tuning. RMON uses the SNMP protocol, ASN.1 encoding, and standard MIB to provide multi-vendor interoperability between monitoring products and management stations, allowing users to mix and match network monitors and management stations from different vendors. The data types recorded are defined into different groups, each with a useful function to a network manager; RMON I supports up to ten groups, RMON II up to 19.

Routers

Unlike bridges, routers operate at level 3 (network layer) of the OSI seven-layer model. Also unlike bridges, routers are protocol-specific, acting on routing information carried by the communications protocol in the network layer. Bridges pass layer 2 (data link) packets directly onto the next segment of a LAN, whereas a router is able to use the information it has about the network topology and so can choose the best route for a

ENTERPRISE NETWORKING

GLOSSARY

layer 3 packet to follow. Because routers operate at level 3, they are independent of the physical level (layer 1) and can be used to link a number of different network types together. They have to be able to exchange information between themselves so that they know the conditions on the network; which links are active and which nodes are available.

Routing

The process of delivering a message across a network or networks via the most appropriate path. While simple in principle, routing is a specialised, complex science, influenced by a plethora of factors. The more networks are joined together, the more esoteric it becomes.

RSVP

ReSerVation Protocol is an IETF protocol (RFC 2205) enabling applications to dynamically reserve network bandwidth. RSVP enables applications to request a specific QoS for a data flow across a router-based network which otherwise could not provide a predictable path or service level. RSVP can support multiple network layer protocols such as TCP/IP, Novell IPX, and AppleTalk.

SAA

IBM's System Application Architecture specifies a set of parameters for the creation of software so that they will run on most IBM computers.

SDLC

Synchronous Data Link Control (SDLC) is an IBM protocol for use in SNA environments. It controls an individual link while catering for other network needs and can operate over full or half duplex lines. SDLC is a bit-orientated protocol, using a variety of patterns to flag the beginning and end of a frame or packet. Different patters are used to convey address, control and header fields that accompany the transmission and guide the frame to its destination.

Segment

Refers to an electrically continuous piece of the bus network. Segments can be joined together using repeaters or bridges.

Segmentation and reassembly (SAR)

Converts frames into appropriate lengths and formats them to fit the payload of an ATM cell.

ENTERPRISE NETWORKING

GLOSSARY

Session

Describes a logical connection between nodes on a network for the exchange of data or any live link between any two data devices, such as a minicomputer and a dumb terminal.

Signal Quality Error (Test)

SQE (T) is a function performed by a transceiver immediately after its attached computer has transmitted onto the LAN. The transceiver sends a simple test signal over the AUI back to the computer, ensuring the computer knows it has a working connection. This continual confidential check or pulse is often referred to as a heartbeat.

Single Mode Fibre

This is a thin core of fibre, often called mono mode fibre cabling, which allows light to enter at a very restricted angle. This fibre supports greater bandwidth than multi-mode fibre but requires laser technology to drive the signal down the fibre. Multi-mode fibre relies on cheaper, light emitting diode (LED) technology.

SLA

Service Level Agreement, an agreement on how any network will perform for an enterprise user. This is the standard way that an ISP or ASP can measure and justify its charges for services delivered to enterprise customers. It can include latency, dropped packets, PoP availability, and other factors

Slotted Ring

A LAN architecture that continually carries a constant number of fixed length packets or slots round the ring. The nodes then use empty slots as they pass through to transmit data. All nodes have the ability to recognise empty slots or packets addressed to them. See Token Ring.

Smart Wiring Hub

This is a network concentrator enabling multiple media to be supported and managed from a central location. When supporting structured wiring systems, smart hubs provide port management.

SMON

The Internet Engineering Task Force's (IETF) time-tested Remote Monitoring and RMON II standards monitor single network segments. RMON was developed for shared

ENTERPRISE NETWORKING

GLOSSARY

media networks and is not appropriate for current implementations. The move to a switched infrastructure where each port on a switch is effectively a separate requires a new monitoring application. This is the function of Switch Monitoring (SMON) standard. SMON provides performance information on virtual LANs, priority levels, quality of service (QoS), differentiated services flows or Layer 3 switching. The SMON module can monitor all traffic moving through the switch, not just the port being copied, as is the case with RMON.

SNMP

The Simple Network Management Protocol consists of three parts: Structure of Management Information (SMI), Management Information Base (MIB) and the protocol itself. The SMI and MIB define and store the set of managed entities; SNMP itself conveys information to and from these entities. The public domain standard is based on the operational experience of TCP/IP inter-networks within DARPA/NSFnet. SNMP is the standard for management and monitoring of network equipment such as hubs, switches and routers. It is used to retrieve status and configuration information from devices with GET commands. It can send information and configuration changes to a device with the SET command and, for unsolicited alerts, TRAPs are used to send these alerts to a network management station. It is similar in concept and purpose to DMI, but comes from a different product set. A PC workstation may implement agents for both DMI and SNMP simultaneously, and a management station may manage both concurrently.

SNMPv3

The IETF Network Management Area has been working to resolve a number of deficiencies of the SNMPv1 protocol to enable better support of the complex networks being deployed, and to meet additional requirements of applications used in today's networked environments. They include better error codes, a fast table retrieval operation, new data types to support faster hardware, better management of very large networks, security keys and access control rules.

SNA

IBM's System Network Architecture is a layered communications protocol for sending data between IBM hardware and software.

Source Routing

LAN bridging standard used by IBM for TRN bridges that describes how data frames are routed within complex TRN networks. Source-route bridging allows the configuration of

ENTERPRISE NETWORKING

GLOSSARY

parallel bridge paths through a network using an ARB (All Routes Broadcast) frame included in the 802.5 frame header. The response to ARB is a RIF (Route information Field) setting. Each RIF contains a source ring number, a bridge number and destination ring number. The mechanism relies on the first response to an ARB frame must have come from the shortest route. SRB (Single Route Broadcast) frames were added to stop broadcast storms and Source-route bridges still require the configuration of a spanning tree for monitoring the network topology, in order to handle single-route broadcast frames.

Star

A network topology where each node is connected to a central hub. The hub establishes, maintains and terminates all connections between the nodes. In a LAN, the hub is likely to be a workstation, whereas in large multi-port networks the hub is more likely to be a multiplexer.

Switched Virtual Circuit

A virtual connection with variable end-points, established through an ATM network. With an SVC, the user defines the end-points when the call is initiated.

Synchronous Digital Hierarchy (SDH)

The international form of Sonet specified by the International Telecommunications Union (ITU). SDH is built on blocks of 155.52Mbit/sec while SONET is 51.84Mbit/sec. Both these standards are specified for a fibre infrastructure and multiples of their basic building block to multi-gigabit speeds.

SONET

SONET (Synchronous Optical Network) is an international suite of standards for transmitting digital information over optical interfaces.

T1

A digital transmission service with a basic data rate of 1.544Mbit/sec.

T3

A digital transmission service with a basic data rate of 44.736Mbit/sec for transport of 28 T1 circuits.

ENTERPRISE NETWORKING

GLOSSARY

TCP/IP

Transmission Control Protocol/Internet Protocol (TCP/IP) is a transport and internetworking protocol that is a de factor networking standard. It was originally developed by the US Department of Defense and is able to operate in most environments. TCP/IP operates at layers 3 and 4 of the OSI model (network and transport respectively) and in 1983, became the protocol for the Internet.

Terminal Adaptor

This is the equivalent of a modem for ISDN lines and other digital telephone circuits. It converts the RS-232 serial data stream used by the computer to the pulse format used over the ISDN line. Terminal emulation software that allows a PC to ape the attributes of a terminal normally attached to a mainframe or minicomputer, so that they can communicate with those machines. The most commonly emulated terminals are CED's VT100 terminal and IBM's 3270.

Terminal Server

A module that connects terminals to a network, used to keep the number of cables to a minimum where several terminals need to be attached to a mainframe. The terminals use the network and then the terminal server to reach the CPU, so that only one cable is necessary between the server and the mainframe.

TKI

Stands for Transmit Immediate Access. Token Ring networks have separate transmit and receive paths but operate in a simplex mode using TKP (Token Passing Protocol). Where one manufacturer's equipment is used or today with common standards for switching full duplex communications is supported with the TKI (Transmit Immediate Access) protocol.

Token

A Token is several bytes of unique information in a packet format, or part of a packet that is passed round a LAN continuously. As it passes, the token gives each workstation the all clear to transmit data.

Token Bus

Token Bus is a LAN with a bus topology that uses the token passing technique as its access method. (MAP falls into this category).

ENTERPRISE NETWORKING

GLOSSARY

Token Passing

An access method where a token is passed from node to node, thereby granting permission to transmit data. The workstation attaches its message to the token that conveys it round the LAN until it finds its destination. The message passes by all of the workstations en route but is only accessed by the addressee. When the recipient has accepted the message, it releases the token so that the next workstation can use it. The whole process is completed almost instantaneously.

Token Ring

A network architecture by which the workstations on the ring are given leave to transmit data while they are in possession of the token that passes from node to node continuously, (see below). It operates at 4 and 16Mbit/sec.

Transceiver

Hardware circuitry that provides the correct electrical/optical connection between computer and IEEE802.3 LAN media. Since transceivers typically support only one type of network media, a choice of transceivers is available to support network or different media. Transceivers can detect carrier and collisions and pass these signals up to the computer. Transceivers can be standalone units or incorporated into a circuit board within a computer. A shortening of transmitter/receiver, its full official title is Medium Attachment Unit (MAU).

Transmission Media

Any means of conveying a signal such as wires and cables, also includes less tangible media such as microwaves.

Trunk

In Token Ring networking, a trunk is the cable that runs between MSAUs and can be either fibre optic or STP cable. STP cable uses two positive transmit wires in normal mode, with no crossover, while fibre has one transmit fibre and one receiver fibre. The positive transmit circuit on the ring out of an MSAU. Thus in normal mode the second pair of wires is not used, and is known as the back up or secondary path. This back up path is used to implement the wrap feature.

Twisted Pair

Two insulated copper wires twisted together with the twists or lays varied in length to

ENTERPRISE NETWORKING

GLOSSARY

reduce potential signal interference between the pairs. Where cables comprise more that 25 pairs, they are usually bundled together and wrapped in a cable sheath. Twisted Pair is the most commonly used medium for connecting telephones, computers and terminals to PABXs, supporting speeds up to 64Kbit/sec per second. Following the IEEE's ratification of 802.3 10BaseT standard for networking 10Mbit/sec Ethernet over Unshielded Twisted Pair (UTP) telephony wiring, Twisted Pair has became standard in most offices. As well as performance at Ethernet rate, it offers cost benefits to the end user through ease of relocation. New data grade Unshielded Twisted Pair is specified for 100Mbit/sec transmissions and category 5e cable can support Gigabit Ethernet (1Gbit/sec).

Tunnel Protocols

Tunnelling involves a network protocol establishing an end to end communications link across an alien protocol. The Internet uses the IP protocol but by using PPTP (Point to Point Tunneling Protocol) developed by Microsoft, 3Com and others, layer 2 data can be sent across the Internet using the PPP and GRE protocol.

Universal Serial Bus

The USB standard was developed by an industry consortium including DEC, IBM, Intel, Microsoft and Compaq. The objective was to clean up the wiring used to connect peripheral devices commonly used in a PC configuration. Supported devices include everything from modems to joysticks. Only one device needs to be actually plugged into your PC and a USB hub, either standalone or embedded, within a peripheral device such as a keyboard or printer can support up to 127 devices. USB has two data rates 12Mbit/sec for devices such as disk drives and 1.5Mbit/sec for devices such as joysticks.

User network interface (UNI)

The protocol adopted by the ATM Forum to define connections between ATM user (end-station) and ATM network (switch). UNI version 3 specifies the complete range of ATM traffic characteristics, including cell structure, addressing, signalling, adaptation layers and traffic management.

UTP

Unshielded Twisted Pair is the generic term for a low cost cabling scheme using Twisted Pair cables. It is the dominant cabling system for Local Area Networking installations. And was the medium of choice for the 90s. Brand names to look out for - PDS (Systimax), OSCA and IBM cabling scheme.

ENTERPRISE NETWORKING

GLOSSARY

VANS - Value Added Network Services

A network that provides specialised facilities above and beyond the normal carrier services, by adding computer control and communications.

Variable Bit Rate (VBR)

Information that can be represented digitally and which can tolerate delays and fluctuating throughput.

Vendor Independent

This describes hardware or software that will work with hardware and software manufactured by other vendors, the opposite of proprietary.

Virtual Channel

Is a defined route between two end-points in an ATM network that may traverse several virtual paths.

Virtual Channel Identifier (VCI)

The unique numerical tag used to identify every virtual channel across an ATM network, defined by a 16-bit field in the ATM cell header.

Virtual Circuit/Connection (VC)

A link that seems and behaves like a dedicated 'point-to-point' line or a system that delivers packets in sequence, as happens on an actual 'point-to-point' network. What really happens is the data is delivered across a network via the most appropriate route. The sending and receiving devices do not have to be aware of the options and the route is chosen only when a message is sent; there is no prearrangement so each virtual connection is in existence only for the duration of that one transmission.

Virtual path

A group of virtual channels, which an support multiple vitual circuits.

Virtual Path Identifier (VPI)

An 8-bit field in the ATM cell header that indicates the virtual path over which a cell is to be routed.

Vulnerability Assessment Scanners

A hacker in a box to give you a measure of your vulnerability to attack providing attack

ENTERPRISE NETWORKING

GLOSSARY

signatures and protocol infringements.

VRRP

Virtual Router Redundancy Protocol is a router-based application that allows a group of routers to appear as one logical router. Users access VRRP which selects the appropriate router or if there is a problem the next best router to fulfil the connection request.

Wave Division Multiplexing WDM

This is a technique used to define technology that is capable of mixing multiple light sources at different wavelengths down a single fibre cable. There are different implementations known as Dense WDM - up to 100 optical channels supported down a single fibre - and Wide WDM - four optical channels supported down a single fibre. This technique increases dramatically the bandwidth capability of the fibre. This is the basis of the new metropolitan area networks that will be built over the next few years at 10Gbit/sec and higher.

Wide Area Network

A network that covers a larger geographical area than a LAN and where telecommunications links are implemented, normally leased from the appropriate PTO(s). Examples of WANs include packet switched networks, public data networks and Value Added Networks (VANs).

Wrap

The trunk cabling used in Token Ring TCUs contains two data paths, a main and backup, with the latter normally being unused. If the trunk cable is faulty, the physical disconnection of the connector at a TCU causes the signal from the main path to wrap around onto the back up path, thus maintaining the loop.

X.400

A store and forward Message Handling System (MHS) standard that allows for the electronic exchange of text as well as other electronic data such as graphics and fax. Mainly provided by suppliers to allow for internetworking between different electronic main systems. X.400 has several protocols, defined to allow the reliable transfer of information between user agents and message transfer agents.

X.500

A directory services standard that permits applications such as electronic mail to access a

ENTERPRISE NETWORKING

GLOSSARY

standard directory to enable global access to users. X.500 was the first attempt to define a global, open standardised directory by a technical sub-committee of ISO/CCITT (CCITT has been renamed the ITU). Initially driven by the world's telephone companies to provide a directory service for the e-mail standard, X.400, it was intended that the directory would automate the world-wide White and Yellow Page telephone directories. However, the ISO participants quickly realised that the standard could be applicable to a far-wider range of applications, particularly in the area of distributed applications running over various network architectures. This lengthened the time the standard took to develop. There are three official versions 1988, 1993 and 1997 each representing increasing complexity. This in turn has resulted in a standard that is very difficult to implement.